Designing with Light

An Introduction to Stage Lighting

FIFTH EDITION

J. Michael Gillette

Professor Emeritus
University of Arizona

Mc
Graw
Hill

Boston   Burr Ridge, IL   Dubuque, IA   Madison, WI   New York
San Francisco   St. Louis   Bangkok   Bogotá   Caracas   Kuala Lumpur
Lisbon   London   Madrid   Mexico City   Milan   Montreal   New Delhi
Santiago   Seoul   Singapore   Sydney   Taipei   Toronto

The *McGraw·Hill* Companies

Higher Education

Published by McGraw-Hill, a business unit of The McGraw-Hill Companies, Inc., 1221 Avenue of the Americas, New York, NY, 10020. Copyright © 2008 by The McGraw-Hill Companies, Inc. All rights reserved. No part of this publication may be reproduced or distributed in any form or by any means, or stored in a database or retrieval system, without the prior written consent of The McGraw-Hill Companies, Inc., including, but not limited to, in any network or other electronic storage or transmission, or broadcast for distance learning. Some ancillaries, including electronic and print components, may not be available to customers outside the United States.

This book is printed on acid-free paper.

1 2 3 4 5 6 7 8 9 0 DOC/DOC 0 9 8 7

ISBN: 978-0-07-351415-4
MHID: 0-07-351415-2

Vice President and Editor-in-Chief: *Emily G. Barrosse*
Publisher: *Lisa Moore*
Senior Sponsoring Editor: *Christopher Freitag*
Senior Marketing Manager: *Pamela Cooper*
Managing Editor: *Jean Dal Porto*
Senior Project Manager: *Emily Hatteberg*
Art Director: *Jeanne M. Schreiber*
Designer: *Marianna Kinigakis*
Manager, photo research: *Brian J. Pecko*
Senior Production Supervisor: *Carol A. Bielski*
Cover credit: *The Theatre School at DePaul University; CLOUD NINE; Directed by Lisa Portes; Lighting Design by Chris Prezas; Scenic Design by Katie Schweiger; Costume Design by Jessica Chesak. Actors Pictured: Adam Poss and Sara Anderson*
Composition: *10/12 Sabon, by G&S Typesetters*
Printing: *45# New Era Matte Plus, R. R. Donnelley & Sons*

Library of Congress Cataloging-in-Publication Data

Gillette, J. Michael.
   Designing with light: an introduction to stage lighting / J. Michael Gillette.—5th ed.
     p. cm.
   Includes bibliographical references and index.
   ISBN-13: 978-0-07-351415-4 (softcover : alk. paper)
   ISBN-10: 0-07-351415-2 (softcover : alk. paper)
   1. Stage lighting. I. Title.
   PN2091.E4G5   2008
   792'.025—dc22

2006034481

The Internet addresses listed in the text were accurate at the time of publication. The inclusion of a Web site does not indicate an endorsement by the authors or McGraw-Hill, and McGraw-Hill does not guarantee the accuracy of the information presented at these sites.

www.mhhe.com

To Joyce Ann who always knows why

Preface

The purpose of this book is to introduce students to stage lighting design, which is an amalgam of technology and art. Without an understanding of the technology used in the craft, it is difficult to design with light. And without an understanding of the theory and processes of design, it is almost impossible to design with light. To be successful, a designer needs to know both.

As with any art form, the basic elements for a successful creation are an understanding of the chosen artistic medium and the inspiration to create. I hope that this text will provide that basic understanding of the design potential of light and give an insight into the sources that inspire a lighting designer to create.

ORGANIZATION
. . . .

Because the study of theatrical lighting design covers two basic areas—technology and design—this text has been divided into two sections. Chapters 1 through 10 present practical information that is essential to developing an understanding of the technological aspects of designing with light. Chapters 11 through 17 provide information on how to design with light as well as how to draft the light plot and execute the other paperwork used by a lighting designer. Chapter 18 provides both technical and design information for lighting film and video.

NEW TO THE FIFTH EDITION
· ·

In the rapidly evolving technological world of lighting design one of the challenges of updating this text is divining which of the new technologies and design innovations—that seem to be appearing at an ever-accelerating pace—are truly significant developments that will become "the new standard," and which are simply interesting ideas that, for one reason or another, will quietly fade away. I've chosen to include explanations of a few of these new developments, such as the IGBT and sine wave dimmers as well as LED-source lighting fixtures because these innovations offer some clear advantages over the existing technologies at what are, or may soon be, competitive costs. As progress is made on similarly exciting new technological developments, they will be included in future editions.

I also find it interesting that, while there have been myriad technological advancements in the past decade, almost no changes have occurred in basic design philosophy—the reason we design light for theatrical presentations in the first place. The core of that design philosophy—to provide visual reinforcement that supports the production concept—hasn't changed. And it probably won't change until such time in the future as, for whatever reason, there is a radical shift in the purpose and nature of theatrical presentation. Because the reason for designing light hasn't really changed, I've chosen to make very few adjustments to the sections of this text dealing with the whole process of creating the lighting design.

It is probably a gross understatement to say that the world of lighting design is a much wider and deeper field than it was when the first edition of this text was published almost 30 years ago. What were once considered subfields of theatrical lighting—concert, club, trade show, TV specials, and event lighting—are now fully developed, energetic, and vital professional fields. And, since the integration of the computer and its related technologies into the lighting industry, we are being constantly bombarded with new technologies and exciting equipment. There is almost too much information to learn. And anyone working in the field needs to know, or at least be aware of, much of it. For this reason I've added a selected bibliography that references a number of excellent sources from across the now-broad field of entertainment lighting design. I hope you will find this additional information helpful and useful.

In this edition, the basic organization of the text remains the same. But there have been several significant changes in content. Because of the increasingly common use of computer drafting in lighting design, a number of the light plots used as illustrative examples, as well as several previously hand-drawn illustrations, have been changed to computer-drafted examples. New technologies have been introduced, old technologies updated, and many of the equipment photos have been changed to show manufacturers' more recent designs and models.

ACKNOWLEDGMENTS
· ·

Once more I would like to thank those students, friends, and colleagues who have offered suggestions for improving *Designing with Light* in the years since the publication of the fourth edition.

I would particularly like to thank Michael McNamara of the School of Theatre Arts at the University of Arizona for undertaking the redrafting of a number of illustrations in this edition as well as providing the excellent computer-drafted lighting design paperwork for shows on which he had worked as an associate lighting designer. Additionally, his suggestions and information about current practices and trends have been invaluable.

The following list of reviewers of the text offered numerous excellent suggestions for improving the book. I've included many of those ideas. I would like to sincerely and humbly thank them for their help.

Andra Bilkey, *Texas Tech University*
Steve Crick, *University of North Texas*
Shane Fuller, *East Texas Baptist University*
Jonet Leighton, *Antelope Valley College*
Merrill J. Lessley, *University of Colorado at Boulder*
Gary Musante, *SUNY College at Brickport*
Robin Schraft, *Drury University*
Melissa Shafer, *East Tennessee State University*
Arden Weaver, *University of Minnesota, Duluth*

Contents

CHAPTER 8

PRACTICALS AND EFFECTS 129

· ·

CHAPTER 9

COLOR 140

· ·

CHAPTER 10
ADVANCED TECHNOLOGY INSTRUMENTS　　　156

CHAPTER 11
THE DESIGN PROCESS　　　173

CHAPTER **16**

DESIGN EXAMPLES   240

. . . .

CHAPTER **17**

REHEARSAL AND PERFORMANCE PROCEDURES   270

. . . .

CHAPTER **18**

AN INTRODUCTION TO LIGHTING FOR FILM AND VIDEO   285

. . . .

CHAPTER 1

An Introduction to Designing with Light

Any dramatic production, unless it is performed outdoors during the day, needs some kind of artificial light. If illumination were the only function of stage lighting, however, you could hang a bank of fluorescent lights over the stage and forget all about the **dimmers**, **control boards**, **cables**, and **instruments**. Obviously, there is more to stage lighting than simple illumination. Effective stage lighting not only lets the spectators see the action on the stage but also ties together all the visual elements of the production and helps create an appropriate mood and atmosphere that heighten the audience's understanding and enjoyment of the play.

Dimmer: An electrical device that controls the intensity of a light source connected to it.

Control board: A console containing controls for a number of dimmers. Also called a control console.

Cable: An electrical extension cord used to connect instruments to dimmers or instruments to permanent stage circuits.

Instruments: Lighting fixtures designed for use in the theatre.

LIGHT AND PERCEPTION

What is lighting design and why do we bother to "design" light in the first place? To understand these questions, we first need to understand what light is, what it does, and how light influences our perceptions and understanding.

We can describe light in terms of its characteristics and physical nature. Visible light can be defined as: (1) something that makes vision possible; (2) that portion of the electromagnetic spectrum that stimulates the visual receptors in the eye; (3) that relatively narrow band of the electromagnetic spectrum between infrared light and ultraviolet radiation. Further, light travels at approximately 186,281 miles per second.[1]

---

[1] *Webster's Ninth New Collegiate Dictionary*, 1986, p. 690.

Although the above describes the physical nature of light, it doesn't tell us what light "does." What does light do? A simplistic, and accurate, answer is that it allows us to see things. It makes objects visible. However, it is probably more important for a student of lighting design to understand that *the manner in which light illuminates an object shapes our impressions and understanding of what we're seeing.* That concept is the crux of the discussion of light and perception as well as the underlying reason that we bother to design with light.

The angle of the light, its intensity, color, and sharpness or diffusion all affect our impression of the object we're seeing. To illustrate, almost everyone has heard of the phrase "the ever-changing face of the mountains." But, if you stop to think about it, unless there is some cataclysmic disaster, the features of any particular mountain or mountain range change very little, if at all, over hundreds or even thousands of years. However, if you were to critically look at a mountain range for even a few days or weeks, you would begin to understand the concept behind the phrase. The appearance of any mountain changes considerably in the course of the day. The patterns of highlight and shadow created by sunlight falling on the ridges and valleys shift continuously as the sun moves across the sky. A steep cliff that is bathed in brilliant morning sunshine slides into deep shadows in the late afternoon. A hillside that hides in morning gloom emerges into brilliant sunshine by midday. Clouds or fog soften or obscure part of the range. In the late afternoon we may be treated to the mountain being bathed in a soft purple or peach twilight at sunset. Thus the manner in which the sun illuminates the mountain controls not only what we see but also, to a great extent, how we feel about what we're seeing.

Intellectually everyone understands that the physical structure of the mountains isn't changing. But our individual perception, our personal understanding, of what those mountains mean to us is based on a complex process involving not only sight and intellectual recognition, but our emotional reaction to what we're seeing. That emotional reaction is controlled, to a great extent, by two primary elements: instinct and learned behavior. Another example may help explain this process. Imagine that it's a pleasant, sunny summer day. You're walking down the sidewalk next to a park. There is a low stone wall, about waist high, between you and the park. The park is inviting, with a thick carpet of grass beneath a canopy of large shade trees. A few benches are randomly scattered on the lawn. A young couple sit on one of the benches quietly talking. Across the street there are several stores—a bookshop, a clothing store, a bank, and a drugstore on the corner.

Now, imagine that you're on this same street at 2:00 A.M. on a moonless night. It's really dark. The only light comes from the window of the all-night drugstore on the far corner at the other end of the park. As you walk beside the stone wall, you peer into the blackness of the park. A little starlight filters through the leaves. You hear a low noise coming from the park. Then you think you see something move. You quicken your stride as you cross the street and almost break into a run as you rush into the drugstore.

As mentioned earlier, our emotional reaction to what we see is controlled by two primary elements: instinct and learned response.

Instinctively, most people are afraid of the dark. This response was genetically programmed into our ancestors tens of thousands of years ago when our progenitors roamed the plains and woodlands looking for food. Our primary defense against being eaten by something larger, stronger, and faster than we were was to be able to see it. If we saw it, we would at least have a chance of defending ourselves. If we couldn't see it, it could jump out of the dark and "get" us. Humans don't see well in the dark, so our ancestors who avoided dark places were more likely to live to pass on their gene pool than those who ventured into the dark and didn't return. With each succeeding generation this healthy act of self-preservation became more and more reinforced in our genetic code.

The second contributor to our reaction to what we see is learned response. From the time that we're infants we are busy learning. A great deal of what we learn is stored in the brain as memories. Almost all of our early learning is experiential—learning by experience. What we learn experientially is a major contributor to how we will react in any given circumstance. Occasionally I have looked outside on a cloudy summer day and absently thought, "It looks like it could snow." Logically, I know that it isn't going to snow, but there is something about the shape and color of the clouds, the direction and speed of the wind, and the color of the light that reminds me of the way it looks before a snowstorm. Our subconscious minds are constantly comparing incoming information—what we're currently seeing—with memories of what we've experienced before in our ongoing struggle to help our conscious minds make sense of our surroundings. An interesting example of this learned response occurred during the University of Arizona production of *Terra Nova*, which primarily is set in Antarctica and chronicles Scott's ill-fated trip to the South Pole. (See Color Plates 11 and 12.) The director wanted the lighting for the Antarctica scenes to be "white and painfully bright." At first I left the lights uncolored, but the white light seemed warm rather than cool. Before the next rehearsal I put a light blue **color media** into all the lights. At rehearsal that night almost all the people in the audience complained of being chilly or cold. The thermostat in the theatre hadn't been changed from the previous day. The only difference was the light blue color in the lights. My assumption is that our subconscious minds saw the blue light, compared it with memories of "the color of cold," and convinced our conscious minds into thinking that the theatre actually was cold. Subsequently we had several comments from the paying audience that the theatre was rather cold. We raised the thermostat a few degrees even though the production occurred in late September in Tucson when the average temperature was in the high 90s. Such is the power of the mind.

Color media: The plastic or glass materials used to color the light emitted by lighting instruments.

Lighting designer:
Person responsible for the appearance of the lighting during the production.

Production concept:
The creative interpretation of the script that will unify the artistic vision of the production design team.

The reason that we design the lighting for an event or a place is to influence the audience's perception and understanding of what they're seeing. That is the reason lighting is thoughtfully designed for theatre, films, and television as well as for rock concerts, theme parks, and retail stores. Lighting influences our perceptions and understanding. Machiavellian, isn't it? Read on and learn how Machiavellian lighting design really is.

DESIGN CHARACTERISTICS OF LIGHT

As you begin to study how to design with light, it is important that you understand what lighting design is, as well as what it is not. Theatrical lighting design is a process and a craft for creating an artistic result. While the lighting design first of all allows the audience to see the stage, it is more than an exercise in illumination. The **lighting designer** uses light to achieve four primary goals: (1) To influence the audience's perception and understanding of what they're seeing; (2) to selectively illuminate the stage; (3) to sculpt, mold, and model actors, settings, and costumes; and (4) to create an environmental atmosphere that is supportive of the play's **production concept**. To achieve these goals the lighting designer uses the tools of lighting design—the instruments, dimmers, color media, and so forth—to create a design that works to support the production concept.

Any creative art, whether in theatre, painting, or sculpture, comprises—in equal parts—inspiration and craft. Inspiration in this case refers to the creative element, the process used to create a conceptual image that the artist "sees" in his or her mind. Craft refers to a mastery of the tools and techniques used to re-create the conceptual image in physical form. Michelangelo is re-

---

Development of the Production Concept

The production concept is the coordinated artistic vision that the members of the production design team—the producer; the director; and the scenic, costume, lighting, and sound designers—develop. This kind of development is possible only if all members of the team freely share their ideas and vision for the production. A regularly scheduled production meeting (discussed more fully in Chapter 2, "Lighting Production Team: Organization and Responsibilities") is probably the most effective method of ensuring that every member's ideas, thoughts, and opinions are heard and understood by every other member of the team.

puted to have said that he released figures that were trapped in the blocks of stone that he sculpted. He first studied the stone, saw the figure entombed within it, and then used chisels and mallet to sculpt away the stone to reveal the form. Michelangelo's statues are the result of the two qualities that any artist has to possess: artistic inspiration/vision and skill in using the tools of the medium to re-create the inspiration.

Actors also use both process and craft. An actor uses many sources to develop the interpretation of a character. Although the character is based on elements in the script, a good actor also uses other sources to conceptualize the role in an effort to make the character portrayal seem more "real" and to create a life beyond that contained in the script. For example, an actor may recall and use characteristics of people he or she has observed; perhaps characters from literature will serve as models for certain aspects of the role; parts of the characterization will certainly be based on emotional memories from the actor's past. Although the process of analysis can lay the foundation for creating a conceptually brilliant character portrayal, if the actor doesn't have a mastery of his own body and voice so that he can move and talk as he has conceived the character would, then it will be impossible for him to fully realize his brilliantly conceived portrayal. To create a great character, an actor employs both process and craft. The intellectual process of character analysis can neither supplant nor negate the need for a basic understanding of how to move and how to talk and vice versa.

In the same way that an actor uses both process and craft to create a character, the lighting designer uses process to develop an understanding of how the lighting should look for a production and uses craft to re-create those images in, hopefully, an artful manner. (A technique used to help the lighting designer "see the light" is discussed at length in Chapter 11, "The Design Process.")

CONTROLLABLE QUALITIES OF LIGHT
· ·

Tharon Musser, a prominent professional lighting designer, has said, "If you ask most people who walk in and tell you they want to be lighting designers, what kind of weather are we having—what's it like outside?—half of them won't know how to describe it, if they remember it at all. They simply don't know how to see."[2] Learning how to see—understanding how light shapes our perception of people and objects—is absolutely essential to learning lighting design.

---

[2]"Tharon Musser," *Lighting Dimensions* 1 (1977): 16.

As Musser indicates, a student of lighting design must learn how to see. Actually, it is relatively easy to train yourself to see things critically. You just need to begin studying and watching how people and objects are lit, then correlate that with your thoughts, impressions, and understanding of that person, situation, or thing. Over time you will begin to notice that relationships exist between light and understanding. Some are subtle; some are overt. But all are interesting, useful, and necessary for a lighting designer to know.

To recognize relationships between light and understanding, you first need to gain an understanding of how objects are lit in the "real world." The following list provides a good beginning point for your study of meaning in light. As you begin to critically examine how things—people, buildings, trees, cars, clouds—are lit, you will undoubtedly come up with additional ideas and criteria that will help you understand how light is shaping your understanding of what you're looking at.

1.   What is the light source illuminating the object you're viewing? For example, is it the sun, a streetlight, a table lamp?

2.   How bright is the light? Is there more than one source? If so, is one of the sources brighter than the other(s)?

3.   From what directions is the light striking the object? For example, light is probably striking the object from multiple directions, some direct, some indirect. What are those directions? Is the light coming from overhead or the side, coming straight from the front, or bouncing off the ground or a nearby wall?

4.   Is the light hard-edged or diffused? Are the edges of the shadows cast by the object sharp or fuzzy?

5.   What color is the light? Is it picking up color by being bounced off something else (grass, building, surface, sidewalk, clothes, furniture, etc.)?

As you begin to develop an understanding of how things are lit, you also need to ask yourself if the way an object is lit has any influence on your perception of that object. An interesting way to check that perception is to imagine the object lit in some other way. For example, if you're studying the way a woman's face is lit as she reads a book while sitting in the library, imagine that same woman reading the same book while sitting by a campfire. Does that change of lighting affect your understanding of that person? If so, how?

The point of the above exercise? Learning to see what's really there and how the manner in which it is lit influences your perception of that object.

Any discussion of how lighting affects understanding needs to have some common terminology. Traditionally the controllable qualities of light—those qualities the lighting designer can manipulate to affect meaning—have been divided into four categories: distribution, intensity, movement, and color.

Distribution

Distribution is a catchall term that refers to several elements: (1) the direction from which the light approaches an area, actor, or object; (2) the shape and size of the area that the light is covering; (3) the quality of the light—its cohesiveness (clarity or diffusion); and (4) the character of the light—its texture (smooth, uneven, patterned, hard- or soft-edged, and so forth). The **focus** of the lighting instruments determines both the pattern and position of highlights and shadows cast on the actors and their environment.

Intensity

Intensity is the actual amount, or level of brightness, of the light that strikes the stage or actor. The lighting designer can control the intensity of all lighting instruments by adjusting appropriate dimmers. The range of intensity can vary from total darkness to painfully brilliant white light. The range of intensity normally lies somewhere between these two extremes and is modified to suit the needs of a particular scene or moment in the play.

Movement

Movement can be divided into three general categories: (1) the timed duration of a **light cue**—that is, the length of time it takes for the lights of one cue to come up or go out; (2) the movement of onstage lights, such as a lantern or candle that an actor carries across the stage; and (3) the movement of an offstage light source, such as a **followspot**.

Color

Color is an extremely powerful tool that will be discussed at length in Chapter 9, "Color." Color media allow the designer to use the full range of the rainbow. The judicious use of colored light onstage can enhance a scene immeasurably. Happy, pastel colors can help to create a pleasant, friendly environment for the production of an old-fashioned musical comedy like *The Boyfriend*. Stark white light etched against a black background can help reinforce the sense of conflict in Anouilh's *Antigone*.

FUNCTIONS OF STAGE LIGHTING

Stage lighting design can be defined as the creative use of illumination to enhance the spectator's understanding and appreciation of the production by visually supporting the production concept. To achieve this goal, stage lighting must perform several basic functions.

Focus: In stage lighting, the location onstage where the light from an instrument is directed.

Light cue: Generally, some type of action involving lighting; usually the raising or lowering of the intensity of one or more lighting instruments.

Followspot: A lighting instrument with a high-intensity, narrow beam of light; mounted on a stand that allows it to tilt and swivel so that the beam can "follow" the actor.

Production design team: The producer; director; and scenic, costume, lighting, and sound designers who develop the visual and aural concept for the production.

Unit set: A single set in which all the play's locations are always visible and the audience's attention is usually shifted by alternately lighting various parts of the set.

Visibility

The lighting for any production must make the actors, costumes, and sets clearly visible to the audience. At the same time, because light affects meaning, it is equally important that the audience see those actors and objects only as the designer, director, and other members of the **production design team** want them to be seen. The dark, brooding, heavily colored shadows that we usually associate with murky tragedies would call for a completely different type of visibility than would the bright, happy look of a farce or musical comedy. One of the real challenges of lighting design is to create a selective visibility that subtly directs the audience's attention to a specific area or location. The intensity of the light as well as its direction and color all affect the visibility of a scene.

Selective Focus

Selective focus means directing the audience's attention to a specific area of the stage. The lighting designer can selectively focus attention in a number of ways but frequently does so by increasing the intensity of the lights on the desired area of interest. When this happens, all areas that are less brightly lit become of secondary importance. A common example of the use of selective focus occurs when the lighting designer reduces the intensity of lights on one area of a **unit set** while increasing it on another. Instinct literally forces the audience to look at the brighter area.

A more subtle use of selective focus can be seen in the lighting designs for most interior settings. In these designs the lights are usually brighter in the major acting areas than they are in the upstage corners of the set where there is little, if any, action during the course of the play. The most extreme use of selective focus can be seen in almost any musical, where the audience's attention is directed to the lead singer by one or more followspots that focus on the singer while the rest of the stage lights dim or change color to emphasize the mood of the song.

Modeling

Light can be thought of as a plastic sculptural medium that is used to reveal form through the creation of a pattern of highlight and shadow. A column is perceived as round because of the smooth gradation of light from the highlights on the sides of the column to the lowlight, or shadow, area in the center (shown in Figure 1.1A). However, if we light the shadow area, effectively creating a smooth, unvarying wash of light over the whole column (Figure 1.1B), then the column appears to be a flat, board-like rectangle with little or no apparent depth.

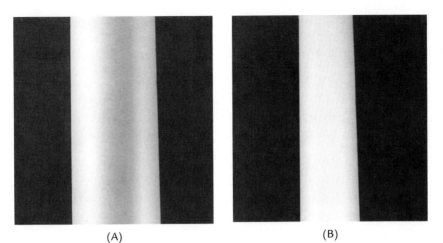

(A)   (B)

Figure 1.1 The modeling effect of light: (A) a column lit from the side; (B) column lit smoothly edge to edge.

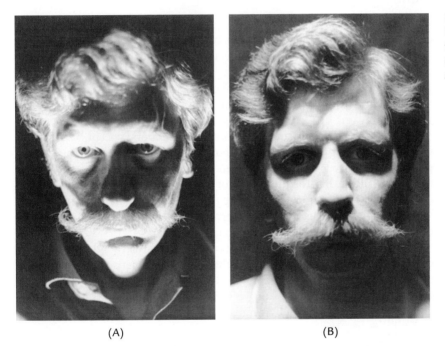

(A)   (B)

Figure 1.2 The modeling effect of light: (A) face lit from beneath; (B) face lit from in front and above.

Almost all of us, at one time or another, have placed a flashlight under our chins and impersonated a monster by shining the light up into our faces. Lighting the face from beneath, as shown in Figure 1.2A, reverses the normal and expected patterns of highlight and shadow that are illustrated in Figure 1.2B. In Figure 1.2A, areas of the face that are normally shaded—the bottom of the nose, the eyebrows, below the chin—are highlighted, while

Sidelight: Any light striking the side of an object relative to the view of the observer.

Kinetic: Having to do with movement. In the case of lighting design, having to do with moving light.

areas that are usually highlighted—the cheekbones, bridge of the nose, and brow—are shaded. This simple example demonstrates the dramatic changes in meaning that can be made by simply reversing the normal pattern of highlight and shadow. In the same manner, our perception of the forms of actors or dancers can be changed or modified by controlling and manipulating the patterns of highlight and shadow on their faces and bodies. The use of **sidelight** highlights and accentuates the edges and vertical line of the body and makes those actors or dancers seem taller and thinner than they are in reality.

Direction is the primary element used in modeling, although intensity, movement, and color all affect modeling to a lesser degree. A change in any or all of these variables will inevitably result in an apparent change of form and feeling in the object being lit.

Mood

Creating a mood with light is one of the easiest and, at the same time, most difficult aspects of stage lighting. It is relatively easy to create a spectacular sunset effect or a sinister feeling of lurking terror; the difficulty comes in integrating these impressive effects with the other elements of the production. Effective stage lighting, even though it greatly affects meaning, is subtle and rarely noticed. Although it is fun to create a sunset or similar breathtaking visual display, the opportunity to do so legitimately doesn't present itself in many plays. Within the parameters of the production concept, stage lighting is usually designed to enhance the mood of the play as unobtrusively as possible. Intensity levels may be varied slightly to shift focus, change color, or create a mood, but the movement of the light must be so restrained that it will be felt by the audience rather than seen. Lighting handled subtly and with precision can be used to create or shift the environmental mood without distracting the audience or calling attention to itself.

An apparent exception to the concept of unobtrusive lighting involves concert and club lighting. Mirroring the vitality and energy of these venues, concert and club lighting is almost always frenetic, bold, and spectacular. But note that these sassy, **kinetic** designs are providing exactly the same function for their productions as their more unobtrusive cousins do for a production of Shakespeare, Williams, or Ayckbourn. A vital function of a successful lighting design is to create a mood that reinforces and supports the production concept.

An understanding of the functions and controllable qualities of light will enable the designer to blend and manipulate light with the subtlety and precision necessary to create a lighting design that uniquely enhances the audience's understanding and appreciation of the production.

PSYCHOLOGICAL EFFECTS OF LIGHT

In lighting design, just as in literature, the concepts of good and evil are often associated with light and darkness. When a scene is lit with dark and murky shadows, most people instinctively react with a sense of foreboding. The suspicion that something could be lurking unseen in the shadows is almost universal. When a scene is brightly lit, we instinctively relax, because we realize that nothing can sneak up on us unseen.

To more fully understand how we see and how we understand what we see, you might want to take courses in perception from your school's psychology department. These courses are appropriate, effective, and helpful to the training of a lighting designer. After you understand the nature of our learned and instinctive responses to light and our environment, you can apply that knowledge to create lighting designs that will effectively manipulate the audience's response to the environment of the production.

Additional information on the psychology of color can be found in Chapter 9.

CHAPTER 2

Lighting Production Team: Organization and Responsibilities

Lighting production team: The personnel who work on lighting for a production.

In some professional theatres, such as the Broadway theatres in New York, unions stipulate the individual jobs for which a **lighting production team** is responsible as well as the number of people necessary to perform a particular job. In regional professional theatres and professionally oriented educational training programs, the demarcation of these responsibilities becomes a little fuzzier. However, this chapter's discussion of the lighting production team's organization and responsibilities generally applies to both professional and educational theatres.

LIGHTING DESIGNER

The lighting designer is responsible for the design, installation, and operation of the lighting and special electrical effects associated with lighting used in the production. Not too long ago, to present their visual ideas, lighting designers frequently drew sketches or showed visual examples—paintings, photographs, and so forth—to demonstrate the type and style of lighting that they intended to create. Many designers still do this, but that method of presentation is being supplemented by the continuing development of previsualization software. These programs allow lighting designers to create pictures or animations of how the lighting is going to look. More specific information on previsualization software can be found in Chapter 10, "Advanced Technology Instruments."

To show where the lighting equipment is to be placed, the lighting designer produces a light plot, which is a scale ground-plan drawing that details the placement of the lighting instruments relative to the physical structure of the theatre and the location of the set (see Figure 2.1). The designer also produces the lighting sectional, which is a composite side view, also drawn to scale, that shows the location of the instruments, the set, and the theatre (see Figure 2.2). Additionally the lighting designer compiles the instrument schedule or hookup sheet, which is a form used to record all of the technical data about each instrument used in the production (see Figure 2.3).

ASSISTANT LIGHTING DESIGNER

Over the past several decades the assistant lighting designer's duties have been divided into several subcategories. The general rules for determining which type of, and how many, assistants are needed on a show are determined by the preferred working style of the designer, the complexity of the design, and, if the assistants are to be hired, the budget. The basic subcategories are these:

> *Assistant to the Lighting Designer*—The assistant to the lighting designer functions as a general assistant to the lighting designer. He or she may draw any or all of the associated paperwork—light plot, lighting sectional, instrument schedule, and so forth—as requested by the lighting designer. Depending on the nature and disposition of the lighting designer, as well as the complexity of the show, the assistant lighting designer may focus or participate in focusing the instruments, write cues, update paperwork, or perform any of the other myriad tasks necessary to make the lighting design come alive onstage.

> *Assistant Lighting Designer*—In addition to performing the duties outlined for the assistant to the lighting designer, the assistant lighting designer may make some minor design decisions, design some of the cues, and substitute for the lighting designer in his or her absence.

> *Associate Lighting Designer*—The associate lighting designer effectively performs all the duties of a lighting designer while under the artistic direction of a more senior designer.

Examples may help explain the associate lighting designer's job. In the professional theatre it has become relatively standard for an associate lighting designer to perform the lighting designer's duties when a show is mounted in a new, or different location than the original theatre. The associate designer follows the artistic vision, light plot, and cuing of the original production as closely as possible. But each new venue requires that some type of adjustments be made. Fixtures normally cannot be hung in exactly the same position as the original production. The associate lighting designer decides the new hanging positions. Changing the location of the lights necessitates adjusting the intensity levels of the dimmers to match the **look** of the original production. This work is also the responsibility of the associate lighting designer. He or she

Look: The appearance—the way the light looks onstage—of a particular cue.

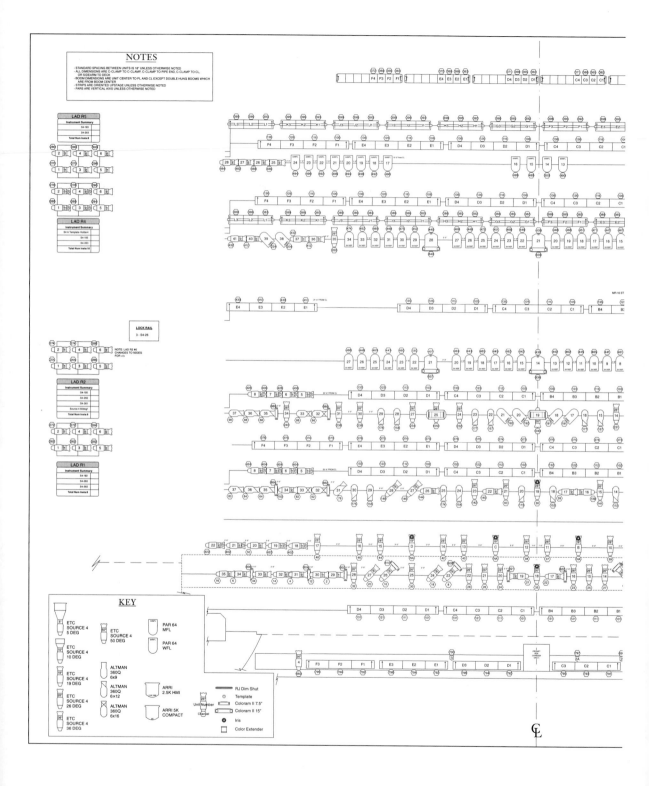

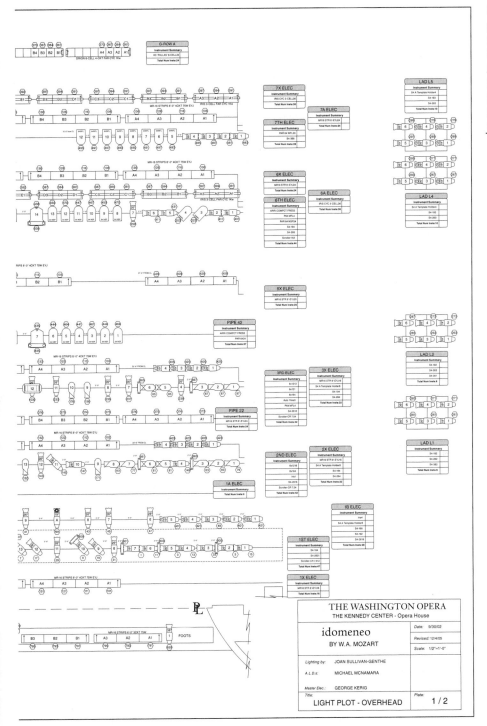

Figure 2.1 The light plot for the 2002 Kennedy Center Opera House production of *Idomeneo*. Lighting design by Joan Sullivan-Genthe. Drafting by Michael McNamara and Laura Jean Wickman.

Figure 2.2 The lighting section for the 2002 Kennedy Center Opera House production of *Idomeneo*. Lighting design by Joan Sullivan-Genthe. Drafting by Michael McNamara and Laura Jean Wickman.

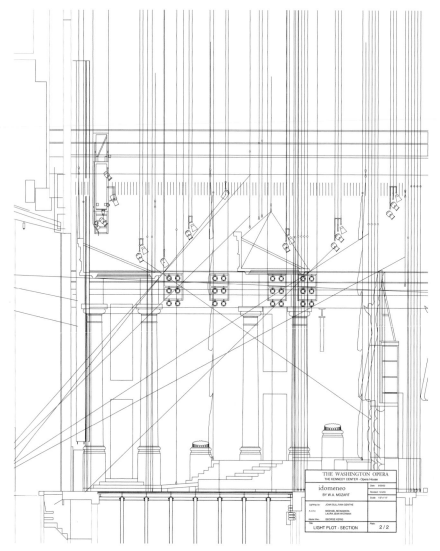

Repertory theatre: A company that presents several different plays alternately in one theatre in the course of a season. In the context of lighting design, adjustments are normally made to the focus and color of lighting instruments for each play each time it is performed.

also updates the paperwork—plot, cues, and so forth—to reflect any changes that have been made. Typically, all paperwork for a traveling or "new venue" production will be stored in a laptop computer so making changes to any of the production's lighting-related paperwork can be accomplished quickly and efficiently.

In a **repertory theatre** situation the lighting designer frequently designs a unit light plot to create basic lighting for each of the plays in the repertory. The lighting design for each play uses this basic plot, but additional instruments will be used and adjustments may be made to the focus and color of

IDOMENEO		CHANNEL HOOKUP				Page 1

LD: Joan Sullivan-Genthe
The Washington Opera
Kennedy Center Opera House

04 Dec 2005
ALD: Michael McNamara
ALD: Laura Jean Wickman
Master Electrician: George Kerig

Channel	Dim	Position	Unit	Type & Accessories & Watts	Purpose	Color & Temp
(1)	149	1ST ELEC	7	S4-19+SCR 575w	X FAR W	SCROLL 1
(2)	224	1ST ELEC	29	S4-19+SCR 575w	X FAR W	SCROLL 1
(3)	146	1ST ELEC	5	S4-26+SCR 575w	X CEN W	SCROLL 1
(4)	178	1ST ELEC	31	S4-26+SCR 575w	X CEN W	SCROLL 1
(5)	143	1ST ELEC	2	S4-26+SCR 575w	X NR W	SCROLL 1
(6)	181	1ST ELEC	34	S4-26+SCR 575w	X NR W	SCROLL 1
(7)	202	1ST ELEC	13	S4-26+SCR 575w	P2 FAR W	SCROLL 1
(8)	169	1ST ELEC	23	S4-26+SCR 575w	P2 FAR W	SCROLL 1
(9)	153	1ST ELEC	10	S4-26+SCR 575w	P2 CEN W	SCROLL 1
(10)	219	1ST ELEC	26	S4-26+SCR 575w	P2 CEN W	SCROLL 1
(11)	147	1ST ELEC	6	S4-19 575w	X FAR C	L161
(12)	179	1ST ELEC	30	S4-19 575w	X FAR C	L161
(13)	145	1ST ELEC	4	S4-26 575w	X CEN C	L161
(14)	227	1ST ELEC	32	S4-26 575w	X CEN C	L161
(15)	186	1ST ELEC	1	S4-26+T 575w	X NR C	L161
(16)	182	1ST ELEC	35	S4-26+T 575w	X NR C	L161
(17)	156	1ST ELEC	12	S4-26 575w	P2 FAR C	L161
(18)	217	1ST ELEC	24	S4-26 575w	P2 FAR C	L161
(19)	194	1ST ELEC	9	S4-26 575w	P2 CEN C	L161
(20)	221	1ST ELEC	27	S4-26 575w	P2 CEN C	L161
(21)	210	1ST ELEC	19	S4-26+SCR 575w	XO RIGHT	SCROLL 1
(22)	206	1ST ELEC	17	S4-26+SCR 575w	XO LEFT	SCROLL 1
(23)	205	1ST ELEC	16	S4-26 575w	SPARE	L202
(24)	211	1ST ELEC	20	S4-26 575w	SPARE	N/C
(25)	203	1ST ELEC	15	S4-26 575w	SPARE	N/C
(26)	212	1ST ELEC	21	S4-26 575w	CHAIR	L202
(27)	160	1ST ELEC	14	S4-26 575w	SPARE	N/C
(28)	214	1ST ELEC	22	S4-26 575w	FACE SL	L161
(29)	155	1ST ELEC	11	S4-26 575w	SPARE	N/C
(30)	172	1ST ELEC	25	S4-26 575w	SPARE	N/C
(31)	152	1ST ELEC	8	S4-26 575w	SPARE	N/C
(32)	223	1ST ELEC	28	S4-26 575w	SPARE	N/C
(35)	207	1ST ELEC	18	S4-26+IRIS 575w	SPARE	L281
(36)	270	2ND ELEC	19	S4-26+IRIS 575w	SPARE	N/C
(37)	239	1B ELEC	11	S4-26 575w	SR MIR	L201
(38)	240	1B ELEC	12	S4-26 575w	SL MIR	L201
(39)	200	1B ELEC	10	S4-26 575w	CR MIR	L201
(40)	215	1B ELEC	13	S4-26 575w	CL MIR	L201
(41)	199	1B ELEC	9	S4-26 575w	FACE SR	L281
(42)	216	1B ELEC	14	S4-26 575w	WCHAIR SP	L161
(43)	197	1B ELEC	8	S4-26 575w	SPARE	L202, T:R7797
(44)	173	1B ELEC	15	S4-26 575w	SPARE	L202, T:R7797
(45)	193	1B ELEC	7	S4-26 575w	MIR ON FLR DR	L202
(46)	222	1B ELEC	16	S4-26 575w	SPARE	N/C
(47)	189	1B ELEC	6	S4-26 575w	SPARE	L202, T:R7797
(48)	225	1B ELEC	17	S4-26 575w	SPARE	L202, T:R7797
(49)	231	1B ELEC	3	S4-26 575w	SPARE	N/C
(50)	230	1B ELEC	20	S4-26 575w	SPARE	N/C

Figure 2.3   A sample page from the instrument schedule (hookup sheet) for the 2002 Kennedy Center Opera House production of *Idomeneo*. Lighting design by Joan Sullivan-Genthe. Drafting by Michael McNamara and Laura Jean Wickman.

some instruments in the basic plot. While these design features will be notated on the plot and paperwork for each play, the physical changes of focus and color media must be accomplished each time that there is a **changeover** between plays. The lighting designer can do this work, or an associate lighting designer may be assigned to each play in the repertory to do the changeover.

Changeover: Changing from one play to another in a repertory theatre situation. Involves exchanging sets, costumes, and properties and making adjustments to lighting and sound.

Scenographic designer: A designer responsible for the entire artistic look—scenery, costumes, lighting, properties—of a production.

Hanging: The process of placing lighting instruments in their specified locations.

Circuiting: The process of connecting a lighting instrument to its specific stage circuit.

An associate lighting designer may also be employed to create the lighting design while working under the artistic supervision of a **scenographic designer** who is focusing his or her design efforts on the scenery and costumes.

PROGRAMMER

Programmers are individuals who program the specialized consoles used to control automated lighting fixtures and projectors. They generally work under the aesthetic direction of the lighting designer. Programmers may be freelance technicians although they are also often associated with companies that manufacture or distribute automated fixtures or projectors. Programmers are usually hired for individual projects in which these highly specialized fixtures and projectors are used rather than being employed by a producing organization for the full run of a show or for an entire season.

Skilled, experienced programmers are normally in great demand. And, on a purely practical note, top-level programmers are usually well paid—a most unusual situation in theatre—because of the high level of expertise required, the short time frames between load-in and performance, and the need for a quick, and accurate, implementation of the designer's visions.

Programmers normally run the console for one-off performances such as television specials and concert events, where making adjustments "on the fly" is frequently the norm rather than the exception. For events with more consistent performance expectations, such as theatre performances with multi-week (or longer) runs, programmers normally train other electricians to serve as board operators for the specialized consoles.

MASTER ELECTRICIAN

The master electrician, under the supervision of the lighting designer, associate or assistant designer, implements the lighting design. He or she is directly responsible for the acquisition, installation, and maintenance of all lighting equipment and the supervision of the crews who hang, focus, and run the lighting equipment during the production.

As head of the lighting crew, the master electrician is responsible for **hanging** and **circuiting** the equipment used in the lighting design. Each instrument is hung in the exact position shown on the light plot and is checked by the master electrician and crew to determine that it is functioning and circuited according to the instructions of the lighting designer.

The importance of the master electrician cannot be overestimated. He or she is not only responsible for making sure that the design is implemented according to the vision of the lighting designer, but for maintaining that look throughout the run of the production. During the run of a production, color media, particularly the darker shades, may bleach out and need to be replaced. Instruments may drift, or be knocked, out of focus. Lamps may burn out and need to be replaced. It is the responsibility of the master electrician, under the direction of the lighting designer (or his or her designate), to notice these discrepancies and correct them. Only if these tasks are accomplished will the design continue to look as it was intended.

ELECTRICIANS

The work of the electricians can be divided into three areas: hanging, focusing, and **running**.

The hanging crew places the lighting instruments and associated equipment in the positions designated by the light plot. This job is very important because the accurate placement of the instruments on the **pipes**, **booms**, and other locations affects the distribution of the light on the stage. The proper wattage and type of **lamp** are also indicated on the plot or hookup sheet, and it is the electrician's responsibility to ensure that the instruments are "lamped" as required. Additionally, the electricians also circuit and **patch** the instruments. The appropriate circuit and dimmer for each instrument are normally indicated on the light plot or instrument schedule, or the master electrician designates the appropriate circuit and dimmer during the hanging sessions. Finally, the electricians who are hanging the show also **gel** the instruments and, under the supervision of the lighting designer or assistant designer, focus the instruments.

The running crew is responsible for the operation of the lighting equipment during rehearsals and performances. Depending on the complexity of the production, as few as one or as many as five or more electricians are needed to run the lights for a production.

Although the electricians who operate the **light board** and specialty equipment during a performance have written instructions regarding the timed duration of each **cue**, they should be able to sense the rhythm of the play and integrate the various **fades** and other movements of the lights into the flow of the performance.

As previously mentioned, musicals and many other kinds of productions frequently require the use of a followspot. It is essential that the electrician who operates this instrument have a good sense of movement and timing as well as steady hands. Nothing is more distracting to an audience than a followspot that moves one way while the actor goes another. A followspot operator must master the mechanical intricacies of the instrument and follow the onstage action in a smooth, fluid, and unobtrusive manner.

Running: Controlling or operating some aspect of a production.

Pipe: A counterweighted batten or fixed metal pipe that holds lighting instruments or equipment.

Boom: A vertical pipe with a heavy base, frequently equipped with horizontal crossbars. Used as a hanging position for lighting instruments.

Lamp: The stage term for "light bulbs" used in stage lighting instruments.

Patch: To connect a stage circuit to a dimmer circuit.

Gel: (verb) To insert color media in a color frame and place on a lighting instrument. (noun) Color media made from gelatin.

Light board: A generic term used to describe all types of lighting control consoles.

Cue: A directive for action; for example, a change in the lighting.

Fade: To increase (fade-in) or decrease (fade-out) the intensity of the lights.

Patch panel: An interconnecting device that allows you to connect any stage circuit into any dimmer.

Repatch: To remove one circuit from a dimmer and replace it with another during a performance.

In theatres with **patch panels**, it may be necessary for the running crew electricians to **repatch** during the performance. Occasionally, a circuit must be patched into or removed from a dimmer during a performance. In patch panel systems that don't have a large number of dimmers, repatching may occur frequently and indeed may be the norm more than the exception.

Running crew electricians are also normally responsible for replacing burned-out lamps and color media that deteriorate during the run of the production, as well as refocusing instruments that have been accidentally knocked out of focus. They also recircuit instruments, move booms, and take care of any other activities involving lighting equipment during rehearsals or performances.

PRODUCTION DESIGN TEAM

The lighting designer is a working member of the production design team. The composition of the team may vary slightly from organization to organization and even from production to production, but the positions of responsibility and the lines of communication among the various members of the team are the same. Close coordination among the producer; director; and scenic, costume, lighting, and sound designers cannot be overemphasized. If there is unity of thought, style, and direction among the various members of this team, then the chances are good that the production concept will also be unified.

The director is the artistic manager and inspirational leader of the production design team. As such, he or she usually makes the final decisions on all artistic aspects of the production. The lighting designer frequently meets with the director during the production meetings (see the box "Production Meeting"). Under ideal conditions, the production concept evolves during these meetings. If the members of the production design team cannot be assembled to jointly develop the production concept, then the director frequently takes a more authoritarian stance and develops the production concept alone. Either way, the lighting designer must meet with the director to learn of his or thoughts regarding the production. If the director decides to change or adapt the script, the lighting designer has to know about it so that the lighting can be adjusted accordingly.

The lighting designer must work closely with the scenic designer because the work of one directly affects the work of the other. In many productions, the same person functions as both scenic and lighting designer. The form of the scenic design dictates, to a certain extent, the positions in which the lighting designer can place the lighting instruments. Obviously, if the set has a ceiling, the use of overhead or top lighting will be restricted, though not necessarily precluded. The scenic and lighting designers could decide, for

✳ Production Meeting

For any theatrical production to be successful it must be well organized, and communication within the group must be excellent. The production meeting is probably the single most important device for ensuring smooth communication between the members of the production design team—the producer; the director; and the scenic, costume, lighting, and sound designers. The initial production meetings will probably be attended only by the production design team. The purpose of these early meetings—ideally held on a daily or relatively frequent basis—is to develop the production concept. After the designers begin to produce their drawings, sketches, and plans, the production meetings decrease in frequency to about once a week, and their main purpose is then to keep other members of the team informed about progress and changes in all production areas. At this time the stage manager normally joins the discussions, although the stage manager may have been a part of the production design team from the beginning. The last production meeting is usually held just before the opening of the production.

example, to place beams on the ceiling. These beams could, in turn, **mask** slots cut on the upstage side of the beams, and instruments could be focused through those slots. Both the scenic and lighting designers will often have to compromise on their designs to achieve a compatible blend of the two.

Mask: To block the audience's view—generally of backstage equipment and space.

Because even moderately saturated color can drastically alter the appearance of delicately colored costumes, the lighting designer must hold discussions with the costume designer to learn of the color palette being used for the costumes. It is the lighting designer's responsibility to see that the costume designer's palette remains unchanged when the costumes appear onstage under the lights.

The ultimate goal of the production design team is the creation of an atmosphere and environment that support the production concept. This goal can be achieved only when each member of the production design team openly communicates his or her concepts and plans to the other members of the team.

Communication among the members of the production design team, as well as effective and conscientious work by every member of the lighting production team, is critical to the successful realization of the entire production. Each member of every team is an important link in the chain, and a chain is only as strong as its weakest link.

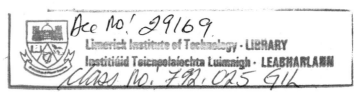

CHAPTER 3

Electrical Theory and Practice

Preset light board: A lighting control console that uses electromechanical variable-resistance switches to control the output of the dimmers.

Computer board: A lighting control console that uses a computer to store and recall dimmer intensity levels and fade times for each cue; it also stores and recalls various other functions.

Atom: The smallest particle of a chemical element that retains the structural properties of that element.

Proton: A fundamental particle in the structure of the nucleus of an atom; possesses a positive charge.

Neutron: A fundamental particle in the structure of an atom; possesses a neutral charge.

Electron: A negatively charged fundamental particle that orbits around the nucleus of an atom.

In the first edition of this book, I wrote, "A thorough understanding of electricity and the component elements of the electromotive force are not essential to a comprehension of basic stage lighting." At the time I wrote those words, the **preset light board** was the standard in the lighting industry; today the **computer board** is king and moving light fixtures are becoming commonplace. Control devices, for light boards and stage equipment as well as shop tools, that 25 years ago were electromechanical are now electronic. Times have changed. It has become a pragmatic reality that students of technical theatre must comprehend the function of electricity and electronics. The discussion that follows differentiates between the terms: electricity generally pertains to the use of the electromotive force to perform work—make lamps glow, motors run, and so on; electronics generally refers to the low-voltage circuits and devices used to control the flow of electricity.

ELECTRICITY—WHAT IS IT?

The study of electricity has to begin with a brief excursion into the not-so-mysterious realm of basic atomic theory. This is because some fundamental laws of electricity are based on the laws of atomic structure. For this reason we need to know a little bit about the atom.

The **atom** is the smallest complete building block in nature. But an atom is composed of even smaller particles: protons, neutrons, and electrons. The subatomic particles possess specific electrical properties. The **proton** has a positive charge, the **neutron** a neutral charge, and the **electron** a negative charge. The physical structure of any atom is very similar to the configura-

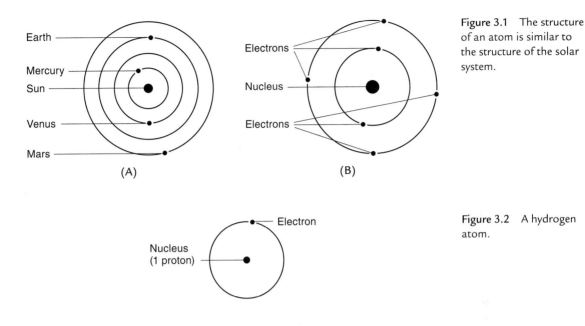

Figure 3.1 The structure of an atom is similar to the structure of the solar system.

Figure 3.2 A hydrogen atom.

tion of our solar system. In the same manner that the earth rotates around the sun (Figure 3.1A), electrons follow a slightly elliptical orbit as they whirl around the nucleus of an atom (Figure 3.1B).

In a stable atom the number of electrons in orbit around the nucleus is equaled by the number of protons in the nucleus. Hydrogen, the lightest and least complex atom, is a perfect example of this principle. Figure 3.2 shows the single electron of the hydrogen atom in orbit around the nucleus, which is composed of a single proton. Because the orbiting electron has a negative charge and the proton in the nucleus has a positive charge, an electrical attraction exists between them. The electron is prevented from being pulled into the nucleus by the centrifugal force of its orbital movement. At the same time, the electron is restrained from breaking out of orbit and flying away by the attraction. This attraction is an important underlying principle of electricity and is the basis for the first important law of electricity, the law of charges: *like charges repel, and unlike charges attract.*

If it were physically possible to isolate two protons, they would defy all attempts to bring them together. The same results would occur if attempts were made to push two electrons together. But if an electron and proton were placed in proximity, they would zip toward each other until they met. The law of charges is the "electrical glue" that holds the atom together.

In atoms that are more complex than hydrogen, such as oxygen (Figure 3.3), additional electrons orbit in several planes around the nucleus. These electrons are counterbalanced by an equal number of protons in the nucleus, so the atom remains in an electrically balanced, or stable, condition.

Figure 3.3 An oxygen atom.

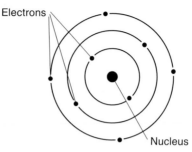

These additional orbiting electrons occupy orderly spherical shells at specific distances from the nucleus. Each of these shells can hold only a certain number of electrons. When each shell is filled with its quota of electrons, a tight bonding takes place, and no additional electrons can be added. Although it is possible to dislodge an electron from one of these filled shells, it takes a relatively large amount of energy to do so.

As the structure and weight of the atom grow, the number of protons in the nucleus increases, as does the corresponding number of electrons orbiting around it. Since the electrons cannot force their way into the already filled shells, they must orbit at a greater distance. The increased distance between the orbiting electron and its counterbalancing proton in the nucleus decreases the attractive force that holds the electron in orbit.

An atom of copper has 29 electrons in orbit around its nucleus. Because of copper's particular atomic structure, only a very weak force holds its outer electrons in orbit, and only a very weak force is needed to dislodge them from the outer shell, or **valence shell**, of the copper atom.

A strand of copper wire is composed of billions upon billions of copper atoms, all having the same characteristically weak valence electron. The atoms in the wire are in such close proximity to one another (most of them are intertwined with their neighbors) that the nuclei of adjacent atoms can exert the same or more attractive force on their neighbors' valence electrons than they do on their own. Consequently, many of the valence electrons break away from their "home" atoms, momentarily attach themselves to other atoms, or float freely within the confines of the wire.

If this cloud of **free electrons** meandering in the wire could be organized to move in the same direction, an **electrical current** would be generated, simply because an electrical current is defined as the flow of electrons from one point to another. The unit of measurement for this electron flow is the **ampere**.

How can free electrons be motivated to move from one point to another? The answer lies in a practical application of the law of charges (like charges repel, and unlike charges attract). Because the electrons have a negative charge, they are attracted to a body that has a positive charge. However,

Valence shell: The outermost plane of orbiting electrons in the structure of an atom.

Free electron: An electron that has broken away from its "home" atom to float free.

Electrical current: The flow or movement of electrons through a conductor.

Ampere: The unit of measurement of electrical current.

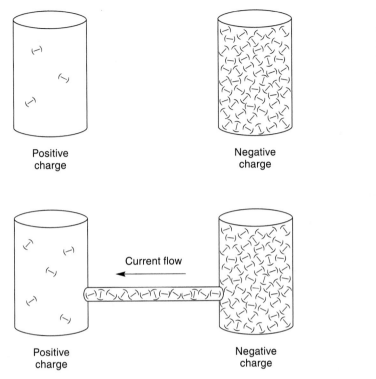

Figure 3.4 An electrical charge is created when electrons are transferred from one place to another.

Positive charge

Negative charge

Figure 3.5 Electrical current flows from a negatively to a positively charged body.

Current flow

Positive charge

Negative charge

it isn't possible to create a positive charge by itself. A negative charge is created simultaneously with the creation of a positive charge, because electrical charges are produced by the transfer of electrons from one point to another. Specifically, when electrons leave one point (creating a positive charge), they move to another point (creating a negative charge). (In the process, electrons are neither created nor destroyed but simply transferred.) Figure 3.4 simplistically illustrates the principle that the positive charge is created by the removal of electrons, and the negative charge is the result of an accumulation of electrons.

If two bodies of opposite charge are created, an electrical current could be generated if a conductor, such as a copper wire, were connected between them. Free electrons would flow from the negatively charged body to the positively charged body, as shown in Figure 3.5. The flow, or current, would continue as long as there was a difference in charge between the two bodies. This difference in the electrical charge between the bodies is called **potential** and is measured in **volts**.

The amount of voltage, or potential strength of the electrical system, is directly related to the difference in potential between the charged bodies. The greater the difference in potential between the charges, the greater that

Potential: The difference in electrical charge between two bodies; measured in volts.

Volt: The unit of measurement of electrical potential.

system's capacity to do work. For example, a system with a rating of 220 volts has a greater potential capacity to do work than does a 117-volt system.

ELECTRICITY AT WORK

To understand how electricity works, you need to first understand a number of separate but interrelated facts about electricity. The following information is set out in an order and manner that will, hopefully, make this task seem a little less daunting.

Direct and Alternating Current

There are two types of electrical current: direct current (DC) and alternating current (AC).

Direct Current   In the last section, Figure 3.5 illustrated the flow of electrons from a negative to a positive charge. The flow of electrons in one direction is known as direct current (DC). Batteries are DC sources. In a battery the negative terminal, [identified by a (−) sign], is created by an excess of electrons; the positive terminal, [marked with a (+) sign], by a dearth of electrons. This electron transfer happens through a chemical reaction. DC power cannot be transmitted over long distances without a severe loss of voltage, but batteries provide an excellent source of power for portable devices.

Alternating Current   Alternating current can be transmitted over long distances with little loss of voltage. In alternating current (AC) the direction of flow of the electrons is reversed on a periodic basis. In the United States utility companies generate power that reverses direction 120 times, or 60 cycles, per second. Figure 3.6 illustrates this process. Each cycle starts with no voltage (point *A*). During the first half-cycle the voltage increases to a maximum (point *B*), then decreases until it is zero again (point *C*). For the second half-cycle the same process is repeated, only on the negative side of the graph. During the positive half of the cycle the electrons can be thought of as moving in one direction and in the other direction during the negative half of the cycle. This reversal of direction occurs 60 times each second.

Source: The origin of electrical potential, such as a battery or 120-volt wall outlet.

Load: A device that converts electrical energy into another form of energy: a lamp converts electrical energy to light and heat; an electrical motor converts electricity to mechanical energy.

Circuit: A conductive path through which electricity flows.

A Simple Electrical Circuit

Every electrical system must have three parts: a **source**, a **load**, and a **circuit**. Figure 3.7 illustrates this concept. The source provides a difference in potential, or voltage. The load is a device that uses electricity to do some type of work. The circuit is a pathway that the current follows as it flows from

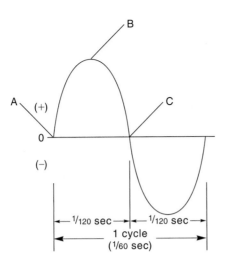

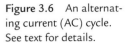

Figure 3.6 An alternating current (AC) cycle. See text for details.

the negative to the positive terminal of the source. Current flows from the source to the lamp through the "hot" wire and returns to the source through the "neutral" wire. In the United States the insulation color of the hot wire normally is black (occasionally red), while the neutral wire is white.

Figure 3.8 illustrates a simple circuit of a battery and a lamp. The source of this system is an ordinary flashlight battery. The load is a small incandescent lamp. The circuit is composed of copper wire. When the wires are attached to the lamp and the terminals of the battery, a current of electrons flows from the negative to the positive terminal of the battery. As the electrons pass through the filament of the lamp, resistance to their flow causes the filament to heat up and incandesce, or give off light. The current will continue to flow as long as the circuit is intact and there is enough voltage left in the battery to overcome the resistance of the circuit and the lamp. When the voltage is reduced to the point that it cannot overcome the resistance the current stops and the lamp no longer glows.

Basic Circuits

Two primary types of circuits, series and parallel, are used to distribute electricity. A third type, known as a combination circuit, combines the principles of the two.

Series Circuit   In a series circuit all of the electricity flows through every element of the circuit, as shown in Figure 3.9. In a series circuit if any of the lamps burn out, the circuit will be broken, the electricity won't flow, and the remaining lamps will go out.

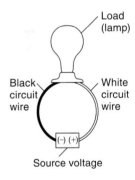

Figure 3.7 A basic electrical circuit.

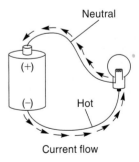

Figure 3.8 A lamp will incandesce when current flows through it.

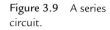

Figure 3.9   A series circuit.

Figure 3.10   A parallel circuit.

Figure 3.11   A combination circuit.

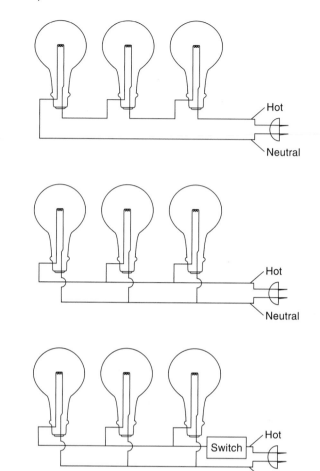

Parallel Circuit   In a parallel circuit only a portion of the electricity flows through each of the branches of the circuit. If one of the lamps shown in Figure 3.10 burns out, the electricity will continue to flow in the rest of the circuit, and the other lamps will continue to glow.

Combination Circuit   Any electrical circuit that uses a switch to control a light is a working example of a combination circuit. In a typical application of a combination circuit in stage lighting, a control device (switch, dimmer, **fuse, circuit breaker**) is used in series with the lamp load, and the lamps are wired in parallel as shown in Figure 3.11. The series arrangement allows the switch or dimmer to exert control over the whole circuit, and the parallel wiring of the lamp outlets allows individual lamps to be inserted or removed from the circuit without affecting its operation.

Fuse: A device to protect a circuit from an over-load; has a soft metal strip that melts, breaking circuit continuity.

Circuit breaker: A device to protect a circuit from an overload; has a bi-metal device that trips open when heated by excess current, breaking circuit continuity.

Power Calculations

The following information can be used to calculate the safe capacities of electrical circuits.

Ohm's Law   Although it's interesting to know that electrons flow within a circuit, unless there is some way of determining how the various parts of the circuit affect one another, there is no real way to understand and predict what will happen in any electrical circuit. Fortunately, a German physicist, Georg Simon Ohm, discovered in the nineteenth century that some very basic rules apply to the functioning of electricity in a circuit. These relationships have been formalized as Ohm's law, and they are the primary mathematical expressions used in determining electron action within a circuit. Ohm's law states: *As voltage increases, current increases; as resistance increases, current decreases.*

The diagrams in Figures 3.12 and 3.13 will help illustrate these relationships. They show very simple schematic diagrams or drawings that substitute symbols for the various parts of the circuit. The ⫤ symbol represents a battery, and the ‑Ⱳ‑ symbol represents **resistance**, or load, within the circuit. Figure 3.12 illustrates the first portion of Ohm's law. The voltage of the battery in Figure 3.12A is 10 volts. With this voltage the 1-ohm resistance allows a current flow of 10 amperes. If the voltage is doubled to 20 volts, as shown in Figure 3.12B, and the resistance is not changed, the current will also double, to 20 amperes.

Figure 3.13 illustrates the second element of Ohm's law. Figure 3.13A is a 10-volt system with a resistance, or load, of 1 ohm. This configuration allows a current flow of 10 amperes. In Figure 3.13B the voltage remains constant at 10 volts, but the resistance has been doubled to 2 ohms, which results in a reduction of the current to 5 amperes.

In both cases it is important to remember that the speed of the electron flow is constant. The increase or decrease in current flow is the result of an increase or decrease in the number of electrons flowing in the circuit.

Another way of looking at the relationships stated in Ohm's law may help understand them. The voltage can be compared to the electrical pressure

Resistance: The opposition to electron flow within a conductor, measured in ohms; the amount of the resistance is dependent on the chemical makeup of the material through which the electricity is flowing.

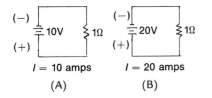

Figure 3.12   As voltage increases, current increases.

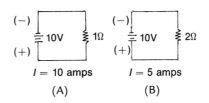

Figure 3.13   As resistance increases, current decreases.

that causes the electrons to flow within the circuit. If more pressure (voltage) is applied, it would be logical for more electrons to flow. Since resistance is defined as opposition to the flow of electrons, any increase in resistance would naturally cause the electron flow, or current, to decrease.

The relationships of Ohm's law can be mathematically expressed as:

$$I = \frac{E}{R}$$

where I = current in amperes, E = voltage in volts, and R = resistance in ohms. This basic formula can be rearranged into two other forms. Each of these can be used to find the value of the other components in the relationship:

$$E = IR$$

$$R = \frac{E}{I}$$

These mathematical expressions of Ohm's law are extremely valuable in working with low-voltage electronic systems such as those found in the control portion of electronic dimmers and sound systems.

The Power Formula   Another formula, which is a derivation of Ohm's law, is more useful when dealing with the higher voltage encountered in stage lighting systems. It is called the power formula. This formula is used when it is necessary to determine how much power an electrical circuit will consume.

Household light bulbs, toasters, stage lamps, and electrical motors all convert electrical energy into mechanical energy, light, or heat in accomplishing their tasks. The amount of electrical energy converted, or consumed, is measured in **watts**. Usually the wattage figure is written on a label located somewhere on the device. Almost all household lamps have both the voltage and wattage printed on the top of the bulb. Toasters, electrical motors, and similar devices usually have a tag or label fixed somewhere on the unit. The label states both the voltage and wattage of the unit. Stage lighting lamps have this information printed on either the metal lamp base or the top of the lamp.

The power formula is usually referred to colloquially as either the "pie" formula:

$$P = IE$$

where

P = power in watts
I = current in amperes
E = voltage in volts

Watt: The unit measurement of power required to do work.

or the "West Virginia" formula:

$$W = VA$$

where

W = power in watts
V = voltage in volts
A = current in amperes

The power formula can be rearranged just as Ohm's law can:

$$P = IE \qquad\qquad W = VA$$

$$E = \frac{P}{I} \qquad\qquad A = \frac{W}{V}$$

$$I = \frac{P}{E} \qquad\qquad V = \frac{W}{A}$$

With these three expressions of the power formula, it is possible to find the unknown quantity in an electrical circuit if the other two factors are known.

An everyday example will help illustrate the point. You want to put a desk lamp on a table, but the lamp's power cord won't reach from the table to the wall outlet. You go to the hardware store to buy an extension cord, and the only information attached to the power cord indicates that it will safely carry 6 amperes of current. You know that the voltage in your apartment is 117 volts. The lamp you plan to use is rated at 150 watts. To determine if the extension cord is safe to use, you will need to find out how many amperes of current the 150-watt lamp will require. To find the answer just plug the known information ($V = 117$, $W = 150$) into the appropriate variation of the power formula—the variation that has the unknown variable (in this case, A) located on the left side of the equal sign:

$$A = \frac{W}{V}$$

$$= \frac{150}{117}$$

$$= 1.28$$

The lamp creates a current of 1.28 amperes, so the extension cord, which can carry 6 amperes, will be safe to use.

Practical Applications of the Power Formula   The following problems illustrate how the power formula can be used to calculate the safe electrical limits of typical stage lighting situations. Remember that when you know two of the three variables of the power formula, the easiest way to solve these types of problems is to place the known information on the right-hand side of the equal sign of the appropriate form ($W = VA$, $V = W/A$, $A = W/V$) of the power formula. In the following problems, and in most situations in the real world, you will be provided with the values of two of the three variables.

Problem No. 1   The output voltage of a dimmer is 120 VAC. The dimmer can handle 20 amperes of current. What is the maximum safe load that can be placed on this dimmer?

$$watts = volts \times amperes \ (W = VA)$$
$$W = 120 \times 20$$
$$= 2{,}400 \ watts$$

The dimmer can safely carry any load up to, but not exceeding, 2,400 watts.

Problem No. 2   The system voltage is 120 VAC. The dimmer can carry 2,400 watts (2.4 kilowatts, or kW). The 14-gauge cable connecting the instruments to the dimmer can carry 15 amperes. Using the 14-gauge cable, how many 500-watt lighting instruments can be safely loaded onto the dimmer?

   We already know that the dimmer can handle 2.4 kW, but we need to determine the load that can be safely carried by the cable. (*Hint:* Insert the two "knowns"—120 VAC system voltage (V) and 15 ampere capacity of the 14-gauge cable (A)—on the right-hand side of the equation.)

$$W = VA$$
$$W = 120 \times 15$$
$$= 1{,}800 \ watts$$

The cable can carry a maximum load of 1,800 watts. To determine the number of 500-watt lighting instruments that can be carried by the cable, divide 1,800 by 500:

$$\frac{1{,}800}{500} = 3.6$$

Theoretically, a 14-gauge cable can safely carry three and six-tenths 500-watt instruments. However, since you can't load six-tenths of a lighting instrument onto a circuit, the "real world" answer is that a 14-gauge cable can safely carry three 500-watt instruments (1,500 total watts). But, since the 2,400-watt dimmer can safely carry four 500-watt instruments (2,000 total watts), the correct answer to Problem 2 is that four 500-watt instruments can be safely loaded onto the dimmer *as long as any one leg of the 14-gauge cable doesn't carry more than three instruments.* Figure 3.14 illustrates three safe (A, B, C) and one unsafe (D) methods of loading four 500-watt instruments onto the dimmer with 14-gauge cable. Figure 3.14D could be made safe if the cable was changed to 12 gauge, which can safely carry 2,400 watts.

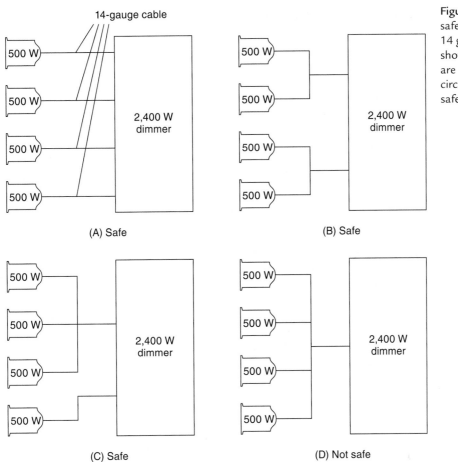

Figure 3.14 Wiring safety. All cables are 14 gauge. The circuits shown in A, B, and C are safe to operate; the circuit shown in D is not safe. See text for details.

More Practical Information

There are additional concepts, terms, and practical information that will help you more thoroughly understand how electricity works.

Conductors and Insulators   An electrical conductor is any material with an abundance of free electrons. Copper, aluminum, gold, and silver are all excellent conductors. Water is also a very good conductor. Conversely, an insulator is a material with few free electrons. The lack of free electrons effectively prevents the flow of electricity through an insulator. Air, glass, paper, rubber, and most plastics are good insulators. In an electrical wire the conductor (usually copper) is surrounded by an insulator (normally rubber or plastic) to keep the electrical flow confined within the conductor and to prevent the conductor from making contact with anything else.

Short circuit: A short circuit, or short, is created when a very large surge of current causes a portion of a conductor to explosively melt.

Pigtail: The electrical cable containing hot, neutral, and ground wires used to connect a lighting instrument to a power source such as a dimming system.

Plug: The male portion of a connecting device.

System ground: The grounding point—usually a metal rod driven into the earth outside the building or an underground metal water pipe—for an electrical system.

Grounding plug: A plug that connects to ground in addition to electrical service. The grounding pin is longer than the energized pins to complete the ground before the electrical service is connected.

Service panel: Also called fuse box or panel box. Normally contains a primary power switch (called the main disconnect) for the area being served by the panel as well as circuit breakers or fuses for the individual circuits in that area.

Disconnect box: Contains a main disconnect, but no circuit breakers for individual circuits. Used as a power source for, normally, 220-VAC equipment.

Grounding   Safety dictates that all electrical equipment be grounded. The purpose of the ground wire, also called the ground circuit, is to provide a low-resistance path for the electricity to follow in case of a **short circuit** between the hot wire and the device's metallic housing. Grounding requires making a direct mechanical connection between the conductive housing of an electrical device and the earth. Devices with metal housings, such as lighting instruments and dimmer packs, have a ground wire mechanically connected to the housing. This wire runs through a **pigtail** and **plug** into the theatre's dimming system where it connects with another ground wire. If you could visually follow that ground wire throughout the system you would see that it eventually makes a mechanical connection to the **system ground**. The purpose of the grounding circuit is to provide a low-resistance path for the electricity to follow in case of a short circuit or accidental connection between the device's hot wire and its housing.

Double Insulation   While stage lighting fixtures and other devices with metal housings have a **grounding plug**, some plug-in electrical hand tools—most frequently those with plastic cases—do not have a grounding pin on the plug. The information plate attached to these tools' casings will probably carry the words "double insulated." These tools don't need grounding, because the casing that you hold is actually a second, or outer, casing. These two layers of plastic insulators (the casings) effectively isolate you from any potential short.

Electrical Power Service   Before beginning this discussion of electric power service, remember: These high-voltage distribution systems can kill; do not work on **service panels** or **disconnect boxes** unless you are a qualified electrician.

Is 120 Volts Really 120 Volts?

Throughout this book you will find references to 120 volt electricity. In reality that figure is an approximate average. The voltage of alternating current (AC) electricity generated by utility companies varies between approximately 115 and 125 volts during the course of a normal day. Those variations are caused by a number of factors including the number of generators creating electricity for the system as well as the load or demand being placed on the system.

Almost all equipment that uses 120 volt electricity—lights, motors, dimmers, computers, and so forth—is designed to work efficiently while the voltage varies between 115 and 125 volts. If, however, the generated voltage moves below 115 or above 125, damage to equipment can occur.

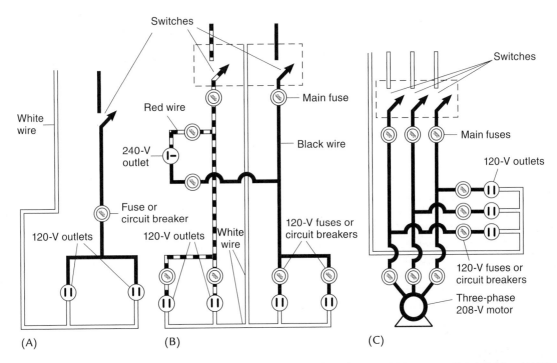

Figure 3.15   (A) Two-wire single-phase 120-VAC system; (B) three-wire single-phase 120/240-VAC system; (C) four-wire three-phase 120/208-VAC system.

A number of wiring configurations are used to distribute AC power. Figure 3.15A illustrates a typical 120-VAC service system. According to National Electrical Code (NEC) practice, in the United States the insulation of the hot wire in this system is colored black (occasionally red) and the insulation of the other wire, the neutral, is colored white.

Notice that the circuit-control devices—switches, fuses/circuit breakers, outlets, or receptacles—are placed on the hot wire in all applications. Control devices are always placed on the hot wire, never on the neutral.

The ground wire is not included in any of these illustrations, because it should not be used as part of the electrical distribution system. However, it needs to be included in the wiring of the system, and, according to code, its color should be green. The ground wire connects the nonelectrical metal parts of the system such as dimmer cases, instrument housings, and receptacle boxes to ground. The ground wire is never used as either a hot or neutral conductor in the system.

Figure 3.15B illustrates a three-wire single-phase 120/240-VAC system. The hot wires are depicted as black and red. In some installations they are both black. The voltage between either of the two hot wires and the neutral (white) will be 120 VAC. The voltage between the two hot wires will range between 220 and 240 VAC. Electrical service is delivered to most houses, buildings, and theatres with this three-wire system. In a typical theatre, the high voltage electricity—220 to 240 VAC—is routed from the service panel to the permanently mounted dimming system as well as shop and stage disconnect boxes. The 120-VAC electricity is distributed to various lighting fixtures and wall outlets throughout the structure.

Figure 3.15C shows a four-wire, three-phase 120/208-VAC service system. This type of service normally is used for large commercial buildings. The voltage between the neutral (white) and any of the three hot lines (black) will be 120 VAC. The voltage between any two of the hot wires will measure 208 VAC.

Theatres normally have one primary service panel where the power enters the building. From that primary service panel, power is routed to subpanels and disconnect boxes throughout the building to serve its various needs—stage, lobby, lighting system, shops, and so forth.

It is important to know the voltage of the system serving your theatre because most electrical equipment is designed to work at a specific voltage. Serious damage may occur to equipment designed to work with 208 VAC when it is connected to 220- to 240-VAC electricity. Similarly, serious damage can occur to 220- to 240-volt equipment run at 208 VAC. Some equipment, such as many portable dimmer packs, have an input voltage switch that will let you select either 208 or 220 to 240 VAC to match the voltage of your power service. It is a fairly easy task to measure the voltage at a disconnect box or receptacle, but, for safety reasons, this work should be accomplished by a supervisor or qualified electrician.

Overload   An overload occurs when the current flowing through a circuit is greater than the maximum current for which the system was designed. An example of an overload is created when a too-heavy load is placed on a circuit—as when a 3,000-watt load is placed on a circuit that was designed to safely carry a load of only 2,400 watts.

Shorts   The difference between an overloaded circuit and a short circuit is really just a matter of degree. A short circuit, or short, is created when a very large surge of current in an overloaded circuit causes a portion of the wire, insulation, or anything else at point of the short to explode. A short happens when a very low resistance alternative to the primary circuit is created. These alternative paths form when a wire breaks or comes loose from its terminal or when the insulation is worn away from the connector, allowing it to touch another conductor or come into contact with the device's metal housing.

If a short occurs in a grounded circuit, the very low resistance path between the circuit and the earth invites the surge of current to follow the ground circuit path. The high current flow activates a fuse or circuit breaker to shut off the electricity to the shorted equipment. If a circuit isn't grounded or if the ground circuit doesn't function properly (perhaps someone clipped off the ground pin from the plug) and you picked up the shorted device, you would be severely shocked or possibly killed, because your body would act as the ground circuit to provide the path of least resistance between the shorted circuit and the earth.

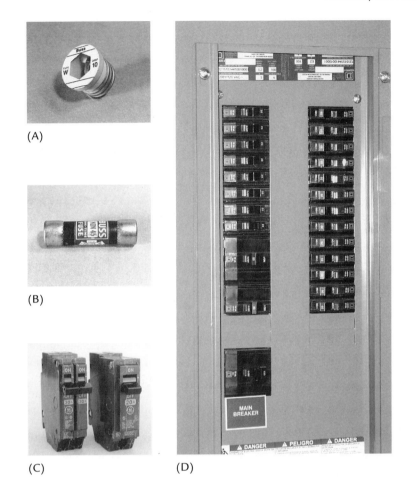

(A)

(B)

(C)   (D)

Figure 3.16 Fuses and circuit breakers protect electrical circuits from overload. (A) Plug fuse, (B) cartridge fuse, (C) circuit breaker, (D) circuit breakers in service panel.

Fuses and Circuit Breakers   Fuses and circuit breakers (see Figure 3.16) are devices designed to protect circuits from overloads. To effectively protect a circuit, a fuse or circuit breaker must have the same amperage rating as the conductors in the circuit as shown in Table 3.1. For example, typical stage lighting circuits have 12-gauge wire that is rated to safely carry 20 amperes (amps) of current. To properly protect this circuit the fuse or circuit breaker must also be rated at 20 amps. When an overload or short occurs both fuses and circuit breakers open or create a physical break in the circuit to stop the flow of electricity. They accomplish this task in two different ways.

A fuse contains a soft metallic strip that becomes a link in the circuit when it is placed in its socket or fuse holder. If the current flowing in the circuit exceeds the rated capacity of the fuse, the strip melts, breaking the circuit and stopping the flow of electricity. Fuses are not reusable. When one "blows" it must be replaced. Always replace blown fuses with ones of the

TABLE 3.1   American Wire Gauge Current Capacity Chart

Gauge of wire	10	12	14	16	18
Capacity in amps	25	20	15	6	3
Capacity in watts (@ 120 VAC)[a]	3,000	2,400	1,800	720	360
Fuses/circuit breakers (in amps)	25	20	15	6	3

[a]The capacities indicated are maximums and assume that all elements in the circuit are in excellent repair. For safety considerations, unless you are absolutely certain that the equipment is in excellent shape, each of these figures should be reduced by approximately 10%.

same rating. If a fuse with a higher rating is used, the fuse won't protect the circuit and a fire may result if the circuit is overloaded.

A circuit breaker basically functions like a switch. It has a handle with which you can turn the circuit on and off. Additionally, when the current flow exceeds the rating of the circuit breaker, an internal bimetal strip flexes and trips a release to open the circuit. The circuit breaker doesn't have to be replaced when it trips. Simply reset the circuit breaker by moving the handle to the off position and then back to the on position.

If a circuit isn't protected by a fuse or circuit breaker and the circuit becomes overloaded, the various elements within the system—conductors, dimmers, plugs, and so on—could heat up. If the overload is sufficiently large, the elements within the system will heat up to the point where they will either melt or catch fire. If combustible material is in the immediate proximity of the overheated elements, it is very possible that a serious fire will occur.

Current-Carrying Capacity of Cable   Electrical wires and cables, and the fuses and circuit breakers designed to protect them from overload, are designed to carry specific current loads. This information is shown in Table 3.1.

Wiring of Control Devices   Control devices such as switches, dimmers, fuses, and circuit breakers are always placed on the hot leg—the black wire—of a circuit.

Input and Output Voltage   Input voltage is the voltage that is fed into a device (dimmer, amplifier, and so forth). The output voltage is the voltage that comes out of the same device. In stage lighting systems, input voltage refers to the voltage that is fed to the dimmer pack (used with portable dimming systems) or rack (used with permanently installed systems) while output voltage refers to the voltage coming out of the dimmers.

The input voltage for most dimming systems in the United States is generally referred to as 220 VAC. (The term 220 VAC is a generic term

SAFETY TIP

Electrical Hazards

Electricity is extremely dangerous. It can burn, maim, and kill. Any piece of equipment that is connected to an electrical outlet should always be handled with caution and common sense. If you follow the safety procedures and work habits outlined below, your work with electricity can be safe and productive.

1. If you don't know what you're doing, don't do it. Ask your supervisor, or consult a trained electrician.

2. When working with electricity, use tools with handles that are covered with plastic or rubber insulation.

3. Use wooden or fiberglass ladders when working on elevated electrical jobs. Electricity will always take the path of least resistance, and a metal ladder (and your body) provides a very-low-resistance path. If metal ladders must be used, insulate them with high-quality rubber foot pads. Movable metal scaffolds or adjustable ladders should have lockable rubber casters.

4. Disconnect any device (lighting instrument, motor, amplifier) from the circuit before you work on it. Unplug any lighting instrument before changing the lamp.

5. Use common sense: Don't touch any bare wires. Don't work in damp locations or put a drink where it could spill on an electrical or electronic component. Don't intentionally overload a circuit. Don't try to bypass fuses or circuit breakers.

6. Maintain the integrity of all ground circuits. Don't clip the ground plug off of any extension cord or power cord. When necessary, use ground plug adapters.

7. Check cables and connectors periodically, and replace any items that show signs of cracking, chipping, or other deterioration. Cracks in the insulation of cables and connectors increase the chances of receiving a shock from the device.

8. Keep the cables and connectors clean. Remove any corrosion, paint, grease, dust, or other accumulations as soon as they become evident. These substances can act as insulation between the contacts of the connector, and—if flammable—they can pose a fire hazard.

9. When stage or microphone cables are not in use, coil them and hang them up. A cable will stay neatly coiled if the connectors

(continued)

SAFETY TIP

Electrical Hazards *(continued)*

are plugged together or if it is tied with light rope or fastened with a Velcro loop.

10. Always disconnect a plug by pulling on the body of the connector, not the cable. Pulling on the cable puts unnecessary strain on the cable clamp and will eventually defeat the clamp. When the cable clamp no longer functions, pulling on the cable places the strain directly on the electrical connections.

11. Be sure that all elements of a cable are of the same electrical rating: 12-gauge cable (capable of carrying 20 amperes of current) should have only 20-ampere-rated connectors.

frequently used, though often inaccurately, to describe voltage in the 208- to 240-VAC range.) The output voltage for dimmers in the United States is 120 VAC. Inside the dimmer pack the input voltage (usually 208 to 240 VAC) is broken down (reduced) so it can be used by the individual dimmers, which, in the United States, are designed to work at an output voltage of 117 to 120 VAC.

Wire Colors   The National Electrical Code (NEC) specifies that, in the United States, the insulation of hot wires in electrical circuits is normally colored black or, under specific circumstances, red. Neutral wires should be white and ground wires should be green. Sometimes these guidelines have not been followed, so it is prudent to always test the wires of a circuit to determine which wires are hot and which are neutral and ground. This testing should be done by, or under the supervision of, a supervisor or qualified electrician.

CHAPTER 4

Lenses, Lamps, Reflectors, and Lighting Instruments

It is very easy to become enamored of the various tools (some would call them toys) of lighting design. However, lighting instruments and dimmers as well as the control and distribution systems are not ends in themselves; they are the metaphorical mallet and chisels that lighting designers use to create their sculptures in light. This chapter will explore the major lighting instruments used in the theatre.

LENSES

The lenses used with most stage lighting instruments control the angle of the beam of light emitted by those instruments. Lenses refract light, which means that they redirect, or deflect, light from its normally straight path. The amount of deflection depends on the angle of intersection between the light ray and the surface of the lens, as well as the density of the medium through which the light is passing.

When a light ray passes from one medium into another medium of greater density (for example, from air into glass), it bends away from its original direction of travel. The direction of the deflection depends on the angle of intersection of the light ray and the boundary between the two media. When the light ray passes through the glass and reenters the air (from more to less dense), it bends back toward its original direction of travel. Figure 4.1 provides an illustration of these principles.

The more pronounced the curvature of the convex face of the lens, the more quickly light rays entering the lens from the convex side will converge, as shown in Figure 4.2. The distance it takes the light to converge into a

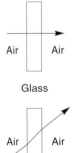

Figure 4.1 Light rays are deflected when they pass through a lens.

41

Figure 4.2 The greater the curvature of the convex face of a lens, the greater the angle of deflection, and vice versa.

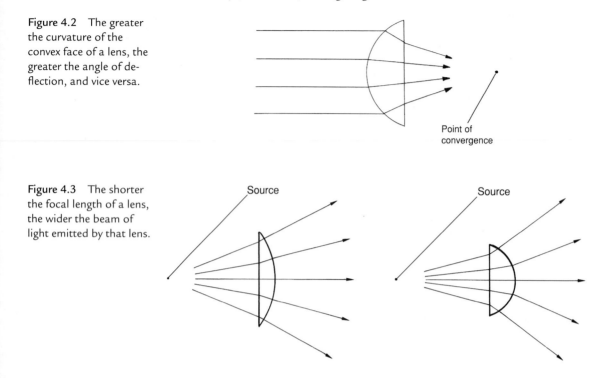

Point of convergence

Figure 4.3 The shorter the focal length of a lens, the wider the beam of light emitted by that lens.

Source

Source

Why So Many Lenses?

Theoretically, a single plano-convex lens would work very nicely in stage lighting instruments, but several practical considerations preclude the use of these lenses. To be optically effective, a single lens would need a severe curvature on its convex side, which would result in a thick lens; and a thick lens has two disadvantages. First, thick lenses are susceptible to heat fracture. During the manufacture of the lens, molten glass is poured into a mold. In the cooling process the outside of the lens cools faster than its inside, setting up stresses inside the lens that can cause it to crack. The internal stresses can be controlled by slow cooling in a special oven that carefully lowers the temperature over a period of hours. In practical theatre applications, however, lenses are quickly heated by the lamps, and there is no controlled heating or cooling. As a result, thick lenses almost always crack. Second, a certain amount of light passing through any lens is absorbed by the glass: the thicker the glass, the more light it absorbs. In reality, double plano-convex lens trains, step lenses, and fresnel lenses all absorb less light than does a single thicker lens of the same focal length.

Figure 4.4 Double plano-convex lens train.

single point is referred to as the **focal length** of the lens. The specific focal length of a **plano-convex lens** is determined by the curvature of the convex face of the lens. The greater the curvature, the shorter the focal length.

The focal length of a lens affects the angle of the beam of light emitted by that lens. When considered in a relationship to the diameter of the lens, the shorter the focal length, the wider the beam of light emitted by that lens, as shown in Figure 4.3. A standard stage lighting instrument—the ellipsoidal reflector spotlight (ERS)—can be used to demonstrate this principle. If it is equipped with a lens 6 inches in diameter that has a focal length of 9 inches (known as a 6 × 9), it will produce a wider beam of light than an instrument equipped with a 6 × 12 lens. Similarly a 6 × 12 ERS produces a wider beam of light than a 6 × 16 ERS. The lens trains on almost all of the newer ERSs are designated by a number that is a close approximation of the angle of beam spread in degrees (20, 30, 50, etc.) for that instrument. For these instruments, the higher the number, the greater the beam spread.

Three primary types of lens systems, all based on the plano-convex lens, are used with theatrical lighting instruments: the double plano-convex lens train, the step lens, and the fresnel lens.

Double Plano-Convex Lens Train

The double plano-convex lens train consists of two plano-convex lenses placed with their convex surfaces toward each other, as shown in Figure 4.4. This double configuration provides the same optical properties as a single lens of greater thickness and curvature, and the total thickness of the two lenses is less than the thickness of the optically comparable single lens. The

Focal length: The distance from the lens at which the light rays converge into a point; for lenses used in stage lighting instruments, the focal length is most frequently measured in even inches.

Plano-convex lens: A lens with one flat and one outward-curving face.

single lens with short focal length is not used in lighting instruments, because its thickness makes it very susceptible to heat fracture. The thicker single lens also transmits less light than does its thinner optical equivalent in the double plano-convex lens system.

Step Lens

A step lens retains the optical characteristics and shape of a plano-convex lens, but the glass on the flat side is cut away in steps, as shown in Figure 4.5. The stepping process gives the lens the optical properties of a thick, short-focal-length, plano-convex lens while eliminating its negative characteristics.

✳ What Color Is Your Clear Lens?

There are two types of glass that are commonly used to make lenses for lighting instruments: Pyrex and borosilicate glass.

For years Pyrex was the only glass used to make the thick lenses used in lighting instruments because it was highly heat resistant and didn't crack in normal use. But Pyrex has always had one problem: like window glass, it has a distinctive green cast. You can see this color by looking at the edge of a piece of glass or lighting instrument lens. The effect of this material coloration is that any light passing through a lens made of Pyrex is going to be tinted green, albeit an almost unnoticeably light green.

Why is this a problem? In many cases it isn't. As explained in Chapter 9, "Color," our brains do a marvelous job of interpreting what our eyes see. If we *think* we should be seeing white, our brain adjusts what we're actually seeing to make it appear white. As long as our fixtures are going to be used only to light theatrical productions, we have no problem. But if those instruments are going to be used to light for film or video, the all-but-invisible-to-the-human-eye tinting of the light may create significant color-matching challenges. Let me hasten to add that these problems are *not* insurmountable. They can be solved through the use of filters. But figuring out the solution will take time, and time, as we all know, is money.

Do you want your light to be uncolored? Borosilicate glass is clear, colorless, and transmits more light than Pyrex. It is also more expensive than Pyrex. But improvements in the design of the latest generation of lighting instruments have offset the additional expense of borosilicate glass by reducing the overall size of the lenses while maintaining and, in most cases, increasing light output. Borosilicate glass is becoming the material of choice for most theatrical instrument lenses.

(A)

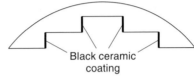

Figure 4.5 Step lens. The shaded area in (B) is eliminated from the lens.

Side view

(B)

Figure 4.6 A black ceramic coating prevents spectral breakdown.

Black ceramic coating

   An inherent property of step lenses is the prismatic effect caused by the steps themselves. Light passing through the steps at a shallow angle tends to create a spectral flare in the same manner that a prism breaks white light into a rainbow. Finishing the edges of the steps with a flat-black ceramic coating eliminates the spectral breakdown in most step lenses and does not interfere with the light passing through the rest of the lens (Figure 4.6).

Fresnel Lens

Originally intended for use in lighthouses by its inventor, Augustin Fresnel, the fresnel lens is a type of step lens with the glass cut away from the convex face of the lens instead of its plano side, as shown in Figure 4.7. The advantages of the fresnel lens are the same as for the step lens; reduction of the thickness of the lens allows more light transmission and lessens the chances of heat fracture.

   Fresnel lenses are used in (surprise!) fresnel spotlights. The plano side of these lenses is finished with a surface treatment to **diffuse** light. The diffusing treatment generally makes the plano side of the lens appear as though it has been sandblasted, or it may be finished with a series of small rectangular or irregular circular indentations. Regardless of the appearance of the treatment, its purpose is to diffuse the light to create the characteristically soft, luminescent light of the fresnel spotlight.

Diffuse: To soften the appearance of light by using a translucent filtering element to scatter the rays.

Figure 4.7 Fresnel lens. The shaded area in (B) is eliminated from the lens.

Side view

(A)   (B)

Filament: The light-producing element of a lamp; usually made of tungsten wire.

Bulb: The Pyrex glass or synthetic quartz container for a lamp filament and gaseous environment.

Fresnel lenses were once used in ellipsoidal reflector spotlights (ERSs). These lenses had a black ceramic coating applied to the vertical faces of the steps to eliminate spectral flare. The plano side of these lenses was smooth and did not have any diffusing treatment. Progress in the optical design of lenses used in ERSs has made this application of the fresnel lens obsolete, as it is not nearly as efficient as the newer designs.

LAMPS

Because many stage lighting instruments are designed to use lamps of specific shapes and characteristics, it makes sense to study about lamps before we discuss lighting instruments.

The two primary sources used for stage lighting instruments are the standard incandescent lamp and the tungsten-halogen lamp.

Incandescent Lamp

The standard incandescent lamp contains a tungsten **filament** that is placed in an inert gas environment inside the lamp **bulb**, as shown in Figure 4.8. The inert gas within the bulb is not pure and contains some oxygen. As an electrical current passes through the filament, heating it to incandescence, particles of tungsten are released. These particles are deposited to form the dark coating frequently found on the inside of older bulbs or envelopes. Eventually the filament weakens sufficiently to cause it to break. The average life expectancy of a regular incandescent lamp designed for use in stage lighting instruments ranges from 50 to approximately 200 hours. The life rating for a lamp does not mean that the light will burn out in the rated time. It means that the original output of the lamp will be reduced by 40 percent by the buildup on the inside of the bulb. Most lamps continue to burn long after their rated life, but at a significantly reduced output.

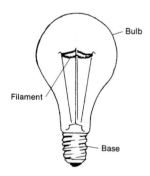

Bulb

Filament

Base

Figure 4.8 A standard incandescent lamp.

Tungsten-Halogen Lamp

Although it looks rather different from its cousin, the tungsten-halogen (T-H) lamp (Figure 4.9) is primarily the same as the standard incandescent lamp in all respects but one: The atmosphere inside the bulb of the T-H lamp is a halogen, or chemically active, gas instead of an inert gas. As the bits of tungsten are released from the tungsten filament, they unite with the halogen gas to form a compound that is attracted back to the filament. The tungsten reunites with the filament, and the halogen gas is released to repeat this chemical action. Because of the halogen cycle, tungsten is not deposited on the inside of the bulb, and the filament of the T-H lamp is constantly being replenished. This results in a significantly longer life expectancy for the T-H lamp. Many T-H lamps designed for stage lighting instruments are rated from 150 to 2,000 hours, as shown in Figure 4.10.

The halogen cycle becomes active only in a high-temperature environment. To achieve this goal the T-H filament is encased within a small, highly heat-resistant synthetic quartz envelope. The heat generated by the filament is confined with the small space, and the resultant temperatures are much higher than if a larger bulb were used.

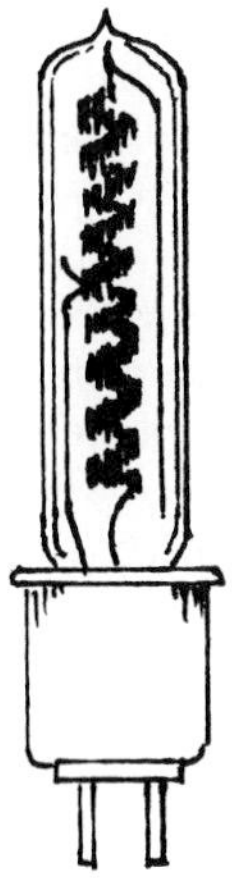

Figure 4.9 A tungsten-halogen incandescent lamp.

Arc Sources

An electric arc that produces a brilliantly blue-white light is created when an electric current jumps the air gap between two electrodes. An **open arc** is used as the source on some followspots.

When an arc is struck in an oxygen-rich environment such as air, the electrodes are consumed in the same way that a welding rod deteriorates during arc welding. If the arc is encapsulated in a noncorrosive atmosphere, however, the electrodes deteriorate extremely slowly. Neither arc nor encapsulated arc sources can be dimmed, so they are not used in "regular" stage-lighting instruments. However, encapsulated arcs such as the xenon and halide metal incandescent (HMI) lamps are frequently used in followspots and moving light fixtures where internally mounted mechanical dimmers allow the light to be dimmed. Followspots are discussed a little later in this chapter while moving light fixtures are discussed in Chapter 10, "Advanced Technology Instruments."

Light-Emitting Diodes

High-output light-emitting diodes (LED) have recently been introduced as sources for some stage-lighting fixtures. The first practical LED, which emitted red light, was developed in 1962 by Nick Holonyak, Jr.[1] LEDs are

Open arc: A light source in which the two electrodes operate in the open air.

---

[1]http://web.mit.edu/invent/a-winners/a-holonyak.html, p. 1.

Figure 4.10 The rated life of tungsten-halogen lamps varies according to their color temperature and output (lumens). Generally, the higher the output, the higher the color temperature and the shorter the life (and conversely). (Courtesy of Sylvania Lighting Products.)

Sylvania Tungsten Halogen Lamps

MEDIUM PREFOCUS – 3½" LCL – REPLACEMENT*

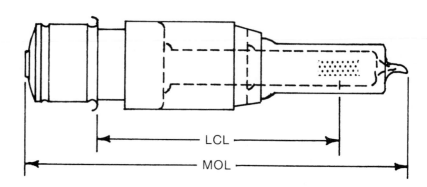

ANSI Code	Watts	Volts	Bulb	Fila-ment	Base	Lumens	Color Temp. (°K)	Avg. Rated Life (Hrs.)	LCL In.	mm	MOL In.	mm
EGC/EGD	500	120	T-4	CC8	Med. Pf.	13,000	3200	150	3½	88.9	5½	139.7
EGE	500	120	T-4	CC8	Med. Pf.	10,000	3000	2000	3½	88.9	5½	139.7
EGF	750	120	T-4	CC8	Med. Pf.	20,000	3200	250	3½	88.9	5½	139.7
EGG	750	120	T-5	CC8	Med. Pf.	15,000	3000	2000	3½	88.9	5½	139.7
DNT/FMD	750	120	—	—	Med. Pf.	17,000	3050	500	3½	88.9	6⅛	155.6
EGJ	1000	120	T-6	CC8	Med. Pf.	25,500	3200	400	3½	88.9	5¾	146.0
EGK	1000	120	T-6†	CC8	Med. Pf.	24,500	3200	400	—	—	5¾	146.0
DNV/FME	1000	120	—	—	Med. Pf.	27,500	3200	200	3½	88.9	6⅛	155.6

*Family of lamps which are replacements for existing incandescent T12 types primarily utilized in ellipsoidal reflector spotlights.
†Frosted

☀ Lamp Diameter Measuring System

The diameter of lamps is described in eighths of an inch. Thus a PAR 64 and an MR 16 (both described later in this chapter) have diameters of 8 inches and 2 inches, respectively. Figure 4.10 provides another example. In the "Bulb" column, you will see that the bulb of the LCL lamp is described as T-4. This means that the lamp has a T (tube) shape and is ⁴⁄₈, or ½ inch in diameter.

If you measure the diameter of lamps with self-contained reflectors such as the PAR 64 and the MR 16, you will find their diameter to be greater than the figure indicated. However, the diameter of the actual reflector will mirror its designation.

now available in a wide variety of colors and output levels, from the relatively low-output LEDs that you see every day in devices such as the red/yellow/green status lights on electronic equipment to high-output applications for outdoor video displays, traffic lights and, now, stage lights.

Microwatt: One millionth of a watt.

A precise explanation of how an LED emits light requires knowledge of electrical engineering beyond the scope of this introductory stage-lighting book.[2] Fortunately, it really isn't necessary to understand *how* an LED emits light to understand how it works. An LED is a special type of semiconducting diode that emits light. The color of the light is determined by the chemical composition of the material from which the LED is made. The amount of light emitted by the LED is directly proportional to the amount of electrical power (wattage) needed to make it produce light. Status-light LEDs typically operate in the 30–60 **microwatt** range. High-output LEDs operate in the 1–5 watt range. Ongoing research indicates that significantly brighter LEDs, with brightness levels equivalent to 50-watt household light bulbs, should be commercially available by the time you read this or in the near future.[4]

Light-emitting diodes have numerous advantages over incandescent sources:

- They produce colored light of a specific wavelength without the use of filters.
- The shape of the LED case can be designed to focus light to a specific beam width.
- They have an expected life of 100,000 hours.
- They dim over time rather than burning out abruptly.
- They provide more light output per watt.
- Their operational temperature is cooler than incandescent lamps.

Three main, but solvable, challenges stand in the way of the quick adoption of LEDs as a primary light source for stage-lighting equipment manufacturers:

1. relatively low brightness of individual LEDs
2. heat
3. LEDs need DC, not AC, power

Further discussion of these issues, and more information about the current stage of LED-sourced stage fixtures, can be found in Chapter 10, "Advanced Technology Instruments."

---

[2]For those technically minded readers who want to know exactly how an LED emits light, a good explanation is offered at http://electronics.howstuffworks.com/led.htm.

[4]http://compoundsemiconductor.net/articles/news/9/9/1/1, p. 1.

Why Are LEDs (Potentially) Good Sources for Stage Lights?

There is one primary characteristic that makes LEDs an exciting potential light source for use in stage lighting fixtures: efficiency. For the amount of power needed to produce a given level of brightness of a specific color, LEDs produce significantly more light when compared with the traditional method—filtering a white light source.

LEDs also offer the possibility of color mixing. Separately controlled LEDs in the primary colors of light—red, blue, and green—if placed in the same housing, can be blended to create any imaginable color.

State-of-the-art high-output LEDs also offer power savings when comparing the amount of light produced by an LED with both incandescent and fluorescent sources producing the same level of brightness. Ongoing research indicates that even higher levels of power savings will be possible in the future.

For all these reasons LEDs are an exciting new class of illumination source that is currently being explored by a large segment of the lighting industry.

Lamp Structure

All incandescent lamps, regardless of shape or type, are composed of three basic parts: bulb, base, and filament, as shown in Figure 4.11.

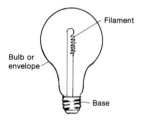

Figure 4.11 Lamp structure.

Bulb   The bulb is the Pyrex or synthetic quartz envelope that encases the filament and acts as a container for the gas-filled atmosphere of the lamp. The shape and size of the bulb are determined by the position and shape of the filament, the burning position of the lamp within the lighting instrument, and the heat dissipation requirements of the lamp. Figure 4.12 illustrates common incandescent bulb shapes. Bulb sizes vary, depending on individual lamp requirements.

Base   The lamp base secures the lamp in the socket and provides the electrical contact points between the socket and the filament. There are several styles of lamp base, as illustrated in Figure 4.13. Generally, large, high-wattage incandescent lamps have the larger bases. Figure 4.13 shows not only the different bases but also the relative size relationship that each base has to the others. The candelabra base is approximately ½ inch in diameter, the medium-size bases are approximately 1 inch in diameter, and the mogul bases are about 1½ inches across.

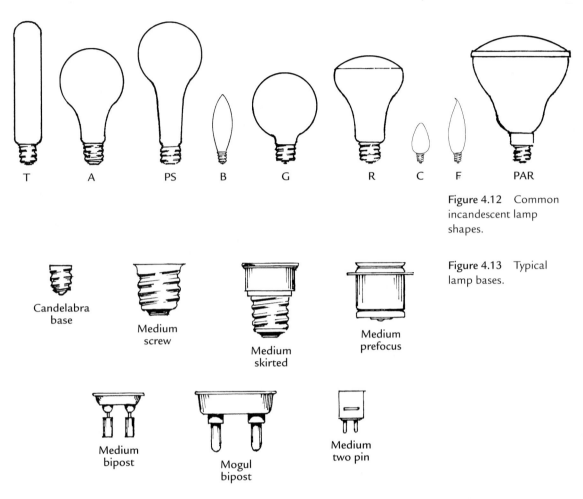

T A PS B G R C F PAR

Figure 4.12 Common incandescent lamp shapes.

Figure 4.13 Typical lamp bases.

Candelabra base

Medium screw

Medium skirted

Medium prefocus

Medium bipost

Mogul bipost

Medium two pin

The prefocus, bipost, and two-pin bases are used for instruments that need the filament in a specific location in relation to the reflector—such as the ERS or fresnel spotlight discussed later in this chapter.

Filament Various lamp filaments are available, each designed to perform a particular function. All filaments for stage lighting instrument lamps are made of tungsten wire, usually tightly coiled, and strung in one of the general configurations shown in Figure 4.14.

Color Temperature

To most humans the light emitted from all artificial sources appears to be the same color—white. In reality these sources—household incandescent bulbs, stage lamps, followspots, and so forth—create light in a relatively wide range

Figure 4.14   Filament
styles.

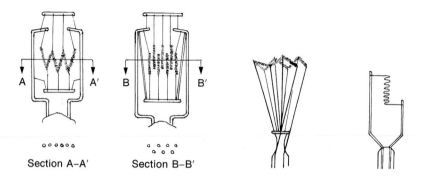

of hues. The reason that these various sources *seem* to be white is because of our brain's ability to interpret the information being transmitted to it by our eyes. We *expect* the light from these sources to be white, so our brain tells us we're seeing white light regardless of its actual color.

The color of light is measured by using the color temperature scale. That scale is based on the concept that heated metal produces colored light. An example of this process can be seen when you turn the burner on an electric stove to high. As the burner heats up it changes from its original grayish black color to dull red, eventually becoming cherry red. The color temperature scale is based on that principle—as a metal object is heated it produces light. To create the color temperature scale, scientists hypothesized that as the heat of a metal object—which they called a blackbody radiator—is increased, the color of the light it emits changes. The precise color of the light—its exact wavelength—can be measured with a device known as a spectrometer. By measuring the precise color of light emitted by the blackbody radiator at very specific temperatures, scientists could create a scale that identified the color of light according to the temperature of that blackbody radiator—the color temperature scale. The only flaw in this theory is the fact that a perfect blackbody radiator doesn't exist. But, actual metal objects—called graybody radiators—do exist and are useful for measuring the temperature/color correlation up to approximately 3,000 kelvins.[6]

The color temperature scale is measured using the Kelvin scale—the temperature in degrees Celsius using absolute zero (–273 degrees Celsius) as the starting point. Table 4.1 shows the color temperature of some common sources.

Because most metals melt by 3,000 kelvins, above that point the correlation between blackbody temperature and the color of light emitted by it is purely theoretical, but the relationship between them still provides a convenient way of precisely describing the color of an object.[7]

---

[6]William B. Warfel and Walter R. Klappert, *Color Science for Lighting the Stage* (New Haven and London: Yale University Press, 1981), pp. 15–16.
[7]Ibid.

TABLE 4.1 Approximate Color Temperature of Some Common Sources

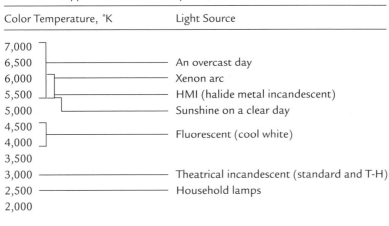

Color Temperature, °K	Light Source
7,000	
6,500	An overcast day
6,000	Xenon arc
5,500	HMI (halide metal incandescent)
5,000	Sunshine on a clear day
4,500	
4,000	Fluorescent (cool white)
3,500	
3,000	Theatrical incandescent (standard and T-H)
2,500	Household lamps
2,000	

TABLE 4.2 Comparison of Same Wattage/Different Output Lamps

Watts	Sylvania Ordering Abbre- viation	Other Designation	NAED Code	Standard Case Quantity	Volts	Color Temper- ature, Kelvins	Nominal Lumens	Average Rated Life, Hours	Filament Class	Fused Silica Bulb Finish	Lighted Length, Inches
1,000	DXW	—	53993	12	120	3,400	33,500	30	CC-8	Clear	1¹⁄₁₆
1,000	DXW	—	53997	12	120	3,200	28,000	150	CC-8	Clear	1³⁄₁₆
1,000	FBY	Frosted DXW	53996	12	120	3,200	26,000	150	CC-8	Frosted	—
1,000	FBZ	Frosted DXN	53999	12	120	3,400	31,500	30	CC-8	Frosted	—
1,000	BRH	—	54563	12	120	3,350	30,000	75	CC-8	Clear	—

SOURCE: *Sylvania Lighting Handbook,* 7th ed.

The color temperature of a lamp decreases with age relative to its rated life. Thus a tungsten halogen lamp with a rated life of 2,000 hours will hold its color temperature for approximately 2,000 hours, whereas a regular incandescent lamp with a rated life of only 50 hours will retain its color temperature for only 50 hours. The average rated life of a lamp (see Table 4.2) refers to the time that a lamp will burn at its designated color temperature and not to the length of time before the lamp burns out.

It is important to understand that there is no relationship between color temperature and brightness or intensity. Just because a particular lamp has a high color temperature does not mean that it will burn brighter than another lamp with a lower color temperature. The sole purpose of the color temperature scale is to accurately describe color.

SAFETY TIP

Lamp Maintenance

Although it is a good idea to keep all lamps clean and free from dirt and grease, it is particularly important to handle tungsten-halogen lamps with extreme care. The bulb of the T-H lamp must be kept free of all fingerprints, grease, or any other foreign substance that could cause a change in the heat-dissipation characteristics of the bulb. Because a T-H lamp reaches a high temperature, any change in its heat-dissipation characteristics could cause the lamp to break or explode.

When installing lamps, grasp the lamp by the base rather than the bulb. If this is not practical, a soft cloth or glove should be used to handle the glass envelope. This practice will protect both your hands and the lamp bulb.

If you happen to touch the lamp envelope with your fingers, or get any other foreign substance on it, be sure to wipe the surface clean with a soft cloth and vinegar or rubbing alcohol. Wiping it with just a soft cloth will only smear the contaminant. The vinegar water or alcohol will normally remove any residue and leave the surface squeaky clean. Do not use commercial glass cleaners, as they frequently leave a film.

Although it is not as important to keep a regular incandescent lamp as scrupulously clean as a T-H bulb, it is good practice to wipe the bulb with a soft cloth and alcohol or vinegar water after handling.

Lamp bases should be kept free of any corrosive buildup or insulating deposits that could interfere with the electrical contact between the socket and base.

While there is no fixed relationship between color temperature and brightness, the measured color temperature of a lamp will match its rated color temperature only if that lamp is being run at its rated voltage. When a dimmer controls a lamp, its measured color temperature will match its rated color temperature only when the dimmer is being run at 100 percent. As the lamp is dimmed, its color temperature decreases.

Why does any of this matter? In stage lighting we frequently want to create a smooth wash of color in a particular area of the stage. However, if the color temperature of all the lamps used to create that wash isn't identical or nearly so, the color of the resultant wash will vary from instrument to instrument. Depending on the specific color you're using, these variations sometimes can be quite significant, particularly when you are dimming. How do you prevent this type of color problem? Equip all the instruments used in your lighting design with lamps of the same color temperature and age.

Light Output of Lamps

The output of an incandescent lamp, while related to the lamp wattage, is primarily a function of the size and composition of the filament. This output is measured in lumens. Generally speaking, if two lamps have the same wattage but one has a smaller filament, the smaller-filament lamp will have a higher lumen output but a shorter life expectancy, as shown in Table 4.2. Table 4.2 also provides additional material about a few lamps. This type of information is typical of the "ordering information" found in lamp catalogs such as the *Sylvania Lighting Handbook*. Perusal of this type of information—with the obvious exception of the "Standard Case Quantity"—is helpful in understanding a little more about the criteria used to evaluate lamps.

Another term that you will encounter in theatrical lighting is **footcandle**. While lumens measure the output of a source—the amount of light being created by a lamp—footcandles measure the light falling on an area. This information is useful to designers when they are selecting instruments to use in a particular design. Lighting equipment manufacturers detail this type of information about every fixture they manufacture in data sheets. These specification sheets, commonly called "spec sheets," provide information about lamp/instrument output—output of the lamps is listed in either candlepower or lumens, output of the fixture is listed in footcandles—at specific **throw distances**, as illustrated in Figure 4.15. This information can be used by the lighting designer to help determine what particular lens/lamp combination of a particular type of instrument should be used in any given situation.

In general, the lowest usable light level of an unfiltered fixture—a lighting instrument without color media—is approximately 50 footcandles. While 50 footcandles provides a good level of visibility, instruments are rarely used without some color. The addition of even a lightly colored gel can reduce the effective output of the fixture by anywhere from 10 to 55 percent. If a heavily saturated color such as indigo or a dark blue is used, the effective output of the instrument can be reduced by more than 90 percent. More information on color and color media is available in Chapter 9, "Color."

Reflectors

A reflector can be defined as any surface that reflects light, but to be useful a reflector needs to redirect light in a specific manner. Two qualities—surface finish and reflector shape—determine the characteristics and effectiveness of any reflector.

The surface finish of a reflector determines the amount of light that will be reflected from it. Smooth surfaces, such as glass or mirror-polished

Footcandle: An international unit of illumination. One footcandle equals one lumen of light falling on a surface area of one square foot.[8]

Throw distance: How far light from an instrument travels from its hanging position to the center of it area of focus.

---

[8]Boylan, Bernard R., *The Lighting Primer*, Iowa State University Press, Ames, Iowa, p. 7.

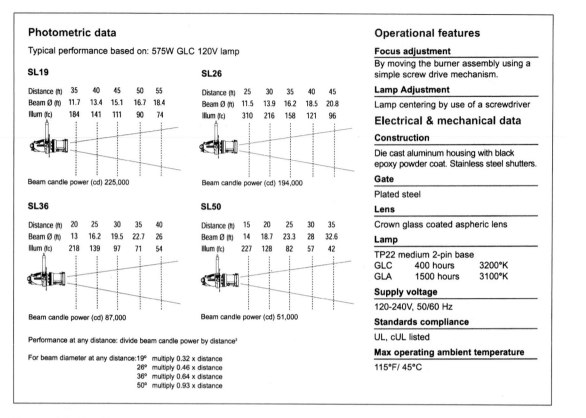

Photometric data

Typical performance based on: 575W GLC 120V lamp

SL19

Distance (ft)	35	40	45	50	55
Beam Ø (ft)	11.7	13.4	15.1	16.7	18.4
Illum (fc)	184	141	111	90	74

Beam candle power (cd) 225,000

SL26

Distance (ft)	25	30	35	40	45
Beam Ø (ft)	11.5	13.9	16.2	18.5	20.8
Illum (fc)	310	216	158	121	96

Beam candle power (cd) 194,000

SL36

Distance (ft)	20	25	30	35	40
Beam Ø (ft)	13	16.2	19.5	22.7	26
Illum (fc)	218	139	97	71	54

Beam candle power (cd) 87,000

SL50

Distance (ft)	15	20	25	30	35
Beam Ø (ft)	14	18.7	23.3	28	32.6
Illum (fc)	227	128	82	57	42

Beam candle power (cd) 51,000

Performance at any distance: divide beam candle power by distance²

For beam diameter at any distance: 19° multiply 0.32 x distance
26° multiply 0.46 x distance
36° multiply 0.64 x distance
50° multiply 0.93 x distance

Operational features

Focus adjustment

By moving the burner assembly using a simple screw drive mechanism.

Lamp Adjustment

Lamp centering by use of a screwdriver

Electrical & mechanical data

Construction

Die cast aluminum housing with black epoxy powder coat. Stainless steel shutters.

Gate

Plated steel

Lens

Crown glass coated aspheric lens

Lamp

TP22 medium 2-pin base
GLC   400 hours   3200°K
GLA   1500 hours   3100°K

Supply voltage

120-240V, 50/60 Hz

Standards compliance

UL, cUL listed

Max operating ambient temperature

115°F/ 45°C

Figure 4.15 Specification sheets graphically depict throw distance and related brightness. (Courtesy of Strand Lighting.)

Point source: A theoretical concept: All light emanates from a single point that has no dimensions. In the real world all light sources, such as filaments, have height, width, and depth.

steel, reflect a higher percentage of the light striking them than surfaces with matte finishes, such as brushed aluminum. Both types of surface finishes are used in theatrical lighting instruments.

All reflectors change the direction of light according to a simple principle: the angle of incidence equals the angle of reflection. This means light striking a surface at a specific angle is reflected from that surface at the same angle. For example, a 45-degree angle of incidence (approach) equals a 45-degree angle of reflection, as shown in Figure 4.16. This principle is used by fixture designers to position the reflector relative to the lamp filament to redirect the light in specific ways.

The properties of the most common types of reflectors used in theatrical lighting fixtures are discussed below.

Spherical Reflectors   The spherical reflector, Figure 4.17A, is shaped like a section of a sphere with the center of the lamp filament placed at the center point of the sphere (F1). If the filament was a **point source**, all light strik-

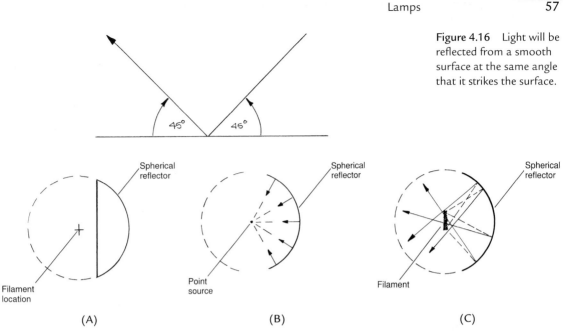

Figure 4.16 Light will be reflected from a smooth surface at the same angle that it strikes the surface.

Figure 4.17 (A) A schematic drawing of a spherical reflector. (B) Light emitted from the focal point of a spherical reflector will be reflected back through that point. (C) Light not emitted from the focal point of a spherical reflector will be reflected around, but not through, that center or focal point.

ing the reflector would do so at a 90-degree angle. The reflector would then bounce that light back through the point source, as shown in Figure 4.17B. But lamp filaments aren't point sources. Tungsten-halogen filaments typically are about ¼ inch wide by 1 inch long. Light is emitted all along that filament, resulting in light striking the reflector from many angles, as shown in Figure 4.17C. But the basic principles still apply. The lamp filament is centered on F1, and the spherical reflector redirects light back through the filament area toward the front of the instrument.

The spherical reflector was quite **efficient** when used with the lamps for which it was originally designed. **Plano-convex spotlights** and, later, fresnel spotlights used the spherical reflector with incandescent lamps that had grid-shaped filaments (see Figure 4.14A, B). The shape of this filament resulted in the majority of the light being emitted out the front or back of the lamp. Positioning the filament at the focal point of the reflector (F1) with the filament grid perpendicular to the axis of the instrument enabled the reflector to redirect the majority of the light because very little light was lost out the sides, top, or bottom of the lamp. When retrofitting older fresnel instruments with tungsten-halogen lamps, it is important to use a lamp with a grid-shaped filament. Doing so will retain the efficiency of the spherical reflector. It is possible to fit a lamp with a coil-shaped filament into these instruments, but the coiled cylindrical shape of the filament, which emits light equally toward the front, back, and sides, significantly reduces the efficiency of the reflector and the light output of the instrument.

Efficient: In this case, refers to a comparison of the intensity of light emitted by the lamp with the intensity of light emitted by the instrument.

Plano-convex spotlight: An archaic instrument with a relatively hard-edged light quality. So called because it used a plano-convex lens.

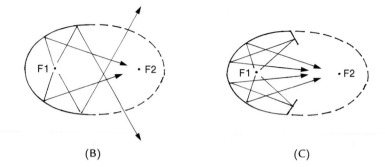

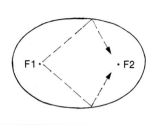

(A)   (B)   (C)

Figure 4.18   Optical properties of a conical ellipse reflector.

Ellipsoidal Reflectors   An ellipsoidal reflector is officially known as a truncated conical ellipse. This shape has properties that are uniquely suited to focusing light. The conical ellipse reflector shown in Figure 4.18A has two focal points, F1 and F2. Light emitted by a light source located at F1 will reflect off the walls of the conical ellipse and pass through F2. If half of the elliptical reflector were removed (Figure 4.18B), light emitted from the source at F1 would again pass through F2, although some of the light would pass out the open end of the reflector.

The ellipsoidal reflector is most prominently used in the fixture that bears its name—the ellipsoidal reflector spotlight (ERS). Most ERSs employ a kickback reflector at the open end of the conical ellipse to redirect any potentially lost light back into the reflector to be channeled into a usable direction, as shown in Figure 4.18C. This feature significantly increases the efficiency of the ERS.

Parabolic Reflectors   If a lamp filament (F1) is placed at the focal point of a conical parabola reflector, the light bounced off that reflector will be directed forward in a relatively coherent beam of light, as shown in Figure 4.19. This characteristic provides a strong "punch" of light with most of the intensity being concentrated in a relatively small diameter area in the center of the beam.

PARs, car headlights, and aircraft landing lights all have parabolic reflectors. In all of these applications the parabolic shape of the reflector creates a beam of light, while the dispersion characteristics—narrow/medium/wide beam spread—and beam shape—round/oval—are controlled by the lensatic properties of the front lens, which also functions as the front cover for the lamp.

PAR: Acronym for parabolic aluminized reflector. A sealed-beam lamp with a parabolic-shaped reflector covered by a thin, reflective, aluminum coating.

Combination Reflectors   Combination reflectors, as you probably expected, combine the characteristics of more than one type of reflector shape. At this writing, few stage lighting instruments utilize combination reflectors, although with the search for increased lighting efficiency it is probably only a matter of time before these reflectors make their way into this segment of the lighting industry. Combination reflectors are used in some specialty lamps such as the MR series, which will be explained later in this chapter.

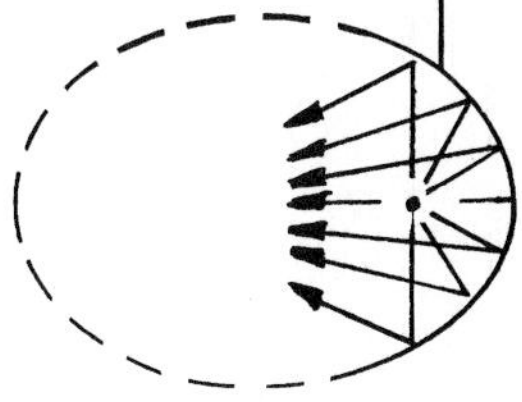

Reflector Materials   There are two primary types of materials used to make reflectors: metal and glass.

Because of the high temperatures associated with tungsten-halogen lamps, most modern metal reflectors are generally made of stainless steel or some other highly heat resistant material. Older instruments originally designed for regular incandescent lamps, which have lower operating temperatures than tungsten-halogen lamps, were sometimes manufactured with spun aluminum reflectors. The surface finish of the reflectors varies considerably and is dependent on the particular requirements of each instrument. Generally the metal finishes vary from coated, highly reflective, mirror-polished surfaces to dull matte. Some reflectors are manufactured with "flatted reflectors." Rather than having a continuous curve, a flatted reflector breaks the surface into a series of flat surfaces that have the same general reflecting characteristics as the curved surface. An example of a flatted reflector can be seen in Figure 4.19.

Glass reflectors are relatively new to the theatrical lighting instrument market. They are becoming widely used in the newer generation of ellipsoidal reflector spotlights in the stage lighting industry. These reflectors are almost all designed with "cold mirror" finishes. A cold mirror is a type of **dichroic filter** that reflects visible light while allowing the infrared (heat) portion of the light spectrum to pass through the reflecting surface, as shown in Figure 4.20. This results in significantly reduced heat at the front of the instrument, which lessens heat-induced deterioration of instrument parts and color media.

Figure 4.19 Light reflected from a conical ellipse reflector creates a strong punch of light.

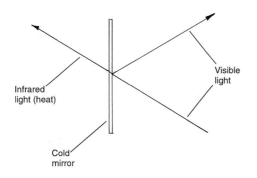

Figure 4.20 A cold mirror reflects visible light but allows infrared light (heat) to pass through it.

Dichroic filter: A filter that reflects, rather than absorbs, unwanted wavelengths of light while allowing the desired wavelengths to pass through the filter.

LIGHTING INSTRUMENTS

Various lighting instruments are used in the theatre, but the ellipsoidal reflector spotlight and the fresnel spotlight are the real workhorses for the lighting designer.

Ellipsoidal Reflector Spotlight

The light produced by an ellipsoidal reflector spotlight (ERS) has a relatively narrow beam width and is capable of traveling long distances. The quality of the light produced by this instrument, also known by the trade name Leko, can be characterized as generally hard edged with little diffusion. The shape of the beam is controlled by internally mounted shutters. The spill light from an ERS (that is, any light that escapes past the edge of the beam) is minimal. Because of all these characteristics, ERSs are the primary lighting tool of the designer. Several manufacturers' versions of the ERS are shown in Figure 4.21.

General Operating Principles   The ERS operates on the basic principle of using an ellipsoidal reflector to gather light from one focal point (F1) and focus it on the second focal point (F2), as described earlier in this chapter. The shutters, made of stainless steel or some other highly heat resistant metal, are located in a plane close to the second focal point to shape the light.

Figure 4.22 shows a cross section of an axial-mount ERS, so called because the lamp is placed on the optical, or centerline, axis of the instrument. This configuration was made possible by the development of the tungsten-halogen lamp. Compare the position of the lamp in the axial-mount instrument (Figure 4.22) with the instrument shown in Figure 4.23, an ERS de-

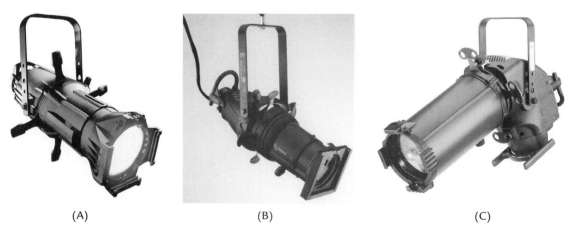

(A)   (B)   (C)

Figure 4.21   Ellipsoidal reflector spotlights: (A) ETC Source Four; (B) Strand Cool beam; (C) Selecon Pacific.
(Courtesy of Electronic Theatre Controls (ETC), Strand Lighting, and Selecon.)

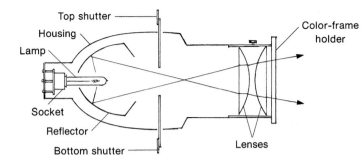

Figure 4.22   Cutaway view of an axial-mount ellipsoidal reflector spotlight.

Figure 4.24   A continuously variable-focal-length ellipsoidal reflector spotlight. (Courtesy of Altman Lighting.)

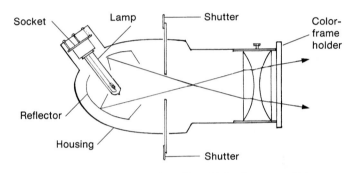

Figure 4.23   Cutaway view of an ellipsoidal reflector spotlight designed for a T-shaped incandescent lamp.

Figure 4.25   A variable-focal-length ellipsoidal reflector spotlight. (Courtesy of Altman Lighting.)

signed for the larger incandescent T-shaped lamp, which predates the T-H lamp. Note how the lamp filament is still located at the focal point of the ellipsoidal reflector even though the lamp is mounted in a different position.

The lens is placed in front of the shutters, as shown in Figures 4.22 and 4.23, to focus the light into the desired field angle. ERSs are equipped with one of three lens systems: a double plano-convex lens train; a step lens; or, on some older models, a fresnel lens. Although there may be slight differences in light output and quality, the three types work equally well.

The **zoom ellipse**, more officially known as the variable-focal-length ERS (Figure 4.24), is an extremely versatile instrument. This variation of the standard ERS has lenses that can slide forward or backward to change the focal length of the instrument. Changing the focal length affects the **beam** and **field angles** of the instrument, with those angles widening as the focal length becomes shorter. The field angle of most zoom ellipses can be varied between approximately 20 and 50 degrees.

Figure 4.25 illustrates another type of variable-focal-length ERS. Its lenses can be moved between slots in the housing to change the field angle between 26, 36, and 50 degrees.

Zoom ellipse: An ellipsoidal reflector spotlight with movable lenses that allow the focal length to be changed.

Beam angle: That point where the light emitted by an instrument is diminished by 50 percent compared to the output of the center of the beam.

Field angle: That point where the light output diminishes to 10 percent of the output of the center of the beam.

TABLE 4.3   Beam and Field Angles for Typical ERSs[a]

Instrument Type	Beam Angle	Field Angle	Maximum Effective Range[b]
6 × 9	16°	37°	25 feet
6 × 12	11°	26°	35 feet
6 × 16	9°	18°	50 feet
20°	10°	20°	65 feet
30°	12°	30°	60 feet
40°	15°	40°	55 feet

[a]All data are approximate but typical. Specifics vary with manufacturer.
[b]Determined by point at which output diminishes to 50 footcandles.

Table 4.3 lists the beam and field angles in degrees of arc for several varieties of 6-inch ERSs. The nomenclature used to describe ERS lenses—for example 6 × 9—indicates that the diameter of the lens is 6 inches and its focal length is 9 inches. Most ERSs manufactured in the past 10 years don't use that traditional nomenclature, but simply identify the fixture by the field angle—20, 30, 23, 50—of the lens. While historically it was safe to assume "the bigger the lens the greater the output," that is no longer true, so the identification of the fixture's field angle, when combined with the light output listed on its spec sheet, will provide a clear picture of the instrument's capabilities.

The beam angle (Figure 4.26) is that point where the intensity of the cone of light emitted by the instrument diminishes to 50 percent of its inten-

Lamp Comparison Chart

Although the specific lamp that is used with any instrument depends on the design of the instrument, some fairly standard wattages are used with various families of instruments.

Instrument	Standard Lamp Wattage Range
4-inch ERS	250–600
6-inch ERS	500–1,000
8-inch ERS	1,000–2,000
6-inch fresnel	250–750
8-inch fresnel	750–2,000
Scoop	350–1,500
Striplight	150–500
Followspot (incandescent)	1,000–2,000

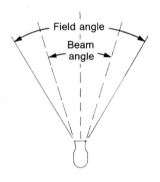

Figure 4.26   Beam and field angles.

sity as compared with the center of the beam. The field angle is that point where the light diminishes to 10 percent of the output of the center of the beam. An explanation of how this information is used is given in Chapter 14, "Using the Lighting Key to Draw the Light Plot."

Two more terms—**flat** and **peak**—are used to help provide a more complete description of a fixture's light output. Every ERS has controls that allow adjustments to be made to the position of the lamp within the reflector. Changing the lamp's position changes the characteristic shape of the cone of light produced by the instrument. The lamp can be manipulated so the light output is essentially smooth from edge to edge across the field, or it can be adjusted so there is a hot spot in the center of the beam. A "flat" field reading defines the output at any point within the smooth edge-to-edge beam. A "peak" field reading refers to the brightest area within the center of the hot-spot-adjusted beam.

Relatively recent additions to the ERS family, such as the ETC Source Four, the Source Four Jr., and the Altman Shakespeare 600 series, use an excellent innovation in theatrical instrument design—cold mirror reflectors. These reflectors, which are made of heavy borosilicate glass, have an applied dichroic coating that reflects visible light while transmitting infrared (heat) wavelengths. This means that the majority of the heat generated by the lamp passes through the reflector rather than being reflected with the visible light. The result is less heat deterioration of the shutters, iris, and gobos, as well as longer color media life. Another feature of the Source Four is the efficiency of its optical design. Most ERS designs that preceded the Source Four used a 750- or 1,000-watt lamp. Interestingly, because of the higher efficiency of its reflector design and its relatively clear, color-free borosilicate lenses, the Source Four generates more light output with a 575-watt lamp than its 1,000-watt predecessors.

More innovative ERS design is evident in the Pacific family of fixtures by Selecon. This instrument has a unique shape because it is designed to reflect light off of a dichroic cold mirror before the light strikes the gate, as shown in Figure 4.27. The cold mirror reflects visible light but passes infrared (heat) and ultraviolet light through the mirror. A heat sink vents the infrared heat outside of the housing. The net effect is a much cooler beam of light, which, in turn, results in longer shutter and color media life. Additionally, the lens rotates 360 degrees, which allows the shutters to be positioned to make the most appropriate **shutter cut**

Accessories The most basic accessory designed for use with an ERS is the **color frame** (Figure 4.28), a lightweight-metal or heat-resistant-fiber holder for plastic colored media. The color frame is inserted into the holder on the front of the ERS to color the light.

The **gobo** (Figure 4.29), also known as a pattern, template, or cookie, is a lightweight metal cutout that turns the ERS into a pattern projector. Most ERSs are equipped with a built-in pattern slot located adjacent to the shutter

Flat: Refers to a beam of light, the output of which is essentially smooth from edge to edge when measured perpendicular to the axis of the beam.

Peak: Refers to a beam of light, the output of which has a noticeable hot spot in its center when measured perpendicular to the axis of the beam. Peak field reading taken at the center of the hotspot.

Shutter cut: The straight-line edge created when an ERS's shutter is inserted into its beam of light.

Color frame: A lightweight metal holder for color media that fits in a holder at the front of a lighting instrument.

Gobo: A thin metal template inserted into an ellipsoidal reflector spotlight to project a shadow pattern of light.

Figure 4.27 Light is bounced off a cold mirror reflector in the Selecon Pacific ERS.
(Courtesy of Selecon.)

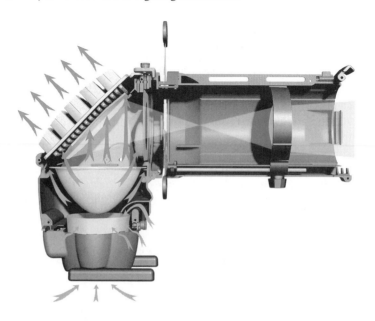

Figure 4.28 A color frame.

Figure 4.29 (A) A gobo and (B) the pattern that the gobo projects.

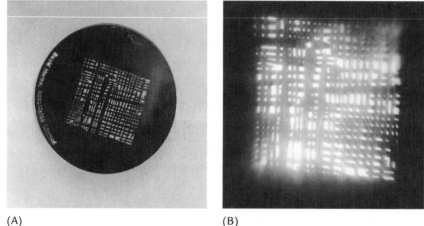

(A)   (B)

Dremel tool: A handheld router similar to a dentist's drill, which can be equipped with a number of bits for grinding, cutting, or carving of wood, plastic, and metal.

plane. A wide variety of commercially designed gobos, usually made of stainless steel, are available from scenic and lighting supply houses. Gobos can be constructed from metal offset printing sheets or from heavyweight disposable aluminum cookware (roasting pans, pie plates), as shown in Figure 4.30. Offset printing sheets are thin, flexible aluminum sheets, which can usually be obtained from local newspaper publishers at low cost. They can withstand the heat generated by an ERS, are stiff enough to prevent flexing or buckling, and can be worked easily with scissors, chisels, or a **Dremel tool**. The

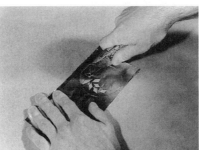

(A)   (B)

(C)   (D)

Figure 4.30 Gobos can be built in the shop by cutting the pattern out of disposable aluminum cookware (A, B, C) using scissors or from offset printing sheets using a Dremel tool (D).

disposable aluminum pie plates are satisfactory for making cloud gobos and similar patterns that have little intricate detail. The aluminum used in these products is about one-third as thick as the offset printing sheets and will vaporize under the high heat generated by the instrument lamp if the pattern is too detailed. It is advisable to make intricately designed gobos from the offset printing sheets or from stainless steel.

Custom gobo designs can be created by using scanned photos, drawings, or designs created with a software program such as Adobe Photoshop. The custom divisions of American Market and Rosco, among others, can produce these self-designed patterns. Additionally, colored-glass patterns—using dichroic filters to create color—are commercilally available from the aforementioned manufacturers, among others. Do an online search or check the trade publications for current manufacturers. Generally, the technical requirements involved in producing glass-mounted images, either black and white or color, that will stand up to the intense heat of an ERS preclude making shop-built glass gobos.

Another useful accessory for an ERS is the iris (Figure 4.31). The **iris** varies the size of the circular pattern produced by an ERS. It is mounted in the shutter plane, and the size of the aperture is controlled by an external handle.

Iris: A device with movable overlapping metal plates, used with an ellipsoidal reflector spotlight to change the size of the circular pattern of light.

Figure 4.31   An ellipsoidal reflector spotlight
equipped with an iris.

Figure 4.32   (A) 6" Die
cast focus Fresnel spot-
light (IKAF-MBP) (Courtesy
of Altman Lighting).
(B) Fresnel spotlight.
(Courtesy of Strand Lighting).

(A)   (B)

Fresnel Spotlight

The fresnel spotlight produces a soft, diffused, luminescent light. Examples
are shown in Figure 4.32. When the instrument is focused on narrow beam,
or spot, as shown in Figure 4.33A, it produces a beam with a central hot spot
that rapidly loses intensity toward the edge. When the instrument is focused
on wide beam, or flood (Figure 4.33B), it produces a smooth wash of light.

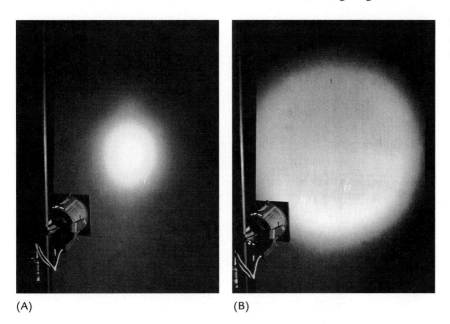

(A)   (B)

Figure 4.33   The fresnel spotlight can be focused on spot (A) or flood (B).

The lens of a standard fresnel spotlight has a diffusing treatment on its plano face that produces a soft, circular beam of light. The oval-beam fresnel lens (Figure 4.34) has the same luminescent and optical qualities as its round-beam counterpart but produces an oval, instead of round, beam of light. The diffusion treatment on fresnel lenses is so strong that it effectively negates the beam-spread characteristics controlled by the focal length of the lens. That is why fresnel lenses are referred to only by their diameter, for example, 6 inch, 8 inch, and so forth.

Figure 4.34   An oval-beam lens for a fresnel spotlight.

General Operating Principles   The fresnel spotlight is simple. The instrument housing holds the lens and provides a mounting platform for the socket, lamp, and small spherical reflector assembly, which are mounted on a small sled that moves closer to or farther from the lens during focusing, as shown in Figure 4.35. Figure 4.36A shows the instrument on spot focus with

Figure 4.35   A cutaway view of a fresnel spotlight.

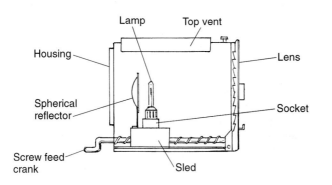

Lamp   Top vent

Housing

Spherical reflector

Screw feed crank

Lens

Socket

Sled

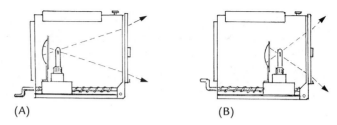

(A)   (B)

Figure 4.36   The sled holding the lamp/reflector assembly is (A) moved backward to produce a hot spot in the middle of the beam or (B) moved forward to produce a relatively smooth wash of light.

the socket and spherical reflector assembly moved toward the back of the instrument housing. In this position most of the light is concentrated into a hot spot in the center of the beam. Figure 4.36B shows the instrument on flood focus, with the socket and reflector assembly moved all the way forward. This creates a relatively smooth wash of light from edge to edge, with only a small, almost undetectable, hot spot in the center of the beam.

Accessories   The primary, and almost indispensable, accessory for the fresnel spotlight is the **barn door** (Figure 4.37). Its flippers are movable and can be swung into the beam of light until they cut off as much light as desired.

Another accessory is the **funnel** (Figure 4.38). The funnel, like the barn door, fits into the color frame slot on the front of the instrument. The circular pattern of light that it creates is dependent on the diameter of the funnel's cone.

Figure 4.37   A four-flipper barn door.

Striplight

The striplight is used to create a smooth wash of light. It resembles a long trough with a series of lamps inside, as shown in Figure 4.39. Striplights are designed to accommodate a specific lamp style such as the 2-inch diameter MR-16 lamp, 5-inch diameter R-40, and 8-inch diameter PAR64 lamps. These and similar lamp families are used because each lamp style is generally available in a variety of beam shapes—spot, flood, oval, and so forth—that allow the designer to pick and choose the appropriate beam shape and

Figure 4.38   Funnels are used to create small circular patterns of light with a fresnel spotlight.

Barn door: An accessory for a fresnel spotlight whose movable flippers are swung into the beam to control it.

Funnel: An accessory for a fresnel spotlight that masks the beam to create a circular pattern; also called a snoot or top hat.

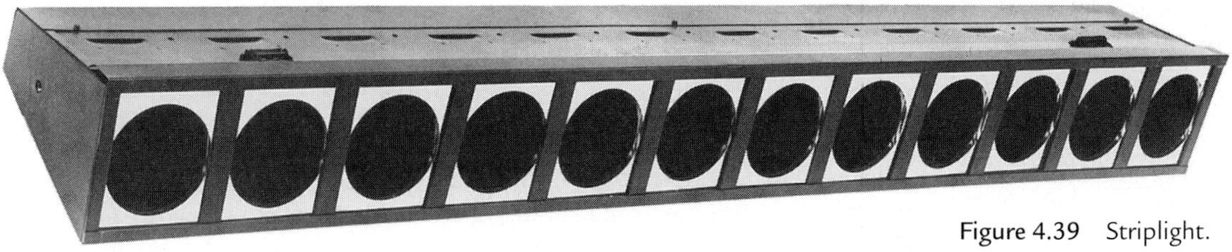

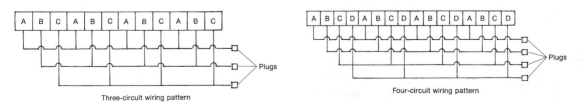

Figure 4.39   Striplight.
(Courtesy of Altman Lighting.)

spread for a specific need. Striplights designed around the MR-16 lamp have a relatively small housing, which allows them to be used in situations where a wash of controllable color is needed and space is limited—club stages, display lighting, and theatrical situations that won't accommodate their larger cousins. Striplights generally are available in a variety of lengths, with 6 to 10 feet being typical, although the MR-16 strips are available in lengths as short as 1 ½ to 2 feet.

The individual lights within the instrument are wired in parallel to form three or four circuits, as shown in the block diagram of Figure 4.40. This type of configuration provides designers with the opportunity to mix and blend color if they gel all the lamps of each circuit with a separate color. By placing each circuit of the striplight on a separate dimmer, designers can manipulate the intensities of the individual colors to mix the desired resultant hue. To create the maximum potential for color mixing, the individual circuits of a three-circuit striplight are frequently colored with the primary colors in light (red, blue, and green). If a four-circuit striplight is used, the fourth circuit is frequently gelled with amber. It is not mandatory that striplights be colored with red, blue, and green; if the designer knows that he or she will be working in a relatively narrow color spectrum, it is usually preferable to color the individual circuits in the appropriate hues.

Striplights are used primarily to light background drops, **cycloramas**, and for top light color washes, although they can be used in any position wherever a diffused, general wash of light is desired. Striplights are equipped to hold plastic color media as well as **roundels** (Figure 4.41), which are glass color media that have diffusing properties to help blend the light. Roundels are available in the primary colors as well as amber, frosted, and clear.

Cyclorama: A large expanse of cloth or drop used to surround the stage. Also called a cyc.

Roundel: A glass color medium for use with striplights; frequently has diffusing properties.

Three-circuit wiring pattern

Four-circuit wiring pattern

Figure 4.40   Circuiting pattern for striplights.

Figure 4.41 Roundels are glass filters used with striplights.

Cyc Light

The cyc light is another tool created to help the lighting designer provide a smooth wash of light. There are two types of cyc lights. One, such as the Aurora Flood by Selecon shown in Figure 4.42A, has a symmetrical reflector which produces a smooth, evenly distributed output of light. This class of instrument is designed for producing color washes on the stage. It can also be used for cyclorama, or cyc, lighting in those rare instances when the fixtures can be placed far enough away from the cyc to produce a smooth wash of light. The other, illustrated by the HUI Cyc, Figure 4.42B, has an asymmetrical reflector that produces an uneven wash of light perfectly suited for cyc lighting. These cyc lights are designed so several of them can be bolted together to create what are essentially striplights, as shown in Figure 4.42C. These joined units can be placed on the floor or hung on battens. If the fixture is hung approximately 16 feet above the stage and about 6½ feet away from the cyc, it will produce a smooth wash of light 16 feet high on the cyc, as illustrated in Figure 4.43. The height of the beamspread becomes proportionately shorter as the instrument is moved closer to the cyc. Even when you can hang the fixtures no further than approximately 3 feet from the cyc, an 18- to 22-foot-tall cyc can be effectively lit by hanging one set of asymmetrically reflectored cyc lights and placing another on the floor.

Ellipsoidal Reflector Floodlight

The ellipsoidal reflector floodlight (Figure 4.44), also known as the scoop, is used primarily to light drops and cycloramas. It is a lensless instrument that has the light-focusing characteristics of a conical ellipsoidal reflector, which provides a wide, smooth wash of light. It is equipped with a large color frame holder that, in many cases, has wire restraining lines crisscrossing over the circular opening to prevent the color medium from falling out. The scoop is available in a variety of sizes, but in the theatre the 14-, 16-, and 18-inch diameters are most commonly used.

(A)   (B)   (C)

Figure 4.42 Cyc lights. (A) Aurora flood. (B) HUI cyc. (C) LUI floodlights. (Courtesy of Selecon Lighting.)

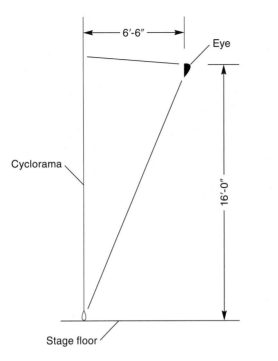

6'-6"

Eye

Cyclorama

16'-0"

Stage floor

Figure 4.43 An instrument with an assymetrical reflector can smoothly light a cyc from an overhead hanging position.

Figure 4.44 An ellipsoidal reflector floodlight. (Courtesy of Altman Lighting.)

Beam Projector

The **beam projector** (Figure 4.45) is a lensless instrument with a parabolic primary reflector and a spherical secondary reflector. It produces a very intense shaft of light that has little diffusion and cannot be easily controlled or modified.

The parabolic reflector focuses the light into parallel rays, and the spherical reflector redirects the light emitted from the front of the lamp back through the filament to the parabolic reflector. The beam projector's characteristically hard-edged, intense beam of light makes it desirable for creating shafts of sunlight and similar illusions.

The beam projector is basically archaic. It requires quite a bit of maintenance and tinkering to get the instrument to produce a smooth beam of light that doesn't have dark spots or holes in it. The PAR lamp and fixtures have largely relegated this once proud instrument to museum displays.

PAR Can

The parabolic aluminized reflector, or PAR, is a sealed-beam lamp similar to the headlight of an automobile. The lamp housing, known as a PAR can (Figure 4.46), performs no function other than safely holding the lamp and its color media.

Figure 4.45 A beam projector. (Courtesy of Kliegl Bros.)

Beam projector: A lensless instrument with a parabolic primary reflector and a spherical secondary reflector that creates an intense shaft of light with little diffusion.

Figure 4.46   PAR cans.
(Courtesy of Strand Lighting and Electronic Theatre Controls [ETC].)

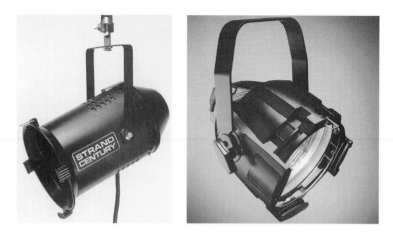

The most widely used size of PAR can is designed to hold the PAR 64, a 1,000-watt lamp 8 inches in diameter. The PAR 64 lamp is available in a variety of beam shapes, as shown in Table 4.4. The PAR 64 produces a powerfully intense punch of light, yet it has a soft edge.

A new development in the PAR family is the ETC Source Four PAR. Instead of using a PAR lamp, this fixture uses a parabolic reflector with a replaceable lamp. The company claims similar performance to a 1,000-watt PAR with its recommended 575-watt lamp. Beam spread is controlled through the use of one of the five replaceable front lenses. Additionally, an optional cold mirror reflector, which significantly enhances color media life, is available.

PARs are used extensively in concert lighting and are finding increased usage in dance lighting because of their characteristic punch of light, relatively low cost, portability, durability, and light weight.

TABLE 4.4   Beam and Field Angles for Various PAR 64 Configurations

PAR 64 Lamp	Beam Angle (in Degrees) (Height × Width)	Field Angle (in Degrees) (Height × Width)
Very Narrow	6 × 12	10 × 24
Narrow	7 × 14	14 × 26
Medium	12 × 28	21 × 44
Wide	24 × 48	45 × 71

Followspot

The followspot is used when a high-intensity, hard-edged beam of light is required to follow a moving performer. Followspots are manufactured in a variety of sizes and styles (see Figure 4.47). The smallest followspot is an incandescent model capable of a useful light throw of about 35 feet. The larger models use high-intensity xenon, HMI, or unencapsulated arc lamp sources and have a useful light throw of up to 300 to 400 feet.

All followspots function on the same general principles, illustrated in Figure 4.48. They have an illumination source—incandescent, tungsten-

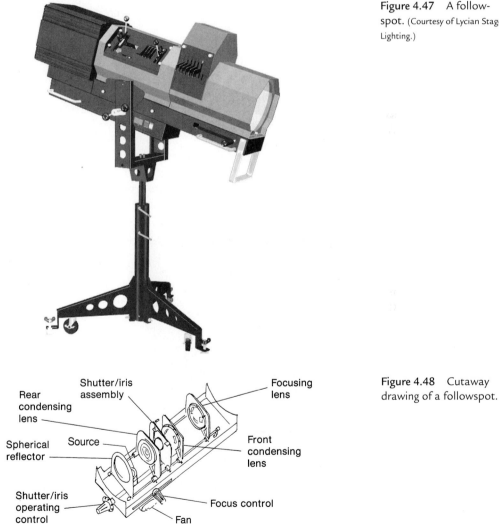

Figure 4.47 A followspot. (Courtesy of Lycian Stage Lighting.)

Figure 4.48 Cutaway drawing of a followspot.

Instrument Maintenance

To function effectively, the various instruments discussed in this chapter must be maintained in good working order, and, as with any delicate piece of equipment, they must be handled with care.

The position of the lamp filament and the reflector must be kept in alignment, particularly in an ellipsoidal reflector spotlight. If this relationship is disturbed, the light output from the instrument will be greatly reduced, and the hot spot will be moved from the center of the beam. One of the significant advantages of the PAR 64 is that the filament and reflector are permanently aligned during the manufacturing process, so when the lamp in a PAR can is changed, there is no need to check the relationship.

The lenses and reflectors need to be kept clean and free from dust and fingerprints, and all nuts and bolts on the housing, yoke, and pipe clamp should be maintained so that the instrument can be locked securely into place.

When not in use, instruments should be hung on pipes or on rolling racks, as shown in the photo, so that they won't be knocked over. If the theatre does not have an instrument storage cage, the instruments can be stored on a counterweight batten above the stage.

Ellipsoidal reflector spotlights should be stored with the shutters pushed all the way in to prevent them from being accidentally bent. When the instruments are in storage, care should be taken that the electrical pigtails are not pinched between the yoke and the instrument housing. The electrical plug and pigtail must be kept in good working order.

Followspots are mounted on a yoke and swivel-stand base that must move smoothly to follow the action of a performer. The base and yoke need to be properly lubricated, usually with graphite rather than oil or grease, and all nuts and bolts must be properly tightened.

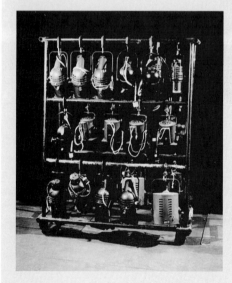

Instrument Storage.

halogen, HMI, xenon, or arc. Many have a forced-air cooling system that helps to dissipate the heat generated by the light source.

The iris and **shutter** are internal control devices used to shape the beam of light. By manipulating them simultaneously, the operator can create a variety of beam edge patterns.

All followspots have some type of lens or reflecting system to gather and shape the light. Portions of the system can be adjusted to focus the light and adjust the crispness of the edge of the beam.

Some followspots are equipped with a dimming device called a **douser**. Because the intensity of some of the light sources used in followspots (unencapsulated arc, xenon, HMI) cannot be adjusted, the douser provides the only way of smoothly dimming those sources. The douser can also be used to achieve a slow fade-in or fade-out of the light. Followspots are also equipped with a color boomerang, which holds five or six color filters that can be easily inserted into the beam of light to control its color.

Shutter: A lever-actuated device used to control the height of the top and bottom edges of a followspot beam; also called a chopper.

Douser: A mechanical dimming device used in followspots.

Transformer: A device that changes the voltage in an electrical system; the output voltage of a step-down transformer is less than its source; a step-up transformer increases it.

SPECIALTY EQUIPMENT
· ·

There are several types of lighting equipment that do not fall conveniently into other categories.

Low-Voltage Systems

A number of specialty lamps use a voltage lower than the 120 output volts of most stage dimmers. The output of these low-voltage lamps is frequently as high as that of their 120-volt cousins. Aircraft landing lights (ACLs) have a very high output and high color temperature, and the parabolic reflector provides a very narrow beam spread. Automobile headlights provide another narrow-beam, low-voltage source.

A primary advantage of lower-voltage lamps is that their filaments are generally much smaller than their higher-voltage counterparts. The smaller filament can be used effectively in some types of scenic projectors discussed in Chapter 7, "Projections."

If used singly, these low-voltage lamps require a **transformer** to decrease the 120-volt source voltage before it reaches the lamp, as shown in Figure 4.49. A step-down transformer of appropriate voltage and capacity to match almost any lamp can be purchased at any electrical supply store. For 12-volt lamps a heavy-duty automotive battery charger can be used as long as the current created by the wattage of the lamp does not exceed the rated capacity of the battery charger or its leads.

Figure 4.49   A low-voltage lamp and transformer.

Figure 4.50   An MR16 lamp.

The low-voltage MR lamp (Figure 4.50), though a relatively recent addition to the theatrical lighting designer's palette, was developed a number of years ago. MRs are quite small. The most common size (MR 16) is 2 inches in diameter, which allows lighting designers to hide them in locations that would be inaccessible to more normally sized instrumentation. MRs are available in what might be considered a surprisingly wide range of voltages and wattages until one realizes that these efficient compact lamps are used in an equally wide range of slide and film projectors. The 12-volt lamp is the most readily available and is the one most commonly used in the theatre. Whereas a single 12-volt lamp requires the use of a transformer as explained earlier, the transformer normally is built into the fixtures that use these lamps.

Although using a single low-voltage lamp with a 120-volt power source such as a stage dimmer requires the use of a transformer, it is possible to wire a number of these low-voltage lamps in series and eliminate the need for a transformer. The method is simple. The total voltage of all the lamps wired in series must equal, or nearly equal, the voltage of the source. The fixture shown in Figure 4.51A has four 28-volt ACL lamps wired in series. The total voltage of the fixture is 112 volts. Although the total voltage is lower than the 120 volts of a stage dimmer, it is close enough to work very effectively. MR16 striplights and other multilamp configurations are also wired in series. The unit shown in Figure 4.51B has ten 12-volt lamps wired in series.

As mentioned in Chapter 3, if one of the lamps in a series circuit burns out, the circuit is broken and the remaining lamps go out. Most modern Christmas tree lights are wired in series, but they also have a circuit feature that allows the remaining lights to remain lit even if one lamp burns out. The whole string goes out only if a lamp is physically removed from its

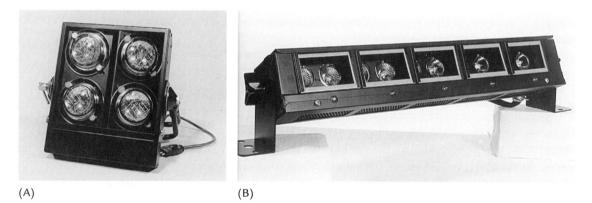

(A)   (B)

Figure 4.51   Series-wired fixtures. (A) An instrument with four aircraft landing lights (ACL) wired in series; (B) A mini strip with ten 12-volt MR16 lamps wired in series. (Courtesy of James Thomas Engineering [A] and Lighting & Electronics [B].)

socket. Most series-wired stage lighting fixtures have some variation of this circuit feature so that the entire instrument doesn't go out if one of the lamps burns out.

The MR lamp demonstrates a very effective use of combination reflectors. The beam spread of these lamps ranges from extremely narrow to flood. The shape of the beam is controlled by the design of the highly mirrored surface of the reflector. The focusing reflector eliminates the need for a front focusing lens, which is one of the reasons that the output of these little lamps is so efficient. Most MR16 lamps also have cold mirror finishes that reflect visible light, but pass infrared light (heat) through the reflector to be vented out the rear of the fixture.

Although the primary market for these lamps is nontheatrical—interior design and display lighting—some manufacturers have created fixtures for MR lamps using traditional theatrical configurations such as striplights and PAR cans (Figure 4.52). Additionally, several designs that are not traditionally thought of as "theatrical" are nonetheless useful in certain situations. The nine light—so called because it normally contains nine individual lamps—is a common fixture in film and television lighting. It is simply an arrangement of nine flood lamps in a rectangular-shaped fixture, and it creates a smooth, soft, reasonably focused wash of light at relatively close range.

Some imaginative thinking will enable you to figure out a wide variety of applications for these useful little lights.

Figure 4.52   An MR16 PAR can. (Courtesy of James Thomas Engineering.)

Booms and Ladders

There are two pieces of equipment that aren't really lighting instruments, but they don't readily fall into any other organizational category either. Booms and ladders are typically shop-built equipment used to hold lighting instruments. They are also commercially available from most lighting manufacturers and stage equipment houses. A boom (Figure 4.53) is a vertical pipe with a heavy base. Typically made from 1¼- or 1½-inch pipe, booms are generally between 14 and 16 feet tall and have adjustable crossbars or side arms on which the instruments are hung. A ladder is similar to a boom in that it is another auxiliary hanging position for lighting instruments; however, the ladder is designed to hang from the end of an onstage electric pipe as shown in Figure 4.54

In **proscenium** theatres, booms are typically used when a design calls for the use of sidelight or when a backstage light needs to be put in a place where there is no permanent hanging position. Ladders are frequently substituted for booms if the placement of the boom might interfere with the movement of large rolling scenic pieces or if the instruments need to be placed higher than about 16 feet. Booms and ladders can be used in conjunction with each other if the design concept calls for the heavy use of sidelight (typical of some types of musicals and dance).

Figure 4.53   A boom.

Proscenium stage: A stage configuration in which the spectators watch the action through a rectangular opening (the proscenium arch) that resembles a picture frame.

Figure 4.54 Ladders are typically hung at the end of pipes.

Figure 4.55 A temporary lighting position can be made from two booms and a pipe.

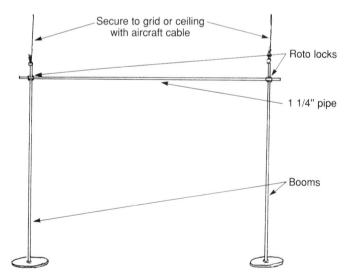

Secure to grid or ceiling with aircraft cable

Roto locks

1 1/4" pipe

Booms

Roto-lock: Specialized clamps used to fasten pipes together for temporary structures such as scaffolding and temporary hanging positions for lighting instruments.

Booms aren't typically used in **thrust** and **arena** theatres because the vertical pipe might interfere with the audience's view of the stage. Ladders can be suspended from the lighting grid whenever there is a need to lower the angle of a particular instrument. However, a temporary lighting pipe can be constructed using two booms to support a crosspipe, as shown in Figure 4.55. If the crosspipe will be longer than about 10 feet or will be holding more than 8 to 10 instruments, a properly engineered truss should be used because the weight of the instruments and cable could bend the pipe. In any case, booms and this type of temporary structure should always be well anchored with **aircraft cable** so that they won't tip over.

Thrust stage: A stage projecting into, and surrounded on three sides by, the audience.

Arena stage: A stage completely surrounded by the audience.

Aircraft cable: Extremely strong, flexible, multistrand, twisted metal cable; $1/8$-inch aircraft cable has a breaking strength of one ton.

CHAPTER 5

Cables and Connectors

In stage lighting, a flexible system for distributing electricity to the lighting instruments is necessary. This chapter discusses the types of cables and connectors that constitute this flexible distribution system, as well as several methods of circuiting, or connecting, the lighting instruments to the dimmers.

ELECTRICAL CABLE FOR STAGE USE

Almost all electrical wires or cables are made up of two basic components: a conductor and an insulator. Basically, a conductor is any material composed of atoms that have many free electrons. With its many free electrons, copper is used extensively in the construction of wires and cables for stage use. In addition to being an excellent conductor, it is flexible and reasonable in cost. Brass, an alloy of copper, zinc, and other elements, possesses the good conductive properties of copper and can be formed into rigid shapes such as **plugs** and **receptacles**. Silver and gold are also excellent conductors, but their cost prohibits their use in all but the most sensitive of electronic applications. Although aluminum is a good conductor, it is not as good a conductor as copper, and it is not used in the types of cable approved by the National Electrical Code (NEC) for temporary stage use.

Insulators are materials that have few free electrons, making it all but impossible for electricity to flow through them. Because it is normal to have several conductors within one cable (see Figure 5.1), each conductor is covered with an insulator to isolate it physically and electrically from the other conductors within the cable; further, all the conductors are encased inside an

Plug: The male portion of a connecting device.

Receptacle: The female portion of a connecting device.

insulating jacket of—usually—the same material. Rubber is a good insulator and also cushions the wire or cable. Some types of thermoplastics are also good insulators, but thermoplastic insulation is usually thin and won't stand up to the physical abuse that rubber insulation can take. Fiber and paper are also good insulators and are frequently used as cushioning material inside multiconductor wire such as the cable shown in Figure 5.1.

There are two basic types of electrical conductors: solid wire and stranded-wire cable (Figure 5.2). Solid wire, which is used in permanent installations such as in-wall house wiring, is semirigid and will break if subjected to repeated flexing. Stranded-wire cable is made up of a number of small wires grouped together to form a large single conductor. This structure is more flexible than solid wire because the individual strands that make up the conductor are very limber. Even when a number of these wires are encased inside an insulator, the resultant conductor is still quite flexible.

The NEC stipulates that the only electrical cables approved for temporary stage wiring are types S, SO, ST, and STO. These cables have stranded copper conductors and are insulated with rubber (S and SO) or thermoplastic (ST and STO). S and SO cables are more commonly used than ST and STO, because their thick rubber jacket can withstand more physical abuse than can the thin, heat-resistant thermoplastic insulation of the ST and STO cable. Type S is generally used for stage lighting, because SO costs more (its only advantage is that it is impervious to oil and gasoline).

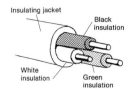

Figure 5.1   An electrical wire.

Figure 5.2   Solid wire (left) and stranded-wire cable.

Wire Gauge

The American Wire Gauge (AWG) system rates wire according to the amount of current that a conductor of a particular size and composition can safely carry. As Chapter 3 explained, the rated current capacity for any given gauge should never be exceeded. Most cables have the gauge and wire type imprinted every foot or so on the insulating jacket.

The amount of current that can be safely carried varies greatly, as shown in Table 5.1. There is no standard size of cable for theatre use, because the load requirements that a typical cable will be required to carry differ—often significantly—from one theatre to another. However, the NEC stipulates

TABLE 5.1   American Wire Gauge Current Capacity Chart

Gauge of wire	10	12	14	16	18
Capacity in amps	25	20	15	6	3
Capacity in watts (@ 120 VAC)[a]	3,000	2,400	1,800	720	360

[a]The capacities indicated are maximums and assume that all elements in the circuit are in excellent repair. For safety considerations, unless you are *absolutely certain* that the equipment is in excellent shape, each of these figures should be reduced by approximately 10%.

First ante-proscenium (AP) cut: A hanging position for lighting instruments; also known as beamport; the slot or opening in the auditorium ceiling closest to the proscenium arch. The second AP is second closest to the proscenium arch, and so on.

Third pipe: When lighting instruments are hung on a batten over the stage, the terminology changes and the batten becomes a pipe. The third pipe is the third batten upstage of the proscenium arch that holds lighting instruments.

that receptacles and conductors used to supply incandescent lamps on stage must be able to carry a minimum current of 20 amperes. Twelve-gauge cable is rated at 20 amperes. Practical or decorative lamps are the only exception to this rule. These lamps may be wired with cable of smaller capacity as long as the lamp load does not exceed the rated capacity of the cable. This means that you can use 18-gauge wire (also known as lamp cord or zip cord) as long as the lamp load doesn't exceed 360 watts (assuming the system voltage is 120 volts: $W = VA$; $360 = 120 \times 3$).

Connecting Devices

Lighting instruments are almost always moved between productions. An instrument that is hung in the **first ante-proscenium cut** for one production may be hung on the **third pipe** for the next. Because of this required flexibility, the electrical cables for both instruments and circuits normally terminate in connecting devices that are quick and easy to connect (or disconnect).

Several different styles of connector are used in stage lighting (Figure 5.3). Twist-lock connectors (Figure 5.3A) are considered by many people to be the best type of stage connector. The male portion, or plug, fits into the

SAFETY TIP

Wiring Continuity, or Green Is for Ground . . .

The types of electrical cables, plugs, and receptacles that are approved for use in the theatre in the United States are color coded. The insulation on the three conductors inside any stage cable is colored black, white, or green. Black is the power (hot) conductor, white is the neutral, and green is for ground. The contacts inside of plugs and receptacles are also color coded, but most of them are colored brass, silver, and green. In this case brass is the power (hot) conductor, silver is neutral, and green is for ground.

Whenever you are repairing cables, connectors, or instruments, make sure that you maintain wiring continuity by following the color coding: *always* connect black to black or brass, white to white or silver, and green to green.

Similarly, never assume that equipment that you've "inherited"— that hasn't been shipped to you directly from the manufacturer—is wired following the color-coding guidelines. Always check any such equipment to make sure that its wiring continuity is maintained.

Maintaining wiring continuity in all of your equipment will prevent a number of electrical problems—shorts, hot grounds, polarity reversals—that are, at best, time-consuming to track down and fix after a show has been hung, but more important, potentially lethal.

(A)   (B)

Figure 5.3   (A) Male and female twist-lock connectors; (B) grounded pin connector; (C) locking grounded pin connector; (D) grounded parallel blade (Edison) connectors. [(B) and (C) courtesy of Union Connector Co.]

(C)   (D)

female portion, or receptacle, and is twisted to lock the two halves together. This locking action prevents most accidental disconnections of the circuit.

Pin connectors are probably more widely used than twist-lock connectors, primarily because they have been in existence longer. Older models of pin connectors (Figure 5.3B) have three distinct disadvantages: (1) they can be easily disconnected by accident; (2) the pins of the plug do not always make a good electrical connection with the receptacle; and (3) if the cable is connected to a live power source, it is very easy to be shocked, because the metal conductors in the receptacle are not deeply recessed. Newer models of the grounded pin connector (Figure 5.3C) overcome these disadvantages. The new designs, which also meet the NEC guidelines, have an excellent locking device that prevents accidental disconnections, and the metal contacts within the receptacle are recessed quite deeply into the insulating body of the connector.

The Edison, or parallel blade, plug (Figure 5.3D), should be used only on decorative lamps or devices that carry a similarly small load.

All connectors, regardless of style, are designed to carry a specific amount of current. The maximum load is usually printed somewhere on the plug, and that limit should be strictly obeyed.

The NEC stipulates that each plug should be equipped with an effective cable-clamping device (see Figure 5.4). The purpose of the cable clamp is to secure the connector to the jacket of the cable. This clamping action

Figure 5.4 Internal and external cable clamps.

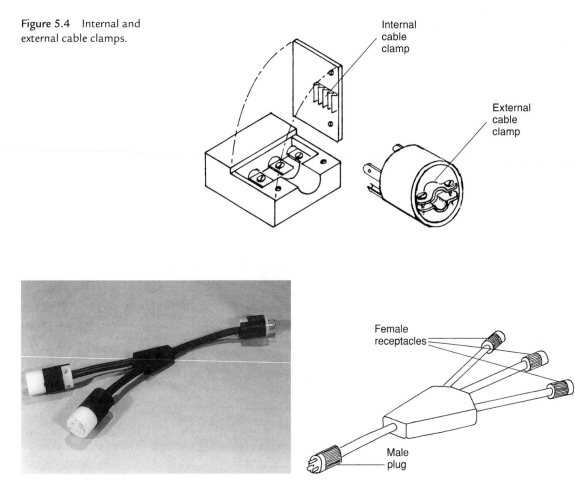

Internal cable clamp

External cable clamp

Figure 5.5 A 'Y,' or two-fer.

Figure 5.6 A martingale, or three-fer.

Female receptacles

Male plug

transfers any physical strain from the plug casing directly to the cable jacket, which effectively eliminates any strain on the electrical connections inside of the plug.

Extension Cables

Extension cables can be purchased, or made in the theatre's electrical shop, in any reasonable length. As noted, they are generally made of type S cable, although types SO, ST, or STO can also be used. Different theatres present differing requirements; but, in general, if a theatre has a permanent lighting

✳ Attaching Cables to Connectors

Several methods are used to attach cables to connectors. Many newer plugs have internal conductor grips, which simply require that you strip the insulation back until about ½ inch of wire is exposed, push the wire into the appropriate hole (black insulation to brass screw; white insulation to silver screw; green insulation, or ground, to green screw) and tighten the screw. The screw tightens a small clamp that firmly connects the conductor to its appropriate terminal.

If you are using an older, exposed-contact connector, the safest method of attachment is to use a closed-end solderless terminal (Figure A). This device is crimped onto the end of the stripped conductor with a plier-like tool called a crimper (Figure B). The seating screw of the plug is inserted through the hole in the solderless terminal and then firmly seated in the plug or receptacle. If you think that you might want to take the plug off the cable at some time in the future, then you might want to use an open-end, or spade-lug, terminal (Figure C).

Another, slightly less safe, method is to twist the conductor into a hook shape and tin the wires by heating the conductor with a soldering gun and applying a small amount of rosin core solder to the wire. By binding the small wires into a solid unit, tinning improves the electrical connection between the conductor and connector. The hook is attached to the plug or receptacle by placing the wire around the screw in the direction of the twist of the screw, as shown in Figure D. This will draw the wire toward the shaft of the screw when the screw is tightened.

The least-acceptable method of attachment is to twist the wires into a hook, omitting the tinning process. When you try to tighten the screw, the wires tend to splay away from the terminal and come in contact with other elements in the connector, thereby creating the potential for a short circuit.

A

B

C

Direction of rotation of the screw

Tinned portion

D

system, an inventory of cables 5, 10, and 20 feet long should meet the needs of most operations.

A **two-fer** is used to connect two instruments to the same circuit. When using two-fers (Figure 5.5) or any other device that can increase the electrical load on a circuit, take particular care not to exceed the maximum current rating of any element (cable, plug, dimmer, and so on) in that circuit.

The three-fer, or martingale (Figure 5.6), is similar in purpose and design to a two-fer except that it is used to connect three instruments to the same circuit. Again, as with the two-fer, you have to be very careful when using a three-fer not to exceed the rated capacity of any element in the circuit.

Two-fer: An electrical Y that has female receptacles at the top of the Y and a male plug at the bottom leg of the Y; used to connect two instruments to the same circuit.

CIRCUITING

· ·

The distribution of electricity from dimmers to lighting instruments creates a complex system. Any complex system is built on compromise, simply because the maximum amount of efficiency that can be built into any system is finite. The compromises on which stage lighting systems are predicated are speed and ease of hanging and circuiting versus flexibility of hanging position. The following methods of stage circuiting demonstrate the effects of tinkering with the variables of this complex equation.

Permanent Wiring

The simplest method of circuiting is to permanently wire the instruments to the dimmers. In this system a few ellipsoidal reflector spotlights are usually hung somewhere on the ceiling of the auditorium, and some striplights or **work lights** over the stage. These instruments are permanently wired to specific dimmers. To operate the system you just turn on the dimmers. The only possible changes or adjustments within the system are changing the color or area of focus for each instrument.

Although this method is certainly the easiest to operate, it provides very little flexibility and just about eliminates any chance for creatively designing with light. Permanently wired lighting systems appear with great frequency in high school auditoriums, music halls, and other facilities where the lighting installation has been guided by criteria other than the needs and requirements of the creative use of designed light.

Spidering

Spidering, also known as direct cabling, originally involved running a cable from each lighting instrument directly to the dimmer to which it was assigned. It got its name from the tangled web of cables created by circuiting a production in this manner. That was back in the old days when Broadway houses and touring shows still used **resistance dimmers**. Currently much of the spiderweb appearance has disappeared by the replacement of almost all the individual cables with multicables that hold numerous conductors in one jacket.

Spidering with multicables is used extensively in Broadway theatres and on touring shows. It provides the greatest flexibility, because it allows the designer to put an instrument wherever it is needed.

Connecting Strips and Patch Panels

An electrical distribution system that utilizes connecting strips and a patch panel provides two advantages in a theatre that has an extensive production program: (1) The light plot can be hung and circuited rapidly and (2) the sys-

Work light: A lighting fixture, frequently a scoop, PAR, or other wide-field-angle instrument, hung over the stage to facilitate work; generally not used to light a production.

Resistance dimmer: An archaic dimmer that functioned as a variable resistor. See page 93 for more information.

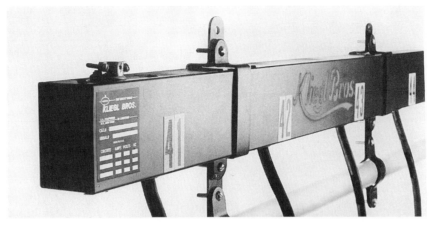

Figure 5.7 A connecting strip.

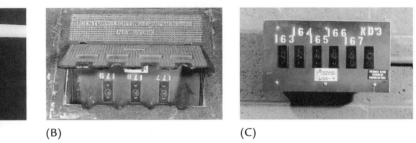

(A)   (B)   (C)

Figure 5.8 (A) Drop box; (B) floor pocket; (C) wall pocket.

tem provides a great deal of flexibility by allowing any circuit to be patched into any dimmer.

Two principle parts make up this system: the stage circuits and a patch panel. Most of the stage circuits are contained in connecting strips, which are sections of wireway, or electrical gutter, that contain a number of circuits (Figure 5.7).

The connecting strips are hung in a variety of positions about the stage and auditorium—counterweighted battens over the stage; various front-of-house positions (ante-proscenium cuts or slots, beamports, coves, boxes); and various locations on the walls of the stage house. Each circuit terminates in a receptacle that is usually mounted at the end of a 2- to 3-foot pigtail, although the receptacles are sometimes mounted flush on the gutter itself.

Additional stage circuit outlets are often contained in **drop boxes, floor pockets,** and **wall pockets** (Figure 5.8). Drop boxes are small connecting strips fed by cables that are attached to the grid above the stage. They usually contain four to eight circuits and are equipped with one or two pipe clamps so that they can be easily attached to pipes or booms. Floor pockets are recessed into the floor while wall pockets can either be recessed into,

Drop box: A small connecting strip, containing four to eight circuits, that can be clamped to a pipe or boom.

Floor pocket: A connecting box, usually containing three to six circuits, the top of which is mounted flush with the stage floor.

Wall pocket: A connecting box similar to a floor pocket but mounted in the wall.

Figure 5.9 In a patch panel system, the stage circuit runs from the female receptacle on the stage outlet to a male plug at the patch panel.

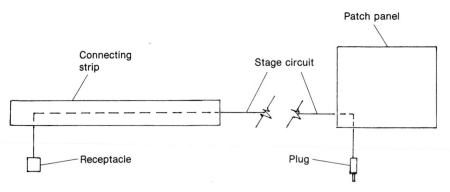

or attached to the surface of, the wall. Both types usually have three to six separate circuits.

All the circuits contained in connecting strips, drop boxes, and floor or wall pockets have certain properties in common. Each circuit is a rather long extension cable that, at the stage end, terminates in a female receptacle. Some connecting strips are designed to provide two receptacles for each circuit. In the patch panel system, the other end of the circuit terminates at the patch panel in a male plug, as shown in Figure 5.9.

The second part of the distribution system is the patch panel, or patch bay. It is an interconnecting device that provides the system with the capability of connecting, or patching, any stage circuit into any dimmer. Patch panels (Figure 5.10) are manufactured in a variety of styles and configurations.

Figure 5.11 illustrates the basic operational design of a patch panel. The lighting instrument is connected into a stage circuit, which terminates at the patch panel in a male plug. The dimmer, which is usually located in another part of the theatre, is permanently wired to a receptacle on the face of the patch panel. To enable the electricity to flow from the dimmer to the lighting instrument, it will be necessary to complete the circuit. This is done by patching the circuit into the appropriate receptacle for the dimmer.

The patch panel is actually very simple to operate. What makes it seem so complex is that it contains many more than the one circuit and one dimmer cited in this example. In fact, a patch panel usually contains between 60 and several hundred stage circuits, and from 40 to several hundred dimmers. In addition, each dimmer is usually provided with several receptacles on the face of the patch panel so that more than one circuit can be patched into each dimmer.

Patch panels usually have some type of electrical overload protection for both the stage circuit and the dimmer circuit. The circuit breaker automatically breaks the continuity of the circuit when an unsafe amount of current is passed through the line. Each stage circuit has a circuit breaker, as shown in Figure 5.12, that provides overload protection. Another circuit breaker is usually located either in the line connecting the patch panel to the dimmer

Figure 5.10 Patch panel. (Courtesy of Colortran.)

Cable and Connector Maintenance

The following steps are suggested to keep cables and connectors in good operating condition and in compliance with NEC and federal regulations.

1. When a cable is not in use, coil it and hang it on the wall of the lighting storage room. The cable will stay neatly coiled if the connectors are plugged together or if it is tied with heavy twine or thin rope.

2. Check cables and connectors periodically, and replace any items that show signs of cracking, chipping, or other deterioration. Cracks in the insulation of cables and connectors increase the chances of someone receiving a shock from the device. Also, dust can accumulate in the crack and may cause an electrical fire.

3. Always disconnect a plug by pulling on the body of the connector, not the cable. Pulling on the cable puts an unnecessary strain on the cable clamp and will eventually defeat the clamp. When the cable clamp no longer functions, pulling on the cable places the strain directly on the electrical connections.

4. Keep the connectors clean. Remove any corrosion, paint, grease, or other accumulations as soon as they become evident. These substances can act as insulation between the contacts of the connector and, if flammable, pose a fire hazard.

5. All elements of a cable should be of the same electrical rating; for example, 12-gauge (AWG) cable (capable of carrying 20 amperes of current) should have only 20-ampere-rated connectors, and so forth.

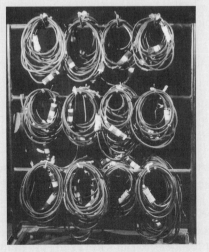

Cable storage.

Figure 5.11 The patch panel allows you to plug more than one circuit into a single dimmer.

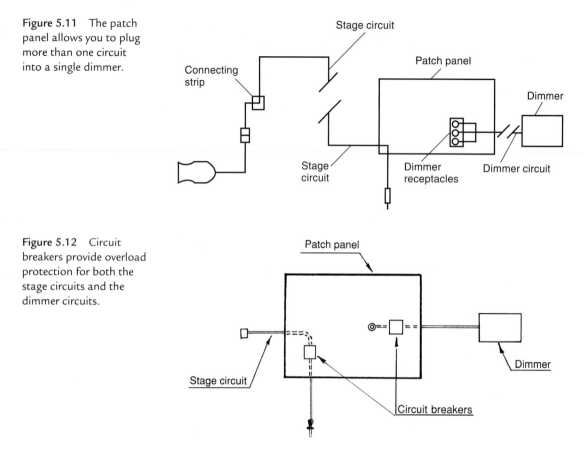

Figure 5.12 Circuit breakers provide overload protection for both the stage circuits and the dimmer circuits.

or in the dimmer itself. This circuit breaker protects the dimmer circuit and dimmer from an overload.

Dimmer per Circuit

The dimmer-per-circuit configuration is probably the most efficient electrical distribution system for stage lighting. It combines the efficiency in hanging and circuiting of the connecting strip with the ease of operation of the permanently wired system.

As in the connecting strip and patch panel system, the onstage end of each circuit terminates in an outlet on a connecting strip, floor pocket, or similar location. The other end of the circuit is directly wired to a dimmer instead of terminating in a male plug at the patch panel.

Before the introduction of the computer-assisted lighting control board, it required a very large and unwieldy control system and three to six—or more—electricians to run all the dimmers required by this type of system.

But the computer board (see Chapter 6, "Intensity Control") makes control of the large number of dimmers associated with this type of system a relatively simple task for one person. The dimmer-per-circuit configuration, when combined with a computer light board, provides what is probably the most efficient electrical system for stage lighting available at this time.

CHAPTER 6

Intensity Control

You're sitting in the auditorium of your favorite regional professional theatre company watching the lights fade out after the final curtain call of a wonderful musical. A number of random thoughts run through your mind—the leads' voices were beautiful, the scenery and costumes were stunning, everybody got whom, or what, they wanted. Probably the last thing you'd think about at this time, if you'd think about it at all, would be the fact that it took between 60 and 200 dimmers, all working in unison, to achieve the smooth fade-out that you'd just witnessed.

Every theatrical lighting system, regardless of size or complexity, is composed of three basic elements: dimmers, dimmer control, and an electrical distribution system. This chapter deals with dimmers and the various systems and methods used to control them. It also contains a discussion of how electricity flows through a stage lighting system in a typical theatre.

DIMMERS

The relatively brief history of electrical stage lighting has seen many different kinds of dimmers used to control the intensity of instruments. Some of the older dimmers, such as the saltwater, saturable core, thyratron tube, and resistance dimmer, have dropped by the wayside. Other older dimmers, such as the autotransformer, have continued in limited use.

✳ Archaic Dimmers

Although the dimmers described in this box are no longer installed in theatres, they do have historical significance in the progress of stage lighting.

SALTWATER DIMMER

The oldest type of dimmer was a frightening contraption. The primary component of this death trap was a bucket of salt water. Metal plates were attached to one leg of the circuit, and one of these plates was completely immersed in the bucket. The current passing through the circuit varied with the depth of immersion of the second plate.

SATURABLE CORE DIMMER

Another old dimmer worked by using a small DC current to magnetize an iron core. The AC load current passed through this iron core. As the level of magnetism was increased, the conductivity of the core also increased, and the lights connected to the dimmer came on.

MAGNETIC AMPLIFIER DIMMER

A more efficient version of the saturable core dimmer, the magnetic amplifier was introduced in the 1950s but was soon relegated to obscurity by the development of the silicon controlled rectifier dimmer.

THYRATRON TUBE DIMMER

The thyratron tube dimmer was the first electronically controlled dimmer, and the first to use the gating principle—a rapid switching on and off of the load current. However, thyratron vacuum tubes were large, had to warm up before they worked, didn't last very long, and were somewhat expensive.

RESISTANCE DIMMER

The resistance dimmer functioned as a large variable-capacity resistor. When lights connected to it were turned off, it converted all the electrical energy flowing to it into heat. As it was turned on, its resistance decreased, and current reached the lamps.

Dimmer Control Techniques

Dimmers can be divided into two groups, based on the type of control used to regulate the current flow through them, mechanical or electronic.

Mechanical Control   Older types such as the resistance and autotransformer dimmers require direct mechanical manipulation of an axle running through the central core of the dimmer to adjust the intensity of a lamp, as shown in Figure 6.1. This method of dimmer control is awkward. When a number of dimmers are linked, as shown in the illustration of an archaic resistance board (Figure 6.2), the resultant dimmer board is noisy, is difficult

Figure 6.1 Some dimmers require a mechanical control technique.

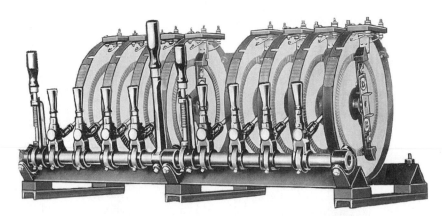

Figure 6.2 A resistance board.

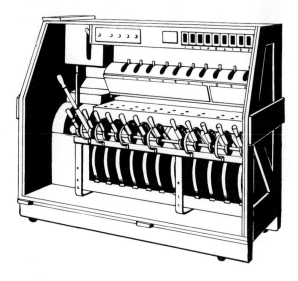

to operate, and requires at least several rather muscular electricians to run even a moderately complex production. You can imagine that a certain delicacy of touch and smoothness of operation are lost when you have to control one dimmer with each hand and try to operate another one with your foot. For the most part mechanically controlled dimmers are no longer used.

Electronic Control   The methods and operating principles vary according to the specific type of dimmer, but all electronically controlled dimmers use a low-voltage control current to regulate the high-voltage load current. The process of controlling the output of the dimmer by electronic rather than mechanical means lets the control console be located some distance away from the dimmers. Additionally, the low-voltage, low-amperage current of the control circuit allows all parts of this electronic circuit to be miniaturized.

Autotransformer Dimmer

Autotransformer dimmers increase or decrease lamp intensity by varying the voltage within the circuit. Although this type of dimmer is only rarely used to control stage lights, houselights in some theatres are controlled by a motorized autotransformer dimmer, as shown in Figure 6.3. A control switch, usually located in the light booth, is used to activate a motor, which runs a mechanical linkage that controls the dimmer and enables it to raise or lower the intensity of the houselights. The only drawback to the motorized autotransformer dimmer occurs when the motor runs at a single speed, which means that the fade time for the houselights cannot be varied.

Figure 6.3 A motorized autotransformer dimmer.

Silicon Controlled Rectifier Dimmer

Until the development of the IGBT and sine wave dimmers, which are explained a little later in this section, the silicon controlled rectifier (SCR) dimmer (Figure 6.4) was considered the most reliable and efficient unit for stage lighting. It still remains the workhorse of the industry. But the operational advantages offered by the IGBT and sine wave dimming suggest that they, or something even more advanced, will ultimately replace the SCR as the dimmer technology of choice.

The SCR dimmer operates on a gating principle (see box, "Gating Principle"), which is simply a rapid switching on and off of the power.

The SCR is a solid-state power transistor, which means that it has no moving parts and no filaments to burn out. The electronic circuitry necessary to switch the SCR to a conducting state is also relatively simple. These properties result in a dimmer that is rugged, long lived, compact, relatively lightweight, moderate in cost, and reasonably quiet in operation.

Figure 6.4 A single CD-80 SCR dimmer.
(Courtesy of Strand Lighting).

Insulated Bipolar Transistor (IGBT) Dimmer

The technology of IGBT dimmers operates on the same gating principle as SCR dimmers but with one significant difference. As described in the box, "Gating Principle" found on page 96, the SCR transistor is used to switch the power *on* at a designated point during each half of the AC cycle. In contrast, the IGBT transistor controls current flow by switching the power *off.* This simple difference results in several significant functional changes. All SCR dimmers use a variety of electronic chokes and most SCR dimmers have fans. Both make noise. IGBT dimmers have neither, resulting in silent operation. Additionally, IGBT dimmers create less filament hum in the lamps of fixtures connected to them.

IGBT dimmers can be rack-mounted in remote dimmer room locations like typical SCR dimmer installations, but, because IGBT dimmers are silent, they can also be mounted in on-stage and in-house locations. Configurations

Gating Principle

If, in a given period of time, you turn a lamp on, then off, then on, off, on, and off, you effectively control the amount of light it puts out for that specific amount of time. If the lamp is turned on, and left on, for 1 second, it burns at full intensity for that 1-second period. If you turn the lamp on for ½ second and turn it off for ½ second, it burns at half intensity for the 1-second span. If you turn the lamp on for ¾ second and off for ¼ second, it burns at three-quarters intensity for the 1-second span. In each of these cases, you will obviously see the lamp being switched on and off. But if the time span for the on-off cycle is reduced to ½₀₀th of a second, you perceive the on-off sequence as being a continuous level of illumination—an average of the on-off cycle ratio.

The SCR dimmer operates on this principle. The SCR is actually an electronic switch. The switch, or gate, opens and allows current to pass through the load circuit when it receives the proper electronic command. The gate stays open until the power is turned off. Sixty-cycle alternating current (AC), the standard current in the United States, alternates its polarity 120 times a second, or twice in each cycle, as illustrated in Figure A. Each time that it alternates its polarity, or crosses the zero point on the graph, there is actually no voltage. The effective result of this "no voltage" situation is that the electricity is turned off. If a command is fed to the SCR to start conduction at the beginning of the cycle, point A in Figure B, the SCR will conduct for the full half cycle, or until the electricity is turned off when it changes polarity at point B. Similarly, if the command specifies that the SCR is to begin conducting halfway through the cycle (Figure C), the transistor conducts for only half the cycle, or half as long.

By varying the time that the SCR is able to conduct electricity, you vary the intensity of any lamp load connected to it. This means that if the SCR conducts for a full half cycle, the lamp will glow at full intensity for the duration of that half cycle. If it conducts for only half of the half cycle, the lamp will be perceived to be glowing at half intensity. Similarly, a quarter-cycle electrical conduction means the lamp will appear to be glowing only one-fourth as brightly. Because each SCR conducts for only half a cycle, two SCRs, one for each half cycle, are necessary to make an effective dimmer. The IGBT dimmer operates on this same gating principle, but rather than beginning conduction, or "turning on," at a specific point during the AC cycle—as the SCR does—the IGBT stops conducting, or "turns off," at a specific point during the AC cycle.

The gating principle.

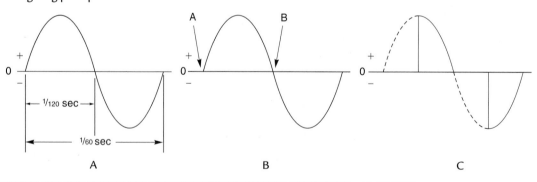

A   B   C

for batten- and wall-mounting, as well as yoke-mounting on individual instruments are available.

Sine Wave Dimmer

Sine wave dimmers are the latest development in dimming technology. The operating principles of the sine wave dimmer are probably best explained by comparing them with SCR and IGBT dimmers.

Both SCR and IGBT dimmers use the gating principle—an abrupt turning on or turning off of the control voltage—to regulate dimmer output. This signal "chopping" generates both audible noise and electrical harmonics. Sine wave dimmers don't use the gating principle to control dimmer output. They use software that varies the amplitude or voltage of the full control signal—which is shaped like a sine wave—to control dimmer output. This change makes these dimmers acoustically silent. They make no noise and the filaments of lamps connected to them don't hum. Additionally, sine wave dimmers don't generate electrical harmonics—radio frequency signals—that can interfere with nearby audio and video signals.

Like the IGBT dimmers, sine wave dimmers can be rack-mounted in dimmer rooms, or they can be located at point-of-use locations both on the stage and in the auditorium.

Digital Control Systems for Electronic Dimmers

As indicated earlier, when you move a controller to increase or decrease the intensity of lights connected to a dimmer you are using a low-voltage control circuit to manipulate the high-voltage output of that dimmer. Until recently analog control systems were the only method available for controlling SCR dimmers. Now digital control has become the new standard.

To appreciate why "digital is better," you first need to understand how both analog and digital systems work and the basic differences between them.

Analog systems work on the following principle: output varies as a continuous function of input. For example, increasing or decreasing the output of the control circuit causes a corresponding increase or decrease in the output of the dimmer. This control signal is sent from the light board over a control **line** to the dimmer. Because the analog system requires a continuous signal, every dimmer in the system must be connected to the light board by its own control line.

Digital systems work on a different principle: Output varies in discrete steps. At first glance the differences in operating principles between analog and digital systems appear relatively inconsequential. But the differences are significant. To understand why, we first need to understand how digital information differs from analog. As stated previously, analog information is continuous. Digital information isn't. Digital information is **discrete**. It is

Line: The wires in low-voltage control systems are frequently called "lines" rather than "wires."

Discrete: Separate and complete; in this case, pertaining to information represented by binary code.

Multiplex: (1) To transmit two or more messages simultaneously on a single channel. (2) To carry out several functions simultaneously in an independent but related manner.

neither continuous nor variable. Digital information exists as binary code—a series of on-off pulses.

The finite nature of the digital signal is very important. It enables digital information to be made up into discrete information or instructional packages. These "packages" can contain any information that we want them to. Further, they can be sent to specific locations. Figure 6.5 is a schematic drawing illustrating a light board and three dimmers using digital control. The light board continuously sends information—instructional packages—to all three dimmers. However, the dimmers "read" only those instructions that are addressed to them. For example, dimmer 1 reads only instructional packages addressed to itself; it pays no attention to the instructions for any other dimmer. Dimmers 2 and 3 react the same way, reading only that information addressed to them. Because each instructional package is read only by the dimmer to which it is addressed, different information can be sent to each dimmer.

The process of sending two or more messages simultaneously on the same channel is called **multiplexing** and is the primary advantage of digital over analog control systems.[1] Figure 6.6 shows the two types of control systems. Figure 6.6A is an analog system. It requires that each dimmer be connected to the light board by its own control line. Figure 6.6B is a digital system. Notice that there is only one control line connecting all three dimmers to the light board. This is because the multiplexed instructional packages are sent to all dimmers but are read by only those dimmers to which they are addressed.

Saving on costs in the wiring of control circuits isn't the only advantage that digital control offers. Multiplexing offers another distinct advan-

Figure 6.5 Digital instructional packages are continuously sent to all dimmers. The dimmers read only those instructions addressed to them.

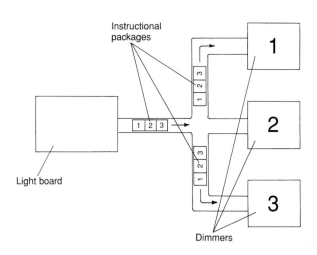

Instructional packages

Light board

Dimmers

1

2

3

---

[1]Analog signals can also be multiplexed, but the quantity of signals that can be multiplexed and the quality of the individual signals are lower than with digital.

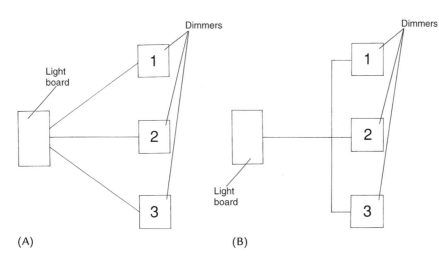

Figure 6.6 Schematic drawing of lighting control systems: (A) analog and (B) digital.

tage with digital control. Some of the moving light fixtures (see Chapter 10, "Advanced Technology Instruments") require up to 20 control channels to function as designed. Digital control requires only one control line to provide instructions to all 20 functions. An analog system would require that 20 separate control lines be connected to the instrument. The final advantage that digital offers over analog is precision of control. Digital instructional packages are finite. Once encoded they don't change. Although analog signals can be remarkably accurate, they aren't as accurate as the unchanging digital code. For all of the preceding reasons, digital is now the mode of choice in almost all dimmer control applications.

CONTROL CONSOLES

The design and style of any control console are dictated by the type of dimmer that will be used with the system. Because the mechanically controlled dimmers are archaic, their control consoles will not be discussed here. However, the types and designs of the electronic control consoles are predicated on the principles that were developed and refined with mechanically controlled dimmers. Electronic control consoles are divided into four main categories: (1) group master, (2) preset, (3) combination, and (4) computer memory.

Group Master

The group master console design is a direct carryover from the control board configurations used with mechanically controlled dimmers. Individual dimmers are controlled by a submaster, which is subsequently controlled by a grand master, as shown in Figure 6.7.

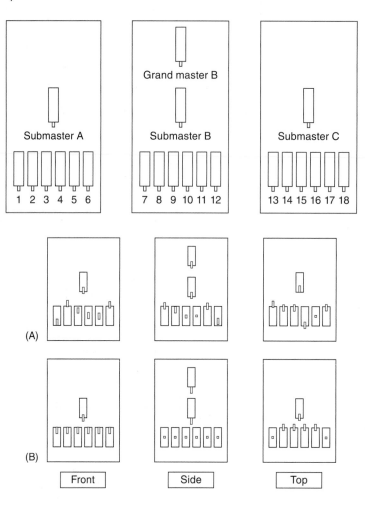

Figure 6.7 Dimmers 1 through 6 are controlled by submaster A; dimmers 7 through 12 by submaster B; dimmers 13 through 18 by submaster C. The grand master acts as a master control for all submasters.

Figure 6.8 Group master operating principles.

Two general operating techniques are used with group master consoles. The first is to set individual dimmer intensity levels on a group of dimmers that are assigned to one particular submaster, as shown in Figure 6.8A. When the submaster is activated, the dimmers will fade up to the previously set levels. This technique is particularly useful when a designer wants to change the color blend of the lighting. For example, group A could be assigned all the lights that are colored red; group B, blue; and group C, green. The color of the onstage light can be changed by varying the intensity of the submaster control for each color group.

The second operating technique involves using the dimmers of one group to control the lighting instruments from a particular direction or location, as shown in Figure 6.8B. For example, group A might control all **front-of-house** instruments; group B, side lights, and group C, the top lights.

Front-of-house:
Describing lights that are hung on the audience side of the proscenium arch.

USITT DMX512

USITT DMX512 is not the title of a bad science fiction movie. It is a standard created by the United States Institute for Theatre Technology (USITT) " . . . as a means to control dimmers from lighting consoles via a standard interface."[1] Basically, DMX512 is a recommended practice that allows the various pieces of a digitally controlled lighting system—computer boards, dimmers, and peripherals—to "talk" to each other. Prior to the adoption of this standard in 1990, each manufacturer had its own proprietary method of control, which made it difficult, if not impossible, for the customer to use a light board from one manufacturer to control dimmers, or any other equipment, made by another manufacturer. DMX512 resolved that issue. Now almost all digitally controlled equipment manufactured for the entertainment industry uses the DMX512 protocol.

To understand DMX512, you first need to understand how digital control works. The example that will be used to explain the process uses dimmers as the controlled device. However, it is important to understand that digital control isn't used solely to control dimmer output. It also can be used to manipulate the functions of any type of electrical equipment, such as the stop/start functions and speed of the electrical motors in moving light fixtures. The signal of most controllers—for example, the slide pots on a light board—is analog. When a controller is set to a specific level, it generates a signal that is an electronic indication of that setting. An analog-to-digital converter reads the controller's signal. Each time the converter reads the signal, it translates that information into binary code, adds the address of the dimmer or equipment associated with that particular command, and sends this "instructional package" to all the dimmers and equipment in the system. Each dimmer and piece of equipment receives all the instructional packages but responds only to those addressed to it. This send/receive process occurs 44,000 times per second—the rate at which the analog-to-digital converter reads the original signal.[2]

DMX512 is simply a technical standard that specifies how much information is sent out on each of the 44,000 cycles that occur every second. DMX512 specifies that the signal shall contain 512 instructional packages and each package will have 256 discrete steps. This protocol has been adopted by the majority of equipment manufacturers and has significantly increased the compatibility of equipment used in the entertainment industry.

---

[1]Adam Bennette, "Recommended Practice for DMX512: A Guide for Users and Installers" (PLASA/USITT, 1994), p. 7.

[2]Some systems create the control signal digitally, which eliminates the need for the analog-to-digital conversion. These signals also are scanned and distributed 44,000 times a second.

Fader: A device, usually electronic, that effects a gradual changeover from one circuit to another; in lighting it gradually changes the intensity of one or more dimmer circuits.

Preset

The primary advantage of a preset control console is that it allows you to keep ahead of the onstage action by presetting the intensity levels for each dimmer before it will be needed. Figure 6.9 is an example of a three-scene lighting control console. Although there may not actually be a control console that works like this one, all preset lighting boards work on the same basic principles being discussed for this hypothetical board.

The controls for dimmers 1 through 6 are repeated three times in the blocks of dimmer controls labeled Preset Scenes I, II, and III. In this simplistic example we will assume that the intensity levels of the lighting for the first cue will be preset on Preset Scene I, the second cue will be assigned to Preset Scene II, and the third cue will be set on Preset Scene III. After the board operator sets the appropriate intensity levels for each dimmer on the three preset scenes, he or she assigns control of Preset Scene I to **fader** A by pushing the button marked I next to fader A. When the cue is called by the stage manager, the operator brings up fader A, which automatically raises the intensity of the lights to the levels that had been preset on the dimmer

**SAFETY
TIP**

Dimmer Maintenance

The greatest enemy of an electronic dimmer such as the SCR is heat. To dissipate heat, some dimmers are equipped with large heat sinks. Heat sinks are metal—usually aluminum—structures that absorb the heat generated by an SCR and radiate it to the atmosphere. Other dimmer packs are equipped with fans.

It is vital for the longevity of dimmers that they have plenty of air circulating around them. Don't pile anything on top of a dimmer rack. If you are working with portable dimmers, be sure that the dimmer pack is raised off the ground so that air can circulate under, as well as over, the case.

If your dimmer system is equipped with fans, be sure that they are running smoothly. The dimmers will frequently function for several hours even if the fan isn't working, but the heat buildup will cause a relatively rapid deterioration of the electronic equipment that will usually lead to premature dimmer failure.

Almost all SCR dimmers need to be adjusted periodically so that they will smoothly increase or decrease their lamp loads. The specific methods vary from manufacturer to manufacturer, but they all involve an adjustment of the low-, middle-, and high-output voltage of the dimmer. These adjustments should be made by a qualified electrician at least annually.

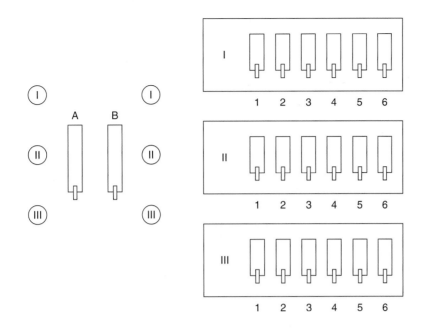

Figure 6.9 Preset board operating principles.

controls of Preset Scene I. The second cue, preset on Scene II, is assigned to fader B. When the cue is called, the operator simultaneously moves fader B up and fader A down, which results in a cross-fade between the lights preset on Preset Scenes I and II. Similarly, before the third cue is called, the operator assigns control of Preset Scene III to fader A. When the cue is called, the operator cross-fades between faders A and B, which results in activation of the dimmer intensity levels associated with Preset Scene III.

To preset the intensity levels for the fourth cue, the operator presets the appropriate intensity levels on Preset Scene I as soon as he or she has cross-faded into the second cue. To run the remaining cues in the show the process of presetting intensity levels on open, or nonactive, preset scenes is repeated as often as necessary. Many preset control consoles have mechanically or electronically interlocked faders, so when either fader A or B fades up, the other fader automatically dims down.

Combination

A fusion of the principles of preset and group master control provides an extremely flexible lighting control system. In the combination console (Figure 6.10), each dimmer channel has an associated switch capable of assigning the dimmer to preset, group master, or independent control. The combination control console provides an operator with more creative choices in controlling dimmer intensities, because it enables him or her to choose the control best suited to each individual production situation.

(A)

(B)

Figure 6.10 Combination control consoles: (A) The ETC SmartFade (Courtesy of Electronic Theatre Controls, Inc.); (B) The Strand 200 series 24/28 channel console. (Courtesy of Strand Lighting.)

Wireless Dimmer Control

The dimming control techniques discussed up to this point all require that a cable be connected from the control console to the dimmer. Wireless dimmers, which transmit the digital control information by radio, are also available. Wireless dimming systems are supplementary to, not replacements for, a theatre's main dimming system. They are generally self-contained, battery-powered component units small enough to be placed inside portable props or, in some cases, hidden in costumes. They are used in special circumstances, such as in portable torches or other situations where a power cord trailing from the prop as it is carried around the stage would create both physical and aesthetic hazards.

Control of wireless dimmers works like it does with any other system. The only difference is that instead of everything being wired together, the digital control information is transmitted by radio. The theatre's control console sends the control information—on/off, dimmer level, fade time, and so forth—to the radio transmitter. Because its transmission distance is quite limited, the transmitter is generally hidden on, or in close proximity to, the stage. Each battery-powered wireless dimmer has a miniaturized receiver associated with it. The receiver gets the control information and passes it to the dimmer. The dimmer then operates whatever device is connected to it.

Although the latest generation of wireless control systems seems to be relatively trouble-free, it is a reality that transmitted signals can be scrambled by interference much more easily than control signals that are sent over a wire. For this reason, wireless control is almost never used to control a theatre's main lighting system.

Computer Memory

Computer memory control for stage lighting has become the standard for the industry. These systems offer much greater control flexibility than does any other method of lighting control, and they are less expensive to manufacture than a preset control console for a comparably sized system.

All computer light boards—computer boards—(Figure 6.11) function in fundamentally the same way: a computer electronically stores the intensity levels of all dimmers for each cue. The computer memory replaces the cumbersome preset board and eliminates the chance of human error in the setting of intensity levels during a show. Even the most basic computer boards have a minimum of about 300 memories for cue storage. More expensive boards may have sufficient storage capacity for up to several thousand cues. The latest generation of control consoles can be used to control automated lighting fixtures in addition to non-moving stage lights. In shows where there are numerous moving lights, it is not uncommon for the production to use two separate light boards—one for the normal stage lights and one for the automated fixtures. Typically there are also two board operators, one for each type of console. Rosco Labs offers a Windows-based lighting-control software program that is used with *your* PC. You use your own PC with Rosco's software and output control devices to control most existing electronic dimmers.

Because most computers will lose their memory when the power is turned off, these systems have an internal battery backup that provides enough power so that the system can retain its memory for a reasonable length of time. This period varies from several hours to several weeks, depending on the manufacturer.

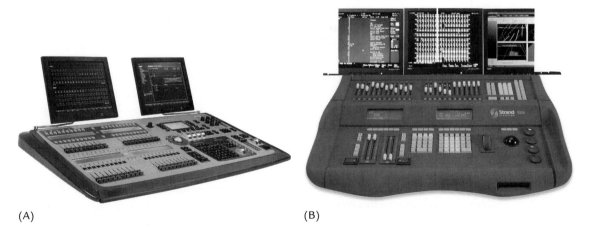

(A)   (B)

Figure 6.11   Full function consoles. (A) The Congo. (Courtesy of Electronic Theatre Controls, Inc.) (B) The Strand 520i portable control console. (Courtesy of Strand Lighting.)

Volatility:
Nonpermanence; in computers, a volatile memory will be lost if the computer loses its power supply.

Hard drive: A device for storing/retrieving digital information.

Crashes: In the context of computers, refers to the hard disk becoming inoperable and the data stored on it nonretrievable.

3½-inch floppy disk: A floppy disk 3½ inches in diameter.

Floppy disk: A thin piece of plastic coated with metal oxide, used to record the information stored in a computer's memory.

Cassette tape: Audio recorder tape, used in computer storage.

Microcassette tape: A tape cassette approximately 1¼ by 2 inches, used in computer storage; identical to microcassette audio tape.

Because of **volatility** almost all computer boards have some method of storing the cuing and programming information. Higher-end computer boards frequently store this information on a **hard drive** while lower-end computer boards typically store information on floppy disks. While even the smallest capacity hard disk will store all the data for just about any show, it is very important to back up the hard disk with some type of library storage in the event that the hard disk **crashes**. The most common methods used for library storage are the **3½-inch floppy disk**, the **floppy disk**, the **cassette tape**, and the **microcassette tape**. It is also essential to make backup copies of the show disks if your computer board uses floppy disks as its storage method. Some designers prefer to record every change on both disks as those changes occur, while others feel that running the backup at the end of every rehearsal or board session is adequate.

Computer Board Control Capabilities

All computer boards have control capabilities that duplicate those of preset control systems. But what makes computer control so dynamic is that these boards have numerous capabilities that simply cannot be duplicated by preset or any other extant control system. This discussion will begin with the most basic memory functions available on almost all computer boards and then proceed to some of the capabilities of more complex, high-end boards.

Before proceeding I need to issue a disclaimer. The terminology and nomenclature associated with computer boards is still evolving. Over the past twenty years, manufacturers have designed a surprisingly large number of computer boards that range from very basic to extremely complex. Each manufacturer has also created what it believes to be "marketable" names for the various functions that their boards perform. As a consequence, there has been very little standardization of terminology. What one company calls a "widget," another company refers to as a "friblick," but, in reality, both the widget and the friblick are, or do, the same thing. In time this sort of thing will be sorted out, but, for now, the terminology will remain a little less than concrete. And you, gentle reader, have the option of calling your widget a friblick or anything else that makes sense. It really doesn't matter as long as you communicate accurately.

Now, let's talk about what these boards can do.

As previously explained, analog or nondigital control systems require that a pair of wires be connected directly from each dimmer to the control console. In these systems increasing or decreasing the level of a control potentiometer, or "pot," on the control board controls the intensity of any instruments connected to a dimmer. In a digitally controlled system, a single pair of control wires runs between all the dimmers and the digital control board. The control circuit of each dimmer is wired in parallel with every other dimmer, and that single pair of control wires runs from

✳ Computer Boards: A Comparison of Features

SMALLER SYSTEMS
1. Memory for up to several hundred cues
2. Capability of controlling 100–150 dimmers
3. Maximum of one video screen for displaying various system functions
4. A timed fader
5. Some type of group or submaster control
6. Control of dimmer intensity by individual sliders
7. Keypad for addressing memory and functions
8. Limited backup system in case of main computer malfunction

These smaller, less expensive systems work well in theatres that have modest production demands.

LARGER SYSTEMS
1. Memory for approximately 1,000 cues
2. Control of 1,000 or more dimmers
3. Expanded functions
   a. Two or more video screens to display more functions simultaneously
   b. Advanced backup systems
   c. Sophisticated group or submastering
   d. More control functions to permit simultaneous cues at different fade rates
4. Dimmer and other functions addressed through a keypad
5. Remote keypad
6. Hard-copy printer for printing data about the lighting design
7. Self-diagnostic program to identify malfunctioning component in case of breakdown

These larger, more expensive systems work well in facilities that have extensive production programs.

---

the dimmer racks to the digital control board. Information about intensity levels and so forth is distributed to all dimmers simultaneously, with the individual dimmers reacting only to information that is addressed specifically to them.

The digital control method just described allows much greater control flexibility than previous systems. To facilitate this flexibility, almost all computer boards employ an electronic patching system, generally referred to as **channel control**. To set the level of a dimmer, you assign it to a control channel, or channel, then adjust the channel level to the desired setting. Channel control allows you to assign any number of dimmers—from one dimmer to all the dimmers in your system—to one particular channel. In practical application there are two primary techniques used with channel

Channel control: An electronic patching system in which one or more dimmers can be assigned to a control channel, which in turn controls the intensity level of those dimmers.

Control System Maintenance

The operating voltage for most electronic lighting control systems is relatively low—normally, between 8 and 24 volts. Because of the low voltage and the miniaturization of the electronic components, the systems need to be kept scrupulously clean and free from dust, dirt, and grease. For this reason, smoking and eating should not be permitted in the lighting control booth. The tar from tobacco smoke can settle on the printed circuit boards and actually change the resistance within the electronic circuits. Even a small change in resistance can cause some elements of the system to malfunction. The obviously disastrous results of spilling a soft drink on a control board don't need further elaboration.

The floppy disks that are used for library storage in many computer systems need to be handled carefully. They should be stored vertically in a dust-free environment away from power lines and electric motors. (The power lines and motors generate magnetic fields that can scramble or erase the information stored on a disk.) Cassette and microcassette library storage tapes should always be replaced in their protective cases and stored in a manner similar to floppy disks. Use only a soft-tip marker to write on the floppy disk label. Pencils and ballpoint pens can dent the recording surface of the disk, and the graphite and ink can interfere with the reading head.

Group: The grouping of two or more dimmers/channels under one controller.

Fade-in: A gradual increase. In lighting, usually from darkness to a predetermined level of brightness. Synonymous with fade-up.

Fade-out: A gradual decrease. In lighting, usually from a set level of brightness to darkness.

Split time fade: A fade in which the fade-up and fade-out are accomplished at different rates or speeds.

Delay: Refers to the time interval that the second part of a split time fade follows the first.

control—one dimmer per channel and ganged dimmers per channel. The one-dimmer-per-channel approach lets you adjust each dimmer, and the instruments connected to it, individually. The ganged-dimmers-per-channel approach involves assigning the dimmers—for example, the six dimmers controlling the blue lights on the cyc—to a single control channel. Another way of controlling the blue cyc lights would be to assign the channels to a **group** controller. The intensity levels of the lights assigned to the individual channels can be adjusted so the blue wash can be balanced as desired, then the group controller is used to raise or lower the intensity of the lights without changing the balance.

All computer boards have some type of timer or time-function capability. The timer is used to assign a fade time to a cue. For example, you could as-sign a time of 5 seconds to a cue so it takes 5 seconds to execute that particular cue, whether it was a **fade-in** or **fade-out**. Most boards facilitate **split time fades** that allow you to, in one action, fade one cue out at a given speed or time while fading in the next cue either faster or slower. When executing a spilt-time fade you frequently want to delay the start of the second or following action. This action is called a **delay**. With this capability the designer can with one board action—pressing the "execute" or "go" button—execute a 15-second fade-out on a scene and, after an 8-second delay, begin a fade-up of another cue with a completely different fade rate.

These board capabilities provide the basic building blocks of creative lighting control for the designer. Many computer light boards have additional capabilities that enhance the designer's ability to control and manipulate light. Some of these will be discussed in Chapter 17, "Rehearsal and Performance Procedures."

It is important to become familiar with the specific capabilities and functions of as many computer boards as possible, because an understanding of those capabilities of the equipment will inform the designer's approach to **cueing** the show.

Cueing: Designing the light cues. Manipulating, and recording, the distribution, intensity, movement, and color of the lights for each cue to create an appropriate look for that moment in the play.

Company switch: A disconnect box to which portable dimmers may be connected. Normally, has 240-VAC power, sometimes higher. Usually located in the wings adjacent to stage.

LIGHTING SYSTEM ELECTRICAL FLOW

Up to this point you've learned about the various individual elements—electricity, instruments, cables, distribution systems, dimmers, control consoles, and so on—of a lighting system. This section demonstrates how all these elements work together.

Figure 6.12 depicts the wiring and elements of a typical theatrical electrical system from the service entrance—where the electricity enters the building—through the dimmer to a lighting instrument. The primary features of our hypothetical electrical system are: (1) permanently installed, rack-mounted, electronic dimmers; (2) a 240-VAC **company switch** disconnect box that can be used to power additional portable dimmers or other equipment needing 240-VAC power; (3) a patch panel; and (4) connecting strips in

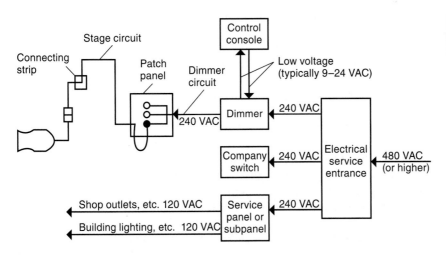

Figure 6.12 Typical path for electrical service in a theatre building.

various locations around the stage and auditorium. The actual locations of all this equipment vary, sometimes greatly, from theatre to theatre.

Depending on the size and complexity of the theatre, high-voltage electricity—normally 480 VAC or higher—enters the building at the electrical service entrance. To save on wiring costs, 240-VAC power is typically routed from the service entrance to subpanels at various locations—shops, offices, dressing rooms, and so forth—throughout the theatre. From the subpanels, 120-VAC wiring is used to power building lighting and wall and shop outlets and similar "infrastructure" uses. In our hypothetical electrical system, 240-VAC electricity is distributed to three places: the permanently mounted dimmer racks, the company switch, and a subpanel for the shops, building lighting, and so forth.

While there doesn't seem to be a typical location for a permanently installed dimmer rack, electrical codes normally require, for safety reasons, that permanently installed dimmers be located in a lockable room. These dimmer rooms can be, and have been, located adjacent to the stage, in the basement, or on a floor above the stage. Ideally, the location will be in an area that can be easily accessed from the stage/auditorium, but far enough, or soundproofed enough, not to be heard in the auditorium. To complicate matters even further, some dimmer systems don't have centralized dimmer racks. Dimmers in these types of systems are located at the hanging positions—on pipes over the stage, in floor and/or wall pockets, and so forth. This type of dimmer-per-circuit system eliminates the need for a patch panel.

Within the dimmer rack, the 240-VAC power is broken down to the 120 VAC utilized by the electronic dimmers. While a dimmer system may have several hundred individual dimmers, each functions in the same way. Every electronic dimmer—regardless of whether it utilizes analog or digital control—has a low-voltage control circuit to regulate the 120-VAC output of that dimmer. That low-voltage circuit is connected to the lighting console. If the dimmers utilize analog control, a hot wire runs from each dimmer to the control panel, while, in a typical analog installation, a common neutral will be used to connect a number of dimmers to the control board. The number of dimmer control circuits clustered onto this common neutral varies from installation to installation. If the dimmers have digital control, a single control circuit—one hot, one neutral, with the hot side wired in parallel to all the dimmers—connects the dimmers to the control console.

The 120-VAC output circuit of each dimmer—the dimmer circuit—runs from the dimmer to the patch panel where it typically terminates in one or more receptacles. The patch panel also contains one end of every stage and house circuit. Each one of these circuits runs from the male plug at the patch panel, through conduit, to terminate at its location in an outlet box or connecting strip somewhere on or around the stage or auditorium. Dimmer-per-circuit systems eliminate the patch panel, so the electrical flow runs straight from the dimmers to the individual stage circuit outlets.

You may remember from Chapter 3, "Electrical Theory and Practice," that electricity will flow within a circuit only if that circuit is complete. The circuit for any lighting instrument is completed when that fixture is connected to a stage circuit, and that stage circuit is patched into a specific dimmer circuit, and power is run from that dimmer to the instrument. This process is repeated for every instrument hung for a production.

While the system may seem complex, remember that it really is a simple system repeated again and again.

Someone once said that the only thing constant is change. So it is in the field of lighting-intensity control. At the present time, the digitally controlled SCR dimmer is state of the art. But we can be assured that it will be supplanted by an even better dimmer at some time in the not-too-distant future. The computer board is similarly state of the art. But new developments in computer science are quickly applied to the lighting industry, and the current state-of-the-art systems, which do more than we could have imagined just 5 years ago, will quickly be outmoded by systems that can do more, in less time, and for less cost.

CHAPTER 7

Projections

Projections enhance the visual texture of a design immeasurably. They can provide the stage with seemingly unlimited depth or create an aura of surrealism as one image dissolves into another. They can be used to replace or complement other visual elements of the setting, or they can be used as an accent.

However, projections aren't a universal panacea. They are simply another tool for the designer to use in the never-ending quest for an evocative visual expression of the production concept.

Both lens and lensless projectors are used in the theatre.

LENSLESS PROJECTORS

If you've ever made shadow pictures by holding your hands in the beam of a slide or movie projector, you understand the principle of lensless projection. As shown in Figure 7.1, a shadow image can be projected when an opaque object is placed in the path of a light source. If the object casting the shadow is colored and transparent rather than opaque, a colored image is projected instead of a shadow.

Several factors determine the sharpness of the projected image, but the primary one is the size of the projection source. Although an arc can provide a very small point source, it isn't particularly practical because its intensity can't be varied through the use of a dimmer. There are two practical lamp sources for lensless projectors:

1. For large-scale projections a 500-, 750-, or 1,000-watt, 120-volt, tungsten-halogen lamp normally used in an ellipsoidal reflector spotlight

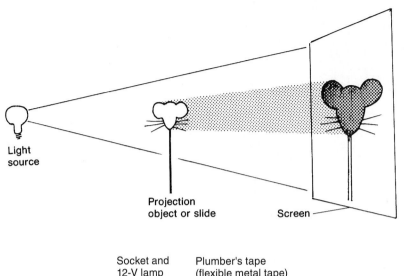

Figure 7.1 Principles of lensless projection.

Light
source

Projection
object or slide   Screen

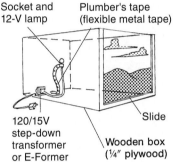

Socket and   Plumber's tape
12-V lamp   (flexible metal tape)

120/15V
step-down   Slide
transformer
or E-Former   Wooden box
                    (¼″ plywood)

Figure 7.2 A low-voltage lamp can provide a high-intensity, small-size source for a lensless projector.

works well. When selecting a specific lamp, remember that the smaller the filament, the sharper the image.

2. For small-scale projections—under 6 feet wide—a single-filament 12-volt lamp (used for automotive brake and turning lights) can provide a high-intensity, small-filament source. For the lamp to provide enough output, it must be run at about 15 volts. This voltage is supplied to the lamp through a 15-volt wire-wound step-down transformer, as shown in Figure 7.2. The transformer may not work properly, however, and the intensity of the 12-volt lamp probably will flutter, or simply switch off, if you try to dim the unit with an SCR dimmer. A smooth fade of a load attached to a wire-wound transformer can be achieved only if the transformer is dimmed with an autotransformer or resistance dimmer. However, the dimmable electronic transformer (E-Former, manufactured by Luminance, Inc.) has made it possible to smoothly dim low-voltage lamps with electronic dimmers such as the SCR. To do so, simply substitute an E-Former of appropriate output voltage for the wire-wound transformer.

Figure 7.3 (A) Sharp image and (B) multiplane image lensless projectors.

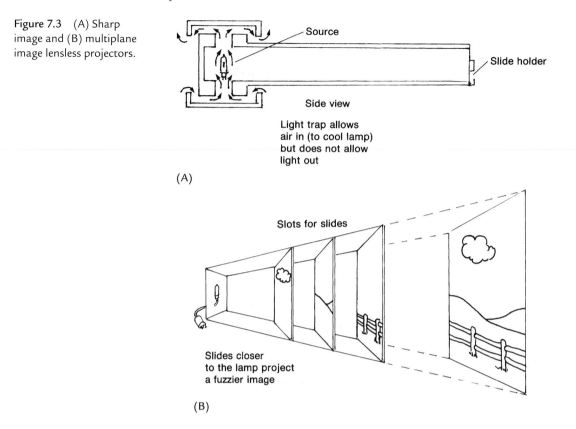

Aerial perspective: An optical phenomenon in which objects that are farther away appear less sharply in focus and less fully saturated in color.

Another important factor in determining image sharpness with a lensless projector is the distance between the slide and the projection surface. The closer the slide is to the screen, the sharper the image. Having the slide closer to the screen does not necessarily mean that the projector is closer to the screen. A relatively long, somewhat skinny projector, as shown in Figure 7.3A, can be built in the shop. If the ratio of the distance between the projection surface and the slide and the distance between the slide and the lamp of this somewhat bizarre projector can be kept at approximately 1:1, an acceptably sharp image can be produced. The multiplane lensless projector (Figure 7.3B) is a natural adaptation of this development. As slides are placed closer to the lamp, the image they project becomes less focused. This phenomenon can be used to good advantage to create **aerial perspective**. In the projection of a landscape, the clouds and distant objects could be painted on one slide and placed relatively close to the lamp to create a soft-edged image. Middle-distance objects, such as hills and a forest, might be painted on a second slide and placed farther from the lamp so that the image they project is more clearly defined. A third slide, with perhaps a fence row and the branch from an overhanging tree, could be painted on a third slide and placed farther away from the lamp so that its image is the sharpest of the three.

Although the multiplane projector might seem to be an ideal solution, there is one very basic problem: slide size. You will remember that for a slide to project a relatively sharp image it needs to be approximately the same distance from the screen as it is from the lamp. If you wanted to project an image 20 feet wide, the sharp-image slide would have to be 10 feet wide! However, if you are trying to project on only a relatively small area (5 feet wide or less), the multiplane projector can provide you with a very realistic aerial perspective effect.

A multiplane projector can be built in the shop using the techniques described later in this chapter for making Linnebach projectors. A 750- or 1,000-watt tungsten-halogen lamp from an ellipsoidal reflector spotlight usually will provide a more-than-adequate light for projections less than 5 feet wide, and the slides can be painted on ⅛-inch Plexiglas with transparent acetate inks.

Linnebach Projector

The primary lensless projector used in the theatre was developed by Adolph Linnebach. All lensless projectors are based on its principles of operation, which are illustrated in Figure 7.4. The metal housing holds the lamp at a fixed distance from the open front of the projector, which is designed to securely hold a removable glass slide. The design is painted on the slide with transparent inks.

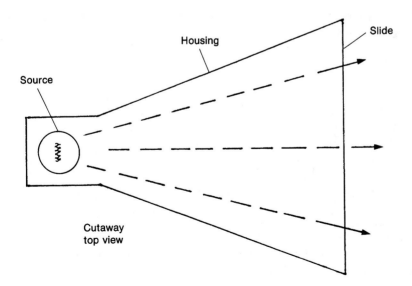

Figure 7.4　Priniciples operation of a Linnebach projector.

Pop riveter: A tool used to secure rivets in thin metal.

Projectors that work on the Linnebach principles can easily be made in the theatre shop using galvanized tin and a **pop riveter.** They can also be fabricated from plywood (Figure 7.5), but the inside of the back and top sides of the plywood box must be lined with tin or some other heat-reflecting or absorbing material. Internally reflected light is the enemy of all lensless projectors. Reflected light passing through the slide will substantially blur or soften the image that you're trying to project. For that reason the inside structure of any shop-built lensless projectors should be painted black. Black matte finish high-temperature engine paint works very well for this purpose and is available at most automotive parts stores.

Linnebach projectors for use with curved cycs can also be shop-built, as shown in Figure 7.6. These projectors, though using only a 1,000-watt FEL

Figure 7.5 Shop-built Linnebach projector.

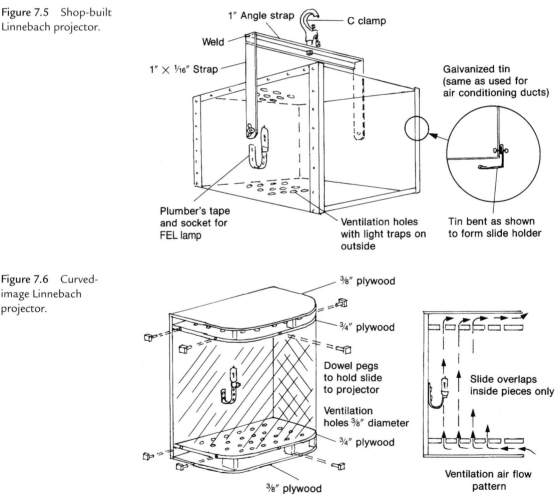

Figure 7.6 Curved-image Linnebach projector.

lamp, can project a patterned wash of pastel color over a full semicircular cyc. Slides for the curved-front Linnebach are made from 20-mil acetate. These slides are fitted to the curved edge of the projector, and the image is painted on the slide with transparent acetate inks. Dr. Martin's Watercolors, when supplemented with a commercial additive that allows the paint to adhere to plastic, work extremely well for this purpose.

Other Lensless Projectors

Small lensless projectors can be made by removing the lens from fresnel or plano-convex spotlights and inserting a slide (painted or photographic transparency) in the instrument's color-frame holder. Although these makeshift projectors won't cover a large surface, they are handy for making relatively soft projections on small surfaces.

LENS PROJECTORS
. . . .

The second basic type of projector uses a lens to control the focus and size of the image on the projection surface. Two primary types of lens projector are used in the theatre, the **scenic projector** and the **slide projector**.

Scenic Projector

The scenic projector is composed of three basic parts: the lamp housing, the optical train, and the slide, as shown in Figure 7.7A.

Lamp Housing A lamp of high intensity is a prime requisite of a good scenic projector. Incandescent lamps of 1,000 to 2,000 watts are fairly typical, and some scenic projectors are designed for xenon or HMI lamps. The

Scenic projector: A high-wattage instrument used for projecting large-format slides or moving images.

Slide projector: A reasonably high-output instrument capable of projecting standard 35-mm slides.

✴ Slide Techniques for Lensless Projectors

A number of systems based on mathematical principles can be used to lay out the slides for lensless, or Linnebach, projectors. However, the fastest and most accurate method is also the easiest. Put a slide into the projector, and place it and the projection screen (usually a cyc or sky tab) in the onstage positions that they will occupy during the production. Turn the projector on, and draw or paint the projection on the slide while watching the projection grow across the screen.

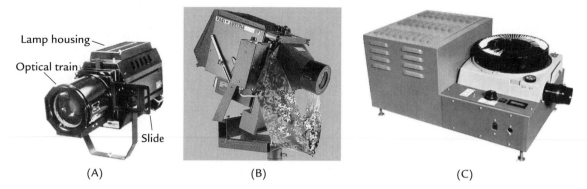

(A)   (B)   (C)

Figure 7.7   (A) A scenic projector is composed of a lamp housing, the optical train, and the slide. (Courtesy of The Great American Market.) (B) Scenic projector. (Courtesy of Pani.) (C) Slide projector. (Courtesy of George R. Snell Associates.)

Figure 7.8   A typical scenic projector optical train.

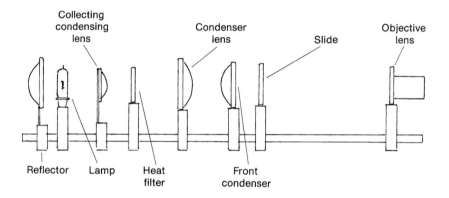

Heat filter: A dichroic glass filter that removes much of the infrared spectrum from light.

Condensing lens: A device that condenses the direct and reflected light from a source and concentrates it on the slide plane aperture of a projector.

Slide plane aperture: The point in a projection system where a slide or other effect is placed.

Objective lens: A device to focus a projected image on a screen or other surface.

housings are frequently equipped with quiet blowers that help dissipate the substantial heat that these powerful sources generate.

Optical Train   The optical train, shown in Figure 7.8, is composed of several parts that perform specific functions. The reflector (usually ellipsoidal or spherical) and collector lens gather and concentrate the light. Most scenic projectors utilize a **heat filter**. The heat filter is a dichroic hot mirror. A hot mirror looks like clear glass but is coated to reflect infrared light (heat) while allowing visible light to pass. The purpose of the heat filter is to remove a substantial amount of the heat from the light before it gets to the slide. The **condensing lenses** focus the light onto the **slide plane aperture**, which is the point where the slide or moving projection effect is placed. The **objective lens** is used to focus the material in the aperture onto the projection surface.

The reflector, lamp, collector lens, and aperture are normally mounted in fixed positions within the lamp housing unit. In contrast, the relative positions of the condensing lens and objective lens are variable on some models of scenic projector to allow the size of the projected image to be changed. Other scenic projectors are available with several **heads**, which hold the condensing and objective lenses in fixed positions to control the image size.

Pani manufacturers a line of large-format scenic projectors for stage use. The slides for these projectors are slightly larger than 7 × 7 inches (18 × 18 cm). The glass slides are normally painted with transparent inks, so the relatively large size of the slide allows for a good level of detail in the projected image. Pani projectors, one of which is shown in Figure 7.9, are available with either halogen or HMI sources. The fans on these high-quality units are extremely quiet. A full line of accessories, such as a mechanical dimmer for the HMI-equipped projectors as well as effects heads, slide changers, and slide painting materials, is available.

Figure 7.9 A Pani projector. (Courtesy of Pani.)

Slide Glass slides are frequently used with scenic projectors to project still images. The image can be painted on a single glass slide, or a photographic transparency can be sandwiched between two glass slides. The longevity of a painted or photographic image on the slide can be increased if a heat filter is placed between the collector lens and the slide.

Moving Effects

A variety of moving effects can be created through the use of **effects heads**. These motorized devices are attached to the lamp housing in place of the slide holder. Effects heads move images in front of the aperture gate of the scenic projector to create abstract or realistic moving images such as the lighted windows of a passing train on the projection surface. The speed of the control motor is usually variable, so the speed of the projected effect can be adjusted to suit the design need. Depending on the specific model, effects heads use either rotating disks or bands to create the specific effect desired. Most scenic effects projectors are equipped to use either Plexiglas or metal disks or plastic bands.

Rosco Labs offers a motion effects machine designed to be used in conjunction with a standard ERS. The system consists of several pieces: a fixed- or variable-speed motor that fits into the instrument's color-frame holder and rotates one of several large, patterned, stainless steel disks mounted in front of the instrument lens; a gobo rotator that rotates a gobo in the gate of the instrument; and a gobo yo-yo that moves a gobo back and forth in the gate. By varying the combination of system elements, you can achieve a variety of motion effects such as waves, flickering flames, rain, and abstract movement patterns that normally require a scenic projector.

City Theatrical offers a highly effective aftermarket effects head to be used in conjunction with the ETC Source Four, Selecon Pacific, or Strand

Head: A housing that holds scenic projector lenses in fixed positions to project images of a specific size.

Effects head: A motor-driven unit capable of producing relatively crude moving images with a scenic projector.

☀ Keystoning

Unless the projector is placed on a perpendicular axis to the projection screen, some linear distortion will be introduced to the projected image. This phenomenon is known as keystoning, because the distortion generally resembles the shape of a keystone.

Keystoning results when the light from one side of the projected image (slide) has to travel farther than the light from the other side of the slide, as illustrated in Figures A and B. Keystoning can be corrected in one of two ways: (1) the screen can be tilted (Figure C) so that the projection axis is perpendicular to the screen, or (2) a

distortion can be introduced to the slide that counteracts the effects of the projection distortion. To correct this you need to determine the angle of intersection between the projection axis and the screen. To introduce the counterdistortion to the slide, place the camera at the same angle, but on the opposite side, when you are taking the picture of the slide material (Figure D). Another advantage of computer projections is that many of the software programs used to create and/or manipulate the images offer keystone correction as part of the package.

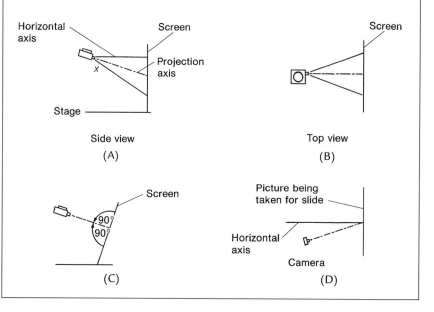

Side view
(A)

Top view
(B)

(C)

(D)

Figure 7.10   The EFX Plus is an after-market effects head for use with ERSs. (Courtesy of City Theatrical.)

SL ellipsoidals. The EFX Plus, Figure 7.10, consists of a housing for two large-format pattern disks. The disks can rotate in the same or opposite directions and the variable speed of each disk is digitally controlled. The unit fits into a modified front barrel of the ERS. Using a single pattern disk produces a single moving image such as clouds. Varying the speed of the disk makes the clouds move slowly or fast. By adding an image from the second disk the clouds can be made to change shape as they move. A distinguishing feature of the EFX Plus is that the projected motion appears linear as opposed to the slightly circular motion of more traditional effects heads.

Moving effects heads for both scenic projectors and ERSs will continue to evolve and will provide many exciting design possibilities.

Slide Projector

Projectors using 35-mm (2 × 2-inch) slides provide another excellent system for producing scenic projections. The challenge of using these projectors, which are designed for audiovisual, not theatrical, purposes, is that the lamp output is frequently not so bright as that of a scenic projector. If you work within the limitations that the lower lamp output imposes, however, the slide projector can be an extremely useful tool.

The Kodak Carousel equipped with a 300-watt lamp provides sufficient light to create a readable image if the slide is of normal contrast and the maximum dimension of the projected image is kept at about 6 to 8 feet.

Adaptations of the basic audiovisual (Ektagraphic) line of Kodak Carousel projectors provide higher-wattage lamps and a number of other interesting features. Although the 300-watt lamp available on the basic models will work adequately for many situations, by all means acquire the higher-output models if your budget can afford them. The image can be significantly brighter.

Other types of 35-mm slide projector can be used, but the carousel types generally offer specific qualities that make them preferable for theatrical projection work: dependable and versatile slide-feeding capabilities, adequate light output, and interchangeable lenses.

☀ Carousel Projector Tips

1. Use the slide tray that holds 80 slides rather than its larger-capacity (140-slide) cousin, because the greater space allocated to each slide in the 80-count tray significantly reduces the chances of the slides becoming stuck in the tray.
2. Mount the slides in plastic, rather than pasteboard, slide holders. The plastic holders are slicker and slightly heavier, which makes it easier for them to be fed into the projector.
3. For the best image use the highest-wattage lamp designed for the specific model with which you are working.
4. Select a lens that will permit you to place the projector as close to the projection surface as possible.

Computer Projectors

Computer projections, more accurately known as digital projections, are rapidly becoming the standard theatrical projection technique. While the image brightness, sharpness, and color clarity of many first- and second-generation digital projectors was not sufficient for stage use, the latest iterations of many of these machines provide brilliant images appropriate for any stage environment. Digital Projection (www.digitalprojection.com) manufacturers an extensive line of digital projectors appropriate for almost every theatrical situation.

I recently saw a portable digital projector—used for business presentations and about the size of a laptop computer—that projected an approximately 12 × 12 foot image that was sufficiently bright and sharp for use in many small- to medium-size theatres.

Digital projections are truly an exciting addition to the designer's toolbox and will probably, in time, replace all other forms of theatrical projection. Why? Because not only can digital projection systems duplicate the image quality of all lensless and lensed film-based still projectors, they can project video as well.

Digital projectors can be used for either front- or rear-screen projection. If the size of the image files is reasonably small they may be able to be stored in the computer (laptop or desktop) that also serves as the control computer (the projection control console) for the system. If the image files are large, complex, or if you have a reasonably large number of individual images, they will need to be stored on separate storage drives. The computer that serves as the projection control console controls the operation of these storage drives as well as the digital projectors. In most cases digital projection systems have their own operating crews that function independently from the light board operators.

The images are produced in the same manner as other computer art. Hand-drawn images can be created on computerized drawing tablets or hand drawn on paper and scanned. Found objects such as fabrics or visually interesting papers or collages can also be scanned. Still photos can be scanned. Images can also be computer generated. Once the image is stored it can be manipulated—colored, textured, redrawn, and so forth—by software programs such as Painter or Photoshop. Digital video can also be used.

The sources for images—both still and moving—to project are almost limitless. And therein lies the trap. Projected images, whether computer-projected or otherwise, have an enormous visual impact. That impact makes it very easy for the projections to upstage the actors. That is a basic no-no. Ideally, the visuals will be integrated into the production concept to *enhance* the overall mood and feeling of the production, not steal focus. Sometimes discretion is the better part of valor.

PROJECTION SCREENS

Actor's bodies, painted scenery, dust motes, smoke, and fog have all been used as projection surfaces. However, they don't work nearly so well as scenic elements that have been specifically designed as front or rear projection screens.

Front-Screen Material

Front-screen projection materials are those surfaces that are designed to reflect light. The best front-projection materials are slide or movie screens. They are white and highly reflective, and the surface is often designed to focus the reflected light in a specific angular pattern. Unless you want a large, glaringly white screen sitting in the middle of the stage, however, it is essential that the screen be lit with either a projection or color wash at all times.

A smooth, white, painted surface (muslin, Masonite, or the like) provides a low-cost alternative to the commercial projection screen. Although the reflected image won't be so crisp as that from the projection screen, it will be more than adequate for most theatrical purposes. When the projections or color washes are turned off, however, the challenge of what to do with the "great white blob" continues.

Unless you are planning on using continuous projections or removing the screen from the set, it is frequently desirable to have the projection screen blend into the surrounding scenic elements until it is time to use it. In these cases, the vertical or horizontal surfaces of the set itself can be used instead of a projection screen. When you are projecting on scenery, the sharpness and brightness of the reflected image will be directly related to the **hue**, **value**, and **texture** of the paint job used on the scenery. Surfaces with low **saturation**, high value, and little texture provide the best reflective surfaces for projected images.

Rear-Screen Material

A major challenge of front-screen projection—actor shadows on the projection surface—is eliminated through the use of rear-screen projection. In this technique, illustrated in Figure 7.11, the projector is placed behind the screen, and the image is transmitted through the screen to the audience.

A significant challenge of rear-screen projection is created by the **hot spot**. If the projector is located within the audience's sight line a small, intensely bright circle of light will appear on the screen as illustrated in Figure 7.12. This bright circle is caused by seeing the actual lens of the projector through the screen material. The hot spot can be eliminated either by positioning the projector so that the hot spot is out of the audience's sight line or by using a screen material that eliminates the hot spot.

Hue: The qualities that differentiate one color from another.

Value: The relative lightness or darkness of an object.

Texture: The relative roughness or smoothness of the finish of an object.

Saturation: The relative purity of a particular hue.

Hot spot: An intense circle of light created when a projector lens is seen through a rear screen.

Figure 7.11 A typical rear-screen projection setup.

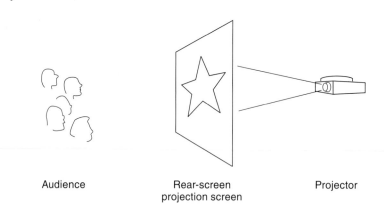

Audience   Rear-screen   Projector
                    projection screen

Figure 7.12 A hot spot, caused by seeing the lens of the projector through the screen, will result unless special rear-screen projection material is used.

Commercial rear-screen materials transmit clear, crisp images while diffusing or eliminating the hot spot. Rosco Labs and Gerriets International offer several types of reasonably priced flexible plastic rear-screen material in rolls 55 inches wide. Wider screens, with invisible seams, can be made by butting strips of the material edge to edge and taping the joints with No. 200 Scotch transparent plastic tape. Unless the atmosphere in your locale is of relatively low humidity, however, the tape seams are only a temporary solution. **Heat welding** of the seams will provide a permanent bond.

If the projector can be placed in a position that will eliminate the hot spot, a variety of translucent materials can be used to receive the projected image. Scenic muslin and other fabrics of similar weight and weave transmit light quite well. The muslin (which will present a crisper image if it is primed with a starch solution—one cup of starch per gallon of hot water) can be painted with dye if it is necessary or desirable for the screen to blend into the set. When using this technique, be sure to use dye, not paint. Dye is transparent and won't interrupt the transmission of the image.

Plain white shower curtains provide another effective, low-cost rear-screen material. The plastic transmits light well, the larger-sized shower curtains are big enough for many scenic uses, and some of the plastics actually diffuse the hot spot.

White (not clear) polyethylene plastic sheeting, sold as plastic drop cloths in paint stores, is also an effective rear-screen material.

SLIDE PREPARATION

Heat welding: The use of a heat gun (a high-temperature air gun, visually similar to a hand-held hair dryer) to fuse two pieces of plastic.

Slides for the various types of commercial and shop-built Linnebachs are generally made from ⅛-inch clear Plexiglas. Slides for the curved-image Linnebach can be made from 0.020-inch acetate. Although still quite flexible, the 0.020-inch thickness provides enough stiffness so that these slides don't bend or flop when secured to the projector.

The slide image can be painted on the acetate with a variety of materials. Transparent acetate inks, available in a wide range of colors, are a standard type of slide paint. If an additive, which makes the water-based dyes adhere to the plastic, is used, Dr. Martin's Watercolors are an excellent choice. As a last resort, Magic Marker inks from refill bottles can also be used. Although the Magic Marker inks remain slightly tacky, they don't smear easily; however, they do attract a great deal of dust.

Scenic projectors can use both photographic and painted slides. To be used in a scenic projector, photographic transparencies should be sandwiched between sheets of projection-grade glass. This type of glass is usually available from photography stores. This "sandwich" accomplishes two things: it reduces the chances of the heat of the lamp crinkling or melting the slide, and it keeps the slide in a vertical plane. Painted scenic projector slides are also usually sandwiched for heat protection. The image is painted on a glass slide, and either that slide is sandwiched between two other clear slides or the painted surface is simply covered with a second slide. The transparent inks mentioned previously will also work on glass. Additionally, silhouettes can be created by using opaque acetate inks. However, you must take care when using opaque inks, simply because they absorb more heat than do transparent ones. The additional heat may crack the glass or cause a deterioration of the other inks.

Thirty-five-millimeter slides shouldn't be used in the cardboard mounts in which they are placed by the film processors. These mounts don't have enough weight to drop the slide into the projector if the projector is mounted at anything other than a perfectly horizontal angle. At a minimum, the slides should be remounted in plastic slide mounts, and ideally you will sandwich them between two layers of slide glass. (The plastic mounts and 35-mm glass mounts are available at photography stores.)

OTHER PROJECTORS

A wide variety of other projectors can be used for special situations in the theatre. However, two of them, the overhead projector (Figure 7.13) and the opaque projector, are arguably the most useful.

A relatively large transparent slide (most overhead projectors will accept slides up to 11×14 inches) is placed on the light table of the overhead projector. A high-output lamp shines through the slide, and the image is redirected and focused on the screen by a mirror mounted in an optical head located a short distance above the light table. The luminance level of this projector is fairly low, but it can work well in short-throw, low-light situations.

Figure 7.13   An overhead projector. (Courtesy of George R. Snell Associates.)

The opaque projector works in generally the same fashion, except that the slide is opaque and the lamp is located above the slide so that the light can be reflected, rather than directly transmitted, to the mirror and optical head. The output of the opaque projector is generally less than that of the overhead projector, because some of the lamp output is lost to absorption and scattering during the reflection process.

GOBOS

Ellipsoidal reflector spotlights equipped with gobos are very effective projection tools available to the lighting designer. Numerous commercially available gobos can be purchased to provide very specific shadow patterns (Figure 7.14). These patterns are generally etched in thin stainless steel. Shop-built gobos can be made from offset printing sheets or disposable aluminum cookware (see Chapter 4 for specific techniques). These "homemade" gobos are frequently as visually effective as their commercial counterparts in creating abstract patterns such as the medium breakup pattern illustrated in Figure 7.15. The only problem is that the shop-built gobos deteriorate within several operating hours, if, as is usual, they are made from aluminum. The stainless steel commercial gobos last much longer because they stand up to the heat generated by the tungsten-halogen lamps much better than do their aluminum counterparts.

The use of textured and patterned light is becoming fairly standard. ERSs with patterns or gobos can be focused on the set, actors, or stage floor to create a variety of visually interesting textures. Placement and focusing direction will dictate whether the audience will see the patterned light on the actors. If the "goboed" ERSs are hung as backlights, and untextured light

257
CLOUD 9

*315
REVERSED TREES

542
PAISLEY BREAKUP

*535
ELIZABETHAN WINDOW

Figure 7.14 Commercial template patterns. (Courtesy of Great American Market. Designs are copyrighted by the Great American Market.)

is used from the front and sides, the audience won't see any shadow patterns on the actors' faces and bodies, but, if the color of the textured light has sufficient contrast with the floor color and other lights, the texture should be clearly visible on the floor. If, however, light from the patterned instruments strikes the actors from the front or sides the audience will see the patterning on the actors. Depending on the template design and color used in the "patterned" instruments and the direction, intensity, and color of the other lights, pattern projection can be interpreted as dappled sunlight, moonlight, or simply an evocative, abstract pattern. Additionally, the visual effect of the shadow image can be varied to a surprisingly large degree simply by changing the sharpness of the shadow image. Obviously, template designs such as the Elizabethan window illustrated in Figure 7.14, are typically used to project an atmospheric image of light coming through a window. The emotional effect of this projection varies depending on the color chosen for the "sunlight" or "moonlight."

Colored glass gobos—using dichroic filters to create the color—are commercially available from manufacturers such as American Market and Rosco. Additionally, custom gobos can be designed with a software program such as Adobe Photoshop and manufactured by the custom divisions of American Market and Rosco, among others.

An automated gobo changer is an accessory that converts an ERS into a moving-light fixture. Basically these devices fit into the gate area of the ERS and permit the operator to change between various gobos. The Goboram, by Wybron, can change between three separate gobos. It also can spin the gobos. It uses a DMX512 signal to control 24-VDC motors to activate the changer and to spin the gobos at rates up to one revolution per second. The Goboram is currently designed to be used with the ETC Source 4 or Altman Shakespeare 600 ellipsoidal reflector spotlight.

Figure 7.15   A shop-built medium breakup gobo (top) and the pattern it projects.

GENERAL PROJECTION TECHNIQUES AND HINTS

It is prudent to test the characteristics of any projection system, technique, or material (commercial or noncommercial) under actual stage conditions before you launch into a design concept that depends on projections. You frequently will discover that your vision of how the projections should look is at odds with the physical reality of how they appear onstage. Some general hints and guidelines may help you in working with projections.

1.   To prevent the projected images from being washed out, keep ambient light off the screen. Be sure that the stage lights for the acting areas in the vicinity of the screen(s) are placed at angles that minimize their effect (direct and reflected) on the screen.

2. To reduce the effects of ambient light and to keep the actors from blocking the spectators' view of the projected image, try to place the screen so that its bottom edge will be no lower than 5 to 7 feet above the stage floor.

3. To maximize the brightness of the image when working with an audiovisual slide projector:

   a. Keep the size of the projection as small as possible.
   b. Use a lens with a low f-stop (3.5 or lower).
   c. Use a short-focal-length lens, and place the projector as close to the screen as possible.

4. Rear-screen projection is affected by ambient light less than front-screen projection is, so try to work with rear-screen techniques whenever possible.

5. Become thoroughly familiar with the equipment that you will be using well before technical rehearsals begin. Shoot your slides early so that you will have time to shoot and process additional slides if it becomes necessary.

CHAPTER 8

Practicals and Effects

Although the lighting designer creates the lighting that simulates whatever—sun, moon, fireplace, table lights, and so forth—is supposed to be the light source for a scene, very frequently those sources are specified by the scene designer or director. However, it is the responsibility of the lighting designer and the lighting crew to see that all of these **practicals** and **effects** are electrically wired and work as they were intended.

Practicals and effects can provide the audience with a wealth of visual information about the time, season, and mood of a play. If a table or floor lamp is turned on, the audience will normally assume that the scene is set in the late afternoon or night. If it's turned off, they'll think it's day. If a fire cheerfully glows in the corner of a brightly lit room, the audience will believe that it's cold in the outside world of the play. If the room lights are dim or off, the mood evoked by that same cheerfully glowing fireplace probably would be interpreted as romantic or sinister depending on the context of the scene. Flickering torches or candles can also be used to create dynamic visual moods.

Regardless of the type of practical or effect that is used, its physical appearance should be appropriate to the period of the play. The shapes, styles, and designs of lamps, lanterns, candles, and fireplaces have all changed through the years. If, in your production situation, the electrical shop is responsible for obtaining or making the practicals and effects as well as wiring them, be sure that you properly research the style of each practical and check its appearance with the scenic and property designers.

One of the lighting shop's more interesting challenges is to create practicals and effects that will look like the source they are simulating. However, a note of caution and a disclaimer are needed before we launch into a discussion of the various techniques used to achieve these effects.

Practical: An onstage working light source such as a table lamp, wall sconce, or oil lamp.

Effect: A specialty device designed to give the appearance of being a light source such as a fire effect, candle, torch, or lightning.

Creating practicals and effects is fun. However, you need to keep everything in perspective. Remember that the audience came to see the play, not the effects. Just like the rest of the lighting, the best practicals and effects will tread that narrow line between being so dynamic that they divert the audience's attention and being obviously fake. The best compliment that you could possibly receive would be that they "looked just like the real thing."

Although the following suggestions aren't exhaustive, they do provide you with a good beginning reference point for producing realistic practicals and effects.

At this point it should be mentioned that the following suggestions for shop-built practicals and effects are far from the only solution. Much of the equipment described in this chapter is available commercially from a number of manufacturers. An Internet search for "theatrical lighting equipment sales" will provide you with a wealth of information on both prime and after-market equipment manufacturers. [I prefer to use Google (www.google.com or ask.com), but any search engine should do.] Peruse the manufacturers' Web pages. You'll learn a lot and may find the exact solution to your design challenge. Additionally, a number of the atmospheric effects—water effects, fire, clouds, and so forth—can be created with moving effects projectors described in Chapter 7, "Projections."

LIGHTING FIXTURES

When you are producing a contemporary production, it isn't particularly difficult to wire table and floor lamps, wall sconces, and chandeliers so that they will work. Run some cable from the fixture to the nearest stage outlet, patch the circuit into a dimmer, and turn it on. The only problem you might have is if the fixture is equipped with a switch. In that case, tape the switch in the "on" position and have the crew check it before each rehearsal or performance.

Lighting designers almost never use lamps of "normal" wattage in these onstage light fixtures because the fixture should be bright enough to look like it's working, but not bright enough to call attention to itself. It is common practice to put in lamps of very low wattage and then further dim them—especially with bare-bulb fixtures such as chandeliers.

When you want or need to see the light output of the fixture, such as when you want to see a splash of light on the wall or floor from a table or floor lamp, you can use a higher-wattage lamp and line the inside of the shade with one or more layers of brown kraft paper.

A greater challenge to your ingenuity comes from trying to re-create realistic-appearing gas, oil lamp, or candle sources.

GAS LAMPS

Gas lamps of the type used for room lighting were almost always housed within glass chimneys. These chimneys were frequently globular in shape and frosted. The gas jet itself had a small flame—between ½ and 2 inches tall—that flickered nonrhythmically. A specialty lamp, called a flicker bulb, available from most home lighting stores, provides a realistic-appearing "gas jet" light. This 4-watt, **F**-shaped lamp with a candelabra base uses two flame-shaped, metallic screen electrodes as the igniters for the neon gas inside the lamp. The resulting yellow-orange light flickers as if it were a gas flame.

CANDLES

Obviously the most realistic-looking candle flame is obtained by simply lighting a candle. However, in many localities fire codes don't allow the use of open flames onstage. Be sure to check with the local fire-safety inspector before using any flames onstage. If candles can be used onstage, be sure to set them away from flammable materials. Although they may look beautiful gracing the mantel above a fireplace, don't put them there because they might set fire to the flat behind them. In fact, candle flames flicker and dance in the slightest breeze and can be very distracting for the audience. Electric candles that use either 120-volt electricity or batteries can be made in the shop. If the candles are going to be stationary, flicker candles—electric candles with a bulb that mimics a flickering candle flame—can be purchased from a theat-

Never use lamps that burn any type of liquid fuel onstage. Their use violates all fire codes and probably would void any insurance coverage your producing organization might have.

SAFETY
TIP

When wiring practicals and effects, be sure to follow the safe wiring procedures outlined in Chapter 5. Try to run all wires in places with the least amount of traffic. To avoid tripping anyone, try to run all wires and cables under rugs (both onstage and offstage) whenever possible. If they have to be run across the bare floor, tape them in place.

SAFETY
TIP

Figure 8.1 (A) 120-volt candle; (B) battery-powered candle.

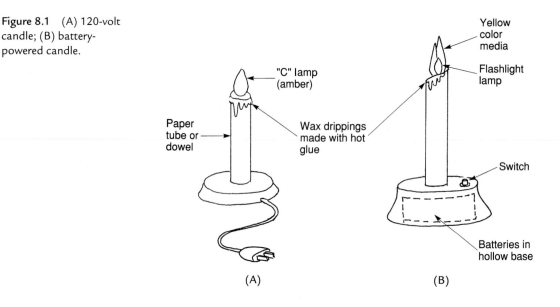

(A) (B)

Ghost-load: To connect an offstage, unseen load to the dimmer. An instrument, usually a 500- to 1,000-watt fresnel, is two-fered with the small onstage load to provide sufficient wattage for the dimmer to operate properly.

rical supply house or novelty shop, or a 120-volt "C" (Christmas tree) lamp can be hot-glued to the end of a dowel or paper tube (see Figure 8.1A). The electric candle can be connected to a stage circuit, and the whole unit can be controlled by a dimmer. Because of the very small wattage of these lamps, it probably will be necessary to **ghost-load** the dimmer in order to keep the lamp from flickering when it is turned on or off.

If the candle is going to be handled or moved, then batteries can be hidden in the base or in the candle itself, and a flashlight lamp of appropriate wattage, painted with amber acetate ink, can be used for the flame (Figure 8.1B). A scrap of flame-shaped yellow gel, lightly sandpapered until it is partially translucent, can be hot-glued to the tip of the candle, around the bulb, to simulate a flame. It's also easy to hide an inconspicuous switch somewhere on the candle base.

LANTERNS

The techniques outlined for candles are equally applicable to most types of lanterns. The candle or battery-and-lamp assembly is hidden in the base of the lantern. The plastic or glass windows can be treated with spray paint so that they appear translucent and smoked around the edges and top.

TORCHES

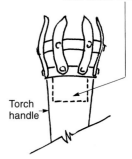

Hollowed out to hold Sterno can

Torch handle

Figure 8.2 Sterno torch.

The same provisos regarding the use of open flames should be applied to the use of torches. Nothing simulates an open flame better than an open flame. If fire regulations permit it (as in some outdoor theatres) and the torches won't be placed anywhere where they might catch scenery, drapes, or costumes on fire, a can of Sterno, or pyro gel, securely fastened to a torch (Figure 8.2) will create an appropriate flame. Under no circumstances should liquid fuels of any type be substituted for the Sterno or pyro gel.

If real flames can't be used and the torches are going to be stationary (for example, the torches lining the walls of a medieval castle hallway), then 120-volt electricity can be used. A single lamp that glows steadily doesn't look like a torch flame; however, a variation of the flickering gas-light effect can provide a fairly realistic torch light. Instead of using a single bulb, closely bunch three of the flicker bulbs together at the tip of the torch (Figure 8.3). If the resultant light output is too "flickery," substitute a clear 3- or 4-watt 120-volt "C" (Christmas tree) lamp for one of the flicker lamps. This "always-on" lamp (which should be painted with yellow or amber transparent acetate inks) will minimize the apparent flicker of the torch. After the desired rate and light output are attained, hot-glue individual pieces of flame-shaped plastic color media between, outside, and over the lamps. Use various tints of yellow/orange/amber, some lightly sanded to make them translucent, some clear, some half and half. The flickering lamps shining through the multiple colors will create a fairly realistic flame. An effective variation on this theme can be achieved by substituting flame-colored chiffon or extremely lightweight silk for some of the plastic color media and blowing the material with a concealed fan. The reasonably silent medium-volume fans used to cool electronic equipment—frequently sold in electronics stores as "stereo fans"—work well in these applications.

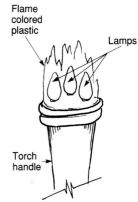

Flame colored plastic

Lamps

Torch handle

Figure 8.3 120-volt torch.

If the torch is going to be hand-carried, it will have to be battery-powered. The challenge here is again to get the torch to flicker realistically. However, if you consult almost any "Basic Electronic Projects" book, it will describe a battery-powered, variable-rate lamp flasher based on the 3909 IC (integrated-circuit) chip. Unfortunately, these flashers have a regular periodic

SAFETY TIP

If it is permissible to use open flames onstage in your locality, and you choose to do so, be sure that you never place candles or torches where their flames will come near anything flammable such as scenery, drapes, or costumes.

rhythm rather than the erratic pulsing of a flame. However, if you use three of these flashers, all set at different rates, and one "always-on" circuit, a fairly realistic flickering effect can be achieved. Be sure that each flasher circuit is set at a slightly different intensity. Some of these circuits make provisions for varying the intensity. If the one you use doesn't, try using flashlight lamps of slightly differing voltage in each circuit. Keep experimenting until the desired results are achieved. A four-D-cell battery holder or the body of a four-battery flashlight can be hidden in the handle of the torch to provide the battery power for the torch. The switch can be concealed in any number of places. Like the 120-volt version, the lamps should be painted with varying tints of flame-colored transparent acetate inks, and they should be surrounded with simulated flames. Additionally, several theatrical specialty houses, such as The Great American Market, sell electric torches or "torch kits" that provide the electrical "guts" that can be inserted into a torch of your own, or the scenic designer's, design.

FIRE EFFECTS

Traditionally, fire effects have been made by building a prop fire of logs and hiding lights of varying colors behind the logs. The resulting steady glow of light isn't realistic. A variation on this theme included a motor-driven, slowly rotating cylinder of crumpled aluminum to reflect the light, which was more realistic but still didn't have the random flicker of a real fire. Figure 8.4 il-

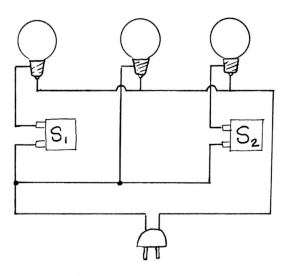

Figure 8.4 Wiring diagram for a random-flicker fire effect.

S_1 and S_2 are fluorescent starters

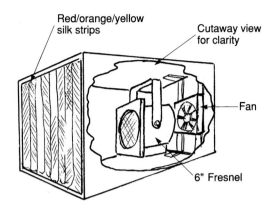

Red/orange/yellow silk strips

Cutaway view for clarity

Fan

6" Fresnel

Figure 8.5 Fire reinforcement effect.

lustrates the wiring diagram for a random-flicker fire effect that can be quite realistic. The random flicker of this system is provided by the starters used with fluorescent-light fixtures. Starters are wired in series with two of the three branches of this 120-volt parallel circuit. There are a number of different-size starters (FS-2, FS-5, FS-25, and so forth), and they all have differing flicker rates. Additionally, the starters are load sensitive, so you can vary the flicker rate (and light output) by changing the wattage of the lamps. Use "A" lamps (regular household) of differing wattages (15, 25, 40, 60, and so forth) to create the specific effect you're looking for. Again, you'll need to paint the lamps with transparent acetate inks to achieve the color appropriate to the type of fire effect you're designing.

A device that reinforces the effect of a flickering fire can be constructed easily with a 6-inch fresnel, a small fan, and some strips of flame-colored lightweight silk, as shown in Figure 8.5. A flame-colored **variegated gel** can be used in the fresnel, and the silk strips are also dyed red and orange. The wavering movements of the silk, caused by the fan, create a realistically flickering light. The unit is normally placed in a hidden corner of the fireplace so that the light will strike anyone approaching the hearth.

Variegated gel: A multi-colored gel made in the shop from strips of color media of differing hues.

MOON EFFECTS

The moon can be re-created in a couple of ways. Traditionally used (and still effective) is the moon box, which is illustrated in Figure 8.6. This wooden box has the silhouette of the desired phase of the moon cut out of the front of the box. The inner face of this cutout is covered with muslin (to diffuse the light), and the cutout is surrounded with between six and eight 25- to 40-watt lamps wired in parallel. (If you use fewer than six lamps, it may be possible to see hot spots from the individual lamps.) The completed moon box is

Figure 8.6 Moon box.

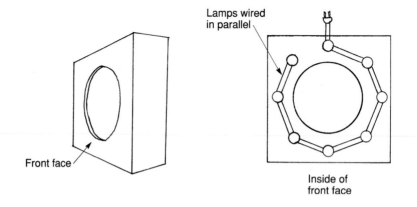

Sky tab: Also sky drop. A large drop made to be hung flat, without fullness; used to simulate the sky.

suspended *in back of* the cyc or **sky tab** and connected to a dimmer, and the intensity is adjusted accordingly. The moon box can also be rigged to move, and so it is possible to have a "rising" or "setting" moon.

Gobos or projections, described in Chapters 4 and 7, can also be used to create the moon. Both gobos and projections can be rear- or front-projected depending on the design and materials from which the set is constructed.

STAR EFFECTS

Stars can be re-created in several ways. Gobos made with lots of very tiny pinpricks, used in an ERS with a wide field angle (such as a 50-degree or $4\frac{1}{2} \times 6\frac{1}{2}$-inch instrument) and thrown a fairly short distance, create reasonably realistic star effects.

If you have an old black curtain or an old drop that you can paint black, you can perforate the curtain or drop with zillions of little "star holes," hang it in front of a cyc or sky tab, and light the cyc. The result can be quite effective.

Grain-of-wheat lamps or white LED lamps (which can usually be purchased at well-equipped lighting, electronics, or hobby stores) can be sewn or hot-glued onto a black cyc or sky tab. These are low-voltage lamps, so an appropriate transformer will have to be used, or they can be wired in series as described in Chapter 4. (See the discussion of the E-Former in Chapter 7 for a transformer that can be dimmed with an electronic dimmer.) Strings of the tiny, clear Christmas tree lights also make very effective, if somewhat larger, stars. Just be sure that the strings are wired in series with a bypass circuit, as described in Chapter 4, so that the whole starlit vista won't disappear if one lamp burns out.

Thin strands of fiber-optic material can be used to create another very effective star effect. Fiber-optic materials, such as Lucite or Plexiglas, act like a light tunnel to conduct light in the same way that copper wire conducts electricity. If you shine a strong light in one end of the fiber-optic strand, a strong light will shine out of the other end regardless of the length of the strand. Light loss in transmission is negligible. To make a "star curtain," hundreds of individual strands are attached to the back of a black drop. One end of each strand is pushed through the fabric to create a pinpoint of light on the audience side, while all the other ends are bundled together and rigidly mounted directly in front of a small, high-intensity light source such as an MR 16 lamp with a cold mirror and cooling fan, a 1½-inch fresnel, or a 3½-inch ERS. The only drawback to the use of fiber optics is the substantial expense of the materials. Star curtains are also commercially available.

LIGHTNING
· ·

Fortunately, bolts of lightning are rarely called for in the theatre. If they are, any number of the production techniques outlined in Chapter 7 can be used. More frequently, lightning will be seen through the windows of the set as intense, erratic bursts of high-intensity light. There are several ways to achieve this effect.

The traditional, and most dangerous, way of creating lightning is by rapidly striking and breaking the contacts of an arc. While this method is effective, it is also very dangerous because an arc of sufficient intensity will use 220-volt electricity, and the brilliance (and ultraviolet emissions) of the arc can severely damage the retina of the operator or anyone looking at the contact zone when the arc is made. For all the obvious reasons this method should never be used. It is included here only to demonstrate how foolish some folks were back in the good old days.

Single-flash heavy-duty strobe lights, also called strobe cannons, provide a brilliant flash of light. These units can be placed where needed and then remotely triggered by an effects operator. Because these units frequently require a "reset" time before they can be fired again, several units may be required to create the erratic, multiple-flash illumination characteristic of lightning. Some aftermarket specialty houses also build strobes that can be retrofit onto ERSs such as the Source Four. These units provide you with the ability to closely focus the strobe's light—something that can't be done with most "regular" strobes—onto a specific area of the set. Large-size flashbulbs, if you can still find them in photo stores, provide about the same amount of light as a strobe.

Any source that has a fast rise time (time that it takes the filament to heat to full incandescence) is a good candidate as a lightning source. The lamps used in most theatrical instruments have fairly large, heavy filaments with resulting slow rise times. However, 200-watt household lamps have fast rise times and reasonably high light output. Several of these lamps mounted

Momentary-on switch:
A push-button switch
without a locking feature.
The circuit remains on
only as long as the button
switch is depressed.

inside the reflector of a scoop (ellipsoidal reflector floodlight), each lamp circuited separately with a **momentary-on switch**, can be used to create a relatively realistic lightning effect.

EXPLOSIONS AND FLASHES

Although the strobes, flashbulbs, and fast-rise-time lamps suggested for lightning can also be used for explosions and flashes, other devices may also be used to create the proper effect.

If you intend to use pyrotechnic devices in any production, whether outdoors or in, you should *always* hire a certified pyrotechnic expert for the work. The primary reason is safety. The secondary reason is liability.

A list of certified pyrotechnic experts should be available from your local fire marshall. These experts may supply their own equipment, or they may ask the producing company to purchase the necessary materials. There are numerous companies that advertise pyrotechnic devices and switching controls in trade magazines such as *Theatre Crafts International (TCI)*, *Lighting Dimensions*, *Stage Directions*, and *Projection Lights & Staging News (PLSN)*.

WATER EFFECTS

Occasionally a production calls for a rippling- or sparkling-water effect. Probably the best way to achieve such an effect is to shine an ERS into a shallow container of water (Figure 8.7) and let the rippling highlights play across the scene. The container must have a highly reflective bottom. You can use a glass dish such as a rectangular Pyrex cake pan and set it on top of a mirror, aluminized mylar, or similar highly reflective surface. The real challenge in this effect is to make the water move, and this can be done in a

Figure 8.7 Rippling-water effect.

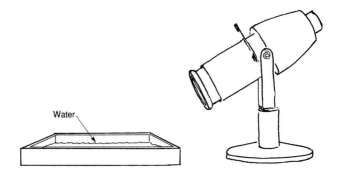

Water

SAFETY
TIP

Working with Pyrotechnic Devices

Flash pots, explosion simulation, and other pyrotechnic devices are extremely dangerous. They can burn, maim, blind, and kill. Pyrotechnics has become highly regulated. It may be illegal for you to work with them if you are not properly licensed. The strong advice offered here is: Hire a pyrotechnic specialist if your production is going to use any explosive or pyrotechnic devices. Do not attempt to operate any pyrotechnic effect unless you are a qualified, and certified, pyrotechnic expert. Pyrotechnic devices are extremely dangerous and must be treated as such.

If, against the advice offered here, you choose to build these devices in your electrical shop rather than purchase commercially available units, be sure to add a warning lamp in-line with the power feed so that anyone who sees the box will know that the power is on.

If you work with any pyrotechnic devices, be sure to adhere to the following common-sense safety guidelines.

1. Always wear eye protection.
2. Always disconnect the power before loading or reloading a flash pot. Do not assume that since the unit is switched off, the power won't reach the detonator. Always unplug the power cord.
3. Never load more than about ½ teaspoon of powder into a flash pot. If you do, the device may explode.
4. Never tamp down the powder. This *probably will* cause an explosion when the device is detonated and *may* cause an explosion *while you are tamping*.
5. Never place any cap or wadding on top of the flash pot. This probably will cause the device to explode.
6. Never place a flash pot directly under or adjacent to any flammable materials.

number of ways. A crew member can jiggle the dish, or you can set up a fan (be sure it's quiet) to blow into the dish, or you can construct a motorized Rube Goldberg-like machine to rock or jiggle the water dish.

The secret to constructing any practical or effect is to understand the appearance of the desired result. When you know what you're looking for, it is usually just a matter of piecing together various elements from known techniques, such as those outlined in this chapter and elsewhere in this book, to create the "look" that is needed.

CHAPTER 9

Color

Color is easily the most noticeable of the elements that a lighting designer can control and is arguably the most dominant. It is also the least understood. We grow up with color all around us, and we see and use it every day. It is probably because of our constant contact with color that we accept it without really thinking about it. This chapter attempts to help you understand the complex subject of color.

DEFINING COLOR

Color has a variety of definitions. It can be defined as a perception created in the brain as a result of stimulation of the retina by light waves of a certain length. It can also be thought of as the intrinsic physical properties of specific objects that allow those objects to reflect and absorb light waves of a certain length. The common denominator for any definition of color is light, because all color is derived from light. The phenomenon that we call light is actually the very narrow portion of the spectrum of electromagnetic radiation that is visible to the human eye. Color Plate 1 shows the position of visible light on this spectrum, as well as the positions of some of the other types of radiation. The visible spectrum stretches in frequency from approximately 750 nanometers to 400. (A nanometer is one-billionth of a meter.) Color Plate 2 shows the approximate wavelengths for the various colors of the visible spectrum.

Color Terminology

Paint chip: A small rectangle of paper or thin cardboard painted in a specific hue.

Without a specific set of terms to describe the various properties of color, almost any discussion of it would quickly degenerate into meaningless comparisons. An example will help explain this phenomenon. If you provided each member of a group of 20 people with 100 **paint chips**, all yellow, but each slightly different, and asked them to identify canary yellow, they probably would select 20 different chips. This is because the connection between the description of any specific color, such as canary yellow, and the brain's understanding of the physical appearance of that color differs, sometimes significantly, from person to person.

The terms that we will be using in our discussion of color are as follows:

- *Hue*—Hue is the quality that differentiates one color from another, such as blue from green or red from yellow.

- *Saturation*—Saturation, also known as chroma, refers to the amount, or percentage, of a particular hue in a color mixture. Fire-engine red has a high, or strong, saturation, because there is a lot of fully saturated color in the mixture. Dusty rose, in contrast, has a low, or weak, saturation, because there isn't a lot of fully saturated color in the mixture; instead, the majority is white or gray.

- *Value*—The relative lightness or darkness of a color is referred to as value. Pale blue has a high value, and dark brown has a low value.

- *Tint*—A color with a high value is referred to as a tint. It is usually achieved by mixing a hue with either white pigment or white light.

- *Shade*—A color with a low value is known as a shade. It is usually created by a mixture of one or more hues and black.

- *Tone*—A color of middle value is frequently referred to as a tone. It is a mixture of a hue with black *and* white.

The color triangle in Color Plate 3 shows the relationships among hue, white, black, gray (the product of mixing black and white), tint, shade, and tone.

SEEING COLOR

· ·

Before we learn how color works, we need to understand how we see color. Human sight comprises a complex series of events. When you look at an object, elements within your eye are stimulated by the light being reflected by, or emitted from, the viewed object. An electrochemical reaction occurs in specialized nerve cells in the retina. Two distinct types of light-receptor

Rods: Nerve cells in the retina that are sensitive to faint light.

Cones: Nerve cells in the retina that are sensitive to bright light; they respond to red, to blue, or to green light.

nerves, **rods** and **cones**, emit minute charges of electricity that are relayed to your brain, where the received data are interpreted as a "picture" that you have seen. The cones are divided into three primary groups: those that respond to the wavelengths of light that correspond to red, blue, and green, respectively.

If a red light enters the eye, the red-responsive cones are stimulated but the others are not. If a light that contains both red and blue wavelengths enters the eye, both the red- and blue-responsive cones are stimulated. In this case the message that is sent to the brain corresponds to the ratio of red and blue light contained in the light mixture the eye receives. If the light contains more red than blue light, that information is transmitted.

Notice that the eye sends information to the brain that corresponds only to the input it has received. The brain is the organ that does the interpretive mixing of the colors. In the example of the red and blue light, the amount of red and blue in the mixture will be interpreted by the brain to be a particular color such as violet, magenta, or purple.

All perceived color is transmitted to the eye by light. If the light is dim, the cones (color sensors) do not function. The best way to demonstrate this effect is by standing outside on a moonlit night and looking at your surroundings. Everything you see will be a monochromatic gray, with perhaps a slight tint of blue or green if the moonlight is sufficiently bright. You will see no vibrant reds, blues, or greens, because the cones require more light than is being transmitted to your eye. If you look at the same scene during the daytime, the bright sunlight will activate the cones in your eye. Unless your eye has some physical dysfunction or the color-interpretive segment of your brain is impaired, you will see colors.

To further illustrate how the eye sees and the brain interprets color, let's assume that you are standing outside in the sunlight looking at a turquoise (blue-green) color chip, as shown in Color Plate 4. The sunlight, which contains all the electromagnetic wavelengths of the visible spectrum, strikes the blue-green surface of the color chip. Some of that light is reflected, and some of it is absorbed by the pigment on the paint chip. A majority of those wavelengths of light that correspond to the color of the chip (blue and green) are reflected. The majority of all other wavelengths of light are absorbed by the paint chip. The reflected blue and green light is received by the eye. The blue and green cones are stimulated by the light, causing them to send electrical impulses to the brain. The relative strength of these signals from the blue and green cones is proportionate to the specific amount of blue and green in the color mix. When the color-sensitive area of the brain is stimulated by these impulses, it interprets that information as a specific color known to that particular brain as turquoise.

Additional hues, which are full chroma equivalents to a mixture of adjacent original hues, can be created and placed between the six principal colors to create a color wheel with twelve specific, fully saturated, hues.

This integrated color wheel can help clarify the interrelationships between pigment and light. For years a semantic problem has hindered easy understanding of these relationships. The use of the same words to describe some of the primary and secondary hues for pigment and light has tended to create some confusion. Although the words red, blue, green, and yellow are used to describe colors in both pigment and light, the specific hues are not identical. The integrated color wheel resolves this problem by renaming the primary colors in light to more accurately reflect the true color relationship that exists between the various hues in pigment and light.

THE PRACTICAL APPLICATION OF COLORED LIGHT IN THE THEATRE

In any discussion of color there is bound to be a disparity between theoretical principles and practical results. Although the principles of color theory are certainly applicable in the practical use of color, the end results will be somewhat different from the results projected by the theory. This is because of the impurities and contaminants found in all stage paints, dyes, lamps, and color media.

Meaning of Color

People react to color. Sometimes that response is subtle and subconscious, and at other times it is overtly physical. Doctors and drug rehabilitation counselors have discovered that an extremely violent patient will often become calm and manageable in about 15 or 20 minutes if placed in an all-pink environment. Many hospitals now have "pink rooms" in which everything—the floor, ceiling, walls, doors—is painted the same hue of pink.

The meanings of color are constantly changing. Color meanings are influenced by many factors: cultural background, personality, adjoining colors, and individual mood. The variability of these factors is the primary reason that the following list of affective meanings is necessarily ambiguous. Moreover, these definitions are simply common interpretations of the meaning of specific colors and should not be thought of as being the "correct" ones.

- Yellow: stimulating, cheerful, exciting, joyful, serene, unpleasant, aggressive, hostile
- Orange: warm, happy, merry, exciting, stimulating, hot, disturbed, distressed, unpleasant

- Red: happy, affectionate, loving, exciting, striking, active, intense, defiant, powerful, masterful, strong, aggressive, hostile
- Green: youthful, fresh, leisurely, secure, calm, peaceful, emotionally controlled, ill
- Blue: pleasant, cool, secure, comfortable, tender, soothing, social, dignified, sad, strong, full, great
- Violet: dignified, stately, vigorous, disagreeable, sad, despondent, melancholy, unhappy, depressing
- Black: sad, melancholy, vague, unhappy, dignified, stately, strong, powerful, hostile, distressed, fearful, old
- White: pure, tender, soothing, solemn, empty
- Brown: secure, comfortable, full, sad, disagreeable

Additional information on light and perception, which is closely related to this discussion of meaning in color, can be found in Chapter 1.

Practical Color Use

Lighting designers normally follow some general color guidelines when selecting their palettes. The following discussion provides a survey of examples and general practices. However, any competent designer will advise you that there are many occasions when it is appropriate, logical, and right to ignore the normal and the conventional if doing so will support the visualization of the production concept.

There are some pragmatic reasons for using colored light on stage. The light from theatre spotlights is relatively bright and harsh. In its uncolored state and at close to full intensity, it will tend to bleach color out of the scenery, costumes, and makeup. If, however, colors that are compatible with the scenery and costumes are used to filter the stage lights the scenic designer's and costume designer's color palettes and values will be maintained.

As we have seen, the mixing of complementary hues creates white light. In the discussion on color theory, this principle was demonstrated with fully saturated hues. In practical application, fully saturated hues are rarely used because of their adverse effect on the other designers' palettes and on actors' skin tones. Complementary hues of low chroma are frequently used, however, because pigments lit with additively mixed white light are enhanced rather than bleached. This color enhancement is caused by the brain's interpretation of retinal stimulation, as demonstrated in Color Plate 9. Color Plate 9A shows white light striking a white surface. Since the white light is composed of all wavelengths of light, the white surface simply reflects all the light rather than absorbing or filtering out any specific portion of the spectrum. Color Plate 9B shows two complementary hues of low saturation (light

How to Create Humidity with Light

A major portion of the lighting designer's job is to create an atmosphere supportive of the production concept. In the box "How Does It Really Look?" in Chapter 11, I discuss the University of Arizona production of *Rain*, in which the lighting designer initially made the set look "desert" hot rather than "tropical" hot. It is fairly easy to manipulate the apparent humidity of the onstage picture. To do so, simply increase the saturation of the color mix used in the acting areas. In *Rain* the lighting designer first lit the whole set with a double-hung (two instruments hung immediately adjacent to each other, each gelled with a different color) complementary mix of very low saturation—No-Color Yellow and No-Color Blue. When we finally stopped tinkering with the colors, that mix had changed to hues of medium saturation—Golden Amber and Steel Blue—and the look of the stage picture had changed to the hot, sticky, moist heat of the tropics. The reason for this change in audience perception has to do with the phenomenon of aerial perspective, which is the visual expression of depth through the gradation of color saturation from more fully saturated in the foreground to less saturated in the background.

According to the principles of aerial perspective, the farther an object is from you, the less saturated it seems to be. As humidity goes up, the effects of aerial perspective are enhanced because there is more moisture in the air to diffuse the reflection of light from objects to your eye. The color of distant objects becomes even less saturated, and their outlines less distinct. All human beings have learned this principle through observation. As a lighting designer, you can play on this unconsciously learned response by increasing the saturation of close objects (in relation to distant objects—background scenes, ground rows, and so forth) in a scene to create the appearance of high humidity. Conversely, to create the appearance of low humidity, all you need to do is decrease the difference in saturation between the light falling on the background and foreground elements of the set.

blue and light yellow) striking the same white surface. These low-saturation hues emphasize a relatively narrow portion of the spectrum (blue and yellow), although there is still a large proportion of the full spectrum (white light) in the mix. The white surface reflects the pale blue and pale yellow, as well as the white light, to your eye. Because blue and yellow are complementary, your brain interprets the mixture of those two lights as white. However, the cones are more strongly stimulated by the blue and yellow light than they would be with plain white light. Interestingly, the brain interprets this stronger color stimulation as a richer, more vibrant color. This phenomenon works for all complementary color mixes. Although the specific color reflectivity and absorption of any colored light from any particular costume or set color will depend on the characteristics of that particular hue, the principles of color vibrancy remain constant.

Because a picture is frequently worth more than a written description, Color Plates 10 to 12 and their accompanying captions are included to help explain some of the practical aspects of creating a lighting design as well as

Source light: The apparent source of light that is illuminating a scene or object.

Double hang: To place two instruments adjacent to each other to light an area that normally would be lit by one instrument. Normally done to allow a color shift during a scene or to provide an additive color mix.

some of the design thoughts and ideas behind the author's lighting design for the University of Arizona Theatre Arts' Department production of Ted Tally's *Terra Nova*.

Warm and Cool Colors

"Warm" and "cool" refer to the psychological effect that certain colors seem to possess. Most people feel a sense of warmth with colors in the red-orange-yellow color range and a sense of coolness with colors in the blue-green-lavender range. Lighting designers frequently make use of these psychological color keys to indicate **source light** (warm) and shadow (cool).

Color Direction

The direction (relative to the audience) from which each color strikes the actor has a great deal to do with how much color blending the audience sees. Basically, light striking an actor from a front light can be seen more readily by the audience than can the light from the side or top. Therefore, the major color impact that the audience sees results from the colors used in the front lights.

Figure 9.1 shows how color blending takes place. Any color that we use on these instruments would additively mix according to the amount of overlap between the instruments and their position relative to the observer. In the proscenium theatre you would see the following: the two side-front lights would blend fairly uniformly; the stage-left side light would blend with the stage-left side-front light and a little bit with the top light; the stage-right side light would similarly blend with its adjacent side-front light and the top light; the top light would additively mix with all four lights, but only on top of the actor's head and shoulders.

There is a theory that having one side of the actor appear to be slightly cool in comparison to the other enhances the modeling qualities of the light. Another theory holds that modeling is more related to distribution and intensity than color and that the color should be evenly distributed on both sides of the actor. Neither practice is necessarily better than the other. They both work well in given circumstances. However, to achieve a smooth blend it will be necessary to have all visible areas of the actor's body covered with light of both colors. This can be accomplished by **double hanging** the lights from each direction, as shown in Figure 9.2A. Double hanging also enables the designer to shift between colors by increasing or decreasing the intensity of one color or the other.

Another method of overlapping the colored light to achieve a relatively uniform additive mix is shown in Figure 9.2B. With this method, however, it isn't possible to do an effective color shift between the warm and cool lights

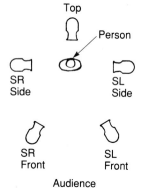

Figure 9.1 Direction of the light (relative to the observer) affects color blending. (See text for details.)

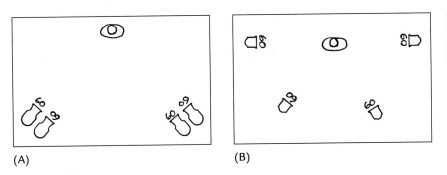

(A) (B)

Figure 9.2 Color-blending techniques: (A) double hanging; (B) alternating colors.

because, with the staggered position of the instruments, the modeling on the actor would change if you were to make one color brighter than the other.

Complementary Tint Theory

The gross oversimplification of the concept of warm and cool colors as directional indicators of source and shadow has unfortunately resulted in some garish stage lighting over the years. When the interaction between hues of a complementary mix is inadequate, as when the angle between the two sources in a two-color mix is so wide that there is almost no overlap of the colors, an uneven additive color mix is the unhappy result. For example, when Roscolux 20, Medium Amber, is used from one side of the stage and Roscolux 68, Sky Blue, is used from the other, the actor will end up looking amber on one side and blue on the other. However, the complementary tint theory works extremely well if approached with care and good judgment. If an actor is lit by two instruments that overlap adequately and are colored with relatively complementary tints, such as Roscolux 09, Pale Amber Gold, and Roscolux 60, No-Color Blue (see Figure 9.3), the majority of his face and body will be washed with both colors, which additively mix to yield a slightly warm white light. Only on the extreme sides of his face, where he is lit by only the Pale Amber Gold or the No-Color Blue, will the actor seem to be slightly warmer or cooler.

When you use a complementary color mix, the additive color mix increases the apparent life in a much wider range of colors than if the scene were lit with a single color that closely approximates the hue resulting from the additive mix.

The palettes used by the scenic and costume designers generally dictate the specific complementary hues that are chosen by a lighting designer. The lighting designer usually selects specific hues that will enhance the primary palettes of the other designers, using the guideline that every hue heightens its own color and suppresses its complementary. If the scenic or costume designer is using a full-spectrum palette, the lighting designer may combine

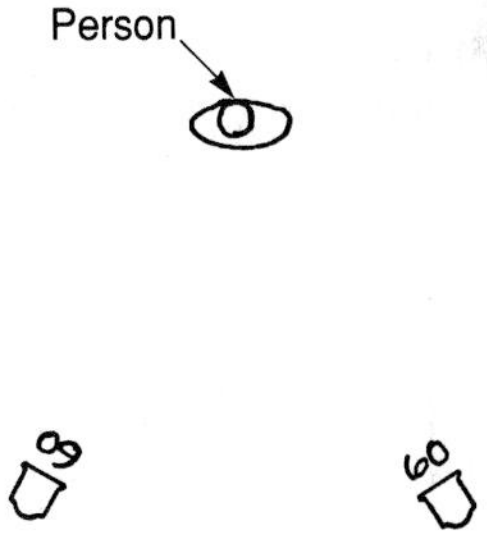

Person

Figure 9.3 Complementary tints can be used to create a more vibrant white light. (See text for details.)

three or more colors, such as low-chroma versions of the three secondary colors—yellow, cyan, and magenta—to create white light. When more specific hues are used to create the white-light mix, the range of hues affected by the color-enrichment characteristics of a complementary mix are similarly broadened.

The lighting designer can also produce a white-light mix that is not exactly complementary—either slightly warm or cool—to create a corresponding warming or cooling of the stage environment. This type of not-quite-complementary color mixing is helpful in establishing an atmospheric feeling of heat or cold on the stage.

Complementary Color Shadowing

Complementary color shadowing is another interesting challenge to the lighting designer. Complementary color shadowing refers to the physiological reaction of seeing shadow colors that are complementary to the specific hue of the source light. An example will help illustrate this phenomenon. Color Plate 13 shows two intersecting light sources, one gelled with a fairly heavily saturated magenta, and the other with a magenta of low saturation. They are projecting onto a white surface. An object has been erected to throw shadows from both beams onto the projection surface. If we were to look at this in "real life," we would see that the shadow of one light is magenta, but the other is green!

The brain constantly tries to balance the input that it receives from the eye to create a white base. The eye recognizes that it is receiving input from multiple sources because of the difference in specific color between the two sources. The only way that the brain can logically create the white base it seeks from these two magenta sources is to interpret one of the hues—the less saturated one—to be the complement of magenta: green.

I've used magenta in this example simply because the magenta/green mix is very visible and provides a startling example. However, the principle holds true for any other related color mix as well: green gels will have magenta shadows, blue gels will have yellow shadows, yellow gels will have blue shadows, and so forth.

While this is an interesting party trick and one that never fails to amaze anyone who sees it, there is a rational, productive reason for lighting designers to understand this phenomenon. When you work with a related tint mix (a color mix in which all of the hues are tints, tones, and shades of one color), you are going to get complementary color shadowing. For example, if you choose to work in a related tint mix of lavender, depending on the specific hues that you select, you probably will have some ugly-looking greenish shadows lurking about the stage. However, if you add a top light in a complementary hue to the mix, you create a resultant white light that reduces the effects of the complementary color shadowing to the point where it isn't visible. Additionally, by putting the complementary hue in the top light, you haven't significantly altered the effects of your related tint design on the sets, costumes, and skin tones.

Color Media

Three transparent color media are used to color the light output of stage lighting instruments. Each medium has its own particular characteristics and advantages.

Gel   Gel has fallen victim to technological progress and is no longer manufactured for use with theatrical lighting instruments. But the name continues to be used. Almost everybody refers to plastic color media as "gel," probably because it is a lot easier to say than "plastic color media." Gel was made from natural gelatin and colored with primarily synthetic dyes. It faded very quickly when used with T-H lamps, was fragile when dry, and was totally destroyed when wet. It was frequently dined upon by vermin—which had an amazing ability to nibble three strategically placed holes in a full 20 × 24-inch sheet, making it almost impossible to salvage an 8-inch gel from the sheet.

Plastic   The primary filters used in stage lighting instruments are generally made from either mylar or polyester because of the rugged, long-lasting, heat-resistant qualities of these plastics. They are available in a wide and ever-increasing variety of colors. The low-saturation tints bleach out very slowly, and the more heavily saturated shades last for a relatively long time, even under the intense ultraviolet radiation emitted by T-H lamps.

Glass   Glass is used infrequently as a filter, although it is certainly the longest lasting and most fade resistant of all the media. Its palette is extremely limited when compared with plastic color media; it is expensive and heavy and will shatter if dropped. The most prominent use of colored glass filters is in rondels, the glass filters used with striplights. These are generally available in red, blue, green, and amber.

Dichroics   Dichroic filters are a relatively new addition to theatrical color media. Dichroics do not work in the same way as other color media. Ordinary filters allow their own color to pass through the filter while *absorbing* the undesired colors. Dichroic filters *reflect* the unwanted colors. To produce a particular color, you use a dichroic filter to remove its complementary. To illustrate, if you want to produce the color red from a beam of white light, you use a dichroic filter that reflects the complementary of red (cyan). Re-

✳ Heat Protection for Plastic Color Media ─────

Heat is one of the prime enemies of plastic color media. A recently developed material, Thermoguard, manufactured by the Artifex Corporation, when placed between the lens of the instrument and the color media, will reflect a high percentage of the infrared radiation (heat) back toward the lamp, while allowing the visible spectrum to pass unimpeded. The material is a dichroic heat-reflective coating bonded to a clear polyester base.

Thermoguard will increase the life of your gels and will actually reduce the heat onstage. When used with heavily saturated gels, a 2-inch air space needs to be maintained between the gel and the Thermoguard material. The reflective coating *must* face the heat source. If the material is put into the instrument backward, the heat from the lamp will melt the polyester base, destroying the filter.

moving cyan from white light produces red light. Although this may seem to be "just another way of doing the same thing," there is a tangible advantage: The output of the resultant light is measurably greater than that produced with traditional filters.

Dichroic filters are made by depositing microscopically thin films onto glass. The particular properties of the films determine which colors are passed and which are reflected. Specific colors are created through the deposition of multiple layers of film.

The advantages of dichroic filters are numerous: The filters are extremely heat-resistant; for all practical purposes, color fade is nonexistent; the colored light transmitted through dichroic filters is extremely pure; dichroics transmit more light when compared (light input/light output) with absorbing filters of the same hue. The primary disadvantage of dichroic filters is their cost.

The property of reflecting rather than absorbing unwanted wavelengths of electromagnetic radiation—remember that light is just a small segment of the electromagnetic spectrum—is another advantage of dichroics. Cold mirrors are dichroic filters that are coated to reflect the visible spectrum and allow infrared radiation (heat) to pass. A reflector made with a cold-mirror finish vents heat *through* the reflector, which makes the reflected light considerably cooler. The use of cold-mirror reflectors in lighting instrument design is discussed in Chapters 4 and 10.

Hot mirrors are, as you would expect, the reverse of cold mirrors. They reflect infrared radiation and allow the visible spectrum to pass. Hot mirrors are used as heat filters in projectors as well as several of the advanced-technology instruments described in Chapter 10.

✳ Gel Books

All media manufacturers offer sample books of the color media that they sell. Most of these books contain plastic swatches of the various colors, transmission information about those gels, and samples of diffusion filters. Some manufacturers include color correction filters normally used in film and video. These filters can be used for theatrical lighting, and they offer some good colors not available in the "regular" theatre product lines.

As indicated above, a gel book contains a sample of each filter color offered by the manufacturer. The sample pieces are typically backed by a piece of white paper that contains information about the transmission characteristics of that particular gel. The figure shows backing sheets from the Roscolux and Lee gel books. The graphs provide visualizations of the proportion of the various colors contained in the gel. Those colors, indicated by light wavelengths measured in nanometers, are listed along the bottom of the graphs. (Color Plate 2 shows the colors of the visible spectrum together with their associated frequencies.) The numbers on the side of the graphs indicate the percentage of the specific colors in the total mix.

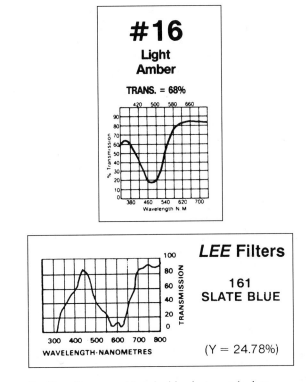

Backing sheets provide valuable photometric data. See text for details.

The percentage of transmission—the amount of light passed through the filter as compared with the unfiltered output of the source fixture—is also listed. In the Lee book the number following the "Y = " is the transmission percentage, while the Roscolux book simply lists "Trans. = " followed by the actual figure.

The color transmission graph is useful in understanding the component colors contained in any gel mix. This information is quite helpful when selecting gel colors because the lighting designer needs to choose colors that are not going to radically change the scenic and costume designers' palettes. For example, if the female lead is always dressed in frothy yellow dresses, you wouldn't want to light those dresses with a gel that had a high percentage

(continued)

✳ Gel Books (*continued*) ───────────────────

of blue. Why? Because the principles of additive color mixing tell us that the blue light will gray out the yellow dress.

You can also use the color transmission graphs to help determine if two gels are complementary. If their graphs are close to mirror images of each other—like the two examples in the figure—the colors will be close to complementary. A somewhat simpler, and probably more accurate, method involves overlaying two gel samples that you think are complementary. If the color of the overlapped area, when viewed while being held above a sheet of white paper, is a neutral gray, then the mix is truly complementary. You can also find "warm" or "cool" complementary mixes—mixes in which the resultant white light is slightly warm or cool rather than truly white—in the same way. The gray of the overlapped area will tend toward a warm brownish-amberish-gray or cool bluish-gray.

Probably the best way to see what the color mixes will look like is to put them in instruments hanging over the stage, run them up on a dimmer, have a friend stand in the pool of light and look at them. Change the dimmer settings. Change colors. Study what you see. Try to figure out why you see what you see.

Unfortunately, life has a way of intruding on our utopian dreams. Stages are normally busy places and we rarely have the luxury of being able to use them as just described. However, you can create your own lighting lab by cutting the gels out of a gel book, mounting them in slide holders, then using slide projectors as "color projectors." This method closely replicates the effect you'd see onstage if you match the color temperature of the projector lamp with the color temperature of the instrument lamps in the fixtures you'll be using. If using more than one projector, make sure that the lamps in each unit are of the same color temperature and have been run for approximately the same length of time. Why? Because to see the best results you want the color temperatures of the lamps to be as close to identical as possible and the color temperature of lamps changes, sometimes drastically, over time. If you don't have, or can't find, slide projectors, use halogen-bulb flashlights with fresh batteries. Overlap the beams. Stick your hand in the light. See what the colors do to your skin tone. Have fun. Again, as with so many facets of stage lighting—or any craft— the best way to learn this stuff is to, as the folks at Nike say, just do it.

Diffusion Filters   Diffusion filters are available in a plethora of densities and types. But they generally fall into two general categories—diffusers and focusers.

Diffusers, such as Roscolux 100–Frost and Lee 216–White Diffusion, soften the quality of the light transmitted through them. The visible result of diffusing is a softening of the edge of the beam of light and, to a lesser extent, the shadows created by that light. The amount of the edge softening and shadow filling is directly dependent on the level of diffusing that is taking place. For this reason every color media manufacturer offers a number of levels of diffusion. This concept is perhaps best illustrated by the Roscolux Tough White filter series: 116–Tough White Diffusion, 117–Tough ½ White Diffusion, and Tough ¼ White Diffusion. The amount of diffusion is di-

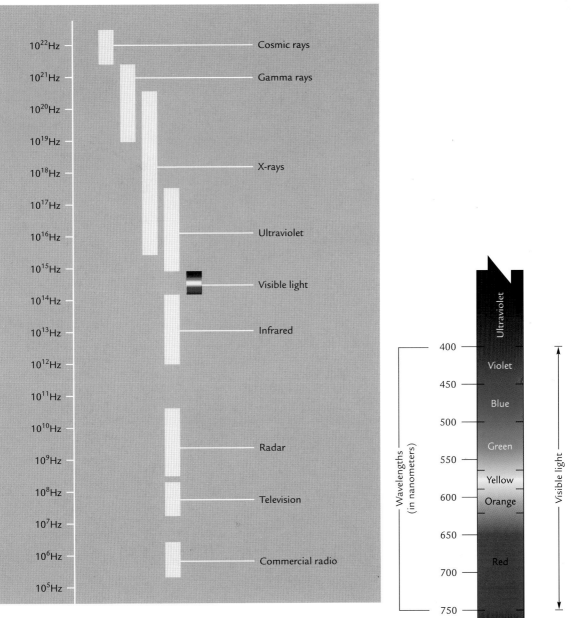

Color Plate 1
The frequency range of selected energy forms contained in the electromagnetic radiation spectrum.

Color Plate 2
The frequency range of visible light.

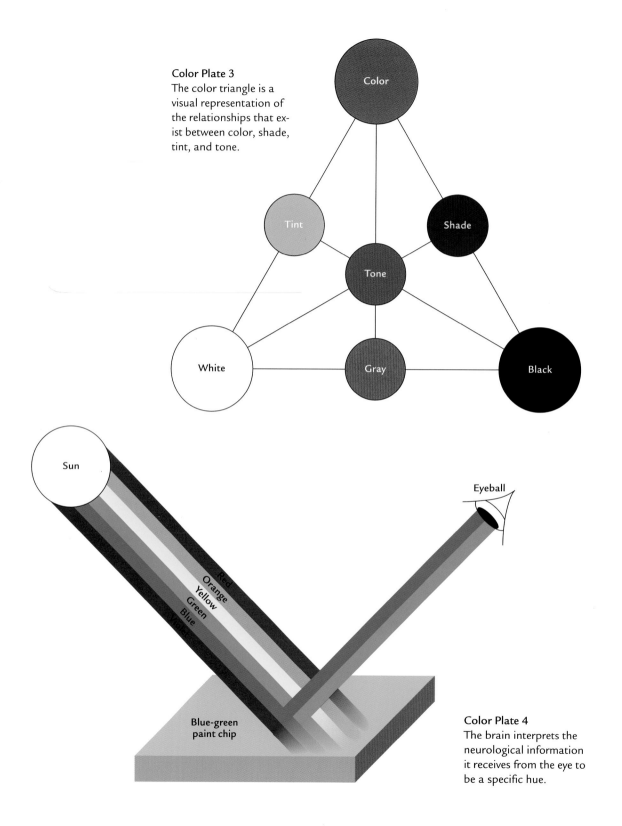

Color Plate 3
The color triangle is a visual representation of the relationships that exist between color, shade, tint, and tone.

Color Plate 4
The brain interprets the neurological information it receives from the eye to be a specific hue.

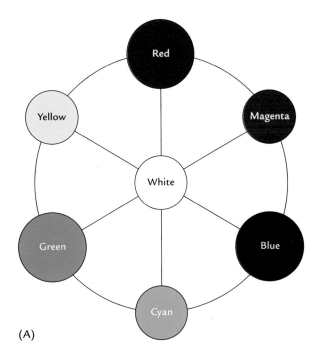

(A)

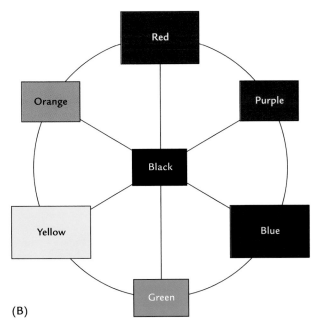

(B)

Color Plate 5
Color wheels for (A) light and (B) pigment.

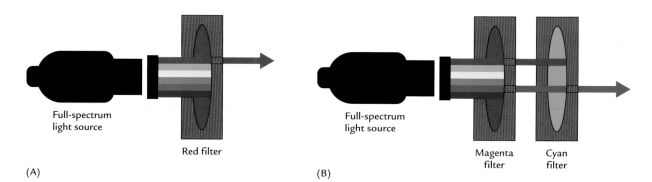

Full-spectrum
light source

Red filter

(A)

Full-spectrum
light source

Magenta
filter

Cyan
filter

(B)

Color Plate 6
Subtractive color mixing in light. A colored filter will allow
its own color to pass but will absorb all others.

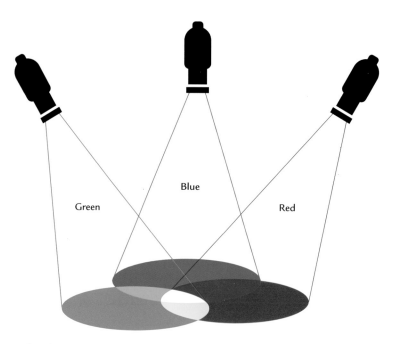

Blue

Green

Red

Color Plate 7
Additive color mixing in light. The eye sees each separate color; the brain
interprets the ratio of the color mix to be a specific hue.

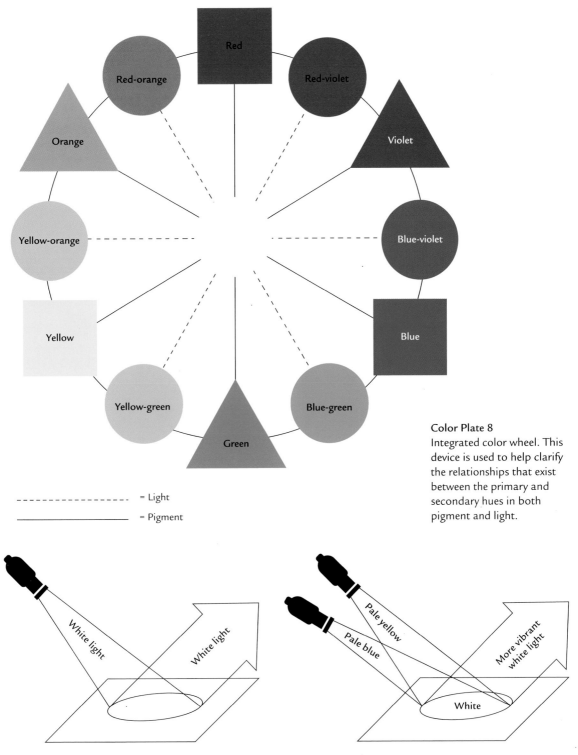

Color Plate 8
Integrated color wheel. This device is used to help clarify the relationships that exist between the primary and secondary hues in both pigment and light.

- - - - - - - - - = Light

——————— = Pigment

Color Plate 9
The use of an additive mix of complementary tints results in a more lively, vibrant light.

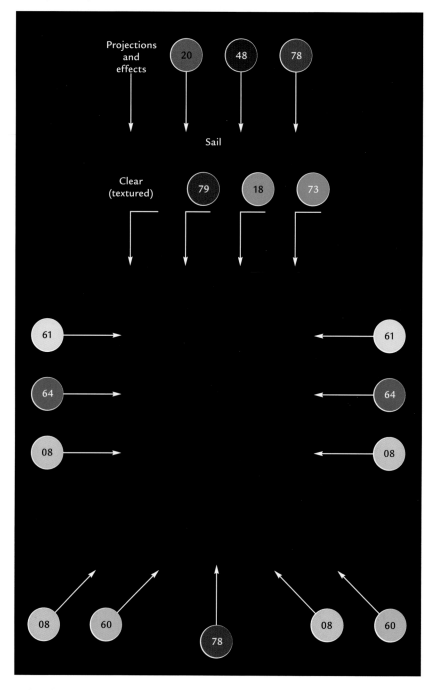

Color Plate 10

The lighting key. The arrows indicate the direction from which the light is traveling toward the stage. The horizontal flags on the arrows in the upper part of the illustration indicate that those lights are coming from above, rather than behind the actors. Note that numbers indicate Roscolux color numbers.

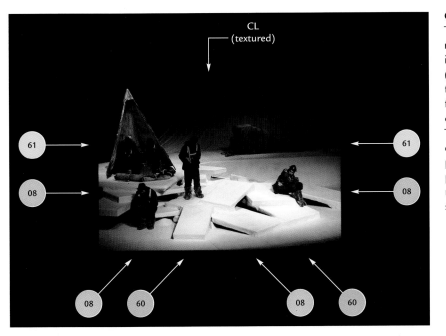

Color Plate 11
The set was white for two reasons: (1) Antarctica is overwhelmingly white; (2) it provided a very effective projection surface for the saturated colors of the dream sequences. The sail was backlit with color washes to provide primary atmospheric and psychological keys to the nature of the individual scenes.

Color Plate 12
The atmosphere of England was created by using textured toplights colored in warm, soft hues (18 and 73) and backlights on the sail (20 and 48), providing a striking contrast with the blue-white coldness of the lighting for Antarctica. Scott and his wife (downstage) were lit with warm-white combinations of 08 and 60 from the front and 08 and 61 from the sides. The figure in the background was side lit with a warm, dim, front/side light. The warm-white light on Scott and his wife provided accurate color rendering of their costumes. The warm light striking the background figure created a fairly accurate rendering of his tuxedo.

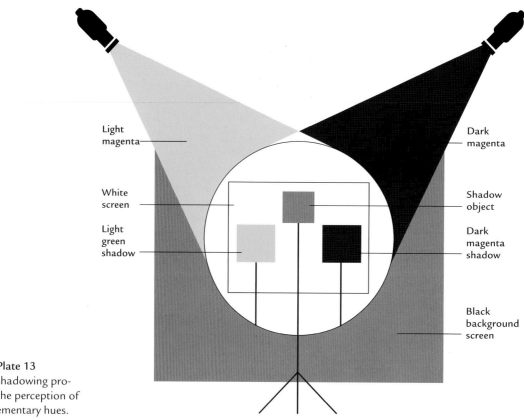

Light
magenta

Dark
magenta

White
screen

Shadow
object

Light
green
shadow

Dark
magenta
shadow

Black
background
screen

Color Plate 13
Color shadowing pro-
duces the perception of
complementary hues.

rectly equivalent to the filter's name—Tough ½ White Diffusion provides half as much diffusing as Tough White Diffusion, and so forth. Other diffusers, such as Lee HT 254–New Hampshire Frost, are intended to reduce hot spots and minimize **color fringes** in addition to providing a light diffusing effect. Diffusing frosts are also available in primary colors—red, blue, green—and amber for use in creating a smooth wash of light on a cyc or sky tab.

Focusing diffusers, such as Lee 228–Brushed Silk and Roscolux 104–Tough Silk, are finished with what looks like very closely spaced striations or scratches on the surface of the media. Light projected through these "silks" is refracted at right angles to the directions of the lines. The effect is to create a roughly horizontal, as opposed to a round, beam of light. This type of effect can be helpful when trying to squirt light into difficult-to-reach places on the set or anytime you want to create a band of light. Silks are also available in the primary colors and amber for use in cyc lighting. One of the great challenges of cyc lighting is being able to achieve a smooth wash of light over the expanse of the cyc from instruments that frequently have to be hung much closer to the cyc than an ideal distance. The directional diffusing effects of the silk diffusers makes this task much easier.

When focusing a show it is not unusual to find that one or two instruments do not produce light of the same type or quality as others in the same group. While the ideal solution would be to provide field maintenance on the pesky instrument and fix whatever is wrong with it, time constraints frequently make this impossible. However, sometimes the "challenges" presented by these troublemakers can be solved by using one of the lighter diffusion filters in addition to the gel specified for the fixture in the lighting design.

Remember that the best way to learn what these, or any other, filters can do is to play with them. Set up an ERS, a Fresnel and, if available, a PAR can. Focus them on something that will have both highlight and shadow areas—a store mannequin would be ideal. Insert the various diffusion filters into their beams of light. See what the resultant light looks like, what it does to the surfaces it strikes and the shadows it creates. Notice the different effects that the media have on the different types of instruments. Observation is a great teacher. And you can have fun while you're actually learning something.

The difference between the theory and practice of color mixing is only a matter of degree, not principle. Although an understanding of the laws of physics that govern the mixing of color is helpful in using color in the theatre, the only way that a lighting designer can develop any real understanding of, and facility in, the use of color is through experimentation and experience.

Color fringes: A rainbow effect seen at the edges of some beams of light. Caused by refraction of the projected light.

CHAPTER 10

Advanced Technology Instruments

As discussed in Chapter 1, one of the primary functions of an effective lighting design is the establishment of a mood that supports the production concept. In the not too distant past, to creatively, and effectively, light a **legitimate theatre** production, the lighting designer generally used the basic tools discussed in Chapter 4—ERSs, fresnels, PARs, scoops, and so forth. With this equipment she or he could create the normally subtle lighting that supported the production concept and covertly affected the audience's understanding of the play. The development of kinetic and intelligent, or moving light, fixtures has skewed this landscape a bit.

In the application of its basic principles, lighting design for **concerts** and **clubs** is no different than lighting design for legitimate theatre. However, there are two substantial differences: the nature of the production concept and the impact of the lighting on the audience. Production concepts for legitimate theatre productions are almost always intellectual, cerebral, and metaphorically introspective. The production concept for rock concerts and clubs is almost always visceral, bold, and extroverted. The atmosphere at a rock concert or club is about as far removed as you can get from a production of Shakespeare, Williams, or Stoppard. The music is fast, hard, and loud. The atmosphere is high energy. So is the lighting. It is overt and spectacular, and the way it affects meaning and mood is anything but subtle. In concert lighting the basic area lighting is normally done with washes of heavily saturated color from PAR 64s. Moving light fixtures provide punch, emphasis, and focus.

The difference in design philosophy between concert/club and legitimate theatre lighting is still valid. And kinetic instruments are still used to provide spectacular effects in concerts and clubs. However, as more design-

Legitimate theatre: Refers to plays that rely on the spoken word to convey their message. Does not include musicals, reviews, dance, opera, or concerts.

Concert: In the context of lighting, primarily refers to touring rock and country shows.

Club: In the context of lighting, refers to night clubs in which high-energy music (live or recorded) is the prime attraction.

ers have had a chance to learn the capabilities of these versatile fixtures, they have learned that these instruments don't always need to be used to spectacular effect. They can also be very effective if used subtly. Consequently, when budgets permit, we are seeing more use of this fascinating class of instrument in legitimate theatre as well. Many colleges and universities now have several moving light fixtures in their basic inventories.

The kinetic instruments and associated support equipment discussed in this chapter provide the lighting designer with the capability to create not only the in-your-face lighting typical of most concerts and clubs, but also the generally more subtle and nuanced lighting associated with legitimate and musical theatre.

MOVING LIGHT FIXTURES

The common feature of this class of instrument is movement: light beams **pan** the stage, zoom in and out, change shape, change color, diffuse, and sharpen; gobos materialize, spin around, change pattern, then disappear. This is an exciting and active class of instrument.

There are a plethora of moving light fixtures available, as shown in Figure 10.1. Obviously, they don't all function in the same way, nor do they all have the same features. But generally they all control light by using a combination of the methods discussed below.

Control

The advent of digital multiplex control (see the discussion of digital control and the box "USITT DMX512" in Chapter 6) facilitated the development of moving light fixtures. Many of these fixtures have up to 20 separate motor functions—pan and **tilt** movement, mechanical dimming, color changers, gobo movement, beam spread, beam diffusion, and so forth. Prior to the development of digital multiplex, these functions could be controlled only with an analog multiplex system (which didn't work well) or with an analog system that required a dedicated control line for each function. Control of all functions of digital-control moving light fixtures is achieved with one control line. A 120- or 208/220-VAC power line is required for the lamp and control motors.

The majority of manufacturers of moving light fixtures use the digital protocol DMX512 to control their equipment. This allows their fixtures to be controlled by any light board that uses this protocol. Those that don't use DMX512 use a proprietary system designed specifically for use with their instruments.

Pan: To rotate horizontally.

Tilt: To rotate vertically.

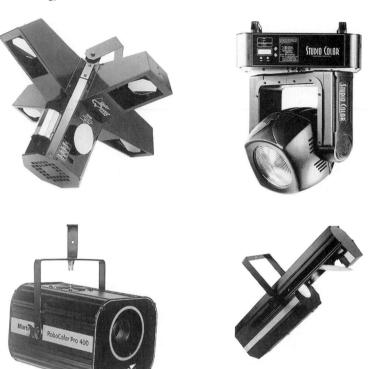

Figure 10.1 Types of moving light fixtures.
(Courtesy of Light Quest, High End, Martin, Elation.)

The light output of some fixtures, primarily those used in club lighting, can be controlled by music. The range of musical criteria to which these instruments react is varied. Some respond to specific notes or a range of notes, others to the beat, others to variations in loudness. In many cases the specific criteria to which they react is programmable. Examples of these fixtures are shown in Figure 10.2. The type of action they perform varies from fixture

Figure 10.2 Moving light fixtures that move in response to music.
(Courtesy of Light Quest and Elation.)

to fixture: some change color, some pan and tilt, others project moving patterns, many do all three simultaneously. The common feature is that they all do whatever they do to music. These fixtures normally are not used in theatrical lighting for precisely the reason they're used to light the dance floor of a club: their light output is random and attention-grabbing. Lighting for legitimate theatre is, for the most part, carefully programmed and choreographed to be subtle and almost unnoticeable. These fixtures are also carefully designed to support a club atmosphere, which is joyously opposite the goals of most theatre lighting. If, however, this quality works in support of the production concept for a particular play, then these instruments should be used.

Lamps

Two types of lamps are used in moving light fixtures: encapsulated arc and incandescent tungsten-halogen. The operational characteristics of both types of lamps were discussed in Chapter 4.

Encapsulated Arc   The encapsulated arc has two characteristics that generally make it the source of choice for moving light fixtures: (1) it creates a very bright, high-color-temperature light (see Chapter 9 for a discussion of color temperature); (2) the point of origin of the light is the very small area between the anode and cathode of the encapsulated arc, which permits the design of small, very efficient light-gathering and focusing structures.

Tungsten-Halogen   The T-H lamp generally is used in lower-output, lower-cost moving light fixtures. Although the output of a T-H lamp is considerably less than that of an encapsulated arc, it does provide two distinct advantages: the lamps are dimmable, and they are less expensive.

Color Changing

Color changing is accomplished with two basic methods: color scrollers and dichroic color changers.

Color Scroller   A color scroller (Figure 10.3A) changes the color of light emitted by an instrument. Generally, they are used with ERSs, fresnels, or PARs—and any other instruments that don't have internal color-changing capability. The scroller, which fits in the color-media holder on the front of the instrument, contains a roll of plastic color media that, if stretched out, would look like a series of different-colored gels taped together. The number of colors that the scroller holds varies with the manufacturer but generally ranges between 8 and 20. The scrolls, which are generally ordered from the manufacturer, are somewhat costly. Although scrolls can be shop built, the

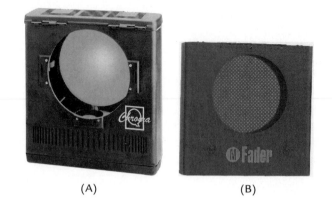

(A)   (B)

practice isn't recommended because if a seam breaks, the unit is useless until a new scroll is installed.

Dichroic Color Changer A dichroic color changer generally uses three dichroic filters (normally cyan, magenta, amber) to change the color of the light. The individual filters can be fully or partially inserted into the beam of light produced by the instrument. The degree of insertion determines the level of saturation of the resultant color. For example, fully inserting a cyan filter produces a fully saturated red light, whereas partially inserting the same filter reduces the degree of red saturation. The three filters can be used in combination to produce any possible hue.

There are two primary advantages to a dichroic color changer when compared to a color scroller: dichroic filters don't bleach out; you can fade or **bump** from any color to any other color in any sequence.

Dichroic color changers are manufactured in both external and internal configurations. The external units (Figure 10.3B), resemble a color scroller and are mounted in the color-frame holder of the instrument. The internal units are mounted inside the fixture.

24-VDC Power Supplies

Externally mounted color changers and retrofitted motion control devices like the gobo spinner that fits into the gate of an ERS, shown in Figure 10.4A, require power and signal control lines that are separate from the "sponsoring" instrument's lamp.

To provide this supplemental power and control, the lighting industry seems to have standardized on the use of the 24VDC power signal and the DMX512 control signal. A power supply, shown in Figure 10.4B, provides the DC power to the units.

To control the color changer or motion control units' movements, DMX cable containing the control signal is run from the lighting console to the

Bump: An instantaneous cue. In this case, refers to bumping from one color to another as opposed to fading from one color to another.

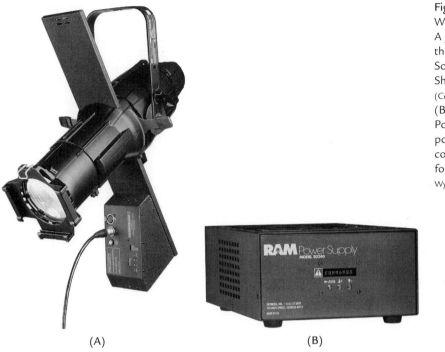

Figure 10.4 (A) The Wybron Goboram II—A gobo changer/rotator that can be retrofitted to Source Four or Altman Shakespeare 600 ERS. (Courtesy of Wybron Inc.) (B) The Wybron RAM Power Supply—a 24VDC power supply for external color changers. See text for details. (Courtesy of Wybron Inc.)

(A)   (B)

power supply. From the power supply, a single cable containing both the control signal and 24-VDC power is connected to the color changer or motion control unit. If, as is common practice, more than one unit is used, additional cables can be run between units to provide both power and control. This practice, generally referred to as **daisy chaining**, eliminates the need to run a separate cable to each unit.

> **daisy chain:** to connect one to another, in a continuous line, like a chain of daisies.

Most manufacturers have equipped their color changers/motion control units with rotary switches or some other type of device so they can be programmed with separate identification addresses. This allows a string of daisy-chained devices each to receive its own discrete set of instructions.

Dimming

Dimming of T-H lamps is simply a matter of connecting the lamp to a dimmer. Encapsulated arc lamps cannot be dimmed like a lamp with a filament. However, they can be dimmed mechanically by inserting something into the beam of light. A mechanical dimmer typically has a series of slats, as illustrated in Figure 10.5, which pivot into the beam to diminish its intensity. The concept of a mechanical dimmer may seem rather archaic. While the concept is over 100 years old, contemporary mechanical dimmers are motor driven, digitally controlled, and very accurate. The digital control facilitates

Figure 10.5 The side view schematic shows how the shutters of a mechanical dimmer can rotate from an open position (A) to closed (B) to reduce light output. The illustrated shutters operate horizontally, but shutters are also made in a circular pattern that opens and closes like a camera iris.

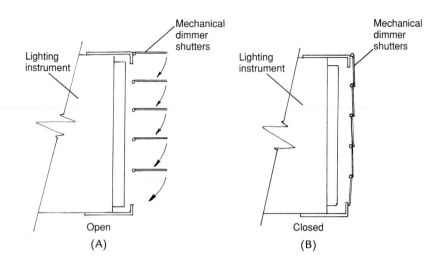

Fade Profiles

Specifically, a fade profile refers to a graphic representation of a fade. It is the line on a graph that shows the relationship between time and the intensity of the light. In a standard "straight-line" fade, 20 percent of the fade will be completed when 20 percent of the time has elapsed, 40 percent of the fade will be completed when 40 percent of the time has elapsed, and so forth, as shown in the Figure. The straight-line fade is the default setting for all computer board faders.

Lighting designers frequently want to adjust fade profiles. They may want a fade-in to start slowly and finish fast, or they may want the lights to rapidly fade for the first part of the cue then linger at a low setting before finally fading out. Most advanced-feature computer boards have 20 or more standard profiles which can either be used as designed or modified. When the lighting designer has chosen the new fade profile, it is linked to its specific cue so that each time that cue is executed the timing of the fade will follow the new profile.

In addition to being used by the lighting designer, fade profiles are used by equipment designers. The output of all electronic dimmers is inherently nonlinear. But each dimmer has on-board electronics that compensate for the nonlinear profile to create a linear output. Likewise, the motor controls of mechanical dimmers, such as those illustrated in Figure 10.4, are inherently nonlinear, but the profile of the motor-control circuit is designed to create a linear light output.

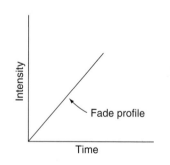

A fade profile is a graphic representation of the relationship between the time and intensity of a fade.

precise regulation of the percentage of light emitted by the fixture, as well as the **profile** and duration of any fades.

Gobos

Gobos, described in Chapter 4, are an integral part of many moving light fixtures. Both metal and glass are used to make these gobos. Generally, each manufacturer has a variety of proprietary patterns available. Because the high-heat environment in these fixtures requires that the gobos be made of fairly exotic metals or heat-resistant glass, they generally cannot be shop built.

If the fixture has the capability of holding more than one gobo, the gobos are mounted in a device called a gobo wheel, illustrated in Figure 10.6A. To project a particular gobo, you rotate the wheel until the desired gobo intersects the optical path. There are two types of gobo wheels: fixed and rotating. Fixed gobos project a motionless pattern. The rotating gobo wheel (Figure 10.6B) allows the selected gobo to be spun. The rate of spin, as well as the direction, is controllable.

Beam Shape

Almost all moving light fixtures have some method of shaping the beam of light emitted by the instrument. Most have a **zoom** feature. Zooming is achieved by varying the focal length of the optical train through a forward/backward adjustment of the distance(s) between the lens(es) and the lamp.

Profile: A fade profile is a linear, graphic representation of a fade. See the box "Fade Profiles" for further explanation.

Zoom: Widening or narrowing of the cone of light emitted by the instrument.

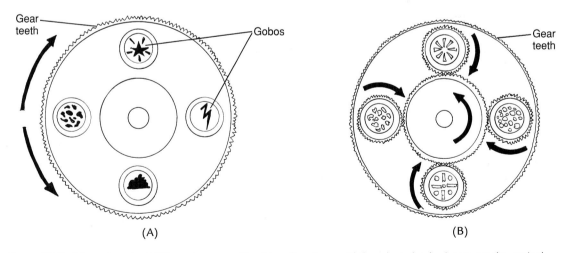

(A)   (B)

Figure 10.6   The gobo wheel (A) can be rotated in either direction until the selected gobo intersects the optical train. The rotating gobo wheel (B) uses a separate motor to control the rotation of the selected gobo.

Prismatic lens: The surface or interior of the glass is scored or beveled to create the desired effect.

Flag: Named for its shape. A roughly rectangularly shaped material—transparent, translucent, or opaque, depending on function—that is inserted into a beam of light to color, shape, or dim the light.

Stepper motor: An electric motor whose movement consists of discrete angular steps rather than continuous rotation. Precision movement is achieved by programming the motor to run, in either direction, for a specific number of steps.

Relay: An electro-mechanical device in which a low-voltage circuit is used to control the opening and/or closing of contacts in a high-voltage on/off system.

Some of these instruments can also vary the shape of the beam from circular to oval as well as other shapes. Beam shaping is normally accomplished with **prismatic lenses** mounted in the gobo wheel or mounted on **flags** that can be inserted into the optical train.

Diffusing flags, used to soften the quality of light and harshness of the beam edge, are also available on some instruments. The degree of diffusion is controlled by the amount that the flag is inserted into the light beam.

Effects Projection

Some moving image fixtures are capable of effects projection. Generally, effects such as multiple images and moving patterns are accomplished with prismatic lenses or etched dichroic filters mounted in a wheel similar to the rotating gobo wheel.

Movement

All of the various movements—color changing, zooming, pan and tilt, and so forth—of a moving light fixture are performed by small, powerful **stepper motors**. Each function, such as the positioning of the slats of the mechanical dimmer or the rotation of a gobo wheel, uses one or more stepper motors or **relays** to create the required movement. The activity of the motor is digitally controlled from a control console. The control console may be a dedicated system used to control any moving light fixtures used in the production, or, if the fixtures are compatible with the lighting system (e.g., if the fixtures and dimmers both use the same protocol, such as USITT DMX512), then the moving lights can be controlled from the same control board used to manipulate the rest of the lights. In a complex production, it is not unusual for the moving light fixtures to be controlled with one board while the static stage lights are controlled with another.

Directional Control

The direction of the beam of light is controlled in one of two ways. Either a mirror is used to direct the beam of light to the focus point or the entire fixture pans and tilts.

The advantage to the mirror system is that you don't have to rotate the entire instrument. Moving light fixtures are heavy—weighing anywhere from 30 to 100+ pounds. The mirror is lightweight, and its movements can be controlled with less powerful motors than would be required to rotate the whole fixture. An added bonus is that the smaller motors and associated hardware generally make less noise. The heavier, and more complex, moving light fixtures such as the High End Technobeam and the Martin Roboscan (Figure 10.7) use mirrors for directional control of the light. Lighter-weight,

Figure 10.7   Some moving light fixtures use a mirror for directional control of the light. (A) Cyberlight Techno-beam. (Courtesy of High End Systems Inc.) (B) Roboscan Pro 918. (Courtesy of Martin Professional.)

(A)   (B)

less optically complex instruments use whole-fixture pan and tilt motion to direct the light.

Examples of Moving Light Fixtures

As mentioned above, the features included in a particular fixture design vary widely.

The Cyberlight (Figure 10.8A) is a complex fixture that uses almost every available feature. Weighing just over 100 pounds, it has an encapsulated arc source, mechanical dimmer, mirror directional control, variable diffusion, motorized zoom and focus, three separate internally mounted dichroic color systems, and both moving and static gobos that can be used independently or in conjunction.

The Varilite VL500 Wash Luminare (Figure 10.8B) can be equipped with either a tungsten-halogen or arc source. The T-H models use the theatre's

(A)   (B)   (C)

Figure 10.8 Moving light fixtures. (A) Cyberlight Turbo by High End. (Courtesy of High End Systems Inc.) (B) Varilite VL500. (Courtesy of Vari-Lite.) (C) MAC 700. (Courtesy of Martin Professional.)

dimming system, or they can be equipped with an internal dimmer. Arc-equipped models have an internal mechanical douser. Both models have a dichroic color changer, interchangeable front lenses for beam control, and an internal diffuser mechanism on some models. Directional control is achieved by panning and tilting the whole fixture.

The Martin MAC 700 Profile (Figure l0.8C) has a arc source, mechanical dimming, motorized zoom and focus, dichroic color mixing, gobo wheel and gobo animation, and strobe effects. Directional control is also achieved by panning and tilting the entire fixture.

The Martin lighting company offers a system that enables up to 64 separate moving light fixtures to track up to four performers as they move about the stage. The system is computer based. Each performer wears a wireless microphone as she moves about the stage. Four ultrasonic speakers are located at the four corners of the performing space. The speakers each emit a sound above the threshold of human hearing. Sound, even ultrasonic sound, travels at 741 miles per hour at sea level. Given that the performer will be a specific distance from each of the four speakers at any given moment, the computer calculates her position by measuring the time it takes the sound to get from each speaker to the wireless mike that she's wearing. The system then relays that information to the moving light fixtures, which follow the performer's every move with the light. Wybron also makes a similar computer-based ultrasonic tracking system.

LED-sourced fixtures

Heat sink a metal device used to draw heat away from, heat-sensitive electronics and vent heat to the air without the use of fans.

Currently, high-output LEDs are being used in several types of theatrical lighting instruments. The basic advantages of LEDs over incandescent lamps were discussed in Chapter 4, "Lenses, Lamps, Reflectors, and Lighting Instruments." But there are several characteristics that make this source very intriguing to those in the lighting industry.

Because of their small physical size, a number of individual LEDs can be clustered together to effectively create a single lamp of sufficient output to be useful for stage lighting. These clusters have already been used to create PAR- and strip-light-type lamps as shown in Figure 10.9. Further development in this area is challenged by one of the by-products of LED clustering—heat. Individual LEDs don't generate much heat, but, when they are clustered together, heat can build to destructive levels, particularly for those units in the center of the cluster. Current fixture design removes this heat with **heat sinks**. Effective heat dissipation will continue to be a primary, but solvable, design challenge as higher wattage, brighter LEDs that generate even more heat are developed.

LEDs require DC power while stage lighting systems use AC power. This requires separate rectifier transformers, such as the unit illustrated in Figure 10.10, are needed to provide DC electricity to the LED units. LEDs can run on AC electricity, but because LEDs only conduct when exposed to a positive electrical charge, and because AC changes polarity 60 times a second, an LED powered with AC electricity produces a noticeable 60-cycle-per-second flicker. Unless an economically viable AC-powered LED is developed, which isn't too likely, the need for a separate DC supply to power these fixtures will probably continue.

Because LEDs can be designed to produce light in a very narrow color range, it is possible—by using separately controlled red, blue, and green LEDs

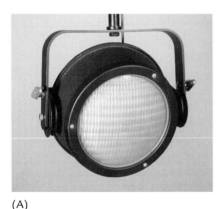

(A)

(B)

Figure 10.9 LED-sourced lighting instruments. (A) Altman SpectraPAR. (Courtesy of Altman Lighting.) (B) Xilver Xolar LT. Both fixtures use LEDs as the light source. Both fixtures control beam spread with changeable lenses. (Courtesy of Xilver.)

Figure 10.10   The LED300 power supply is used to distribute control data and 24 volt DC power to LED-lamped fixtures. (Courtesy of Doug Fleenor Design.)

in the same housing—to produce over 16 million colors. The previously mentioned Altman SpectraPAR fixture, shown in Figure 10.9, has this color-mixing capability.

The high-output, color-mixing capabilities of LED sources, as well as their inherent lower electrical consumption, are the primary reasons that many people in the lighting industry, not only those in theatre, but in media and architectural lighting as well, are excited about the developments in this area. There don't appear to be any insurmountable impediments to the continued development of LEDs for use in stage-lighting instruments. It will be exciting to watch what happens in this arena in the next few years.

FOG AND HAZE

Imagine 20 or 30 beams of light randomly sweeping the large stage and vast audience of a rock concert in an apparently aimless pattern. Suddenly, in a single beat, the lights simultaneously change color, zoom in, and focus on a seemingly tiny performer standing at the front of the huge stage. The effect is startling, dynamic, and impressive. But without fog or haze effects the effect would be lost because, to be seen, light must be reflected from something. Filling the air with fog or haze makes the moving hard-edged shafts of light visible.

Most commercially available **fog** or **haze** generators use environmentally safe solutions to generate the smoke used to create their effects. However, prior to using any smoke, fog, or haze effects, you should be absolutely certain that the solution you're using is safe for both performers and audience.

The smoke generated by fog and haze machines is created by heating the atomized vapor of the smoke formula or solution. A fan is needed to push the smoke out of the machine, and many machines use a variable-speed fan so

SAFETY TIP

Fog: A low-lying smoke effect.

Haze: A smoke effect that fills the entire stage space.

There are several common-sense rules that should be followed when you are using fog or haze effects. First, be sure that the liquid to be used with the machine is environmentally safe and safe for people to breathe. Second, be sure that the liquid you're intending to use was designed for use with the specific machine you'll be using. Third, if the fog or haze is going to cover any surface on which the talent moves or dances, make sure it doesn't make that surface slick. Be sure to thoroughly read, and understand, the material safety data sheets (MSDSs) for the various fog products that you will be using *before* using them.

that the volume of smoke can be adjusted. Although most smoke generators operate on 120 VAC, some have built-in battery packs and aerosol drivers so that they can be disconnected from the power cord for easy movement around the stage.

Fog effects are generated by cooling the smoke so that it will hug the stage floor. Commercially available machines like those shown in Figure 10.11 generally use either liquid carbon dioxide or air conditioning–like refrigerating components to cool the smoke. When the smoke isn't cooled, it disperses throughout the stage house. Examples of commercial haze generators are shown in Figure 10.12.

(A)

(B)

Figure 10.11   Fog machines. (A) Fog Machine: Fogger Pro. (B) Fog Machine: G300 Mark II. (Courtesy of Le Maitre Special Effects Inc.)

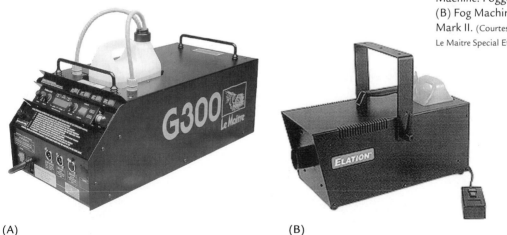

(A)

(B)

Figure 10.12   Haze generators. (A) Radiance Hazer (water-base hazer). (Courtesy of Le Maitre Special Effects Inc.) (B) Elation haze generator. (Courtesy of Elation Professional.)

Truss: An engineered structure, usually made out of metal tubing, suspended above the stage or auditorium. Used as a hanging position for lighting equipment.

STAGE SCAFFOLDING

It may seem incongruous to include stage scaffolding in a lighting book. But stage scaffolding, particularly **trusses**, is commonly used with moving light fixtures.

One of the basic laws of physics states that every action has an equal and opposite reaction. When a moving light fixture pans or tilts, an equal force is exerted in the opposite direction. The strength of that force increases with the speed of the movement and the weight of the fixture. If a number of fixtures mounted on the same pipe, stand, or truss are performing the same movement at the same time, the resultant forces can be surprisingly high.

Single pipes suspended from cables—the standard rig for a stage flying system—are designed to lift and lower static scenery such as drops, flats, and nonmoving lighting instruments like ERSs, fresnels, and PARs. Panning or tilting even one moving light fixture would start the whole pipe swinging like a giant pendulum each time you ran it. A group of moving light fixtures would only exacerbate the situation. To stabilize the pipe, you could anchor it to the stage floor and stage-house wall, but you would have to make certain that the rig didn't interfere with other flying pipes or the movement of scenery or talent on the stage floor.

The stable platform that a scaffolding/truss system provides is one reason that scaffolding is used for concert tours. Another is portability. Concert tours normally play one- or two-night stands, and the stage and grid structures must be assembled and disassembled quickly. For the foregoing reasons, scaffolding and truss systems are the mode of choice for all traveling shows that erect their own stage and grid systems.

PREVISUALIZATION SOFTWARE

A relatively new development in computer support for lighting design is previsualization software. This software enables the designer to see what the lighting is going to look like before the show is hung. Currently avail-

SAFETY TIP

Any time you are planning to work with trusses or scaffolding it is essential that the system be properly engineered. For your protection, and for the protection of people working on the stage and the audience, be sure to consult with an appropriately qualified engineer from a reputable supplier of theatrical truss systems in the design and construction of your system.

able programs such as WYSIWYG (a software program and an acronym for What You See Is What You Get) and VectorWorks Spotlight with ESP Vision make it possible, using 3D model files of the scenic design, to see what the lighting will look like before you ever set foot in the performance space. You create the lighting by using the plot, section, and instrument schedule files and setting dimmer levels for the various instruments. It is possible to create stills to show how the lighting will look at any given moment in the production. You can also create real-time animations to show what cue transitions will look like.

You can download trial versions of either or both programs mentioned above, take a tour, and get an "up close and personal" view of this useful and exciting new tool for the lighting designer. Alternatively, your school's computer lab may already have copies of these programs that you can access.

Neither WYSIWYG nor ESP Vision was originally developed to help lighting designers present their visual concepts to other members of the production team. Their original purpose was, and still is, to enable designers to preprogram cues, primarily for moving light fixtures. An example may help explain. In the real world, time is money. Time that is available to the lighting personnel in performance spaces is normally very limited because it is quite expensive. So lighting designers are rarely afforded the luxury of having enough time in the actual performance space to set cues after load-in. Enter the previsualization programs. They allow the designers to see what light cues are going to look like on a computer screen before the lighting equipment is ever moved into the theatre. Those cues are loaded into the light boards prior to move-in. When the equipment is in the performance space, the limited time available is used to make any of the necessary adjustments that inevitably crop up in any production.

Even given the above, it should be clear to anyone who has seen the capabilities of these various previsualization programs that digital imagery has the potential to provide an extremely accurate, evocative visualization of the designer's intentions that simply wasn't available before.

Unfortunately, right now, the fly-in-the-ointment for the animation/time-based visualizations is the amount of time that it takes to create them. You can't produce these visualizations without a 3D computer file of the scenic design. If the scenic designer has not created one you're often stuck because, as a rule, lighting designers don't have the time to create one in addition to their own work. On top of that, unless you have a computer specifically equipped for high-speed rendering, each animation can take hours to create. Then again, because software development and computer technology advance so rapidly, it shouldn't be too long before this "rendering time" issue ceases to be a problem. And it probably won't be too long before the majority of scenic designers use computer drafting and rendering, so the availability of 3D digital models of scenic designs won't be an issue either.

Even by the time you read this, these programs and others like them may enable you to quickly see the evocative difference that results in a cross fade when you change the fade time from, for example, three to ten seconds. When you can make those kinds of changes quickly and easily, these programs will really have come of age.

However, once again, I feel compelled to issue a caveat: remember that these programs are simply tools of the designer. While they can provide an exciting visualization of what the lighting will look like once the instruments are hung and the cues programmed, they in no way substitute for the designer's need to have a clear vision of what he/she wants to do with the light to support the production concept and the knowledge to accomplish that vision.

In the next chapter we will begin the exciting exploration of the knowledge and information needed to create a lighting design.

CHAPTER 11

The Design Process

Design is a process, not an art. But the steps in that process are easily understood. This chapter and the next two explore the process of creating a lighting design by investigating three concepts: the design process, the image of light, and the lighting key.

However, before you learn these concepts, you need to fully understand their purpose and function. They are simply road maps. They provide directions to your destination if you don't know the way. Once you learn the route you won't need the map. But the map is always available if you get lost.

Just as a road map isn't the trip, the process isn't the design. After you've learned these processes and concepts and used them several times, you would be well served to consciously forget about them. Why? Because an unfettered mind—one that isn't concentrating on slavishly following each step in a process—is more creative. Unconsciously, when you start a design project, you'll still be guided by the principles and steps that you learned, but you will be concentrating more on the concept and appearance of the design and less on how to create it. But, just like a road map is useful when you're lost, you can always come back to the process if you find yourself stuck in the visual equivalent of writer's block. It will help you get to your destination: a functional, artful, lighting design.

As mentioned above, design is not an art, but rather a process, a series of steps through which we pursue the goal of creating what we hope will be a work of art—a lighting design. The design process is a method for finding answers to questions. Although the examples and terms used in this chapter will direct your thinking toward lighting design and production, the principles of the design process can be applied with equally productive results to other theatrical design areas, acting, directing, and—for that matter—life

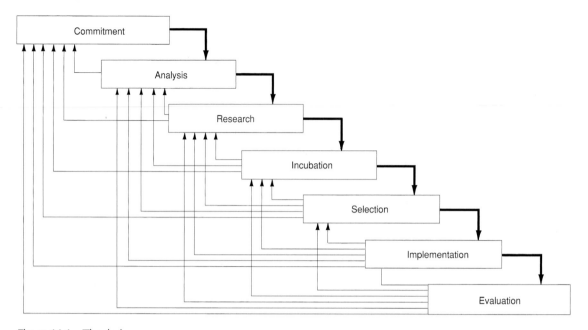

Figure 11.1   The design process is not simply a linear progression. As you move through the steps of the design process, you monitor your progress by continually checking back to see where you have been.

in general. These principles and techniques can help you discover an appropriate and creative solution to almost any design problem. This problem-solving model consists of seven distinct phases:

1. Commitment

2. Analysis

3. Research

4. Incubation

5. Selection

6. Implementation

7. Evaluation.

Unfortunately, the design process isn't a simple, linear progression. As you move from step to step, you must check back on your previous steps to make sure that you are headed in the right direction with your proposed solution. Figure 11.1 shows the back-and-forth movement that occurs as you move through the various stages of the design process. Although Satchel Paige, the wise old pitcher, once advised, "Don't look back; something may be gaining on you," you would do well to look back during your progression through the design process, because the thing that might be gaining on you could be a new thought, a better mousetrap.

COMMITMENT
. . . .

Commitment is the most important step in the whole design process. If you wholeheartedly *commit* your energies to an assignment, you are promising yourself that you will do the best work you can possibly do. Your quality of effort is a direct reflection of your level of commitment.

A simple semantic game may help you commit yourself to an assignment. Use the word *problem* as infrequently as possible—it has a negative connotation—and substitute the word *challenge*. Everybody likes a challenge: the word itself hints at fun, games, and competition. When your problem has been transformed into a challenge, it automatically becomes more interesting and manageable.

ANALYSIS
. . . .

The analysis step in the design process has two objectives: (1) gathering information that will help clarify and refine the definition of the challenge you are facing and (2) identifying areas that will require further research. Analysis in theatrical production is primarily a search for information and an objective evaluation of the data you discover. Prime sources of this information are members of the production design team—the producer, director, and your fellow designers. In your discussions with them, you need to examine everything—production style, concepts, budgets, schedules—that is relevant to your design project. "*Who* is producing the play? *What* is the production budget? *Where* is the play being produced? *When* is the design due? *Why* are we doing this play? *How* is the lighting equipment we're renting being moved to the theatre?" The answers to these questions will provide you with information that will further define and clarify your challenge. Each answer should also raise another question or two in your mind. Ask them. This **stream-of-consciousness questioning** can provide you with invaluable information about your challenge.

Carry a small notebook or **PDA** with you. Whenever a thought or an idea pops into your mind, regardless of how inconsequential it seems, put it into your notebook. These thoughts can be anything relevant to the design challenge. A thought about a character's texture—"He is rough like burlap"—is an idea that should be noted. An impression that the atmosphere of

Stream-of-consciousness questioning: Asking whatever relevant questions pop into your mind in the course of a discussion.

PDA: Personal Digital Assistant. A small, hand-held computer.

Talk It Over

The most unified production concepts are developed as a result of talking. In a production of *Cabaret* at the University of Arizona, the production design team began preliminary concept discussions in early January for a production that was to open on April 25.

The director indicated at the first meeting that he wanted to stress the decadence of Berlin society. Our initial informal discussions centered on what this decadence should look like. Someone said that the cabaret should appear to be below ground level (to subliminally support the idea of descending into the hell that was about to engulf Germany). Another person mentioned that it could be useful to have four towers onstage with followspots on top, because the audience might make a connection between them and the guard towers in a concentration camp. The di-

rector said he wanted to have the cabaret audience watching the onstage action (cabaret and noncabaret scenes) at all times. He thought that this device would add an appropriately voyeuristic quality. Ideas just seemed to pop up as we all became more excited about the project.

Within a month we developed the production concept through our discussions at these once-a-week meetings. We all brought rough sketches, photos, and ideas to every meeting. We discussed everything—acting style, acting areas, color, visual motifs, atmosphere, history. When the deadline for final designs arrived, we all knew what everyone else was thinking and doing.

This example shows what can happen when the production design team, under the leadership and coordination of the director, works together to

evolve the production concept. For a variety of reasons, however, it frequently isn't possible for the director and designers to sit around a table and work together to develop the production concept. When this happens, a good director usually adopts a more authoritarian posture in the development of the production concept. He or she develops a primary production concept and discusses it in individual meetings with the designers. The designers then work toward this concept.

The two methods work equally well. Quality productions can be achieved with either method. The common denominator is communication. A good production concept can evolve only if the director and designers talk to one another and share their ideas, thoughts, and imagination.

the play is hot, heavy, and sticky is important. Your sense that the play is soft and curved, not sharp and hard, should also be noted.

The Questioning Process

Questioning is one of the keys to creativity. Your drive to create is based, to a great extent, on your perceived need for change, or your creative discontent with the status quo. If you are satisfied with everything in your world, you will see no need to change, modify, or create anything.

To analyze effectively it is necessary to shed fear—fear of criticism, fear of making mistakes, fear of seeming less than brilliant, fear of being thought

✳ How Does It Really Look?

Several years ago I designed the sets for a production of Somerset Maugham's venerable play *Rain* at the University of Arizona. One of my graduate students was doing the lighting design. The play is set in an old hotel on the tropical Pacific island of Pago Pago. Everything to do with this production was rushed, and we didn't take much time for production meetings. When the student lighting designer asked me what kind of atmosphere the lights should suggest, I told him that it should be hot, oppressively hot. When we got to the lighting rehearsal the set looked hot, but it was a dry desert heat, not the sticky closeness of the tropics. After talking with the lighting designer, I discovered that he had never been out of Arizona, and so he had no firsthand experience with the wet heat of the tropics.

The moral of this story is that lighting designers need to do research. You need to know about the climate and color of the sunlight in the locale of the play. Ideally, you would be able to experience the locale firsthand; but because most production budgets don't include travel money for the lighting designer to do research, you'll have to accomplish it in other ways. The excellent photos that accompany *National Geographic* stories about various locales provide a wealth of information about the quality and color of light as well as the density of the air (humidity). Look at other picture magazines. Study any and all sources that can tell you what it *looks like* in the locale of the play.

You can also make reasonable comparisons between different geographic areas. With any lighting design you're trying to create the psychological impression of an atmosphere in the audience's mind. You're not trying to replicate the climate of an actual place. If you're designing a show set in Pago Pago and you've never been there, think of where you've been that is similar. Florida during the summer is humid and tropical. If you've been there, try to remember the quality of the light and use that as a base. Chances are very good you've never been to the upper reaches of the Himalayas. So what do you do if you have to design *K-2?* Anyone who's been to the Rockies has seen the clarity and crisp brilliance of sunlight in mountain air. If you've experienced January in one of our northern states, you know what cold looks and feels like. Translate those experiences.

When designing lights, you have to do research and then imaginatively translate that research to create a new reality that will exist on the stage.

a fool or somehow different. Fear inhibits thinking and makes us afraid to ask questions. All too frequently I hear students in my classes say, "I don't want to ask a dumb question, but. . . ." As far as I am concerned, the only dumb question is one that isn't asked.

Analyze the script, question the director, question the other members of the production design team, and question the producer. Learn what they are thinking, feeling, and planning for the production. Analyze what they say. See how it fits in with your reactions and plans. The more information you receive, the more source material you will have to draw on when you finally begin to design.

Pigment: Material that imparts color to a substance such as paint or dye.

RESEARCH

As you gather information, you will discover small pockets of knowledge in which your personal experience and background are weak. List them in your notebook as the areas in which research is necessary. You will be doing both background research and conceptual research.

Background Research

Designers have to study the historical background of each production they design. This type of research involves searching the library for books, catalogs, paintings, periodicals, and other sources of information about the era.

Your historical research should include reading about previous productions of the play and may include looking at photos and sketches of those prior productions. Don't fall prey, however, to the temptation to simply duplicate someone else's design. That practice squelches your creativity and, more pragmatically, it is illegal in most states.

Additional background research in the field of color will also be necessary. A thorough understanding of this extremely important area will enable the designer to match and blend colors in **pigment** and light. Further, by studying the psychology of color, you will be able to select colors for the lights that will help establish the mood and atmosphere of the production. Color is discussed in detail in Chapter 9.

Conceptual Research

Conceptual research involves devising multiple solutions to specific design challenges. In reading a script, for example, you may discover that the first act takes place in a seedy apartment at night. The second act occurs in the same apartment the following morning. Through conceptual research you would resolve this challenge in as many ways as possible.

Unfortunately, we all seem to have difficulty conceiving of any more than two or three possible solutions to any given challenge. Too often our brains go numb and refuse to dream up new ideas. Psychologists refer to this type of nonthinking state as a perceptual block. If the perceptual block can be eliminated, our ability to devise, or create, additional solutions to any given problem greatly improves. In other words, removing perceptual blocks significantly increases our personal creative ability.

INCUBATION

How many times have you left an examination room and then suddenly remembered the answer to a question that eluded you while you were writing the test? How many times have you come up with the solution to a problem

❋ Unblock Your Thinking

How can we get rid of our perceptual blocks? By eliminating the cause, we can usually eliminate the block. Proper identification of the real challenge is extremely important. Many times challenges are not what they first seem to be. If a play has three scenes, the first during late afternoon, the second at sunset, and the third in early evening, one of your design challenges would be to devise ways of making the audience accept and believe the three different time periods. To most of us that would mean gelling the basic acting-area lights with daytime colors and gelling some additional instruments with night colors and adjusting the levels between the two to make the night scene look more "shadowy." Maybe we'd throw in a sunset effect for fun. That's fairly normal. This type of scene is lit that way all the time. But couldn't the challenge be solved just as well by designing three separate plots for each scene? Wouldn't it be possible to produce the play outdoors and start it just before sunset so that it could be lit realistically as the big instrument in the sky slips below the horizon? How about having each scene in a different theatre and moving the audience between them? These additional solutions to the challenge are the

result of nothing more than a careful examination of the specific questions being posed in the challenge.

DEFINE YOUR CHALLENGE MORE BROADLY

If you thought about the traditional way of cross-fading between daytime and nighttime colors in the previous problem, you were actually defining the challenge too closely. By unconsciously limiting your quest for possible solutions to the traditionally accepted methods, you were shutting off a whole realm of new, effective (if somewhat quirky) solutions to the challenge. Think creatively about the elements of the challenge, and don't accept only the commonplace answers to the questions posed by the challenge.

OVERCOME TUNNEL VISION

When you are working on a design, it is easy (and egocentrically convenient) to fail to see your assignment from the viewpoint of others involved in the challenge. It's easy to forget, when selecting a predominately amber/yellow palette for the lights, that the costumer has the heroine in a lavender gown. The result will be a gown that's gray instead of lavender. The thoughtless selection of pink as your predominate hue for the lights will similarly kill the light-green walls that the scene

designer labored so hard to achieve.

Tunnel vision can be avoided if members of the production design team discuss their ideas in production meetings. By conferring on a regular basis, the director and designers can remain aware of everyone else's work as it progresses from conception to completion.

AVOID VISUAL STEREOTYPING

Visual stereotyping refers to seeing what you expect to see rather than what is actually in front of you. It limits your ability to conceive of existing elements in new combinations. If you think of the nighttime sky as simply being blue, then you probably won't experiment with various tones of green and dark lavender, which can provide you with luminescent and realistic nighttime hues. Don't cut yourself off before you start. Critically look at the night sky and you'll see it contains a whole host of colors, tints, and shades.

REMEMBER DETAILS SELECTIVELY

People remember things selectively. If we decide that something doesn't have great personal significance, we tend to forget it. To demonstrate this principle, try to recall the lighting patterns in your dorm room, apartment, or home.

(continued)

✳ Unblocking Your Thinking (*continued*)

Where are the sources? What is their distribution pattern? Where are the highlights and shadows? You pass through this place every day, but you don't look at it very closely.

All of us remember details that we have determined are important for us to recall. Albert Einstein was reputed not to have known his own telephone number. When asked why, he reportedly said that he didn't want to clutter up his mind with information that he could look up.

Although it is very important for a lighting designer to have a thorough knowledge of the various areas directly and indirectly related to the field, it is equally important to follow Einstein's dictum and not clutter up your mind with details that can be found in a reference work.

---

after having "slept on it"? In both cases the information necessary to answer the questions was locked in your subconscious and only needed time and a little stress reduction to allow the answer to float into your conscious mind.

Incubation provides you with time to let ideas hatch. During this period you should basically forget about the project. Your subconscious mind will use the time to sort through the information you've gathered in the previous steps and may actually construct a solution to the design challenge or at least point you in a valid direction.

Give yourself enough time to let your subconscious mind mull over the data that you have absorbed. It isn't possible to do your best work if you wait for a deadline and then rush through an assignment. Quality work happens more easily if you allow time for incubation.

SELECTION
. . . .

Selection is the step in the design process in which you sift through all the data you've accumulated and decide on your specific design concept. Because each designer's choices affect the work of all members of the production design team, all the designs need to be discussed in another production meeting.

The lighting designer can submit sketches showing the general characteristics of the concept for the lighting design, if such sketches are appropriate. Or she or he can fire up a computer and, using WYSIWYG or a similar program (see Chapter 10 for more details), provide a computer simulation of the lighting. At the least, the lighting designer presents the intended palette and a verbal description of the atmospheric effect of the lighting during the production meeting.

The Gobo Trick

A lot of art is the result of happy accident. When designing the lights for some forgotten production, I noticed that one area of the stage seemed to have a rough texture. I went up on stage and looked more closely. The floor didn't have any texture; it was painted a smooth, flat color. Then I looked up at the lights. One of the instruments had a gobo (a thin metal template that creates a shadow pattern) left in it from a previous production. That instrument was creating the texture. Although I took the gobo out of the instrument, I remembered the effect. Now whenever I want to create a textured atmosphere I put gobos in the instruments.

The moral? Always evaluate what you've done, even if you think it's a "mistake." Just because something isn't right for one situation doesn't mean it won't be right for another.

The selection phase of the design process is finished when the director feels satisfied that all design areas support the production design concept.

IMPLEMENTATION

Quite simply, the implementation phase begins when you stop planning and start doing. At this time you produce the light plot, lighting sectional, and instrument schedule, as well as the other paperwork associated with the lighting design. The lighting designer then supervises the hanging and focusing of the lights and determines the intensity levels and timing for all lighting cues.

EVALUATION

Evaluation takes place within each step of the design process, and it also occurs when the project is completed. This final evaluation, or review, is not so much a back-patting session as an examination of the methods and materials used to reach the final design goal. You need to evaluate your selections to see if they were really appropriate and to determine if they could be used in the future in another context.

You need to look objectively at the communication process that took place inside and outside the various production conferences. Examine the

Design Process Checklist

The following checklist provides a review that will help you use each step of the design process.

COMMITMENT
1. Make a commitment to yourself to do your best work on the project.
2. Overcome any negative feelings toward the project.

ANALYSIS
1. Gather information to clarify and refine the definition of the challenge.
2. Identify areas needing further research.
3. Read the play.
4. Talk to other members of the production design team.

RESEARCH
1. Background research
   a. Study the social and artistic history of the period of the play.
   b. Study all the trends and styles of the architecture, lighting fixtures, and the like for the period.
2. Conceptual research
   a. Be a mental pack rat. Think up as many potential solutions to the challenge as possible.
   b. Don't judge or discard any idea. Save them all.

INCUBATION
1. Just forget about the project. Do something else.
2. Allow enough time for your subconscious mind to work on the challenge.

SELECTION
1. Develop your solution to the challenge.
2. Don't be afraid to take a piece of one idea and a piece of another to create the most effective solution.

IMPLEMENTATION
1. Stop thinking and start doing.
2. Produce all necessary drawings, sketches, and plans to facilitate the realization of the design.
3. Hang, focus, and run the show.

EVALUATION
1. Reflect on the challenge. Did you do everything you could to make it succeed?
2. Review your use of the design process. Did you fully analyze the question? Did you do sufficient background and conceptual research?
3. Did you effectively communicate your ideas and thoughts to the other members of the design team?

various interchanges between yourself and the director, producer, and other designers to see if communication can be improved the next time around. Also evaluate the judgments you made to see if anything that might have helped was left out, ignored, or rejected.

As you become more familiar with the design process, you will discover that your own work is more creative and that you can produce it faster and more easily. The design process is a valuable, efficient, time-saving, and frustration-reducing tool. Use it and enjoy.

CHAPTER 12

The Image of Light

Image of light: A picture or concept of what the light should look like for a production.

The **image of light** is a metaphor. It is a mental picture or concept of the quality of the light for a specific production. Frequently the image is abstracted. Very often it will have no direct connection with any specific visual element in the play. However (and this is important), the image of light is based on the production concept that has been evolved by all members of the production design team.

The purposes of the image of light are twofold: (1) to provide the designer with a visual image that summarizes his or her thoughts about the lighting for a production; (2) as a guide that helps determine placement, coloring, and intensity balance of instruments used in the lighting design. An example may help explain the first concept. The second concept will be discussed later in this chapter. The image of light that I evolved for a production of *King Lear* was the profile of an ancient crone, her long filthy hair streaming behind her as she tightly clutched her shawl and stared defiantly into the teeth of a gale. Her deeply wrinkled skin had a strange, translucent gray pallor.

The above-described image of light was a visual synthesis of my thoughts about the play, sort of a visual shorthand. It was created from information I gained during the analysis and research steps of the design process. That information came from reading the script, attending production conferences, asking a lot of questions, listening to input from the director and other designers, and doing background research in the library.

The image of light doesn't just magically appear as a fully developed concept. Normally, bits and pieces come to you as you learn about the play and your production. And the image of light evolves as you gather more information. For example, the first part of the image of which I was consciously aware was the gale-force wind. For me the cold, raw wind of a North Atlantic gale symbolizes the strong sense of desolation and isolation I got from the script. Only later, after a production-meeting discussion about the characters' psychological makeup, did I see the image of the crone, chin upthrust and defiant, glaring into the gale as if daring it to blow harder.

The incubation period of the design process is significant to the development of the image of light. Each time you stop working on the project—whether to sleep, eat, or do something else—your subconscious mind sifts through the information you've gathered and tries to put it into some kind of order. For many people the "answers" that are developed during this subconscious solution-finding process are symbolic rather than specific. That is why the image of light normally does not spring full-blown from your mind. Each time you work on the project your subconscious develops a "solution" to the information you've gathered. As you acquire more information you get more "solutions." Eventually, after you've consciously completed the information-gathering and conceptual research phases of your project, your subconscious will, if you allow it sufficient incubation time, synthesize all of the information into a "recommended" solution. For many people, that solution will be a symbolic visualization such as the image of light.

As indicated above, an important part of the information-gathering phase of the design process is script analysis. Script analysis comprises two distinct processes. The first process is the textual analysis—the script is read (usually several times) for the intellectual and emotional stimuli that will create specific visual images in the mind of the designer. These images are the creative seeds of the lighting design. The second process is a visual analysis of those images. The designer analyzes the specific visual images obtained from textual analysis into the four controllable qualities of light—distribution, intensity, movement, and color.

The visual concept of a production frequently starts with ideas gleaned from the script; however, it is always modified and enhanced through discussions with the other members of the production design team during the initial production meetings. In these meetings the director and designers freely exchange ideas on the style and context of the production concept. (See the box "Talk It Over" in Chapter 11 for more information on the evolution of the production concept.) In these production meetings, the lighting designer also sees the color palettes being used by both the scenic and costume designers.

It is equally important that the lighting designer conduct background research of the type suggested in Chapter 11. Assuming that the production style is relatively realistic, it is imperative that the designer understand what light actually looks like in the physical location of the play. An understanding of the emotional basis—tragic, happy, sad, and so forth—of the play as a whole, as well as the individual scenes and moments within those scenes, is essential. Probably more than any other element, the emotional tone of these segments determines the duration or timing of the fades used with the cues that light these scenes.

From the information gathered from the script and production meetings, as well as from background research, the lighting designer should have evolved an image of light. Some designers like to translate the image of light into a written statement that helps communicate the intent of the lighting design to other members of the production design team.

SCRIPT ANALYSIS

It is not at all unusual for a designer to read the script of a show that she or he is going to design many times. Generally, when they read the script, designers are looking for some specific information. This information-gathering process can be divided into three steps, which I've metaphorically labeled as first, second, and third readings of the script.

First Reading

The first time you sit down with the script, just read it for fun. Discover the flavor of the play. Learn its general story line, the nature of its characters, their socioeconomic status, and their interrelationships. One of the first things you see when you open the script is the description of the physical environment of the play. Usually written in italics just before the opening lines,

In the Beginning, Think Creatively

If the lighting is to be an integral, creative part of the production concept, you need to let the words, images, and music of the production meetings and script stimulate your imagination into creating a visual image, or series of images, that support the production concept. To help that process along, think in terms of the functions of light (visibility, selective focus, modeling, mood) that will help or enhance the production concept.

Probably the last things you should think about during the early stages of the creative process are the tools of the designer (instruments, dimmers, cable, and so forth). This type of tunnel-vision thinking will inevitably limit your creative thought processes. If you count your instruments before you have developed your concept, you're erecting an almost insurmountable roadblock to creativity. An effective concept can always be adapted to equipment limitations, but thinking about the limitations before developing a concept blocks creativity.

it describes the set and, occasionally, the costumes, sound, and lights. Unless you are working from an original script, these descriptions are usually taken from the stage manager's prompt book for the first major professional production of the play and explain the specific designs for that particular production. These descriptions shouldn't be thought of as the correct design solutions for the play; they are just one way that the show can be designed. Your production is entitled to a fresh design treatment that will be appropriate to its personnel, time, place, and budget. To believe that you have to, or should, copy the original design is an insult to your creative ability. Use the descriptive information in the script along with the other information you gather to synthesize an original design concept.

Second Reading

During the second reading of the script you should be looking for specific moments and incidents within the play that stimulate your imagination and provide you with strong visual and textural images and feelings. These inspirations are random, often disconnected, thoughts and impressions about the appearance of the various design elements. Jot them in your notebook or PDA. If they are more visual than verbal, sketch them.

As you continue to reread the play you will get more ideas. Ideas will also appear when you are not reading the script. They can materialize when you are talking to the director, discussing the play with another designer, eating breakfast, or walking to class. Don't judge the ideas at this point. Gather information now, and weed later.

Third Reading

In the third reading you are looking for specific mechanical information rather than broad-based concepts. Specifically, you are looking for any special lighting requirements, such as the appearance of the ghost in Shakespeare's *Hamlet* or the electric cross in Preston Jones's *The Last Meeting of the Knights of the White Magnolia*. At this time you also begin marking the location of both motivated and unmotivated light cues. A motivated light cue is caused by some specific action contained within the script, like the beginnings and endings of scenes or acts or a character's turning a light switch on or off. Unmotivated light cues are changes in the lights that are not specifically called for in the script. They are harder to detect; and, in fact, you may not see the need for any until you watch a rehearsal or two. For example, you're watching a rehearsal of *The Petrified Forest*, which is set in a lonely roadside diner in northern Arizona. The set is fairly large, and two of the main characters have some important dialogue while they sit at a small table on one side of the set. Other characters are onstage but are unimportant to the scene. You decide to help focus the audience's attention on the couple by boosting the intensity of the lights on the table just a little bit. This specific use of selective focus is an unmotivated light cue. Mark your script with the location of both motivated and unmotivated cues.

Information regarding any special effects—fires, battery-powered torches, wall sconces, or other practicals, special projections, and so forth—that influences the budgets (both time and fiscal) should also be noted at this time.

Information from the third reading is gathered not only from reading the script but also from production meetings and additional conferences with other members of the production design team. As with the first and second readings, put all the information you collect in your notebook or PDA.

It isn't intended that you rigidly adhere to the organization of the above-outlined three-step process. You may find that you think about where a wall switch or an atmosphere cue should be placed during your first reading of the script. That's fine. Note it and move on. What *is* important is that regardless of how many times you read the script you glean all the above-referenced information and material from it.

ANALYSIS OF THE IMAGE OF LIGHT

So far, this chapter has explained what the image of light is and has provided you with a method for analyzing the script. As you analyze the script, you should begin to gather images that will help you design the light for your production. To help you visualize how the lighting should look, now is a good time to go back and review the sections on "Light and Perception," "Controllable Qualities of Light," and "Functions of Stage Lighting" in Chapter 1. The concepts explained there are at the heart of visualizing an image of light.

To transfer the image of light from your mind's eye onto paper, you must be able to analyze the image of light for its component elements of distribution, intensity, movement, and color. This is the first step in using the image of light to guide the creation of your lighting design.

Analysis for Distribution and Intensity

The analysis of the image of light for distribution and intensity is one of the prime factors in determining the location of the lighting instruments for a production. Modeling of actors and settings is principally a function of the direction and intensity of the light that strikes them. For these reasons it is

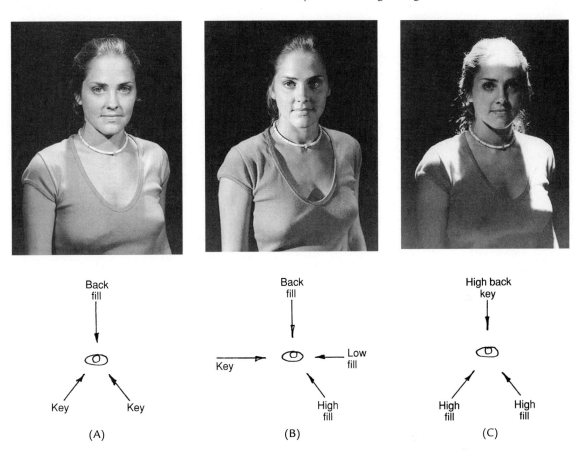

Figure 12.1   Analysis of photographs for distribution and intensity. The length of the arrows indicates the relative intensity of the individual lights.

essential that you be able to determine the direction and relative intensities of the **key** and **fill lights** that are illuminating your image of light if you hope to re-create that image onstage.

Figure 12.1 demonstrates how an image can be analyzed for distribution and intensity and the results codified through the use of the lighting key. Each picture has a different emotional impact on the viewer; but the perceived differences are caused only by lighting, for the model's pose is the same in all three. The model in Figure 12.1A is lit with a relatively smooth light evenly keyed from each front-side as shown in the accompanying lighting key. A back fill light provides some extra depth to the figure. In Figure 12.1B the model is strongly key lit from the left side. The fill lights from high front-side and low side smoothly fill the shadows. Again, a high back light helps to separate the model from the background and provides depth to her face. In Figure 12.1C the model is lit with a high back key light. The smooth front fill makes her face visible.

Key light: The brightest light in a scene.

Fill light: Light used to fill the shadows created by the key light.

☀ Key and Fill Lights

The terms *key* and *fill* are used to describe the relationship between the direction and relative intensity of light striking an object. The key light is the most intense, primary source of light for a scene; and the fill light is the slightly dimmer or more diffused light used to fill the shadows created by the key.

The concept of key and fill lights is an organizational tool. It can help codify your thinking as you struggle to determine the direction, intensity, color, and movement of the various sources that are illuminating your image of light.

The application of the concept of key and fill lights can best be explained by example. When you are analyzing the image of light, you should either see or rationalize a source light—a source or sources of illumination for the image. If your image consists of a picture of the set as it is lit for a particular (or hypothetical) moment in the play, you should be able to look around that picture and pick out the sources—table lamps, windows, fireplaces, and so forth. If your image of light is more abstract—the face of a tired old woman staring off into the distance—you should be able to analyze that face and see where the dominant light is coming from (her left, right, center, or front). In either case, the dominant light in the scene will be the key light; the less intense lights will be the fill lights.

Analysis for Movement

During the analysis phase the lighting designer usually considers movement of light only in terms of his or her feelings about the rhythm and flow of the production. After seeing a finished blocking rehearsal, the designer will have a much better feeling for the specific rhythm, flow, and movement of the production. As movement is probably the most easily adjusted of all the qualities of light, the setting of the times for the various cues is customarily done during the lighting rehearsal and adjusted during the technical and dress rehearsals (see Chapter 17, "Rehearsal and Performance Procedures").

Analysis for Color

The designer needs to pay close attention to the indications of color in his or her image of light, because those color clues provide the basis for creating the color portion of the lighting key. Color is probably the primary means that the lighting designer has for indicating the climate and temperature of a scene. It is also a key element in creating psychological atmosphere. Chapter 9 provided a number of practical tips for the use and application of color in lighting.

This chapter has introduced you to the concept of the image of light as well as a procedure that can be used for analyzing the script. Additionally, you have been provided with a method for analyzing the component elements of the image of light, which is the first step in creating the lighting design. The next chapter contains specific information about converting the image of light into a lighting key and use of the lighting key to create the lighting design.

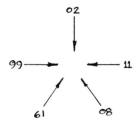

CHAPTER 13

The Lighting Key

Figure 13.1   A lighting key.

Lighting key: A drawing that indicates the plan angle and color of the various sources that illuminate the image of light.

Plan angle: The ground-plan view of an object.

Hanging positions: The various locations around the stage and auditorium where lighting instruments are placed.

Sectional angle: The angle of intersection between the axis of the cone of light emitted by an instrument and the working height—usually the height of an actor's face (about 5 feet 6 inches)—of the lighting area.

The **lighting key** (Figure 13.1) is a codification of the image of light. Specifically, it is a drawing that indicates the **plan angle** and color of the various sources that illuminate the image of light. The lighting key is used by the designer as the primary guide for determining the **hanging positions** of the lights and can be an effective tool when discussing the design with other members of the production design team. To be able to translate the image of light into a meaningful symbol, you have to understand how light works. Specifically, you have to be able to *see* light.

Light is a molding medium; it sculpts and shapes our perception and understanding of people, objects, and things. In the first section of this chapter we'll explore (with visual aids) the effects that can be achieved by manipulating two of the controllable qualities of light—distribution and intensity—to affect the functions of light: visibility, selective focus, modeling, and mood.

MODELING WITH LIGHT

As I said before, light affects the appearance of objects. Before you can hope to be a lighting designer, you have to understand the modeling effects of light. The series of photographs in Figure 13.2 illustrates how varying the direction of a single source of light affects the pattern of highlight and shadows on a model's face. To help you begin to understand how changing the direction and angle of a light affects the modeling characteristics of that light, each photograph is accompanied by a drawing that shows the relative plan and **sectional angles** of the light.

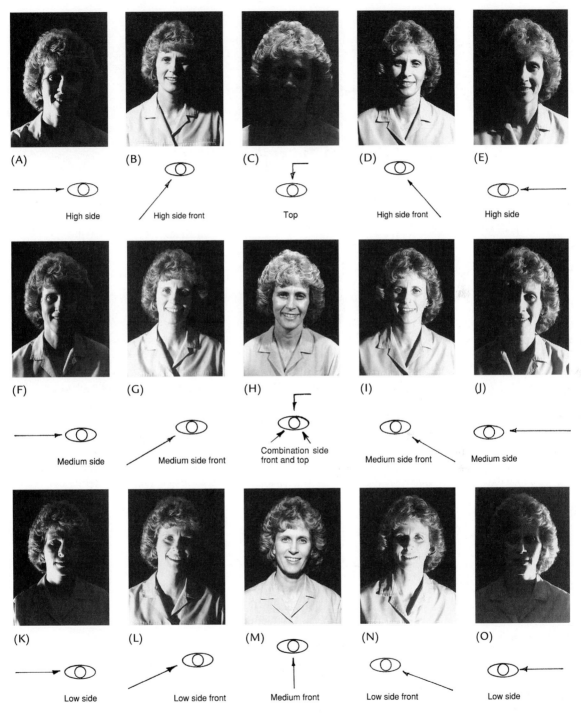

Figure 13.2 Effects of varying the direction of the light.

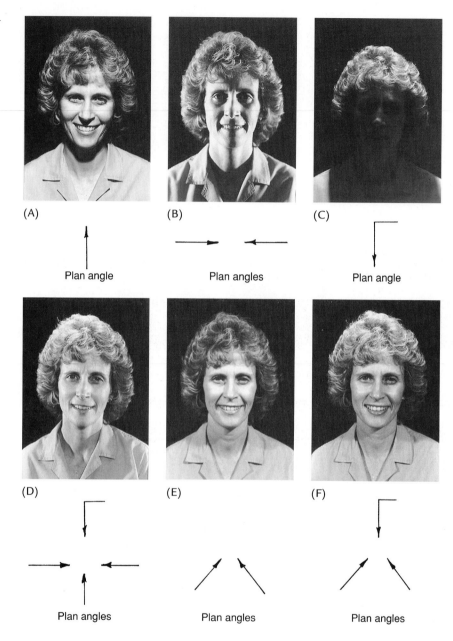

Figure 13.3 Surrounding an actor with light creates the most potential for modeling.

(A)   Plan angle

(B)   Plan angles

(C)   Plan angle

(D)   Plan angles

(E)   Plan angles

(F)   Plan angles

Stage picture: The visual appearance of the stage during a specific moment in a play.

When analyzing a photo, or a **stage picture**, it is almost impossible to discuss one quality or function of light without touching on another. Changing the direction (distribution) of the light affects both selective focus and mood. As you compare the photos in Figure 13.2, notice how you almost invariably look at the area of highlight first. Glance away from the photos;

then try to look at a shadow area first. It is almost impossible. Even when you concentrate and tell yourself, "I'm going to look at a shadow area first," you *will*, in all probability, see the highlight first. This graphic demonstration of selective focus shows the power of the instinctive human reaction that designers understand and use to manipulate the focus of the audience's attention.

Notice how your emotional response to the photos changes with the visibility of the model's face. Most people will feel relatively at ease looking at those photos where her face is fully visible. They will feel a little uncomfortable or uneasy looking at those photos where her face is fully or partially shadowed because they cannot read her facial nonverbal communication—the thoughts and intentions mirrored in her eyes and facial expressions. Again, by learning or intuition, lighting designers know, understand, and use the powerful effects of visibility on the creation of mood in the stage picture.

Surrounding an actor with a number of light sources provides the potential for modeling with light. In Figure 13.3 the direction of the light varies, but the intensity of those individual lights is held constant. A front light (Figure 13.3A) by itself is unflattering; it tends to flatten and compress facial and bodily features. Side lights (Figure 13.3B) and top light (Figure 13.3C) create highlights along the edges of the head and body but cause deep shadows across the face and front of the body. A combination of side and top lights (Figure 13.3D), together with a front light that fills the shadows created by the side and top lights, reveals the form of the model by surrounding her with light.

When lit from the side-front at about 45 degrees in plan and section (Figure 13.3E), the model is smoothly illuminated, but her facial and bodily features are slightly compressed. If a top light or back light is added to the side-front light (Figure 13.3F), the resultant rim or edge light creates a highlight that adds depth to the face and body. As you can see, the greatest potential for variations in modeling, and subsequently meaning, occurs when you position lighting instruments on all sides of the model.

CREATING THE LIGHTING KEY

After you have analyzed your image of light, you must address yourself to the challenge of codifying your thoughts on the direction and placement of the key and fill lights as dictated by that image. This process can best be described through example. Suppose that we want to light somebody standing in the middle of an otherwise bare stage. To light her effectively, we have to create an image of light—a mental picture of how we want her to look. My mental image of the scene is as follows: It's a bitterly cold, January day in Minnesota. A young girl is standing in the middle of a snow-crusted field. The sun is frozen close to the horizon; its pale, washed-out color etches

☀ More About Modeling with Light

An excellent way to learn more about the modeling capabilities of light is to develop a lighting morgue—a collection of photographs of people, objects, and paintings that you analyze for the direction, intensity, and color of their key and fill lights.

Another simple way to learn about light is to look at everyday objects—buildings, statues, trees, parked cars, and so forth—and critically examine the way they are illuminated. See how the appearance of a ball field changes from early morning to noon, noon to afternoon, and late afternoon to dusk. Notice how the range of contrast between the highlights and shadows on a statue in a park is compressed on cloudy days (as compared with clear days). Notice how the sharp-edged shadow that you see under a car on a clear day has no clearly definable edge, is softer, and is not so black on a cloudy day. Look at the same building on a clear day and on a cloudy day and notice how the vibrancy has gone from the colors on the cloudy day—how the building looks more dreary. Notice how the appearance of a city street changes radically between daytime and night—how the patterns of highlight and shadow radically alter when the streetlights and shop windows are the primary sources of light.

Only when you begin to develop your critical eye, when you begin to see how things *really* look—how light shapes our perception of what we see—can you begin to use light to manipulate the audience's understanding of the actors, sets, and costumes of the play they are watching.

jagged shadows across the field. (Specific descriptive information about the scene is vitally important, for the quality of light varies for different locales, times of the day, and times of the year.) So far, this description should provide you with enough information to "see" the scene in your mind's eye.

A cautionary note is appropriate before we launch into an analysis of this scene or *any* image of light. Each analysis is a product of an individual's imagination. Every design is a unique creation of an individual designer. Therefore, when designing for a specific play, you could have 13 different designers create 13 equally competent designs. The only proviso to this scenario would be that each of those 13 designers would have to adhere to the stylistic parameters dictated by the production concept. If they do, then, even though the designs may look significantly different, each of them is equally valid. With this proviso firmly in mind, my analysis of this scene follows: The key light is the sunlight coming from a fairly low angle in back of, and slightly to the side of, the young girl. This light should have a harsher, more strident quality than the light reflected from the snow (front), which is both soft and directionless and seems to insinuate itself into the strong shadows created by the key light.

The quality of the light chosen for a scene generally dictates the type of lighting instruments used, because, although the quality of light is determined by the intensity, color, and level of diffusion of the light, initially you need to choose instruments capable of generating the type of light you need. The back-side key light (sunlight) calls for an ERS, because the light emitted by that instrument produces the hard-edged, cohesive light needed to mimic the quality of sunlight needed for this scene. The soft, directionless quality of the front fill light suggests that a fresnel spotlight, with its soft, diffused light, would be a good choice for this light. Alternatively, ERSs could be gelled with a light diffusion to create the requisite soft-quality light for the front fill. The sunlight (key light) in our image strikes the girl over her left shoulder and from slightly above the horizontal axis, or stage floor, as illustrated in Figure 13.4. To re-create this effect, you have to place the instrument at the same angle relative to the actress as the sunlight seen in the image of light.

The fill light in our image of light is directionless and smoothly fills the shadows. To re-create this effect, we can place two fresnel spotlights in positions where they will provide a smooth, apparently directionless light on the front of the girl, although ERSs with a light diffusion gel could also be used. Instruments placed at a sectional angle of about 45 degrees provide a fairly normal angle of light. This sectional angle provides a feeling of directionless light, particularly when the two instruments are placed between 60 and 90 degrees apart so that they smoothly cover the front of the girl with light but don't override the intensity of the key light (see Figure 13.5).

If the key light ERS and the two fill light fresnels are each circuited into separate dimmers, then the relative intensities of the three instruments can be varied independently until the proper relationship (as determined by your mental picture of the image of light) is established.

While the selection and placement of the instruments and the setting of intensities for the individual lights are of primary importance in the re-creation of the image of light, the selection of color will greatly enhance the overall mood and feeling of the scene. Again, remember that there isn't a "correct" solution to this challenge. Each designer may select a different color palette, but all palettes should be based on an interpretation of the image of light. A realistic interpretation of this scene might find us selecting Roscolux 06, No-Color Straw, for the sunlight or key light. Because the shadow of a color is usually perceived as the complement of that color, Roscolux 53, Pale Lavender, might be selected for the front fill lights. The use of these colors will produce a realistic, thin tint of yellow for the sunlight and a cool, relatively complementary lavender tint for the shadow fill.

The selection of other colors will create different psychological impacts on the audience. If, for some strange reason, you decide that you want the

Figure 13.4   Key light for the "girl in the snowfield" exercise.

Figure 13.5   Fill lights for the "girl in the snowfield" exercise.

scene to have a warm or soft feeling, then you might want to go to warmer colors, say Roscolux 09, Pale Amber Gold, for the sunlight and use a not-quite-complementary hue such as Roscolux 55, Lilac, for the fill lights. (When additively mixed, Roscolux 09 and 55 produce a warm-white hue rather than the pure white that a truly complementary blend would yield.) On the other hand, you might want to enhance the bitterly cold feeling of the scene. In this case you might want to select Roscolux 61, Mist Blue, for the sunlight, and use a related, but more saturated hue such as a Roscolux 64, Light Steel Blue, or Roscolux 57, Lavender, for the fill. Working with a palette composed of closely related tints can have a significant psychological impact on your audience, but you need to remember that using a very narrow range of related (rather than complementary) colors on your lights will suppress any complementary colors in both the sets and costumes. Additionally, you probably will find that the use of related hues, particularly if they are more saturated than a thin tint, will create complementary color shadowing as described in Chapter 9. You can use related tints as long as the set and costume designers are aware of the effects that your narrow color selection will have on their palettes and approve of this restriction.

"Normal" Lighting Angles

I've mentioned "normal" lighting angles several times in this text. Normal is a relative term, but for most people a "normal" sectional angle for light striking the face is between 30 and 60 degrees. The reason for this is simple. If you live in the temperate regions of the world (where some 80 to 90 percent of the world's population lives), the sun angle relative to your body position varies between these two extremes during most daylight hours. Forty-five degrees is an average of these two extremes, and so when you re-create onstage that "average" sectional sun angle, you are in effect creating a situation that duplicates what we've learned to identify as ordinary or "normal."

In the theatre a lighting designer rarely has an opportunity to create an isolated design such as the one just described. Plays exist in time as well as space, and the lighting designer must adapt the lighting key to accommodate the full production, not just an isolated moment in the play. We will use *The Playboy of the Western World*, by John Millington Synge, to illustrate the development of a lighting key for a complete production.

Let's assume that the image of light for this production could be stated as "a bright, twinkling Irish morning." Our analysis of this statement leads us to conclude that achieving the concept of a bright, twinkling Irish morning on the stage will require creation of (1) a light and cheerful atmosphere, (2) no shadows, and (3) thin tints of springlike colors.

If an actor in our play were surrounded with light, as shown in Figure 13.6, we would have achieved one of our stated objectives—no shadows. If we adjusted the dimmers that control those lights to a fairly bright setting, we would achieve another of our objectives—a bright atmosphere. By selecting happy, springtime, pastel colors we would also meet the third objective—a cheerful springlike atmosphere.

This brief analysis of the image of light has already given us much of the information needed for completing the basic lighting key for our production. Specifically, we have determined the distribution for the basic lighting of each lighting area (four diagonal cross lights) and the basic range of the color palette (pastel tints). Let me hasten to add that this particular solution is not the "correct" analysis of the image of light. There are myriad other possibilities, all of them equally "correct." You could have light from more or fewer directions (Figure 13.7A and B). You could also interpret the concept of "springtime pastel colors" to mean thin tints of cool colors as opposed to warm—it just depends on your personal understanding of the idea of a springtime atmosphere.

With the foregoing proviso firmly in mind, we make the conscious decision that our lighting key is going to be based on a five-sided distribution

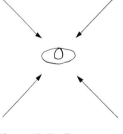

Figure 13.6 Four-source lighting key for *The Playboy of the Western World*.

Figure 13.7 Six- and three-source lighting keys for *The Playboy of the Western World*.

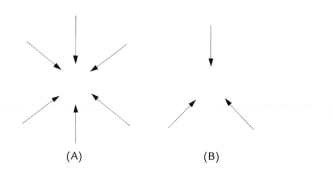

(A)   (B)

pattern (Figure 13.8). This pattern will provide a smooth, shadowless light that will support our interpretation of the image of light. Additionally, the top or back light (the arrow at the top of the pentagon) will provide a nice rim or halo light around the head and shoulders of the actors to prevent them from blending into the set.

Before the specific colors for the lighting instruments are selected, the color palettes of the scenic and costume designers must be studied. This color study normally occurs during the various production conferences as each designer (scenic, costume, lighting) presents his or her design and color concepts. The reason the lighting designer must know what colors the other designers are using is relatively straightforward. Colored light can drastically alter the apparent color of the sets and costumes, and it isn't in the interests of a unified production concept to change the other designers' work without their knowledge and consent.

During the initial conferences of our hypothetical *Playboy* production, the design team decided that the play would be produced in a realistic style. Based on this concept, the lighting designer will want the set to appear as though it were being lit by the source lights that are located on the set. To determine the nature of these sources, and their locations, it will be necessary to look at a scenic rendering or model of the set. The scenic sketch (Figure 13.9) shows that there are oil lamps on the counter and each table, there is a peat fire glowing in the fireplace, and the window and door are open. Each of these sources would provide light of differing hues. The sunlight, according to our analysis of the image of light, is cool-white, bright, and cheerful. The fireplace is warmer and redder than the sunlight, and the oil lamps give off a soft, amber glow.

Using this analysis and information as a guide, Roscolux 61, Mist Blue, is selected to represent the bright, clean sunlight. Roscolux 02, Bastard Amber, is chosen for the firelight, and Roscolux 09, Pale Amber Gold, is selected to represent the color emitted by the oil lamps.

Now that the colors have been selected to represent the various sources, they need to be applied to the lighting key. The application of color to the

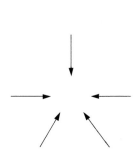

Figure 13.8 Five-source lighting key for *The Playboy of the Western World*.

Figure 13.9   The set design for *The Playboy of the Western World*.

basic distribution pattern of the lighting key should support the thesis that the source lights are providing the light for the environment of the play. To achieve this goal, the light from stage left should be colored to represent the fireplace color, Bastard Amber, because the fireplace is on the stage-left side of the set. The oil lamp color (Pale Amber Gold) is used from a direction (stage right) that supports the visual impression that the oil lamps are primarily on the downstage-right part of the set. The light approaching the stage from an upstage direction should represent the sunlight (Mist Blue), because the window and doorway are on the upstage wall of the set.

Figure 13.10 shows the colors assigned to the specific distribution pattern that we had previously determined from our analysis of the image of light. The stage-left side light is assigned Bastard Amber, to support the concept that the fireplace is lighting the room from this direction. The top-back light is colored with Roscolux 61, Mist Blue, because this supports the idea that any light approaching the stage from this direction would be sunlight coming

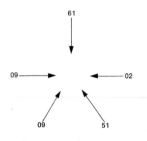

Figure 13.10 Five-source lighting key, with color, for *The Playboy of the Western World*.

through the window or door. The stage-right side light and the stage-right front light are colored with Pale Amber Gold, to support the notion that the primary source light for this side of the stage comes from the oil lamps.

This leaves the stage-left front light as the only uncolored instrument. Because there is no specific source light coming from this direction, it will be necessary to refer back to the image of light to determine the appropriate color for this instrument. The image of light specifies that the atmosphere should resemble a "twinkling spring morning." Roscolux 51, Surprise Pink, is selected for use from this direction, because this bright, cheerful color will blend with the Pale Amber Gold (used in the other front light) to produce a warm white light that supports the concept of a cheery morning that is dictated by the image of light.

A close scrutiny of the set reveals the peat fire (stage left) probably would not have much effect on an actor standing stage right of the center line of the set. In this case you could modify the lighting key for the stage right half (or third) of the set by replacing the Roscolux 02, which is the color selected to represent the fire light, with Roscolux 09, the oil lamp color. There is no rule that states the lighting key must remain static or identical for all areas of the stage. Nor is there any rule that says the lighting key can't remain static. Those are design options and are choices to be made by the designer.

In this chapter you've learned how to translate your image of light into a lighting key. In the next chapter you'll learn how to use the lighting key as the basis for creating the light plot.

CHAPTER 14

Using the Lighting Key to Draw the Light Plot

Before we get into the practical matters of using the lighting key to draw the light plot, you need to know something about acting areas and lighting areas.

ACTING AND LIGHTING AREAS

Acting areas are those spaces on the stage where specific scenes, or parts of scenes, are played. In some plays the entire setting is the acting area (usually the case with a realistic interior setting). In other plays the setting may be divided into several smaller acting areas. A unit set for Anouilh's *Becket*, where one part of the set is used for scenes in Canterbury Cathedral, another for the French seacoast, and another for a hovel in an English forest, illustrates the use of many separate acting areas in one setting. The shape and size of an acting area (Figure 14.1), although roughly determined by the shape of the setting, are specifically determined by the blocking patterns used by the actors.

A lighting area is a cylindrical space (Figure 14.2) whose size is roughly determined by the diameter of the cone of light made by the instruments used to light the area. Generally, a lighting area is approximately 8 to 12 feet in diameter and about 7 feet tall.

In order to provide a uniform base of lighting for the acting area (so that actors will look the same regardless of where they move within the acting area), we will need to subdivide the acting areas into lighting areas as shown in Figure 14.3.

At this point, we'll digress further to explain *how* the process of subdividing acting areas into lighting areas facilitates smooth lighting. To achieve

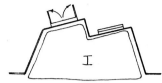

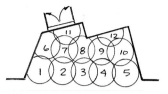

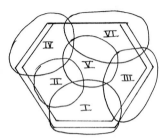

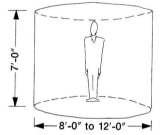

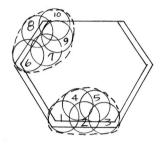

Figure 14.1　Acting areas.

Figure 14.2　A lighting area.

Figure 14.3　Acting areas are subdivided into lighting areas.

Figure 14.4　Lighting areas are overlapped in an acting area to facilitate the creation of a smooth wash of light.

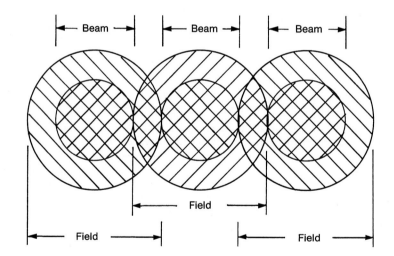

a smooth wash of light throughout the acting area, light from instruments in adjacent lighting areas is overlapped by about one-third, as shown in Figure 14.4. If the light from the field of these two instruments is overlapped, it will nearly equal the intensity of the light from the beam of a single instrument. If the light from all the instruments lighting the individual lighting areas within an acting area is overlapped according to this plan, a smooth wash of light will be achieved for the entire acting area. (Further explanation of this process is offered in the box "Beam and Field Angles Explained.")

Beam and Field Angles Explained

There is a rational reason why lighting designers need to know the beam and field angles for the various instruments they will be using. You may remember from Chapter 4 that the beam angle is the central cone of light whose outer limit is defined as that point where the light diminishes to 50 percent of its intensity when compared with the center of the beam. The field angle is the portion of the cone of light outside the beam angle whose outer limit is defined as that point where the light diminishes to 10 percent of the output of t he center of the beam.

As shown in Table 4.3, the field angle for any ellipsoidal reflector spotlight (the most commonly used stage lighting instrument) is approximately twice its beam angle. In practical terms this relationship means that when adjacent lighting areas are overlapped by one-third, the beam angle of the instruments lighting those areas will illuminate the central, or "un-overlapped," portion of the lighting area, and the field angle will illuminate the overlapped area. The result of the overlap of the adjacent fields is an additive effect that brings the intensity level of the overlapped areas up to approximately the same as the central "un-overlapped" areas. This results in a relatively smooth, consistent level of illumination throughout the acting area.

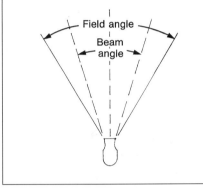

USING THE LIGHTING KEY TO DRAW THE LIGHT PLOT

Now you know that the acting areas are subdivided into lighting areas to facilitate the production of a smooth wash of light throughout the acting area. But where do you go from here? You use the lighting key as a guide for placing and coloring the instruments that will be used to illuminate each lighting area. Again, this process is best explained by example. We've learned that the shape of the acting areas determines the number and arrangement of the lighting areas. In our hypothetical production of *The Playboy of the Western World*, discussed in Chapter 13, the whole set is a single acting area. In order to draw the light plot, it will be necessary to subdivide that acting area into lighting areas, as shown in Figure 14.5.

To create a smooth wash of light over the entire acting area, the lighting designer needs to replicate the lighting key (Figure 13.10, page 202) in each of the lighting areas.

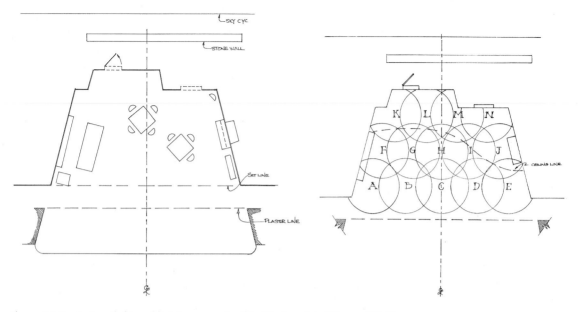

Figure 14.5   Acting (left) and lighting areas for *The Playboy of the Western World*.

DETERMINING THE SECTIONAL ANGLE

The lighting key indicates the plan angle for each instrument, but it provides no information about the sectional angle. We need to know both to effectively replicate the lighting key. The sectional angle for any light should be informed by an analysis of the desired appearance of the light, but reality dictates that the sectional angles for almost all lighting instruments (except top/back lights) is usually somewhere between 30 and 60 degrees, with 45 degrees being fairly normal and typical. (See the box " 'Normal' Lighting Angles" in Chapter 13 for the reason for this apparently arbitrarily selected angle.) Our visual analysis of *The Playboy of the Western World* would suggest that the use of "typical and normal" sectional angles for the front and sidelights would be appropriate.

Figure 14.6 is a plan view showing where instruments could be placed to effectively replicate the lighting key for lighting area C. To complete the process we need to determine if the sectional angles for those instruments will meet our "typical and normal" criteria. If they do, then we can use that information to begin replicating the lighting key in all the lighting areas.

A **working sectional** shows what the sectional angle of the light looks like. You don't need drafting equipment to draw a working sectional. You just need a ruler, a pencil and a piece of typing or notebook paper. If you let ¼ inch represent 1 foot—1 inch equals 4 feet and so forth—a working sectional

Working sectional:
A drawing showing the sectional angle for a lighting instrument; used to determine its trim height or hanging position; not to be confused with the lighting section.

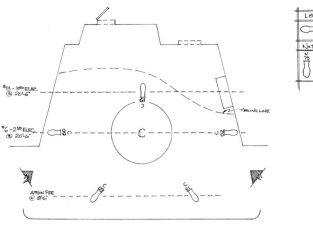

Figure 14.6 Replication of the lighting key in a lighting area for *The Playboy of the Western World*.

for most situations can be drawn on a sheet of 8½ × 11-inch paper. You can use the ruler for your straightedge.

Figure 14.7 is a working sectional of one of the front lights from Figure 14.6. It is a sectional view taken at right angles to the axis of the instrument. It shows the **trim height** of the apron pipe, the ERS hanging below the pipe, and a scale 6′–0″ actor standing in the middle of lighting area C. In the hypothetical theatre of this project, the **fixed** trim height of the apron pipe is 18′–6″ above the stage floor. The center of the ERS's lens hangs 1′–6″ below the pipe.[1] You draw the actor in the lighting area to remind yourself that you're lighting actors' faces, not a circle on the floor. The floor distance—the horizontal 16′–0″ measurement—represents the distance from the center of the lighting area to a point on the stage floor directly beneath the instrument's hanging position. The line drawn from the instrument lens to the actor's head gives us the sectional angle, relative to the stage floor, of the central axis of that instrument's light. Since that angle—about 35 degrees—falls within the previously determined design criteria, this hanging position will work for the front light. Since the plan angles for both front lights are mirror images of each other their sectional angles will also be identical. Therefore, you only need to make a working sectional for one of them.

A related aside: Before finalizing your thinking about where to hang the front lights—or any other lights—you need to examine all the available hanging possibilities. For example, Figure 14.6 shows the front lights hung on the apron pipe. But that isn't the only possible hanging location in most theatres. Our hypothetical theatre also has a first anteproscenium (AP) cut. You could hang the front lights there. Examine both possibilities. Check

Trim height: Height above the stage floor at which an instrument will be hung.

Fixed: In the context of fixed trim height, fixed means unmovable.

---

[1]This figure is normally "guesstimated" because the actual position of the lens is determined when the instrument is focused. But the difference between a drawing done using the "guesstimated" height and the actual height would be too small to be noticed by the audience.

Figure 14.7 A typical working sectional. See text for details.

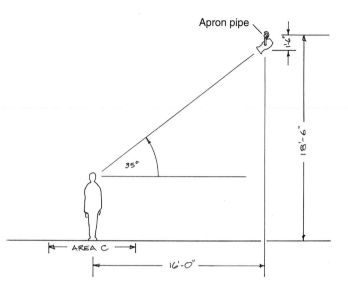

House plot: A scale plan view of a theatre's stage and auditorium showing all hanging positions and related circuiting information.

Second electric: The onstage pipe for lighting instruments that is second closest, from the onstage side, to the proscenium arch.

the sectional angle for both locations. If the theatre of this project were real rather than imaginary, a **house plot** would provide the information—pipe locations, trim heights of permanently mounted hanging locations, and so forth—needed to make working sectionals for both positions. After you've made both drawings, compare them, then use the hanging location in which the sectional angle most closely matches your design criteria.

Working sectionals can be used for other tasks as well. If, for example, we decide that the ideal sectional angle for the sidelight for area C is 45 degrees, we could use a working sectional to determine where on the **second electric** we should hang instruments so their light would hit area C from 45 degrees. Figure 14.8A shows the first step we would take in this process. We would still place our 6'–0"actor in the middle of area C to help remind us that we're lighting actors, not circles on the floor.[2] The predetermined ideal sectional angle for the sidelight—45 degrees—is shown as a line drawn upward from the actor's head at 45 degrees relative to the stage floor. Normally, we would have a rough idea of the trim height for the second electric based on the height of the set, audience sightlines and so forth. From that information we determine a preliminary trim height—20'–6";—for the second electric. Remembering that the lens of any ERS sidelight will be about 1'–6'" below the trim height of the second electric, we draw a horizontal "lens line" at that height—19'–0"—as shown in Figure 14.8B. Extend the 45-degree line from the actor's head until it intersects both the lens line and the second electric.

---

[2] Lighting area C can also be visualized as a 6-foot-tall cylinder. With that image, our 6-foot-tall actor would be effectively lit anywhere he or she goes inside the area.

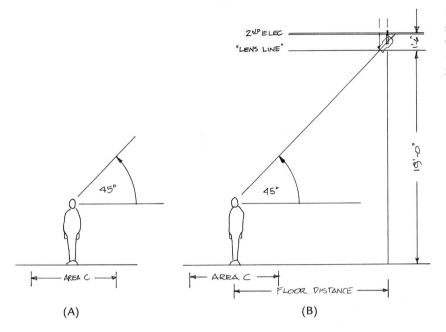

2ⁿᵈ ELEC
"LENS LINE"

45°

45°

19'-0"

AREA C

AREA C

FLOOR DISTANCE

(A)

(B)

Figure 14.8 A working sectional can be used to determine an instrument's hanging position. See text for details.

What Determines a Pipe's Trim Height?

The trim height of any instrument or pipe will be determined by a number of factors. In many arena and thrust theatres, a permanent lighting grid hangs over the stage. Because the height of these grids is rarely adjustable, the trim height for any instruments attached to them is also fixed. Most proscenium arch theatres also have some fixed positions such as the anteproscenium cuts, balcony rails, and other "in-house" positions. However, the counterweight system that is part of most proscenium arch theatres' permanent equipment provides the means for the lighting designer to specify the trim height for onstage lighting instruments.

A pipe's trim height should be specified on the light plot to be the specific height above the stage floor that the pipe actually will be trimmed. The lens of most lighting instruments will hang approximately 18 inches below that height.

Any number of factors will contribute to a designer's decision to trim a particular pipe at a specific height. Among the more practical considerations are the size of the stage, the height of the scenery, the height of any fixed hanging positions, the throw distance of the instruments being used, the maximum safe working height of equipment used to focus the instruments, and so forth. Aesthetic considerations such as whether the production concept calls for the instruments to be masked or seen by the audience would also be considered. After factoring all the available information, the lighting designer will specify the trim height for any movable pipes.

Given all the elements that need to be considered when making this important decision, onstage electrics for productions in medium-sized theatres with counterweight systems are normally trimmed at a height between 18 and 26 feet.

From the intersection of the 45-degree-angle line and lens line, draw a vertical upward until it intersects the second electric. The hanging location on the second electric for that instrument will be halfway between the intersection of that vertical and the second electric and the intersection of the 45-degree-angle line and the second electric. From that point draw a vertical down until it intersects the stage floor. The distance from that intersection to the center of lighting area C—the floor distance—shows how far from the center of area C the ERS must be hung on the second electric to produce the desired effect.

SELECTING INSTRUMENT SIZE

At the same time the sectional angle is being determined, the lighting designer can also determine the appropriate size of instrument to use. From the beam and field angle information (see the box "Beam and Field Angles Explained" or from the manufacturer's specification sheets for specific lighting instruments, beam and field angle templates can be constructed. These thin, triangular pieces of cardboard (Figure 14.9A) are actually sectional representations of the cone of light emitted by a specific instrument. The angle is cut to match the field angle of the instrument; and the length matches, in scale, the **maximum throw distance** of that particular instrument. A composite template (Figure 14.9B), made from acetate, consolidates all the information onto one template. The center line, which coincides with the instrument axial line, is a scale rule marked with 5-foot increments. Fanning out on either side of the center line are lines noting degrees of arc.

Figure 14.10 shows how to use the composite beam and field angle template. After the working sectional for an instrument has been drawn, the apex of the template is placed at the hanging point specified for that instrument. An appropriately sized instrument will have a field angle that slightly overlaps the lighting area and a maximum throw distance longer than the **throw distance** measured to the center of the lighting area.

This method of instrument selection is suggested only as a general guide. In the final analysis, the designer needs to make instrument selections based on what is aesthetically appropriate for the particular situation.

Unfortunately, it isn't always possible to achieve an exact duplication of the lighting key in every lighting area, because the walls of the set prevent the use of sidelight in the lighting areas adjacent to the walls, and the ceiling interferes with a great deal of the top and back light. More challenges are imposed by the physical limitations of the auditorium, which generally inhibit some of the front-of-house hanging positions.

When a situation occurs that makes it difficult to place an instrument exactly where it is needed, the lighting designer must make a design

Maximum throw distance: The point at which the output of a stage lighting instrument drops to 50 footcandles.

Throw distance: How far light from an instrument travels from its hanging position to the center of its area of focus.

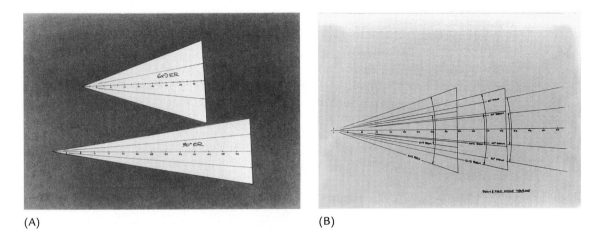

(A)   (B)

Figure 14.9 Beam and field angle templates. (A) Cardboard templates for 6 × 9 and 6 × 16 ERSs. (B) A composite plastic template.

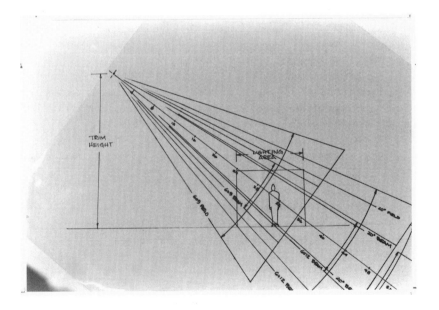

Figure 14.10 How to use a beam and field angle template.

decision. If the light can't be placed in a position where it will replicate the angle specified in the lighting key, the compromise solution should be guided by the principles outlined in the lighting key and the designer's interpretation of the image of light. For example, it isn't possible to use direct stage-left sidelight for area J (see Figure 14.11), because the wall gets

Lighting-Instrument Specification Sheets

It is extremely useful for a lighting designer to assemble a collection of data sheets that specify the photometric data (beam, field angle, light output at specific throw distances, and the like) for the instruments of the various manufacturers (see example). The maximum throw distance is the farthest distance at which the instrument can effectively be used. At this distance the light emitted by the instrument measures 50 foot-candles, which is used as the industry standard and is considered to be the lowest effective illumination level for stage use.

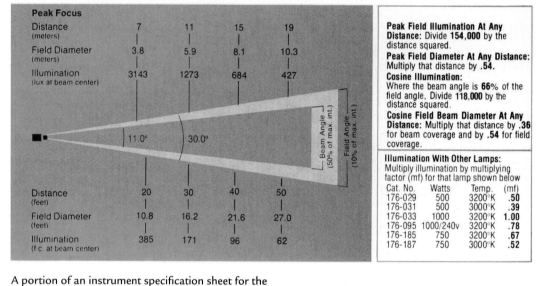

A portion of an instrument specification sheet for the Colortran 30-degree ellipsoidal reflector spotlight.

Figure 14.11 Replication of the lighting key for *The Playboy of the Western World* in a lighting area that is difficult to light.

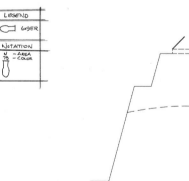

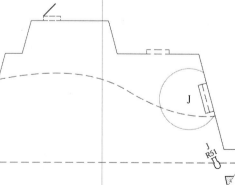

in the way. Two possible compromise solutions to this challenge might be: (1) put an instrument on the stage-left end of the **first electric**, as shown in Figure 14.11; (2) eliminate the instrument. The choice of which solution to use should be guided by your interpretation of the image of light and the lighting key.

To complete the basic, or first, layer of the lighting design it will be necessary to duplicate as closely as possible the lighting key in each lighting area. This process of replication results in a basic light plot that creates the atmosphere and look dictated by the image of light.

First electric: The onstage pipe for lighting instruments that is closest, from the onstage side, to the proscenium arch.

LAYERING

A lighting design exists in time as well as space. It ebbs and flows as the mood of the play changes. To create a temporal development in the lighting design, it is necessary to design mechanisms into the light plot.

Layering is primarily an organizational tool of the lighting designer. It refers specifically to the process of designing layers of light.

The first layer of light for our hypothetical production of *Playboy* was created when we implemented our interpretation of the image of light—"a bright, twinkling Irish morning." This image works well for Acts II and III, which take place in the morning and afternoon, respectively. However, Act I takes place in the early evening. The "twinkling morning" look simply doesn't translate as night. In order to create an appropriate look of early evening for Act I, it will be necessary to do one of two things: (1) create a completely separate lighting key and design for Act I or (2) create some supplemental "early evening" lighting that can be used in conjunction with the basic "twinkling Irish morning" lights.

From an aesthetic standpoint a completely separate plot for Act I would be the preferred solution, but a separate design would necessitate a very large instrument inventory.

The supplemental lighting solution would achieve relatively similar results with a considerably smaller number of instruments. The instruments used to create this second layer of light need to be positioned and colored to create the look of "indoor evening" in the pub, where the principal sources of light are oil lamps and the peat fire. Any light coming in the window and door should have the appearance of "night light" rather than daylight.

Since this second layer of light needs to be integrated with the "twinkling Irish morning" lights to achieve the look of "early evening," it will be necessary to select angles and colors that work to support the premise that the pub is actually lit by the oil lamps and the peat fire.

☀ Effects and Support Lights

Apparent onstage sources of light—windows, table lamps, fireplaces, and so forth—can be thought of as psychological key lights. They are, apparently, the source of illumination for the set. According to the definition of key and fill lights, any lights used to fill the shadows caused by these key lights would be fill lights. That's the principle, and it works.

However, at this point an interesting paradox raises its ugly head. In practice, apparent onstage sources—lamps, fires in fireplaces, and so forth—are deliberately kept dim so that they won't be the center of the audience's attention. (As you learned in Chapters 1 and 2, the audience is compelled to look at the brightest spot in a stage picture.) While the apparent sources, called effects or effects lights, are relatively dim, lighting designers normally place stage lights (ERSs, fresnels, PARs, and so forth) in positions where they can create light that looks as if it is emanating from, and the color of, the effects light. These support lights (lights used to support or reinforce an effect) can be thought of as keys, and the acting area lights can be thought of as fills. These support lights are usually gelled in a hue that is more saturated than, but in the same color range as, the color of the lights approaching the acting areas from the same general direction as the effect. The color of these acting-area lights will be suggested by the lighting key. The reason for the disparity in saturation is so that the influence of the support light will be more noticeable as the actors get closer to the effect—table lamp, fireplace—that the support light is reinforcing.

A wash of "night" colors (Roscolux 79, Bright Blue) could be used to flood the stage from the front-of-house positions, as shown in Figure 14.12A. By balancing the intensities of these night colors with those of the basic lighting key, we can ensure that the blue lights won't override the basic hues that were selected for the lighting key. They will, however, provide a blue wash over the whole acting area that will fill any shadow or underlit areas with a blue light to help create the illusion of nighttime.

Additional instruments could be hung to augment the color selected to reinforce the source lights—the oil lamps and peat fire—in the first layer of the plot. These instruments, as shown in Figure 14.12B, should be colored in more fully saturated hues than their "first layer" counterparts, and they should be hung in positions that will support the effects of the source lights.

Additional layers of light can be used for a variety of purposes. Figure 14.12C shows the location of those instruments that are used to create the "daylight" and "night light" that come through the window and door.

As indicated at the beginning of this discussion, layering is primarily an organizational tool of the lighting designer. It isn't necessary to divide your thinking about the design into segments, but many designers find that this compartmentalization of the design into specific segments, or layers, makes it easier to concentrate on solving the challenges imposed by the individual elements of the design. Figure 14.13 shows the finished light plot for *The Playboy of the Western World*.

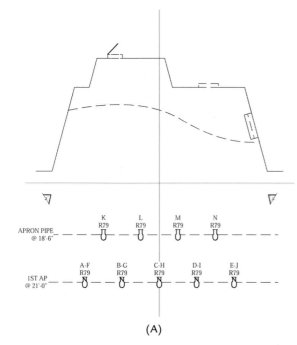

APRON PIPE
@ 18'-6"

K	L	M	N
R79	R79	R79	R79

1ST AP
@ 21'-0"

A-F	B-G	C-H	D-I	E-J
R79	R79	R79	R79	R79

(A)

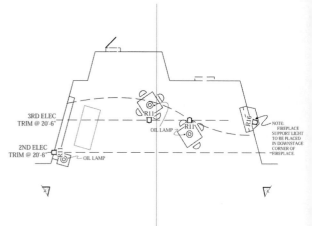

3RD ELEC
TRIM @ 20'-6"

R11
OIL LAMP

R11

R16

NOTE:
FIREPLACE
SUPPORT LIGHT
TO BE PLACED
IN DOWNSTAGE
CORNER OF
FIREPLACE

2ND ELEC
TRIM @ 20'-6"

R11
OIL LAMP

(B)

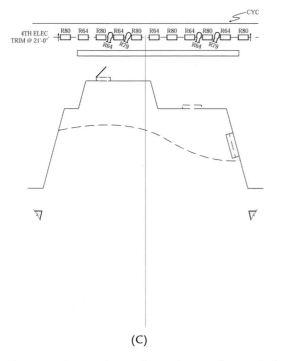

CYC

4TH ELEC
TRIM @ 21'-0"

R80 R64 R80 R64 R80   R64 R80 R64 R80   R64 R80
R64   R79   R64   R79

(C)

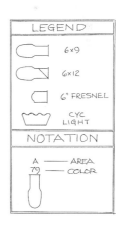

LEGEND

6×9

6×12

6" FRESNEL

CYC
LIGHT

NOTATION

A —— AREA
79 —— COLOR

Figure 14.12   Layering can be used to supplement the basic design key.

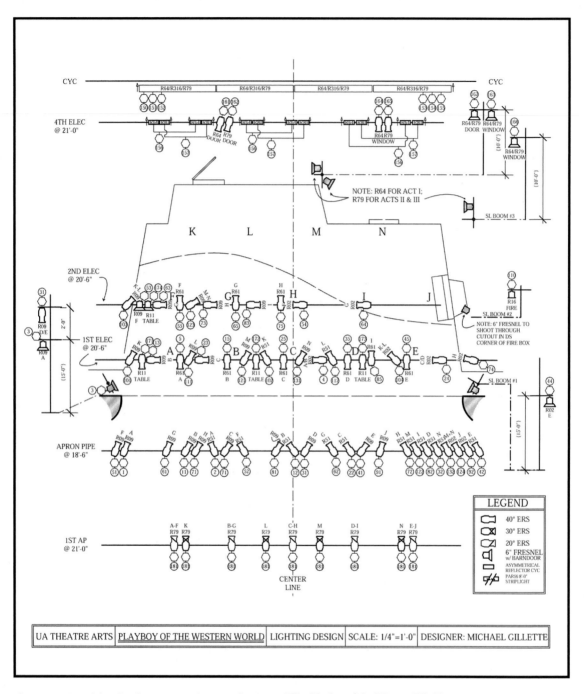

Figure 14.13 Light plot for a proscenium production of *The Playboy of the Western World*. Lighting Design by J. Michael Gillete. Drafting by Michael McNamara.

DESIGNING LIGHTING KEYS FOR THRUST AND ARENA STAGES

Designing lights for an arena or thrust stage is not significantly different from designing for a proscenium theatre. The only substantive difference is the location of the audience. In the thrust configuration, as you will recall, the audience sits on three sides of the stage, and in an arena theatre it surrounds the stage. It is the lighting designer's responsibility to light the stage so that all spectators, regardless of where they are sitting, are able to see the production equally well.

We can use our hypothetical production of *The Playboy of the Western World* to demonstrate the relative lack of difference between designing lighting for the three modes of stages. Figure 14.14 shows a sketch of the modified scenic design that would work for a thrust production of our play. Note that the side walls have been removed so that the spectators sitting on the sides of the thrust stage can see all the action. Also notice that because the walls are gone, the ceiling has been eliminated.

The image of light remains the same as before, simply because the concept of how we are going to produce the play hasn't changed. The distribution of the design key has been slightly modified because of the position of the audience relative to the stage. We are still surrounding the actors with light to re-create our "bright, twinkling Irish morning," as shown in Figure 14.15A. The color of the design key also remains relatively unchanged, although we will lower the saturation of the "warm" color because of the proximity of the audience, as shown in Figure 14.15B.

The second layer for our thrust production could concentrate on enhancing the source lights—oil lamps, fireplace, window, and door (Figure 14.16A). The third layer (Figure 14.16B) would concentrate on creating the "night" wash.

The lighting design for an arena production of our play would be very similar to the thrust design. The set for the arena production is shown in Figure 14.17. Notice how all the walls that might in any way interfere with the spectators' sight lines have been removed. The scenic design has been essentially reduced to a furniture arrangement, with just enough set left to provide a hint of what the cottage or pub actually looks like. The set has been shifted to a diagonal angle so that the entrances are lined up with the auditorium entryways.

The distribution of the lighting key for the arena production is no different from the thrust stage configurations (Figure 14.18A). The color portion of the design key is different, but only because we want everyone looking at the play to get the same feeling. For the proscenium and thrust productions, we were able to have the light coming from the direction of the door and window gelled with colors that would support the "outdoors" look of

Figure 14.14 Scenic design for a thrust production of *The Playboy of the Western World*.

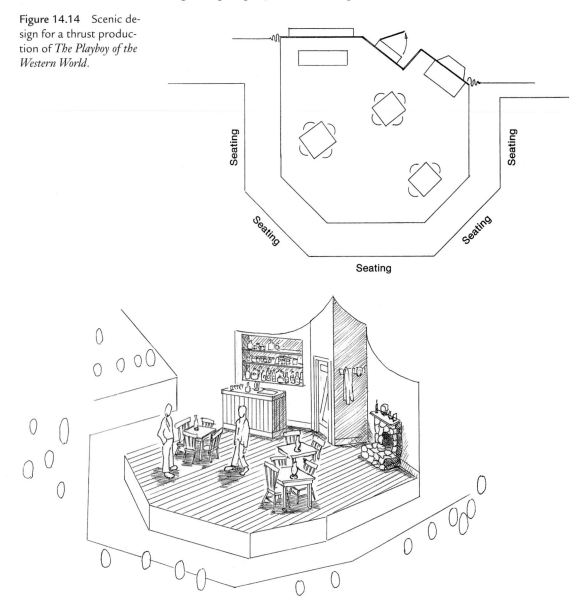

the light coming through the window and door. Because we now have the audience surrounding the stage, however, we need to create the same feeling of "interior" lighting from all angles. These changes are shown in the color selection for the design key illustrated in Figure 14.18B.

Similarly, the "night" layers must place lights in positions that will enhance the idea of "night" for all the viewing audience, as shown in

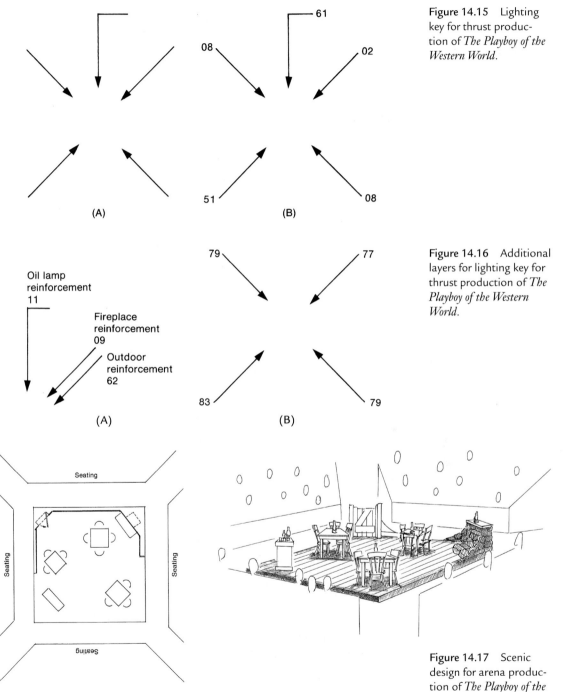

(A)

(B)

Figure 14.15 Lighting key for thrust production of *The Playboy of the Western World*.

61

08

02

51

08

Oil lamp reinforcement 11

Fireplace reinforcement 09

Outdoor reinforcement 62

(A)

79

77

83

79

(B)

Figure 14.16 Additional layers for lighting key for thrust production of *The Playboy of the Western World*.

Seating

Seating

Seating

Seating

Figure 14.17 Scenic design for arena production of *The Playboy of the Western World*.

Figure 14.18 Lighting key for arena production of *The Playboy of the Western World*.

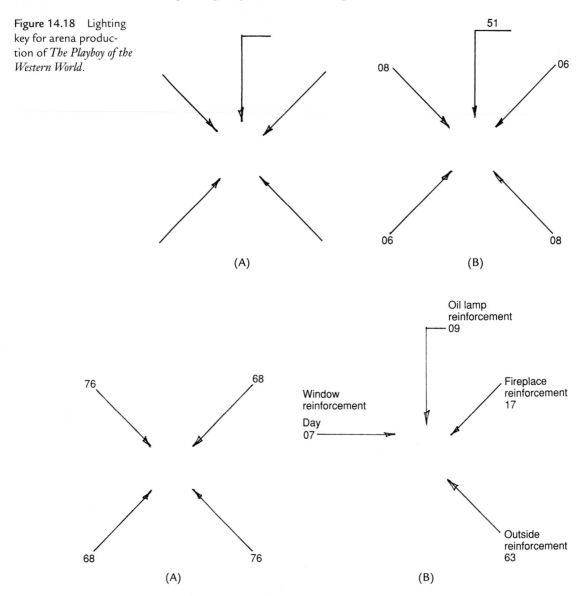

Figure 14.19 Additional layers for lighting key for arena production of *The Playboy of the Western World*.

Figure 14.19A. In this particular design the third layer of light is used to support both the internal and external source lights. These lights need to be reasonably directional, as shown in Figure 14.19B, because the apparent source lights that they are reinforcing (sunlight, moonlight, peat fire) are also directional. The instruments that are reinforcing the oil lamps are placed over the general area of the lamps, simply because the light from the oil lamps illuminates everything around it.

The only other type of design modification that needs to be made when working in an arena theatre is caused by the fact that the instruments are probably hung closer to the actors than in either a thrust or proscenium configuration. Because of this situation you will want to use less-saturated color media, since the closer the instrument is to the actor, the stronger the effect of any color that is used with that instrument.

Other than these relatively minor adjustments required by the positioning and proximity of the audience, there aren't any significant changes in philosophy, practice, or techniques when designing for thrust or arena theatres.

CHAPTER 15

Drafting the Lighting Design

Because the product of lighting design—light—is probably the most intangible and abstract of all the theatrical design elements, some specialized paperwork is needed to help carry out the designer's intentions.

GRAPHIC STANDARDS FOR LIGHTING DESIGN

The purpose of the paperwork associated with the drafting of a lighting design—light plot, lighting section, instrument schedule, or hook up sheet,—is to provide sufficient information to the master electrician and crew to enable them to hang and circuit the lighting equipment for the entire production. There are some definitions, conventions, and standards that you need to know before you begin to draw the light plot.

The Light Plot

The light plot is a scale mechanical drawing—a "road map"—that indicates where the lighting instruments should be placed (Figure 15.1). More specifically, the light plot is a "horizontal offset section with the cutting plane passing at whatever levels are required to produce the most descriptive view of the instrumentation in relation to the set(s)," according to the United States Institute of Theatre Technology's (USITT's) graphic standards for stage lighting.

Although there is no universally accepted style of drafting light plots, all good plots will have certain things in common. The primary purpose of a light plot is to depict, in scale (usually ½ or ¼ inch to foot), the exact location of all lighting instruments being used in the production. The plot shows the location of the set(s) in relation to the physical structure of the theatre. The plot also includes a legend describing each of the symbols used on the plot, as well as a title block that details pertinent information about the production. (More information about the legend and title block is provided later in this chapter.)

Center line: A leader line that runs perpendicular to the set line from the midpoint or center of the opening of the proscenium arch.

The Lighting Section

The lighting section (Figure 15.2) is usually a composite side-view drawing (if the set is basically symmetrical) that shows the position of the lighting equipment in relation to the set and the physical structure of the theatre. If the set is significantly asymmetrical, then two sections will normally be drawn, one looking stage right from the **center line**, the other looking stage left. This drawing, used primarily by the lighting designer, has several purposes: to check sightlines of the lighting instruments, to assist in determining the appropriate trim height for horizontal masking, and to ensure that the lighting equipment won't interfere with any scenic elements and vice versa.

The Instrument Schedules and Hookup Sheets

The instrument schedule (Figure 15.3), also known as the hookup sheet, is a specification sheet that contains everything you might want or need to know about every instrument used on the production. It identifies each instrument by its instrument number and specifies its type, hanging location, focus area, circuit, dimmer, lamp wattage, and color. A section for special remarks is used to note anything else that might be appropriate, such as focusing notes, auxiliary or nonstandard equipment that needs to be attached to the instrument, and so forth.

Some designers differentiate between instrument schedules and hookup sheets. While they both contain the same basic information, they order the information differently: generally instrument schedules are ordered by the *position of the instrument* whereas hookup sheets are ordered by *dimmer* or *channel number.*

Standards for Drafting in Lighting Design

Because so much data must be included on a light plot or lighting section, the USITT has developed a set of standards and conventions for drafting in lighting design. This section details some of the pertinent elements of those recommendations. The full text of the standard, including the currently

Figure 15.1 The light plot for the Canadian Opera Company Hummingbird Centre production of *Il Trovatore*. Lighting design by Joan Sullivan-Genthe. Associate lighting designer: Michael McNamara. Drafting by Joshua Windhausen.

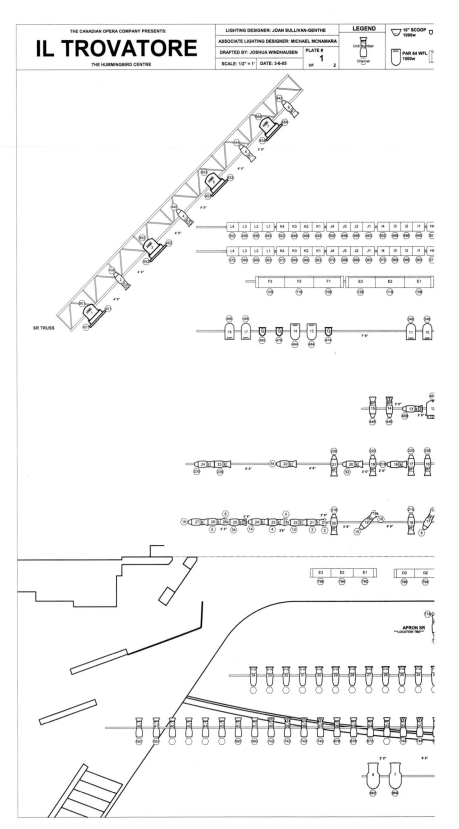

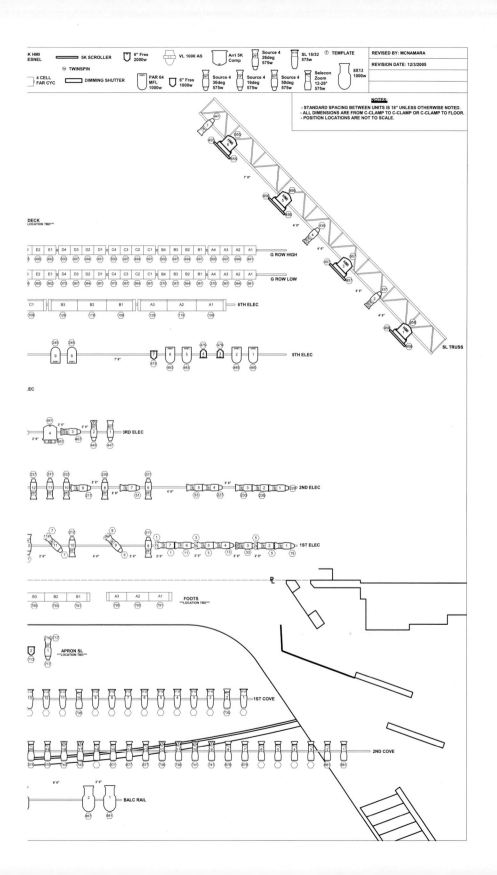

K HMI
ESNEL

5K SCROLLER

6" Fres 2000w

VL 1000 AS

Arri 5K Comp

Source 4 26deg 575w

SL 15/32 575w

TEMPLATE

4 CELL FAR CYC

TWINSPIN

DIMMING SHUTTER

PAR 64 MFL 1000w

6" Fres 1000w

Source 4 36deg 575w

Source 4 19deg 575w

Source 4 50deg 575w

Selecon Zoom 12-28" 575w

8X13 1000w

REVISED BY: MCNAMARA

REVISION DATE: 12/3/2005

NOTES:
- STANDARD SPACING BETWEEN UNITS IS 18" UNLESS OTHERWISE NOTED.
- ALL DIMENSIONS ARE FROM C-CLAMP TO C-CLAMP OR C-CLAMP TO FLOOR.
- POSITION LOCATIONS ARE NOT TO SCALE.

DECK
LOCATION TBD***

G ROW HIGH

G ROW LOW

6TH ELEC

5TH ELEC

SL TRUSS

.EC

3RD ELEC

2ND ELEC

1ST ELEC

FOOTS
LOCATION TBD

APRON SL
LOCATION TBD

1ST COVE

2ND COVE

BALC RAIL

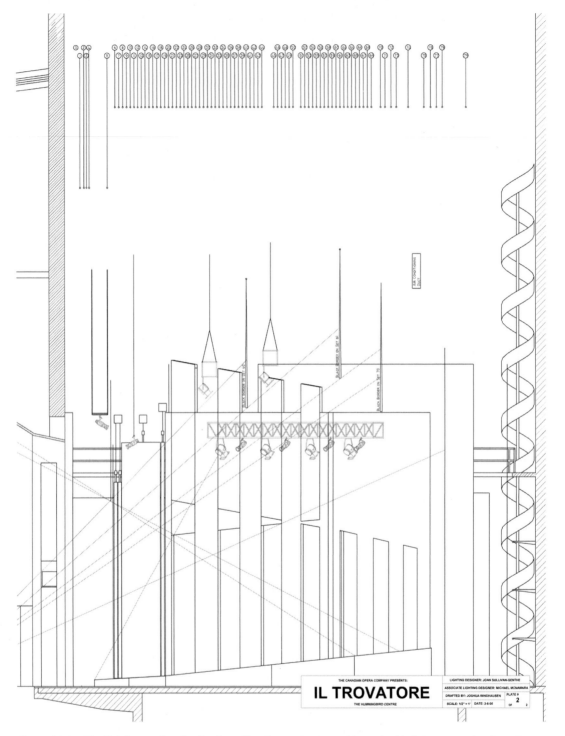

Figure 15.2   The lighting section for the Canadian Opera Company Hummingbird Centre production of *Il Trovatore*. Lighting design by Joan Sullivan-Genthe. Associate lighting designer: Michael McNamara. Drafting by Joshua Windhausen.

IL TROVATORE		CHANNEL HOOKUP			Page 1

03 Dec 2005

Canadian Opera Company
Production: Stephen Lawless
LD: Joan Sullivan-Genthe & Michael McNamara

Hummingbird Centre
ALD: Wendy Greenwood
ALD: Heidi Lingren

Channel	Dim Position	Unit	Type & Accessories & Watts	Purpose	Color & Tmp
(1)	1st ELEC	7	ETC S4 19° 575w	X FAR W	
	1st ELEC	7s	Wybron C-Ram II S4 Scroller	1E #7 Scroller	SCROLL 1
(2)	1st ELEC	21	ETC S4 19° 575w	X FAR W	
	1st ELEC	21s	Wybron C-Ram II S4 Scroller	1E #21 Scroller	SCROLL 1
(3)	1st ELEC	5	ETC S4 26° 575w	X CEN W	
	1st ELEC	5s	Wybron C-Ram II S4 Scroller	1E #5 Scroller	SCROLL 1
(4)	1st ELEC	23	ETC S4 26° 575w	X CEN W	
	1st ELEC	23s	Wybron C-Ram II S4 Scroller	1E #23 Scroller	SCROLL 1
(5)	1st ELEC	2	ETC S4 26° 575w	X NR W	
	1st ELEC	2s	Wybron C-Ram II S4 Scroller	1E #2 Scroller	SCROLL 1
(6)	1st ELEC	26	ETC S4 26° 575w	X NR W	
	1st ELEC	26s	Wybron C-Ram II S4 Scroller	1E #26 Scroller	SCROLL 1
(7)	1st ELEC	11	ETC S4 26° 575w	P2 FAR W	
	1st ELEC	11s	Wybron C-Ram II S4 Scroller	1E #11 Scroller	SCROLL 1
(8)	1st ELEC	17	ETC S4 26° 575w	P2 FAR W	
	1st ELEC	17s	Wybron C-Ram II S4 Scroller	1E #17 Scroller	SCROLL 1
(9)	1st ELEC	9	ETC S4 26° 575w	P2 CEN W	
	1st ELEC	9s	Wybron C-Ram II S4 Scroller	1E #9 Scroller	SCROLL 1
(10)	1st ELEC	19	ETC S4 26° 575w	P2 CEN W	
	1st ELEC	19s	Wybron C-Ram II S4 Scroller	1E #19 Scroller	SCROLL 1
(11)	1st ELEC	6	ETC S4 19° 575w	X FAR C	L161
(12)	1st ELEC	22	ETC S4 19° 575w	X FAR C	L161
(13)	1st ELEC	4	ETC S4 26° 575w	X CEN C	L161
(14)	1st ELEC	24	ETC S4 26° 575w	X CEN C	L161
(15)	1st ELEC	1	ETC S4 26° 575w	X NR C (Slash Slider)	L161
(16)	1st ELEC	27	ETC S4 26° 575w	X NR C (Slash Slider)	L161
(21)	1st ELEC	15	ETC S4 26° 575w	XO RIGHT	
	1st ELEC	15s	Wybron C-Ram II S4 Scroller	1E #15 Scroller	SCROLL 1
(22)	1st ELEC	14	ETC S4 26° 575w	XO LEFT	
	1st ELEC	14s	Wybron C-Ram II S4 Scroller	1E #14 Scroller	SCROLL 1
(27)	1st ELEC	12	ETC S4 26° 575w	42 Cell	L161
(33)	1st ELEC	3	ETC S4 26° 575w	Temp X Mid Cen	R99+R99, T: R7806
(34)	1st ELEC	25	ETC S4 26° 575w	Temp X Mid Cen	R99+R99, T: R7806
(51)	2nd ELEC	7	ETC S4 26° 575w	X FAR IN 2	G841
(52)	2nd ELEC	20	ETC S4 26° 575w	X FAR IN 2	G841
(53)	2nd ELEC	5	ETC S4 26° 575w	X CEN IN 2	G841
(54)	2nd ELEC	22	ETC S4 26° 575w	X CEN IN 2	G841

Figure 15.3 A sample page from the instrument schedule (hookup sheet) for the Canadian Opera Company Hummingbird Centre production of *Il Trovatore*. Lighting design by Joan Sullivan-Genthe. Associate lighting designer: Michael McNamara. Drafting by Joshua Windhausen.

suggested lighting instrument symbols, is contained in Appendix A. It is recommended that you closely read this information.

Lettering All lettering, whether handwritten or computer-generated, should be legible and easy to read. Characters that generally conform to the single-stroke gothic style (Figure 15.4) meet these requirements. In general, only uppercase letters should be used, although lowercase letters can be used for special purposes.

Figure 15.4 Single-stroke gothic lettering.

ABCDEF GHIJKLM
NOPQRSTUVWXYZ
1234567890

Figure 15.5 A title block.

University of Arizona School of Theatre Arts	
SCUBA DUBA	
LIGHT PLOT	PLATE 1 OF 1
SCALE: 1/2" = 1'-0"	
SC DES: T. WARING	LT DES: F. SMYTH
DIRECTOR: R. HOWE	DRAFTED: 11/21/05

Title Block   The title block (Figure 15.5) should be in the same location on all drawings of a single project. The title block should be located either in the lower-right-hand corner or in a strip vertically spanning the right side of the drawing. In either case, the block should include the following information:

1. Name of producing organization and/or theatre
2. Name of production
3. Drawing title
4. Drawing number
5. Predominant scale of the drawing
6. Date the sheet was drafted
7. Designer(s) of the production
8. Drafter, if different from designer
9. Approval of drawing, if applicable
10. Dates of revisions

Symbols   The normal procedure in drawing a light plot is to use symbols to represent the various types of lighting instrument being used. The USITT-recommended symbols are illustrated in Appendix A. As part of the process of determining which symbol to use for a particular instrument, you may find it helpful to read the material found under the heading, "Symbol Guidelines," in the text portion of Appendix A. That material really helps explain the whole symbol-selection process.

Legend   Each light plot must have a legend, or instrument key (Figure 15.6), which explains the meaning of each symbol used on the plot. The legend, or instrument key, can be placed in any location on the light plot that does not interfere with other information. A perusal of the information in the Appendix A text under the heading, "Legend or Instrument Key," will help explain the specific types of information that need to be included.

Instrument Notation   The symbol for each instrument drawn on a light plot normally has a great deal of information associated with it: the area of focus, color, instrument number, lamp wattage, circuit, channel, dimmer, and so forth. Figure 15.7 shows the specific location where this information should be placed relative to an ellipsoidal reflector spotlight symbol. For PAR-lamped instruments, strip lights and cyclorama lights, see the graphic information in Appendix A under those headings. Again, you are encouraged to not only look at the illustrated symbols but read the related text in Appendix A as well. The meaning of each follows:

- *Focus area*—The focus area for each instrument, identified by a letter placed in front of the lens housing, corresponds to the same letter that identifies a specific lighting area on the plot.
- *Color*—This reference is to the number of the specific color medium that will be used on that instrument.
- *Beam designation*—This symbol provides an indication of an instrument's focal length or beam angle. This symbol is used with all ERS's but generally isn't used with fresnels.
- *Gate accessory*—Used to indicate if an ERS has an accessory, such as a gobo or other device, placed in the instrument's gate-accessory slot.
- *Instrument number*—Each instrument is assigned a number so that it can be cross-referenced with the instrument schedule. (See the box "Instrument Numbers" for specific information on instrument numbering.)
- *Lamp wattage*—Because most instruments will accommodate lamps with a variety of wattages, it is important that the specific wattage of the lamp used for each instrument in the production be noted.
- *Circuit and/or dimmer number*—This identifies the stage circuit into which the instrument should be plugged. The appropriate circuit or dimmer number can be assigned in this space by the lighting designer, or the space can be left blank to be filled in by the electrician when he or she hangs and circuits the instrument.

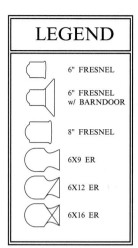

Figure 15.6   A sample legend.

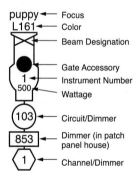

Figure 15.7 Recommended instrument notation style.

- *Dimmer*—This identifies the specific dimmer that will control this instrument. If the theatre is equipped with a patch panel, the circuit number is usually assigned to the circuit/dimmer space (see above) and that space is used for the assignment of the specific dimmer used with this instrument. Again, the dimmer number can be assigned by the lighting designer but is frequently left to the discretion of the master electrician.

- *Channel/dimmer*—If the theatre has a computer board, this space is normally used for the assignment of the control channel related to a specific instrument.

Instrument Numbers

The specific number assigned to each lighting instrument is determined by two factors: (1) its hanging location and (2) its position relative to the other instruments on that pipe. On the portion of the instrument schedule shown below (A), you'll notice that the instrument numbers are specified as 1E1, 1E2, and so on. The first portion of the number, 1E, refers to its hanging location—in this case, the first electric. The second portion of the number (1, 2, and so forth) refers to the instrument's sequential position on the pipe. In the proscenium theatre, the numbering of any electric starts at the left end of the pipe when viewed as if you were standing with your back against the upstage portion of the stage house (B). See material under the heading, "Numbering Luminaires within Conventional Mounting Positions," in Appendix A for additional information pertaining to instrument numbering.

If you compare the instrument notation used on the partial batten in this box (B) with the recommended practice shown in Figure 15.7 you'll notice that some of the recommended items such as lamp wattage, circuit/dimmer, and dimmer are missing. That's okay. It's the designer's choice to include what she believes is necessary to make the plot "communicate clearly." This example still subscribes to the recommended practice of assuming that the house for which this plot was drawn has a dimmer-per-circuit system and that control of the dimmers are assigned on a channel-per-dimmer basis. That way the channel number noted on the drawing—denoted by the hexagon at the rear of the instrument—is also reflective of the dimmer and circuit numbers. Other notation techniques are also possible. The one overriding consideration is that whatever elements of the recommended notation system that a designer chooses to use, those items are clear and consistent throughout all the drawings—plot(s), section(s), and so forth—for that particular production and that they clearly communicate the designer's intentions.

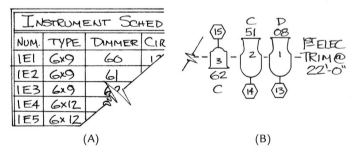

(A)   (B)

The above-referenced stipulations should be thought of as guidelines and not as rules that must be slavishly followed. The only *real* criteria pertaining to what information is located in each position, and inside of each type of circular/square/hexagonal space, is that there be consistency, and that that visual logic be applied to all symbols throughout all the drawings for a single design. Realistically, there are so many variables possible for each lighting design—a theatre's in-house equipment (type of control system, dimmer per circuit or dimmers and patch panel circuiting, etc.) as well as the instrument inventory available (in-house only, in-house and rental, or all rental) for any particular design, that it is almost impossible to create a standard that can realistically be applied to all design possibilities.

Only relevant information need be included in the symbol notation. For example, if the theatre for which you're designing has a dimmer-per-circuit system, then it would be unnecessarily redundant to include both the circuit and dimmer number. Similarly, if you've made a note in the legend that all 6 × 9 ERSs are to be equipped with 500-watt lamps, then you won't have to include the lamp wattage in each 6 × 9 symbol.

If a producing organization has the budget to rent all the instruments for a particular production, then the designer can specify the manufacturer and model number of every instrument he/she wants to use in his/her design. Unfortunately, that situation occurs only rarely. Most lighting designers have to create their designs using an "in-house" inventory of equipment. Additionally, in most situations, inventory has been accumulated over a number of years and will include, for example, ERSs made by a number of different manufacturers, or a number of different models. Each model of instrument creates its own quality of light, and rarely will the quality of light from one model or manufacturer match the light from a different model or manufacturer. For this reason, it is incumbent on the designer, when devising symbols for use on the light plot, to create something that differentiates between those various models and manufacturers so the specific instruments can be placed where he/she wants them to create the desired effect. While the USITT recommendations offer suggestions for doing this, it is the designer's responsibility to create some type of symbology that clearly communicates his/her intentions. For example, if you are using both older Century 6 × 9s and new 30-degree Source Fours you have to create clearly differentiated symbols for both, indicate both symbols in the legend, and use both on the plot. You also have to note those differences in the instrument schedule.

Under normal circumstances, instrument notations such as those described are made only on the light plot, not on the lighting section. The lighting section is used mainly as a guide for checking the physical compatibility of the various elements of the design—lighting equipment, set, theatre structure, masking—and the inclusion of any of these technical data would be unnecessary.

Ground plan: A scale mechanical drawing in the form of a horizontal offset section with the cutting plane passing at whatever level, normally a height of 4 feet above the stage floor, required to produce the most descriptive view of the set.

Lighting Templates   Lighting templates (Figure 15.8) are used to facilitate the drawing of the various stage lighting symbols. Templates are readily available in scales of ¼ inch = 1 foot and ½ inch = 1 foot.

Line Weights   The USITT recommends the following line weights be used for drafting light plots and sections.

Pencil:	Thin:	0.3 mm
	Thick:	0.5 mm
Pen:	Thin:	0.010 inch–0.0125 inch
	Thick:	0.020 inch–0.025 inch

In either pen or pencil, an extra-thick line, 0.035 inch to 0.040 inch (0.9 mm) may be used, as necessary, for emphasis (plate border, suitable section cutting-plane line, and so forth).

Drafting Conventions   The drafting conventions for lighting design generally subscribe to the USITT-recommended graphic standards for scenic design and production shown in Figure 15.9.

Although it is normal and convenient to have the outline of the set on the light plot, the most important visual elements on the light plot are the lighting symbols; therefore, those symbols should be drawn with a solid thick line. So that it recedes in visual importance, the set should be drawn with a solid thin line. Any portion of the set that would interfere with the lighting symbols or notes should be eliminated. Lighting pipes should be drawn with a hidden-construction-line style.

Lighting booms offer an interesting challenge to the general rule that a light plot is a **ground-plan** view. Typically, booms are drawn in front elevation (using a thick line) to show the height of the boom and the placement of the instruments. If there is enough space on the plot, the elevation is drawn with its base marking the place onstage where the boom will stand. However, booms are often located in cramped areas between the set and

Figure 15.8   Lighting templates.

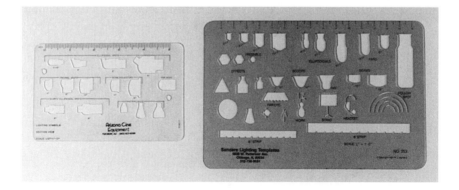

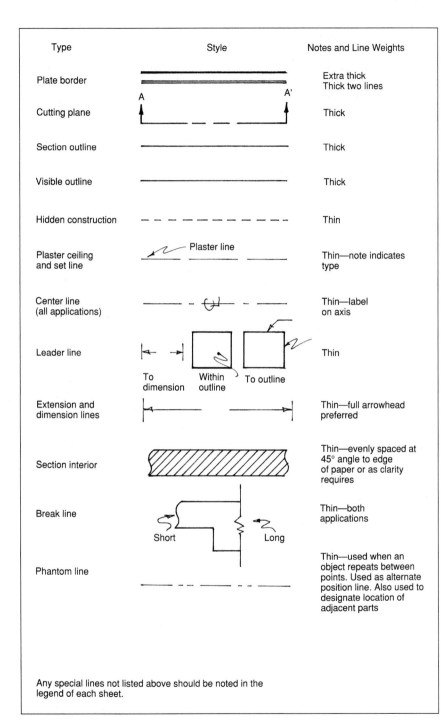

Type	Style	Notes and Line Weights
Plate border		Extra thick Thick two lines
Cutting plane	A — A'	Thick
Section outline		Thick
Visible outline		Thick
Hidden construction		Thin
Plaster ceiling and set line	Plaster line	Thin—note indicates type
Center line (all applications)		Thin—label on axis
Leader line	To dimension — Within outline — To outline	Thin
Extension and dimension lines		Thin—full arrowhead preferred
Section interior		Thin—evenly spaced at 45° angle to edge of paper or as clarity requires
Break line	Short — Long	Thin—both applications
Phantom line		Thin—used when an object repeats between points. Used as alternate position line. Also used to designate location of adjacent parts

Any special lines not listed above should be noted in the legend of each sheet.

Figure 15.9 Drafting conventions.

masking where there is no room on the plot to draw an "in situ" elevation. In these cases the elevation is frequently drawn toward the side of the plot, and an alternate position line is drawn from the base of the elevation to the place where the boom will stand, as shown in Figure 15.10. A plan view of the boom, including the instruments (use the hidden-construction-line style), is drawn in position on the plot.

Figure 15.10 Alternate-position drafting technique for depicting booms.

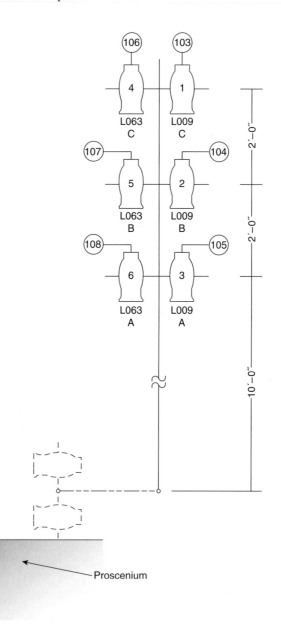

DRAFTING THE PLOT
· ·

The lighting designer needs to acquire several specific drawings from other members of the production design team before he or she can start to draw the light plot:

- the ground plan(s) of the scenic design
- the **sectional(s)** of the scenic design
- a scale ground plan of the stage and auditorium
- a scale sectional drawing of the stage and auditorium
- a layout of, and specifications for, the stage lighting system(s) of the theatre

The ground plans of the theatre and set are traced, using a thin line, onto the tracing paper to be used for the light plot. The layout of the stage lighting system provides information about the location of the various stage circuits (connecting strips, floor and wall pockets, and so on). The sectionals of the set and the stage/auditorium are traced to create the basic visual information necessary for the lighting section.

Information regarding the lighting key, beam and field angles, and lighting areas was presented in Chapters 13 and 14.

Computer Graphics

I doubt that there is any research to verify the following statement, but nevertheless, it is probably true that significantly more light plots and their associated paperwork are now computer-, rather than hand-drafted. The reason is simple and straightforward. The computer saves time. Drafting the original light plot, whether by hand or with a computer, is still a labor-intensive effort. But the computer saves a tremendous amount of time when it comes to producing the seemingly endless lists—hookup sheet/instrument schedule, **cut list**, rental schedule, and so forth—that make up the paperwork associated with the design. The computer also is an incomparable timesaver when it comes to revising the plot. Rather than erasing and redrawing whatever needs to be changed on the plot, then changing the associated paperwork, most computer drafting programs let you make changes by simply "pointing and clicking."

Reality dictates that young designers just beginning their careers *must* know computer drafting. The more programs you're acquainted with the better. At the present time, being highly proficient at several programs, such as VectorWorks Spotlight, SoftPlot by Crescit Software, and Lightwright by John McKernon Software, could land you a job. It's happened numerous times in recent years as established lighting designers, who, for any number of reasons can't, or don't want to, take the time to become computer-proficient, hire young assistants to do the computer work for them.

Sectional: A drawing, usually in scale, of an object that shows what it would look like if cut straight through at a given plane.

Cut list: A list that details the number of gels of specific size and color that will be used on a production; for example, 12 pieces of Roscolux 09 for 6-inch ERSs, 6 pieces of Lee 154 for 8-inch fresnels, and so forth.

> ⁕ Drafting for Lighting Design
>
> As we have seen, the lighting designer uses two principal mechanical draw-ings to record the information that is needed to hang, circuit, and focus the lighting design: the light plot and the lighting section. The purpose of these drawings is to guide the master electrician and crew. The amount and kind of information shown on the paperwork associated with a light-ing design varies greatly from production to production and designer to designer. But a set of basic criteria pertains to the drawings associated with any lighting design.
>
> 1. The light plot and lighting section should be drawn to scale.
> 2. The light plot should show the location of the lighting instruments in relation to the set and the physical structure of the theatre.
> 3. All drawings should adhere to the tenets of good mechanical drafting techniques.
> 4. Lighting instrument symbols and associated lettering should be repre-sented by a thick line; all other elements should be drawn using a thin line, unless a thick or extra-thick line is needed for emphasis.
> 5. A legend should be used to explain all symbols used on the plot.
> 6. Each lighting instrument or fixture should be numbered to allow for its easy identification on the hookup sheet, or instrument schedule.
> 7. All pertinent data regarding each instrument should be included on the instrument schedule.
> 8. The title block should adhere to the criteria noted in the text.

The following illustrates the capabilities of the principal types of light-ing design software programs.

Drafting Programs   The features available on any lighting design drafting software differ from manufacturer to manufacturer. The following synopsis highlights the types of features generally available on these programs.

Drafting programs for lighting design generally allow you to import CAD files of the scenic design drawings—ground plans, sectionals, and so forth—as well as the architectural drawings of the stage and auditorium. Conceptually, you can think of the imported drawings as a stack of acetate drawings. Stack them the way you want, select needed graphic information from each layer, then, building on that base, create your own drawing—the light plot layout or the sectional.

After creating the basic layout, including any permanent and temporary hanging positions, you start placing instruments. Effective drafting pro-grams will have extensive symbol libraries for the myriad lighting and scenic elements commonly used in drafting for lighting design such as fixtures, accessories, stage drapes, trusses, and scenic elements. They will also have

2D drafting capabilities. More sophisticated programs will also include 3D drafting and visualization capabilities.

To place an instrument on the plot, most programs let you select the symbol for an instrument from a toolbar or window. This symbol may be generic, or it may be so specific that it identifies the manufacturer and model type. After placing the instrument symbol on the plot you assign notational information—color, circuiting, instrument number, focus, and so forth—to each unit. Most programs automatically update instrument numbering so if you remove an instrument from a pipe, or change its location on the same pipe, the instruments on that pipe are automatically renumbered. Every time you select/place/edit an instrument or create any of the associated notational information, most drafting programs will list that information in an embedded database. That information is either added to the various lists needed to organize and track the equipment by the software program, or it will allow you to export data to specialized database programs such as Lightwright for more sophisticated paperwork management.

Some of the more popular integrated programs—programs that automatically generate paperwork lists when you draft the plot—include Vector-Works's Spotlight, MacLux Pro by Claude Heintz Design, and SoftPlot from Crescit Software.

Data Management Programs   There are two types of data management programs for lighting design. The first is the sophisticated spreadsheet/database program used to organize the data associated with a lighting design—instrument, circuiting, dimmer control, and cueing information—into the seemingly endless list of lists that lighting designers are so fond of generating. The second type is a utility. These programs provide types of information not normally included in drafting programs.

Lightwright is a popular data management program for lighting design. Available for both PC and Macintosh, it provides advanced features not available in the data management software of most drafting programs. "It can find mistakes, compare two sets of paperwork, figure your circuit and dimmer needs, automatically renumber a pipe, renumber or rearrange your channels and dimmers, or even assign dimmers automatically based on your channels. You can enter text almost any way you want and use footnotes and ditto marks to cut down on typing and wasted paper."[1] Database information generated by a drafting program such as Vectorworks Spotlight is imported into Lightwright for manipulation, organization, and printing.

As mentioned above, utilities provide the designer with ancillary information. Almost all utility programs are stand-alone products that don't work in conjunction with other programs. Beamwright, by John McKernon

---

[1]http://www.mckernon.com/whatis.htm, "Lightwright and Beamwright Introduction," p. 1.

Hey Gillette, Why Don't You Tell Us What These Programs Can Do?

I've been asked numerous times to include a discussion of the specific capabilities of the various lighting design software programs—drafting, paperwork management, visualization, and so forth—in this text. I've always declined. Here's why: discussing the specific capabilities of these programs really isn't practical. Updated versions of the software programs typically are released once every year or so. This book is revised every three to five years so if I were to write that, "Program A can do such and such," by the time you read what I wrote, it would be grossly out of date. Besides, learning how to run a software program and its capabilities is best accomplished with hands-on learning rather than reading about it in a textbook.

Most of these software programs have online trials. You can download them and work with them in the comfort of your own home for a specific length of time before the trial ends. Then, if you decide not to buy, the program is disabled. Additionally, I cannot recommend strongly enough that you take a computer drafting class and become really proficient in whatever relevant program(s) your school has available. Your school's computer lab may also have one or more of these programs. If so, spend time in the lab playing with the software. Learn what it can do. You may actually discover that it can do a whole bunch of things that you never even thought about and that playing with it is fun!

Software, is a program that helps the designer choose the correct instrument for a given situation. For example, if you input the distance from an instrument to a lighting area and the size of that lighting area, the software develops a list of fixtures that would provide an effective solution in those circumstances. Another utility, LightShop, a Rosco product, provides photometric data for the 1,500 instruments in its inventory. On the basis of lamp used, the gel color, the trim height of the fixture, and its floor distance from the subject, the program will tell you the resultant beam diameter, throw, and light output for that instrument.

Additional information about these and similar software products for lighting design can be found online and in articles and advertisements in trade magazines such as *Lighting Dimensions*, *Entertainment Design*, *Stage Directions*, and *Pro Lights & Staging News*.

Computer drafting for lighting design is clearly the way of the future. What is equally clear is that at the present time, as well as in the foreseeable future, lighting designers will need to know how to do both—draft by hand and draft on a computer.

Hand-Drawing the Plot: A Suggested Sequence

It is easy to be apprehensive when confronted with the challenge of drawing a light plot. The following sequence may help ease some of that frustration. However, remember that this is only a suggested procedure. It isn't the "only" way to do it, nor does it provide for every contingency. Nevertheless, it does provide a reasonably accurate list of "what to do first" and should help you through the necessarily complex job of producing the lighting designer's preliminary paperwork—the light plot, lighting section, and instrument schedule. While this description is specifically written for hand-drawing plots, the process works equally well for computer drafting.

1. Draw a "rough" plot first. You can make all sorts of smudges, erasures, and corrections on this copy. Then, when you have the plot the way you want it, lay another piece of Clearprint over it and trace your final clean copy.
2. Draw the theatre structure and set using a thin line.
3. Draw in your lighting areas using a thin line. On your rough plot, you can draw circles for the lighting areas if doing so will help you visualize. Most designers assign each area a letter to differentiate between them. When you draw the final plot, don't draw the circles; just place the appropriate letters in the center of the areas. If placing the letters in the center of the area interferes with the location of any lighting equipment, move the letter, not the equipment.
4. Replicate the lighting key in each area. Use a thick line for the symbols for all lighting equipment. (If you, as lighting designer, are going to be assigning circuits to each instrument, do so when you draw each instrument.) When you plot the location of the instruments, it is usually easiest to start with an area that will be the least encumbered by set pieces and masking. For proscenium and thrust productions, this is usually one of the areas down center. For arena productions, the least encumbered areas are usually center stage. If you're a little hazy on how to replicate the key in the lighting areas, you might want to review Chapter 14.
5. Proceed to replicate the keys for any additional layers of lights, such as the support lights for any sources (practical lamps, windows, fireplaces, and so forth); washes; cyc and ground-row lighting; offstage atmospheric lights such as hallways, adjoining rooms, and so forth. Don't forget to circuit each instrument, practical, and effect.
6. When you've laid in all your lights and made any necessary adjustments, number all of your instruments according to the guidelines laid down earlier in this chapter.
7. Using your light plot and the ground plans of the set(s) and theatre as your guides, draw a rough lighting section. If you find that some lighting equipment interferes with the set or masking, make any necessary adjustments to the section *and the plot*.
8. Trace the final copies of the light plot and section.
9. Fill in all necessary data on the instrument schedule or hookup sheet.

CHAPTER 16

Design Examples

Form: In the context of theatre, elements that have similar physical characteristics. For example, arena, thrust, and proscenium theatres have different *forms* of stage configuration.

The design process (see Chapter 11) provides a useful analytical approach to the process of design. That methodology will remain the same regardless of the **form** (proscenium, thrust arena) or type (drama, musical theatre, dance) of production situation in which you find yourself. However, there are some pragmatic differences between these forms and types of theatre that will affect your work as a designer. Chapter 14 showed how the lighting key varies with the form of stage; this chapter will expand on that beginning and show how the form of theatre and type of production affect the lighting design.

DESIGNING FOR THEATRE TYPE

Theatre in the twentieth century inherited the proscenium stage that had developed, in various ways and through various detours, from the days of Greek drama. Nevertheless, as a ripple effect of the Little Theatre movement of the 1920s and 1930s, fledgling companies, with little money, began to produce theatre in "found" spaces. Existing barns, churches, feed stores, grocery stores, libraries, old movie houses, and other large, relatively open buildings were all candidates for takeover. Many of these groups relished the enforced intimacy between the actors and audience that shoehorning theatres into these cramped spaces provided. Whether by accident or design, many of these converted theatre spaces didn't have the room to erect a proscenium stage and auditorium. For whatever reasons, thrust and arena stages sprang up all over the country, and all three forms prevail today.

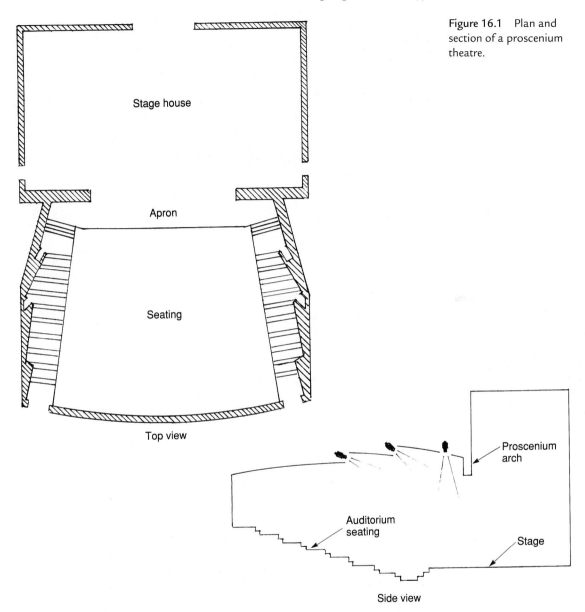

Figure 16.1 Plan and section of a proscenium theatre.

Stage house

Apron

Seating

Top view

Proscenium arch

Auditorium seating

Stage

Side view

Proscenium Stage

The proscenium arch is essentially a picture frame through which the audience views the play (Figure 16.1). Proscenium staging forces a separation between the audience and the action of the production, creating the least intimate observer-action relationship of the three basic forms of stage.

Figure 16.2   A proscenium theatre and auditorium. University of Arizona, Department of Drama.

Style: In this context, refers to the specific compositional characteristics that distinguish the appearance of one type of design from another. Using this definition, the various design styles—realism, expressionism, surrealism, and so forth—are delineated by the differences in their compositional principles.

The traditional proscenium production preserves the "magic" of the theatre. In many of the more elaborate productions, the scenery and set props are moved mechanically. The audience doesn't see the stagehands or stage machinery that moves the scenery; they just see the settings "magically" transformed before their eyes. To help create the magical mood essential to this style of production, the lighting instruments are frequently masked so that the audience won't be aware of the source of the lighting. Although it can be aesthetically pleasing to have the instruments hidden from view, this practice frequently compromises the lighting by reducing the number of hanging locations available to the designer. It is reasonably easy to adequately mask onstage instruments behind borders or in the wings without adversely affecting the lighting to any serious degree. Attempting to hide the front-of-house positions is another matter. Almost any attempt to conceal the instruments will have a negative effect on the flexibility of the designer's choices. Most Broadway and regional professional houses have many, if not all, of the front-of-house instruments exposed to view by some members of the audience (Figure 16.2). Although the instruments aren't particularly attractive, the audience usually doesn't notice them once the production is under way.

The **style** and form of the setting in a proscenium production will, to a great extent, determine the availability of hanging positions. The traditional box setting with a ceiling severely limits side-, top-, and back-lighting ap-

✳ When Possible, Compromise

Many times you will be able to create better designs if you sit down and chat. If the scene designer has created an elegant living room design, but the set has a ceiling, your overhead hanging positions are obviously gone. Right? Not necessarily. Sit down and chat with the designer. See if he or she would be able to put beams or some other visual elements on the ceiling that would enable a hole or slot to be cut through which you could focus your instruments. If holes or slots can't be cut, perhaps you could hide small instruments, such as 6-inch fresnels, PAR 38s, or MR lamps behind the beams.

Remember that theatre is a collaborative art, but collaboration can't happen without communication.

---

proaches. Box settings without ceilings still restrict the use of sidelight but open the set to both top- and some back-light angles. **Drop-and-wing sets** (frequently used in traditional musicals and ballet) enable the designer to make effective use of side, top, and some back lighting. An open setting, one that is essentially a series of platforms with few vertical elements, provides the designer with the most flexibility because it opens the playing area to approaches from all directions—front, side, top, and back.

Thrust Stage

A thrust stage can be loosely defined as any form of playing area that is surrounded on three sides by the audience. Because the audience views the action of the play from three sides, as shown in Figure 16.3, the designer generally needs to surround the actors with light more completely than would be necessary on a proscenium stage. On a thrust stage, the downstage areas (the space toward the front of the thrust) usually contain only furniture pieces, as shown in Figure 16.4. Because there are usually no large walls or other vertical elements to interrupt the lighting-approach angles on the three open sides of the stage, it would seem that the designer would have more flexibility to select the appropriate angle of approach for each instrument. This flexibility can be limited if the theatre doesn't have a well-designed **grid** system above and beyond the stage area. All is not lost, however, because the judicious and creative use of booms and lighting ladders to provide temporary lighting positions in unusual places can solve a multitude of difficulties.

The challenge of masking lighting instruments for a thrust-stage production is considerable. In fact, it is almost impossible to mask the instruments from every seat in the house; and if all instruments *are* effectively

Drop-and-wing set: A setting primarily composed of two-dimensional scenery, normally one or more drops upstage and a series of portals placed between the drops and the proscenium.

Grid: A network of steel I beams supporting elements of the counterweight system.

Figure 16.3 A typical thrust-stage arrangement.

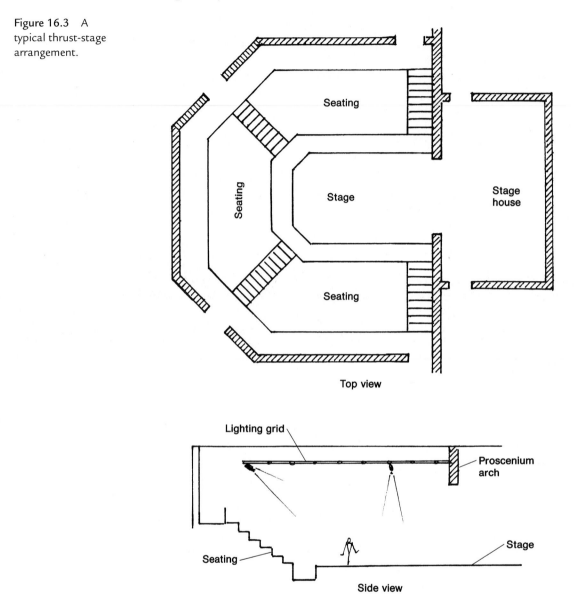

masked, it is often at the expense of the lighting design. In such cases, it is preferable to sacrifice the masking. Although members of the audience may see the instruments, if they aren't lit directly (see the box "Try to Avoid Blinding Your Audience,) and can't clearly see the audience on the opposite side of the stage, they will generally accept the exposed instruments as a convention and concentrate on the action of the play.

Figure 16.4 Thrust theatre. Tyrone Guthrie Theatre, Minneapolis, Minnesota. Seating an audience of 1,441, no seat is farther than 52 feet from the stage. (Photo by Robert Ashley Wilson.)

✳ Try to Avoid Blinding Your Audience

When working on a thrust or arena stage, you always confront the challenge of light shining from the opposite side of the stage into the eyes of the audience. Although, ideally, you'd like to keep the light off the audience entirely, the audience's proximity to the stage normally makes it impossible to prevent some spill. If the light falls on the feet, shins, or maybe the knees of audience members closest to the stage, they probably will not be bothered by the light; if it gets much higher, they will tend to become distracted by it.

To reduce ambient spill, and to keep the audience from seeing the hot spots of the lenses, use snoots or top hats on all ERSs and on those fresnels that don't have barn doors.

Arena Stage

An arena stage can be defined as any stage space surrounded on all sides by the audience, as shown in Figure 16.5. It is unusual to find an arena theatre where the last row of seats is more than 20 to 25 feet from the stage. The Arena Stage in Washington, D.C., is a large example of this type of theatre,

Figure 16.5 A typical arena theatre configuration.

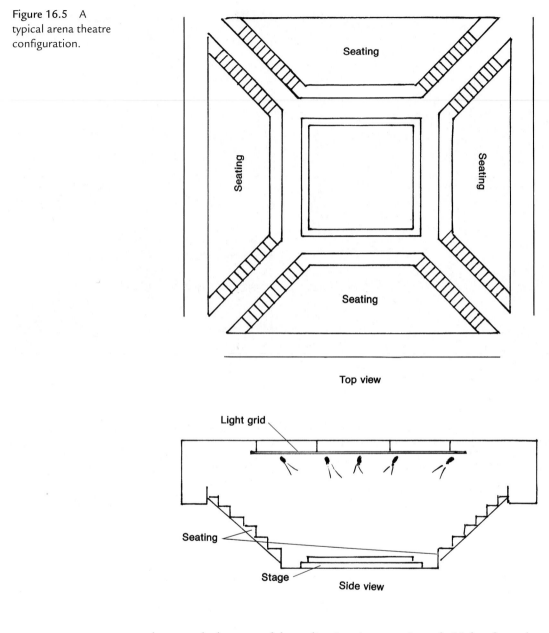

Top view

Side view

because the last row of the auditorium is approximately 35 feet from the stage (Figure 16.6). This intimate observer-action relationship dictates that most of the acting-area instruments, which are hung relatively close to the actors, will serve double duty. Wide field-angle instruments, such as 6 × 9 and 40- or 50-degree ERSs and 6-inch fresnels, provide front lights for one section of

Figure 16.6 Arena the-
atre. The interior of the
827-seat Arena Stage in
Washington, D.C.

the audience while they backlight the action for the audience on the opposite side of the stage.

The use of color in lighting for the arena stage probably requires more subtlety, both in design and execution, than does the lighting for either proscenium or thrust stages. Pale tints and colors of lower-than-normal saturation are generally used in arena productions because hues of even medium saturation have a tendency to overwhelm skin tones and the palettes of the scenic and costume designers if used at the close ranges generally dictated by the proximity of instruments to the stage.

The settings used in arena productions are generally limited to furniture and low-profile pieces that offer little interference with the approach angles for the light. The challenge of inadequate hanging locations can be solved with the same type of creative ingenuity recommended during the discussion of booms and ladders in the section on thrust stages.

Although fairly steep sectional angles are normally used to prevent light from shining on the audience, there is rarely a problem with heavy facial shadows on arena stages because each lighting area is usually lit from at least three (and more normally four) sides, and the bounce light from the floor (even when it's painted black) tends to fill any remaining shadows.

DESIGNING FOR THEATRICAL FORM

The previous section was devoted to a general discussion of how the different forms of theatre affect the execution of the lighting design. Because craft principles are best demonstrated through example, in this section we will study lighting designs for proscenium, thrust, and arena productions of Tennessee Williams's *The Glass Menagerie*. We will discuss the musical *Cabaret* and use *The Nutcracker* to illustrate lighting principles for dance production.

An advisory digression before we begin. Each lighting design is a product of a unique set of circumstances: the theatre in which the play is produced, the personalities and creativity of the production design team, the production budgets (both time and fiscal), the dedication and talent of the lighting crew, and so forth. No design should ever be thought of as "correct" as the only solution to the design challenge. In that vein, these designs are only examples. They show one designer's reaction to the production circumstances. They work; but they aren't "right" and they aren't wrong. They are simply what they are: examples.

Drama: *The Glass Menagerie*

Notes about *The Glass Menagerie* in my designer's notebook (see Chapter 11) might look like the following:

> *The Glass Menagerie* is primarily a memory play. Memories are usually soft and faded, like tattered, forgotten baby blankets. The mind plays gentle tricks with harsh reality of what has been. It smooths off the painful edge of injury and mutes the high points of happiness. Pleasant moments from the past well up in gentle colors and soft focus. Even the unwatchable can be seen through the soft diffusion and blending of time and distance. Memories, both good and bad,

change and fade with the passage of time. Reality is nonexistent. Only special moments remain.

Laura is soft and gentle. She possesses the depth and transparent delicacy of her menagerie of tiny animals. If one personality could combine the brilliant clarity of delicate crystal wind chimes with the velvet kiss of a soft summer night, that person would be Laura. Like glass, she appears hard but can, with only a little pressure, shatter into a thousand shimmering pieces.

Amanda is also soft. She has the softness of a chiffon gown lazily twirling to the music of a waltz at the cotillion on a warm, long ago, Mississippi summer night. Whereas Laura is clear and bell-like, Amanda is delicate pale tints of blue and lavender. A faded memory of herself, she lives in the past because the present is too hard, too harsh. We wonder if her memories of Blue Mountain are based on her past, or if she created the reality of her past to get through her present. Even the stridency and harshness of Amanda is softened through the dimness of memory.

This play belongs to Laura and Amanda. It's Tom's memory of them. As it is his memory, he only wanders through the play to act as a foil to them; he is the narrator of his own memory. He is more real than any of the others. At the beginning of the play and during those moments when he steps out of the play to narrate, he is real. He is contemporary. There must be a separation between Tom and the portrayal of his remembered self.

The Gentleman Caller is also a memory. He is more vibrant than Laura and Amanda because he was a swirl of activity in Tom's memory. He was the All-American ideal, the go-getter, the positive I'm-going-to-succeed young man that Amanda wanted her children to be.

The world of Tom's memory and Tom's world as the narrator must be visually separated by the quality of the light. The world of memory should be soft and faded. The Wingfield's apartment should be lit with out-of-focus ERSs and soft fresnels. No hard edges should be evident anywhere. Colors in the memory scenes should be mostly tints of pale lavenders, blues, pinks, and a little **neutralizing** amber. The candlelight scene will need soft but deep shadows and some "candle color" support for Laura's and the Gentleman Caller's faces. The street of Tom's memories must also be soft, but Tom must always be hard, clear, and real.

Tom's world as a narrator should have the harsh glare of reality about it. The light should be hard-edged; and, to help create Tom's sense of isolation, it should have the look of night about it.

General Design Notes A different lighting key is used for each design to show how the same stimuli can result in a number of equally effective solutions to the design challenge. Notice how the saturation of the colors decreases as we move from the proscenium to the thrust and finally the arena design.

Neutralization: The result of mixing complementary hues. In light, the creation of white. In pigment, the creation of dark gray.

Notes on the Proscenium Production   The lighting key for the proscenium production of *The Glass Menagerie* is shown in Figure 16.7. The scenic sketch, light plot, section, and instrument schedule are shown in Figures 16.8 to 16.11.

The production concept specifies soft pastels and color shifts to enhance the moods of the individual scenes. Because front lights provide the most reflectivity to the audience, the medium-saturation color washes—Roscolux 20, Medium Amber; 43, Dark Pink; and 78, Trudy Blue—are hung in the second AP to provide the dominant color-change mechanism. The side-front lights provide good facial modeling and visibility. They are double hung into

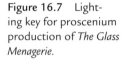

Figure 16.7 Lighting key for proscenium production of *The Glass Menagerie.*

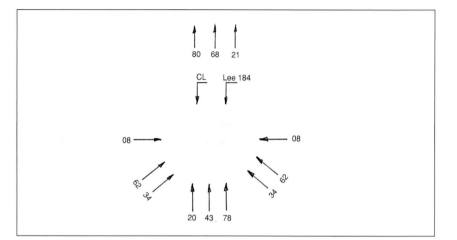

Figure 16.8 Scenic design for proscenium production of *The Glass Menagerie.*

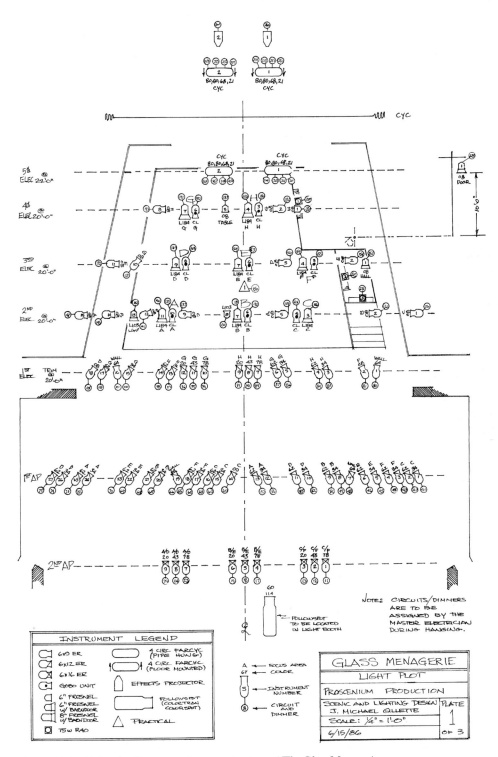

Figure 16.9 Light plot for proscenium production of *The Glass Menagerie*.

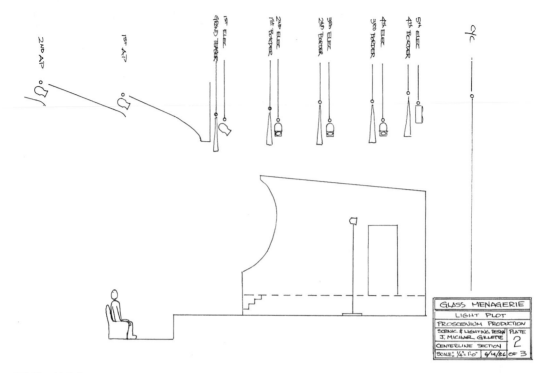

Figure 16.10 Lighting section for proscenium production of *The Glass Menagerie.*

each lighting area with Roscolux 34, Flesh Pink, and 62, Booster Blue, to enhance the color-shift capabilities. (When used together, these two colors result in a warm-white mix. When used separately, they enhance either the warm or cool color-shift capabilities of the design.) The side lights provide good body definition and help to separate the actors from the background. They are gelled with 08, Pale Amber Gold, which is a warm, low-saturation tint that will combine with the R62 to produce a white edge or rim light. The R08 is neutral enough that it won't create any strange shadow colors (see the box "Complementary Color Shadowing, in Chapter 9) when combined with any of the front or side-front lights. The top lights highlight the head and shoulders and help separate the actors from their background. They are gelled with Lee 184, Cosmetic Peach, because its very pale cool-brown hue is an excellent neutral blending color and its soft diffused quality will help fill shadows. The clear top light with the medium breakup gobo is used to provide texture—primarily in combination with the saturated washes during Tom's narrative sequences.

The R-40 (flood) lamps hung over the door arches simply light the doorways. The light from these lamps, which are normally run at low intensity, is very diffused and puts a little fill light into the archways to soften the harsh shadow lines frequently encountered here.

Instrument Schedule — Production: Glass Menagerie – Proscenium, Page 1 of 4

INST #	TYPE	LOCATION	AREA	COLOR	CIR	DIM	LAMP	REMARKS
2AP1	6x16	2ND AP	C/E		11	11	"	
2AP2	6x16	"	C/E		12	12	"	
2AP3	6x16	"	C/E		13	13	"	
2AP4	6x16	"	B/E		17	17	"	
2AP5	6x16	"	B/E		18	18	"	
2AP6	6x16	"	B/E		19	19	"	
2AP7	6x16	"	A/D		23	23	"	
2AP8	6x16	"	A/D		24	24	"	
2AP9	6x16	"	A/D		25	25	"	
1AP1	6x12	1ST AP	C	34	41	41	1000W	
1AP2	6x12	"	C	62	42	42	"	
1AP3	6x12	"	F	39	43	43	"	
1AP4	6x12	"	F	62	44	44	"	
1AP5	6x12	"	E	34	45	45	"	
1AP6	6x12	"	E	62	46	46	"	
1AP7	6x12	"	S.L WALL	64	48	48	"	
1AP8	6x12	"	B	34	49	49	"	
1AP9	6x12	"	B	62	51	51	"	
1AP10	6x12	"	D	34	52	52	"	
1AP11	6x12	"	D	62	53	53	"	
1AP12	6x12	"	A	34	56	56	"	
1AP13	6x12	"	A	62	57	57	"	
1AP14	6x12	"	C	09	60	60	"	
1AP15	6x12	"	C	34	62	62	"	
1AP16	6x12	"	C	62	63	63	"	
1AP17	6x12	"	F	34	64	64	"	
1AP18	6x12	"	F	62	65	65	"	
1AP19	6x12	"	S.R WALL	64	66	66	"	
1AP20	6x12	"	B	34	67	67	"	
1AP21	6x12	"	B	62	68	68	"	
1AP22	6x12	"	E	34	69	69	"	
1AP23	6x12	"	E	62	70	70	"	
1AP24	6x12	"	A	34	72	72	"	

Instrument Schedule — Production: Glass Menagerie – Proscenium, Page 2 of 4

INST #	TYPE	LOCATION	AREA	COLOR	CIR	DIM	LAMP	REMARKS
1AP25	6x12	1ST AP	A	62	73	73	1000W	
1AP26	6x12	"	D	34	74	74	"	
1AP27	6x12	"	D	62	75	75	"	
1E1	6x9	1ST ELEC	S.L WALL	64	80	80	1000W	KEEP FOCUS OFF "
1E2	6x9	"	F	08	81	81	"	
1E3	6x12	"	H	34	83	83	"	
1E4	6x12	"	H	62	84	84	"	
1E5	6x12	"	G	34	86	86	"	
1E6	6x12	"	G	62	87	87	"	
1E7	6x12	"	H	78	89	89	"	
1E8	6x12	"	H	43	90	90	"	
1E9	6x12	"	H	20	91	91	"	
1E10	6x12	"	G	78	94	94	"	
1E11	6x12	"	G	43	95	95	"	
1E12	6x12	"	G	20	96	96	"	
1E13	6x12	"	H	34	97	97	"	
1E14	6x12	"	H	62	98	98	"	
1E15	6x12	"	G	34	100	100	"	
1E16	6x9	"	S.R WALL	64	101	101		KEEP FOCUS OFF "APT."
1E17	6x12	"	G	62	103	103	"	
1E18	6x9	"	D	08	105	105	"	
2E1	6"F	2ND ELEC	C	08	120	120	750W	
2E2	6x9	"	B	08	122	122	750W	
2E3	6x9	"		L184	126	126	750W	
2E4	8"F	"	C	NONE	128	128	1000W	
2E5	6x9	"	A	08	129	129	750W	
2E6	6x9	"	B	NONE	132	132	750W	
2E7	8"F	"	B	L184	133	133	1000W	
2E8	6"F	"	E	L103	134	134	500W	CHANDELIER "SUPPORT"
2E9	6x9	"	C	08	137	137	750W	
2E10	6x9	"	A	NONE	139	139	750W	
2E11	8"F	"	A	L184	140	140	1000W	

Instrument Schedule — Production: Glass Menagerie – Proscenium, Page 3 of 4

INST #	TYPE	LOCATION	AREA	COLOR	CIR	DIM	LAMP	REMARKS
2E12	6x9	2ND ELEC	F	08			750W	
2E13	6"F	"	LAMP SUPPORT	L103			500W	
2E14	6x9	"	B	08			750W	
2E15	6x9	"	A	08			750W	
3E1	6"F	3RD ELEC	HALL	08			500W	
3E2	6x9	"	E	08			750W	
3E3	6x9	"	F	NONE				GOBO - MEDIUM BREAKUP
3E4	8"F	"	F	L184			1000W	BARNDOOR
3E5	6x9	"	D	08			750W	
3E6	6x9	"	E	NONE			750W	GOBO - MED. BREAKUP
3E7	8"F	"	E	L184			1000W	
3E8	6x9	"	D	NONE			750W	GOBO - MED. BREAKUP
3E9	8"F	"	D	L184			1000W	
3E10	6x9	"	G	08			750W	
3E11	6x9	"	E	08			750W	
4E1	6"F	4TH ELEC	H	08			500W	
4E2	6x9	"	G	08			750W	
4E3	6x9	"	H	NONE			750W	GOBO - MED. BREAKUP
4E4	8"F	"	H	L184			1000W	
4E5	6"F	"	TABLE SPEC	08			500W	FULL FLOOD
4E6	6x9	"	G	NONE			750W	GOBO - MED. BREAKUP
4E7	8"F	"	G	L184			1000W	
4E8	6x9	"	H	08			750W	
5E1	PAR FLOOD	5TH ELEC	CYC	80/80/48/21			4-1K	
5E2	PAR FLOOD	"	CYC	80/80/48/21			4-1K	
SL1	6"F	STAGE FLOOR	DINING DOOR	08			500W	BARNDOOR TO DOOR EDGE
SPEC	SIDE ARM		LINE B				8-25W	CHANDELIER
US1	PAR FLOOD	US OF CYC	CYC	80/80/48/21			4-1K	
US2	PAR FLOOD	"	CYC	80/80/48/21			4-1K	
US3	EFFECTS PROJ	"						DISCUSS SLIDES W/ DESIGNER
US4	EFFECTS PROJ	"						"

Instrument Schedule — Production: Glass Menagerie – Proscenium, Page 4 of 4

INST #	TYPE	LOCATION	AREA	COLOR	CIR	DIM	LAMP	REMARKS
DOOR	R40	US DOOR	-		-		75W	ANGLE DOWN @ 60°
DOOR	R40	MIDDLE DOOR	-		-		75W	"
DOOR	R40	DS DOOR	-		-		75W	"

Figure 16.11 Instrument schedule for proscenium production of *The Glass Menagerie*.

The support light for the floor lamp is a 6-inch fresnel hung directly above the practical and gelled with Lee 103 to provide a warm pool of light around the floor lamp when it is on. Support lights for the candles used in the scene between Laura and the Gentleman Caller are hung in the first AP and focused on area C.

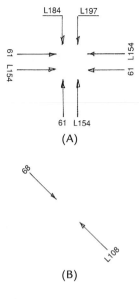

Figure 16.12 Lighting key for thrust production of *The Glass Menagerie.*

Figure 16.13 Scenic design for thrust production of *The Glass Menagerie.*

The followspot focuses tightly on Tom's head during his narration sequences. The specified Colortran Colorspot doesn't have a fan, and the lamp is incandescent so that it can be put on a dimmer to unobtrusively dim it out when Tom segues from narrator to participant in the scene. It is gelled with Roscolux 114, Hamburg Frost, to soften the edge of the beam and Roscolux 60, No-Color Blue, to help it cut through the warm pinks and lavenders of the other lights.

The cyc lights are used to wash the building flats on either side of the set and the cyc in back of it. Each four-lamp cyc light is gelled with two dark blues (Roscolux 80, Primary Blue, and Roscolux 84, Zephyr Blue), one medium blue (Roscolux 68, Sky Blue), and a neutralizing complementary (Roscolux 21, Golden Amber).

The seamless plastic projection screen cyc is painted with dyes and paint. It is lit from front and back to give greater depth to the scene during the evening and storm scenes. The effects projectors contain slides showing the building of storm clouds during the dinner scene.

Because of the number of instruments and the complexity of the color shifts, this production should be equipped with a dimmer-per-circuit lighting system equipped with a computer board.

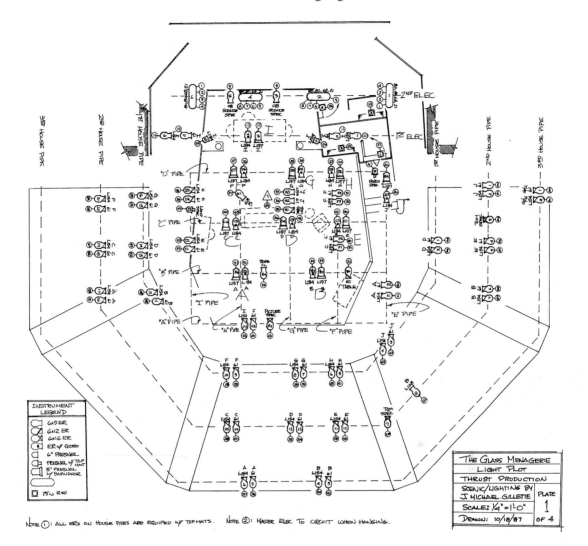

Figure 16.14   Light plot for thrust production of *The Glass Menagerie*.

Notes on the Thrust Production   The lighting key for the thrust production is shown in Figure 16.12. The scenic sketch, light plot, lighting section, and instrument schedule are shown in Figures 16.13 to 16.16.

The thrust-production lighting design uses a two-color shift. The two colors—Lee 154, Pale Rose, and Roscolux 61, Mist Blue—are double hung, as shown in Figure 16.12A, to give a color range from soft pink through lavender to pale blue. The top lights (Lee 184, Cosmetic Peach, with a medium breakup pattern) are a compromise solution. They provide the color

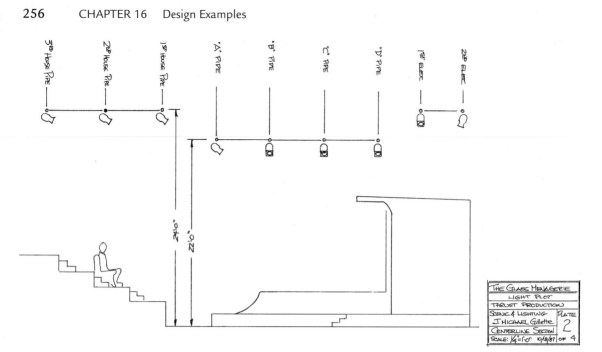

Figure 16.15 Lighting section for thrust production of *The Glass Menagerie.*

neutralization of the Lee 184 with the textural effects of the medium breakup pattern. The Lee 197, Alice Blue, top wash is used in conjunction with the goboed top light during Tom's narrative sequences.

For the candlelit scene between Laura and the Gentleman Caller, area C is crosslit according to the lighting key shown in Figure 16.12B. The Lee 108, Straw, is a candlelight support and the Roscolux 68, Sky Blue, provides visibility while still maintaining the idea of "shadow."

Father's picture, the sofa, and the table holding Laura's menagerie are lit with specials to highlight those areas when necessary. Instead of using followspots for Tom's narrative sequences, a location just in front of the stoop is designated as the "narrative spot." Three ungelled specials are triangulated on that spot. Additional specials provide support lights for the floor lamp, porch light, and wall sconces.

The method of circuiting the dimmers is based on the area color-shift concept. Each lighting area has all three instruments of the same color patched into the same dimmer. The top lights are ganged by areas—AB, CDE, FGH, I, and J. This method uses a moderate number of dimmers while still allowing for color shifting.

Notes on the Arena Production   Figure 16.17 is the lighting key for the arena production. Figures 16.18 to 16.21 are the scenic sketch, light plot, lighting section, and instrument schedule for this production.

INSTRUMENT SCHEDULE

PRODUCTION: GLASS MENAGERIE – THRUST   PAGE 1 of 4

INST#	TYPE	LOCATION	AREA	COLOR	CIR	DIM	LAMP	REMARKS
3P1	6x12	2ND HOUSE PIPE	G/4	G1	300	7	1KW	
3P2	6x12	"	G/4	L154	301	17	1KW	
3P3	6x12	"	B	G1	333	2	1KW	
3P4	6x12	"	B	L154	334	12	1KW	
3P5	6x12	"	A	G1	336	1	1KW	
3P6	6x12	"	A	L154	337	11	1KW	
2P1	6x9	2ND HOUSE PIPE	J	G1	200	10	750W	
2P2	6x12	"	J	L154	201	20	750W	
2P3	6x16	"	TOM SPEC	None	204	41	1KW	PATCH w/ 2P9 & G1
2P4	6x12	L	E	G1	205	5	1KW	
2P5	6x12	L	E	L154	207	15	1KW	
2P6	6x12	"	B	G1	208	2	1KW	
2P7	6x12	"	B	L154	209	12	1KW	
2P8	6x9	"	B	L108	227	31	750W	PATCH w/ H1
2P9	6x16	"	TOM SPEC	None	230	41	1KW	PATCH w/ 2P3 & G1
2P10	6x12	"	E	G1	232	5	1KW	
2P11	6x12	"	E	L154	233	15	1KW	
2P12	6x12	"	D	G1	234	4	1KW	
2P13	6x12	"	D	L154	235	14	1KW	
2P14	6x12	"	C	G1	237	3	1KW	
2P15	6x12	"	C	L154	238	13	1KW	
2P16	6x12	"	A	G1	251	1	1KW	
2P17	6x12	"	A	L154	253	11	1KW	
2P18	6x12	"	C	G1	254	3	1KW	
2P19	6x12	"	C	L154	257	13	1KW	
2P20	6x12	"	F	G1	258	6	1KW	
2P21	6x12	"	F	L154	259	16	1KW	
1P1	6x12	1ST HOUSE PIPE	D	G1	102	4	1KW	
1P2	6x12	"	D	L154	104	14	1KW	
1P3	6x12	"	J	G1	123	10	1KW	
1P4	6x12	"	J	L154	125	20	1KW	
1P5	6x12	"	H	G1	131	8	1KW	

INSTRUMENT SCHEDULE

PRODUCTION: GLASS MENAGERIE – THRUST   PAGE 2 OF 4

INST#	TYPE	LOCATION	AREA	COLOR	CIR	DIM	LAMP	REMARKS
1P6	6x12	1ST HOUSE PIPE	H	L154	133	18	1KW	
1P7	6x12	"	B	G1	134	7	1KW	
1P8	6x12	"	G	L154	135	17	1KW	
1P9	6x12	"	F	G1	138	6	1KW	
1P10	6x12	"	F	L154	139	16	1KW	
1P11	6x12	"	B	G1	148	2	1KW	
1P12	6x12	"	B	L154	149	12	1KW	
1P13	6x12	"	D	G1	152	4	1KW	
1P14	6x12	"	D	L154	153	14	1KW	
1P15	6x12	"	G	G1	158	7	1KW	
1P16	6x12	"	G	L154	159	17	1KW	
A1	6x16	GRID PIPE A	PICTURE SPEC	None	23	34	1KW	
A2	6x12	"	I	G1	64	9	1KW	
A3	6x12	"	I	L154	65	19	1KW	
B1	6x12	GRID PIPE B	TABLE	None	52	32	500W	
B2	8°F	"	B	L197	53	25	1KW	w/ BARNDOOR
B3	6x9	"	B	L184	54	21	750W	w/ MED. BREAKUP GOBO
B4	6x9	"	SOFA	None	55	33	500W	
B5	6x9	"	A	L184	56	21	750W	w/ MED. BREAKUP GOBO
B6	8°F	"	A	L197	57	25	1KW	w/ BARNDOOR
C1	8°F	GRID PIPE C	E	L197	40	26	1KW	w/ BARNDOOR
C2	6x9	"	E	L184	41	22	750W	w/ MED. BREAKUP GOBO
C3	6x9	"	D	L184	42	22	750W	
C4	8°F	"	D	L197	36	26	1KW	w/ BARNDOOR
C5	6x9	"	C	L184	43	22	750W	w/ MED. BREAKUP GOBO
C6	8°F	"	C	L197	44	26	1KW	w/ BARNDOOR
D1	6°F	GRID PIPE D	PORCH SPEC	None	104	35	750W	w/ 2" TOP HAT
D2	8°F	"	H	L197	22	27	1KW	w/ BARNDOOR
D3	6x9	"	H	L184	23	23	750W	w/ MED. BREAKUP GOBO
D4	6x9	"	G	L184	24	23	750W	

INSTRUMENT SCHEDULE

PRODUCTION: GLASS MENAGERIE – THRUST   PAGE 3 OF 4

INST#	TYPE	LOCATION	AREA	COLOR	CIR	DIM	LAMP	REMARKS
D5	8°F	GRID PIPE D	G	L197	25	27	1KW	w/ BARNDOOR
D6	6x9	"	F	L184	26	23	750W	w/ MED. BREAKUP GOBO
D7	8°F	"	F	L197	27	27	1KW	w/ BARNDOOR
E1	6x9	GRID PIPE E	A	L154	61	11	750W	
E2	6x9	"	A	G1	60	1	750W	
E3	6x9	"	J	L184	30	29	750W	w/ MED. BREAKUP GOBO
E4	8°F	"	U	L197	20	30	1KW	w/ BARNDOOR
F1	6x9	GRID PIPE F	C	L154	51	13	750W	
F2	6x9	"	C	G1	50	3	750W	
F3	6x9	"	F	L154	32	16	750W	
F4	6x9	"	F	G1	31	6	750W	
G1	6x12	GRID PIPE G	TOM SPEC	None	35	41	1KW	PATCH w/ 2P9 & 2P3
G2	6x9	"	U	G1	34	10	750W	
G3	6x9	"	U	L154	33	20	750W	
H1	6x9	GRID PIPE H	B	68	37	31	1KW	PATCH w/ 2P8
I1	6x12	GRID PIPE I	E	G1	59	5	1KW	
I2	6x12	"	E	L154	58	15	1KW	
I3	6°F	"	LAMP SPEC		49	36	500W	w/ 2" TOP HAT
I4	6x12	"	H	G1	39	8	1KW	
I5	6x12	"	H	L154	38	18	1KW	
1E1	6x9	1ST ELEC	I	L154	10	19	750W	
1E2	6x9	"	I	G1	11	9	750W	
1E3	8°F	"	I	L197	12	28	1KW	w/ BARNDOOR
1E4	6x9	"	I	L184	13	24	750W	w/ MED. BREAKUP GOBO
1E5	6x9	"	I	G1	14	9	750W	
1E6	6x9	"	I	L154	15	19	750W	

INSTRUMENT SCHEDULE

PRODUCTION: GLASS MENAGERIE – THRUST   PAGE 4 OF 4

INST#	TYPE	LOCATION	AREA	COLOR	CIR	DIM	LAMP	REMARKS
2E1	PANEL	2ND ELEC	SL WALL	80,20,02,21	1-4	22,42,43,44	4-1KW	PATCH w/ 2E6 (BY COLOR)
2E2	PANEL	"	US WALL	80,20,02,21	5-8	46,47,48,49	4-1KW	PATCH w/ 2E4 (BY COLOR)
2E3	6x9	"	SCONCE SPEC	OB	9	37	500W	PATCH w/ 2E5
2E4	6x9	"	US WALL	80,20,02,21	5-8	46,47,48,49	4-1KW	PATCH w/ 2E2 (BY COLOR)
2E5	6x9	"	SCONCE SPEC	OB	9	37	500W	PATCH w/ 2E3
2E6	PANEL	"	SR WALL	80,20,02,21	1-4	22,42,43,44	4-1KW	PATCH w/ 2E1 (BY COLOR)
1	R40	FRONT DOOR	—	—	F1	38	75W	ANGLE DOWN @ 45°
2	R40	L.R. ARCH	—	—	F2	38	75W	" " "
3	R40	U.L. ARCH	—	—	F3	38	75W	" " "
4	B40	DINING RM NOOK	—	—	F4	38	75W	" " "
5	6°F	PAKING RM	I	L154	F6	39	500W	TWOFER w/ 6
6	6°F	"	I	L154	F10	39	500W	TWOFER w/ 5
7	—	PRACTICAL PIPES C/D	—	—	45	40	8-15W	CHANDELIER

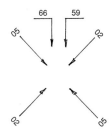

Figure 16.16 Instrument schedule for thrust production of *The Glass Menagerie*.

Figure 16.17 Lighting key for arena production of *The Glass Menagerie*.

The color-shift technique used in this production relies on a close interplay between the saturated overhead color wash (Roscolux 59, Indigo) and the diagonally crossing acting-area lights (Roscolux 02, Bastard Amber, and 05, Rose Tint). By varying the intensity differential between these two sets of lights, colors that range between a very delicate rose-pink and deep purple

Figure 16.18 Scenic design for arena production of *The Glass Menagerie*.

can be achieved. The goboed top light gelled with Roscolux 66, Cool Blue, provides a complementary hue to enliven the mix and provide some needed texture for Tom's narrative sequences.

The diagonal orientation of the lighting in the apartment area results in a slightly different look compared with the "on-axis" orientation of the lights outside the apartment.

Candlelight support lights are not used for the scene between Laura and the Gentleman Caller because the lights from the candles should provide the needed light. The dark blue "Alley specials, will be used to help create the concept of night outside the apartment. Various other support lights and specials are used as necessary.

Again, as in the thrust production, a "narrative spot" will be established, and that location will be lit with specials rather than followspots.

The circuiting of the dimmers will be similar to that for the thrust production. Each lighting area has all four of the instruments gelled with R02

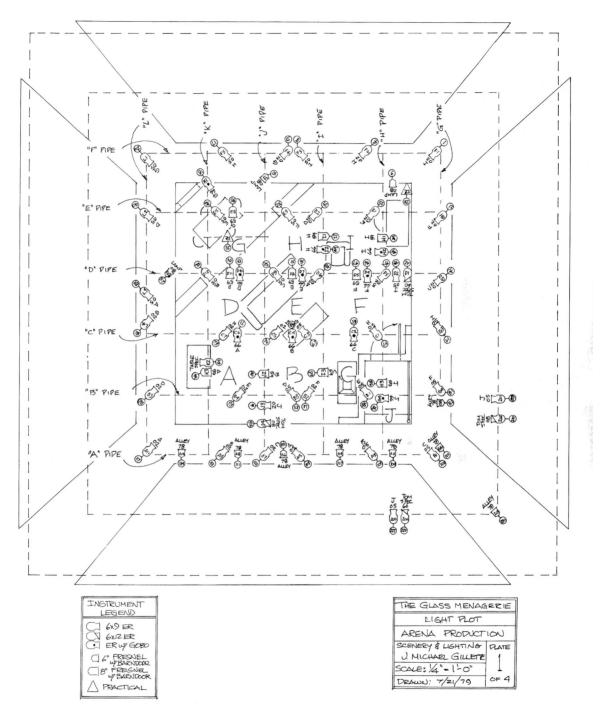

Figure 16.19 Light plot for arena production of *The Glass Menagerie*.

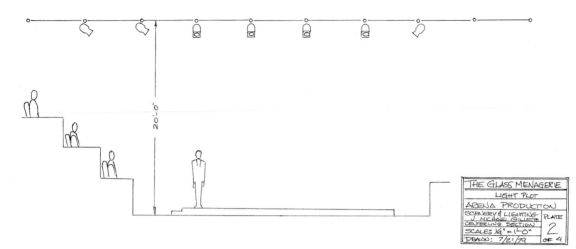

Figure 16.20 Lighting section for arena production of *The Glass Menagerie.*

and R05 patched into the same dimmer. The top lights are ganged by areas—ABC, DEF, G, HI, and J.

Musicals: *Cabaret*

The lighting key for *Cabaret* is shown in Figure 16.22. Figures 16.23 to 16.26 show the scenic sketch, light plot, lighting section, and instrument schedule.

There are two significant differences between most musical and nonmusical forms of theatre: the use of (1) songs and (2) dance within the context of the story to further the plot, provide character development, and so forth. As a consequence, the style of most musicals is generally less realistic than is that of nonmusical theatre. This "less realistic" style frequently results in a color palette that is more saturated than its more realistic counterparts; the addition of dance requires that principles of dance lighting, which focuses on illuminating the whole body, be integrated with those of dramatic lighting, which (to a great extent) focuses on lighting the face.

The colors selected for lighting design in this particular production of *Cabaret* were dictated by three primary considerations: (1) the full-spectrum colors of the costume and set; (2) the heavy, smoke-filled, sensuous atmosphere needed for the cabaret; and (3) the need for a lighter, more realistic atmosphere for those scenes outside the cabaret.

Complementary colors of light saturation (Roscolux 62, Booster Blue, and 02, Bastard Amber) were selected for the front lights because they would be appropriately neutral for both the cabaret scenes and those more intimate scenes outside the cabaret. However, those colors had enough saturation to enhance the costume and set colors in both locations. By balancing the color

INSTRUMENT SCHEDULE

Production: GLASS MENAGERIE - ARENA   Page 1 of 3

INST #	TYPE	LOCATION	AREA	COLOR	CIR	DIM	LAMP	REMARKS
A1	6x9	"A" PIPE	C	05	102	3	500W	
A2	6"F	"	ALLEY	78	104	22	500W	
A3	6x9	"	"	78	105	2	500W	
A4	6"F	"	ALLEY	78	107	23	500W	
A5	6x9	"	A	05	108	1	500W	
A6	6"F	"	ALLEY	78	109	23	500W	
A7	6x9	"	C	05	110	3	500W	
A8	6"F	"	ALLEY	78	111	23	500W	
A9	6x9	"	B	05	113	2	500W	
A10	6"F	"	ALLEY	78	114	23	500W	
A11	6x9	"	A	02	117	1	500W	
B1	6x9	"B" PIPE	E	05	85	5	500W	
B2	6x9	"	F	02	87	6	500W	
B3	6x9	"	D	05	88	4	500W	
B4	6x9	"	E	02	93	5	500W	
B5	6x9	"	D	02	98	4	500W	
C1	6x9	"C" PIPE	H	05	64	8	500W	
C2	6x9	"	C	66	65	11	500W	w/ MED. BREAKUP GOBO
C3	6x9	"	G	05	67	7	500W	
C4	6x9	"	B	66	68	11	500W	w/ MED. BREAKUP GOBO
C5	6x9	"	I	02	70	9	500W	
C6	6x9	"	A	66	71	11	500W	w/ MED. BREAKUP GOBO
C7	6x9	"	H	02	73	8	500W	
D1	6x12	"D" PIPE	TBM SPEC	60	42	21	500W	
D2	6x9	"	J	05	43	10	500W	
D3	6x9	"	B	02	45	2	500W	
D4	6x9	"	F	66	46	12	500W	w/ MED. BREAKUP GOBO
D5	8"F	"	E	05	47	17	1KW	
D6	6x9	"	A	02	48	1	500W	
D7	6x9	"	E	66	50	12	500W	w/ MED. BREAKUP GOBO
D8	8"F	"	E	59	51	17	1KW	

INSTRUMENT SCHEDULE

Production: GLASS MENAGERIE - ARENA   Page 2 of 3

INST #	TYPE	LOCATION	AREA	COLOR	CIR	DIM	LAMP	REMARKS
D9	6x9	"D" PIPE	C	05	52	3	500W	
D10	6x9	"	D	66	53	12	500W	w/ MED. BREAKUP GOBO
D11	8"F	"	D	59	54	17	1KW	
D12	6x9	"	B	05	56	2	500W	
D13	6"F	LAMP SPEC	08	57	24	500W		CHANDELIER SUPPORT
E1	6x9	"E" PIPE	E	02	25	5	500W	
E2	6x9	"	D	02	29	4	500W	
E3	6x9	"	F	05	32	6	500W	
E4	8"F	"	G	59	35	18	1KW	
E5	6x9	"	E	05	36	5	500W	
F1	6x9	"F" PIPE	I	02	1	9	500W	
F2	6x9	"	H	02	4	8	500W	
F3	6x9	"	I	05	8	9	500W	
F4	6x9	"	G	02	9	7	500W	
F5	6x9	"	H	05	17	8	500W	
G1	6x9	"G" PIPE	F	02	21	8	500W	
G2	6x9	"	C	02	41	3	500W	
G3	6x9	"	I	05	61	9	500W	
G4	6x9	"	F	05	81	6	500W	
G5	6"F	"	ALLEY	78	82	22	500W	
G6	6"F	"	ALLEY	78	101	22	500W	
H1	8"F	"H" PIPE	I	59	24	19	1KW	
H2	6x9	"	I	66	44	14	500W	w/ MED. BREAKUP GOBO
H3	8"F	"	J	59	86	20	1KW	
H4	6x9	"	J	66	84	15	500W	w/ MED. BREAKUP GOBO
I1	8"F	"I" PIPE	H	59	27	19	1KW	
I2	6x9	"	H	66	49	14	500W	w/ MED. BREAKUP GOBO
I3	8"F	"	C	59	89	16	1KW	

INSTRUMENT SCHEDULE

Production: GLASS MENAGERIE - ARENA   Page 3 of 3

INST #	TYPE	LOCATION	AREA	COLOR	CIR	DIM	LAMP	REMARKS
J1	6"F	"J" PIPE	LAMP SPEC	08	10	24	500W	CHANDELIER SUPPORT
J2	8"F	"	B	59	90	16	1KW	
J3	6x9	"	J	02	91	10	500W	
J4	6x12	"	TBM SPEC	08	92	21	500W	
K1	6x9	"K" PIPE	G	66	18	13	500W	w/ MED BREAKUP GOBO
K2	6x9	"	TABLE SPEC	-	64	25	500W	
K3	8"F	"	A	59	94	16	1KW	
L1	6x9	"L" PIPE	G	05	20	7	500W	
L2	6x9	"	D	05	40	4	500W	
L3	6x9	"	A	05	58	1	500W	
L4	6x9	"	G	02	78	7	500W	
Z1	CHANDELIER	NEW PIPE	-	-	26	75W		HANG NEW PIPE BETWEEN "J" & "K"
Z2	FLOOD LAMP	BY DESK	-	-	27	60W		
201	6x9	1ST HOUSE PIPE	J		209	10	500W	
202	6x12	"			210	21	500W	
203	6"F	"	ALLEY		220	22	500W	
204	6x12	"	TBM SPEC		224	21	500W	
205	6x9	"	J		225	10	500W	

INSTRUMENT SCHEDULE

Production: _____   Page __ of __

INST #	TYPE	LOCATION	AREA	COLOR	CIR	DIM	LAMP	REMARKS

Figure 16.21 Instrument schedule for arena production of *The Glass Menagerie*.

mix between the 02 and 62, the stage could be made neutral, cool, or warm as appropriate. The full saturation necessary for the scenes inside the cabaret was supplied by the Roscolux 20 (Medium Amber), 57A (Lavender), and 93 (Blue Green) used on the vertical striplights and fresnels on either side of the stage. These saturated color washes, used in conjunction with the acting-area

Figure 16.22   The lighting key for *Cabaret*.

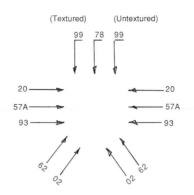

Figure 16.23   Scenic de-
sign for *Cabaret*, by Tom
Benson. Produced at the
University of Arizona.

lights, enhanced the costumes and scenery and provided the sidelight necessary to outline the bodies of the dancers during the production numbers.

During the musical numbers, the set was generally lit with psychologi-
cally appropriate color washes, and the six followspots, using white or lightly
tinted light, were used to highlight the various leads.

The downstage area of the cabaret audience was lit with a textured top
wash (Roscolux 99, Chocolate) to support the concept that the area was lit by

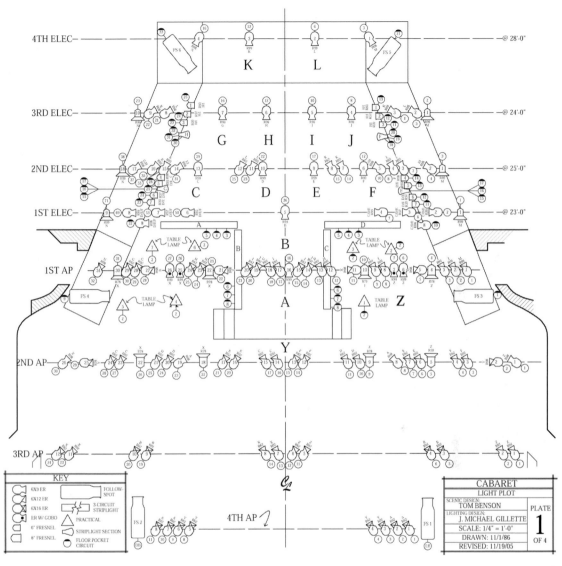

Figure 16.24 Light plot for *Cabaret*. Lighting design by J. Michael Gillette. Drafting by Michael McNamara.

the practical lamps on each table. Because the director wanted the onstage "audience" to be visible at all times, during the out-of-the-cabaret scenes, the textured top light was combined with a deep blue (Roscolux 78, Trudy Blue) to reduce the area's apparent visibility. (The deep blue looks like a shadow color but allows the real audience to see the shadow detail.)

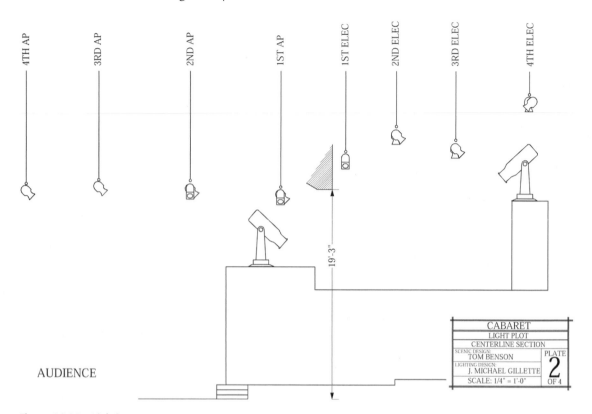

Figure 16.25 Lighting section for *Cabaret*. Lighting design by J. Michael Gillette. Drafting by Michael McNamara.

Dance: *The Nutcracker*

If there is a difference in lighting for dance, as opposed to lighting for legitimate theatre, it is a matter of degree, not principle.

As indicated during the discussion of *Cabaret*, in legitimate theatre you are concerned with lighting the face so that the audience can see the thoughts and emotions of the actors, whereas in dance you are more concerned in revealing the form of the body. To achieve this goal, the axis of the light should be parallel with the axis of the dancer's movement, and it should light the dancer's whole body.

Although, ideally, you would place lights parallel with the axis of every movement in a dance, that ideal is also impractical. However, much of dance movement happens in any number of combinations based on the three patterns illustrated in Figure 16.27. These areas can be effectively covered with the use of side lights, top lights, and side-front lights, with a few front lights

INSTRUMENT SCHEDULE — 21 Nov 2005 — PRODUCTION CABARET — PAGE 1 OF 6

1st ELEC

U#	Dim	Chn	Type & Accessories	W	Purpose	Color	Template
1	56		6" FRES+BARNDOOR	500w	M	R08	
2	63		6X9	500w	C/D/E	R20	
3	65		6X9	500w	C/D/E	R57	
4	67		6X9	500w	C/D/E	R93	
5	38		6X9	500w	B	R99	
6	66		6X9	500w	D/E/F	R93	
7	64		6X9	500w	D/E/F	R57	
8	60		6X9	500w	D/E/F	R20	
9	51		6" FRES+BARNDOOR	500w	N		

2nd ELEC

U#	Dim	Chn	Type & Accessories	W	Purpose	Color	Template
1	57		6" FRES	500w	M	R99	
2	32		6X9	500w	I/J	R08	
3	12		6X9	500w	L	R02	
4	24		6X9	500w	L	R62	
5	31		6X9	500w	G/H	R08	
6	42		6X9	500w	F	R99	
7	11		6X9	500w	K	R62	
8	23		6X9	500w	K	R62	
9	41		6X9	500w	D	R99	
10	40		6X9	500w	D	R99	
11	12		6X9	500w	L	R02	
12	24		6X9	500w	L	R62	
13	39		6X9	500w	C	R99	
14	32		6X9	500w	I/J	R08	
15	11		6X9	500w	K	R02	
16	23		6X9	500w	K	R62	
17	31		6X9	500w	G/H	R08	
18	52		6" FRES	500w	N	R99	

INSTRUMENT SCHEDULE — 21 Nov 2005 — PRODUCTION CABARET — PAGE 2 OF 6

3rd ELEC

U#	Dim	Chn	Type & Accessories	W	Purpose	Color	Template
1	58		6" FRES	500w	M	R99	
2	36		6X9	500w	L	R08	
3	35		6X9	500w	K	R08	
4	46		6X9	500w	J	R99	
5	45		6X9	500w	I	R99	
6	44		6X9	500w	H	R99	
7	43		6X9	500w	G	R99	
8	34		6X9	500w	K	R08	
9	33		6X9	500w	K	R08	
10	53		6" FRES	500w	N	R99	

4th ELEC

U#	Dim	Chn	Type & Accessories	W	Purpose	Color	Template
1	55		6X9	500w	M	R08	
2	48		6X9	500w	L	R99	
3	47		6X9	500w	K	R99	
4	50		6X9	500w	N	R08	

1st AP

U#	Dim	Chn	Type & Accessories	W	Purpose	Color	Template
1	54		6X12	750w	M	R08	
2	10		6X12	750w	J	R02	
3	22		6X12	750w	J	R62	
4	85		8" FRES	1kw	Z	R78	
5	26		6X12	750w	B	R08	
6	82		6X9	500w	Z	R99	Med. Breakup
7	820		6X9	500w	Z	R99	Med. Breakup
8	9		6X12	750w	I	R02	
9	21		6X12	750w	I	R62	
10	85		8" FRES	1kw	Z	R78	
11	78		6X12	750w	X	R08	
12	8		6" FRES+BARNDOOR	750w	H	R02	
13	12		6X12	750w	H	R62	
14	10		6X12	750w	J	R02	

INSTRUMENT SCHEDULE — 21 Nov 2005 — PRODUCTION CABARET — PAGE 3 OF 6

U#	Dim	Chn	Type & Accessories	W	Purpose	Color	Template
15	22		6X12	750w	J	R62	
16	37		6X12	500w	A	R99	
17	7		6X9	750w	G	R02	
18	19		6X12	750w	G	R62	
19	9		6X12	750w	I	R02	
20	21		6X12	750w	I	R62	
21	79		6X12	750w	X	R08	
22	83		8" FRES	750w	X	R02	
23	18		8" FRES	750w	H	R02	
24	20		6X12	750w	H	R62	
25	81		6X9	500w	Y	R99	Med. Breakup
26	81		6X9	500w	X	R99	Med. Breakup
27	26		6X12	750w	B	R08	
28	7		6X12	750w	G	R02	
29	19		6X12	750w	G	R62	
30	83		8" FRES	1kw	X	R78	
31	49		6X12	750w	N	R08	

2nd AP

U#	Dim	Chn	Type & Accessories	W	Purpose	Color	Template
1	80		6X9	500w	Z	R08	
2	88		6X12	750w	Y	R62	
3	6		6X12	750w	F	R02	
4	18		6X12	750w	F	R62	
5	84		8" FRES+BARNDOOR	1kw	E	R02	
6	17		6X12	750w	E	R62	
7	17		6X12	750w	E	R62	
8	25		6X9	500w	A	R08	
9	84		8" FRES+BARNDOOR	1kw	D	R78	
10	4		6X12	750w	D	R02	
11	16		6X12	750w	D	R62	
12	6		6X12	750w	F	R02	
13	18		6X12	750w	F	R62	
14	5		6X12	750w	C	R02	
15	15		6X12	750w	C	R62	

INSTRUMENT SCHEDULE — 21 Nov 2005 — PRODUCTION CABARET — PAGE 4 OF 6

U#	Dim	Chn	Type & Accessories	W	Purpose	Color	Template
16	5		6X12	750w	E	R02	
17	17		6X12	750w	E	R62	
18	82		8" FRES+BARNDOOR	1kw	X	R78	
19	25		6X9	500w	A	R08	
20	4		6X12	750w	D	R02	
21	16		6X12	750w	D	R62	
22	82		8" FRES+BARNDOOR	1kw	X	R78	
23	5		6X12	750w	C	R02	
24	15		6X12	750w	C	R62	
25	88		6X12	750w	Y	R08	
26	77		6X9	500w	X	R08	

3rd AP

U#	Dim	Chn	Type & Accessories	W	Purpose	Color	Template
1	75		6X12	750w	Z	R02	
2	76		6X12	750w	Z	R62	
3	2		6X16	750w	B	R02	
4	14		6X12	750w	B	R62	
5	75		6X12	750w	Z	R02	
6	76		6X12	750w	Z	R62	
7	75		6X12	750w	X	R02	
8	76		6X12	750w	X	R62	
9	2		6X16	750w	B	R02	
10	14		6X16	750w	B	R62	
11	75		6X12	750w	X	R02	
12	76		6X12	750w	X	R62	

4th AP

U#	Dim	Chn	Type & Accessories	W	Purpose	Color	Template
1	13		6X16	750w	A	R62	
2	1		6X16	750w	A	R02	
3	86		6X16	750w	Y	R62	
4	87		6X16	750w	Y	R02	
5	87		6X16	750w	Y	R62	
6	86		6X16	750w	Y	R02	

INSTRUMENT SCHEDULE — 21 Nov 2005 — PRODUCTION CABARET — PAGE 5 OF 6

U#	Dim	Chn	Type & Accessories	W	Purpose	Color	Template
7	2		6X16	750w	A	R02	
8	13		6X16	750w	A	R62	

— SL WALKWAY RAIL —

U#	Dim	Chn	Type & Accessories	W	Purpose	Color	Template
1	67		6" FRES	500w	H/I	R93	
2	65		6" FRES	500w	H/I	R57	
3	63		6" FRES	500w	H/I	R20	
4	28		6" FRES	500w	F	R08	
5	67		6" FRES	500w	D/E	R93	
6	65		6" FRES	500w	D/E	R57	
7	63		6" FRES	500w	D/E	R20	
8	30		6X9	500w	C/D/E	R08	

— SR WALKWAY RAIL —

U#	Dim	Chn	Type & Accessories	W	Purpose	Color	Template
1	66		6" FRES	500w	H/I	R93	
2	64		6" FRES	500w	H/I	R57	
3	61		6" FRES	500w	H/I	R20	
4	27		6" FRES	500w	C	R08	
5	66		6" FRES	500w	D/E	R93	
6	64		6" FRES	500w	D/E	R57	
7	61		6" FRES	500w	D/E	R20	
8	29		6X9	500w	D/E/F	R08	

— STRIPLIGHTS —

U#	Dim	Chn	Type & Accessories	W	Purpose	Color	Template
A1	68		Striplight	500w	Floor	R20	
A2	69		Striplight	500w	Floor	R57	
A3	70		Striplight	500w	Floor	R93	
B1	71		Striplight	500w	Runway	R20	
B2	72		Striplight	500w	Runway	R57	
B3	73		Striplight	500w	Runway	R93	
C1	71		Striplight	500w	Runway	R20	
C2	72		Striplight	500w	Runway	R57	

INSTRUMENT SCHEDULE — 21 Nov 2005 — PRODUCTION CABARET — PAGE 6 OF 6

U#	Dim	Chn	Type & Accessories	W	Purpose	Color	Template
C3	73		Striplight	500w	Runway	R93	
D1	68		Striplight	500w	Floor	R20	
D2	69		Striplight	500w	Floor	R57	
D3	70		Striplight	500w	Floor	R93	
E1	63		Striplight	500w	DL-Vert	R20	
E2	65		Striplight	500w	DL-Vert	R57	
E3	69		Striplight	500w	DL-Vert	R93	
F1	63		Striplight	500w	UR-Vert	R20	
F2	65		Striplight	500w	UR-Vert	R57	
F3	69		Striplight	500w	UR-Vert	R93	
G1	62		Striplight	500w	DR-Vert	R20	
G2	64		Striplight	500w	DR-Vert	R57	
G3	66		Striplight	500w	DR-Vert	R93	
H1	62		Striplight	500w	UR-Vert	R20	
H2	64		Striplight	500w	UR-Vert	R57	
H3	66		Striplight	500w	UR-Vert	R93	

— FOLLOWSPOTS —

U#	Dim	Chn	Type & Accessories	W	Purpose	Color	Template
1	90		Colorgods	1kw	Fgot	Note 1	
2	91		Colorgods	1kw	Fgot	Note 1	
3	92		Colorgods	1kw	Fgot	Note 1	
4	93		Colorgods	1kw	Fgot	Note 1	
5	94		Colorgods	1kw	Fgot	Note 1	
6	96		Colorgods	1kw	Fgot	Note 1	

"AUDIENCE" TABLE LTS

U#	Dim	Chn	Type & Accessories	W	Purpose	Color	Template
1	89		Practical	25w	Practical	N/C	
2	89		Practical	25w	Practical	N/C	
3	89		Practical	25w	Practical	N/C	
4	89		Practical	25w	Practical	N/C	
5	89		Practical	25w	Practical	N/C	
6	89		Practical	25w	Practical	N/C	
7	89		Practical	25w	Practical	N/C	

Figure 16.26 Instrument schedule for *Cabaret*. Lighting design by J. Michael Gillette. Drafting (Lightwright) by Michael McNamara.

for visibility, as shown in the lighting key and plot for *The Nutcracker* (Figures 16.28 and 16.29). The lighting section and instrument schedule for *The Nutcracker* are shown in Figures 16.30 and 16.31.

The Nutcracker could be described as a collection of individual dances, each possessing its own particular emotional quality and style. A flexible design based on color shifts over a wide range of hues provides a good solution to this challenge. Four color washes (Roscolux 20, Golden Amber; 26, Light Red; 58A, Deep Lavender; and 68, Sky Blue) are used in striplights from the

Figure 16.27 Typical dance movement patterns: (A) side to side or cross-stage; (B) up and down stage; (C) diagonal.

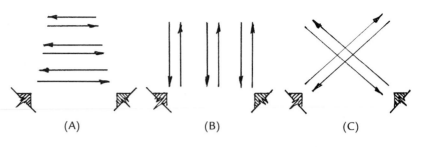

(A)   (B)   (C)

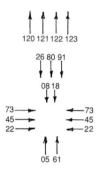

Figure 16.28 Lighting key for *The Nutcracker*.

✳ Dance Booms

Almost every lighting design for dance will have six to eight booms located in the slots (the spaces between the wings [legs] in a drop-and-wing setting). The figure illustrates a typical dance boom. The lowest lights on the boom, frequently referred to as shinkickers or shinbusters (for obvious reasons), light the legs of the dancers when they are at the sides of the stage. Because the dancers work closer to these lights than to those mounted higher on the boom, the shinkickers should be circuited separately so that they can be run at lower intensities. The instruments higher up the boom are focused farther out on the stage so that they shine over the dancers' heads when they are close to the wings.

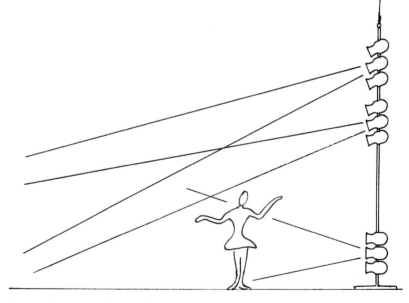

Sectional drawing of a typical dance boom.

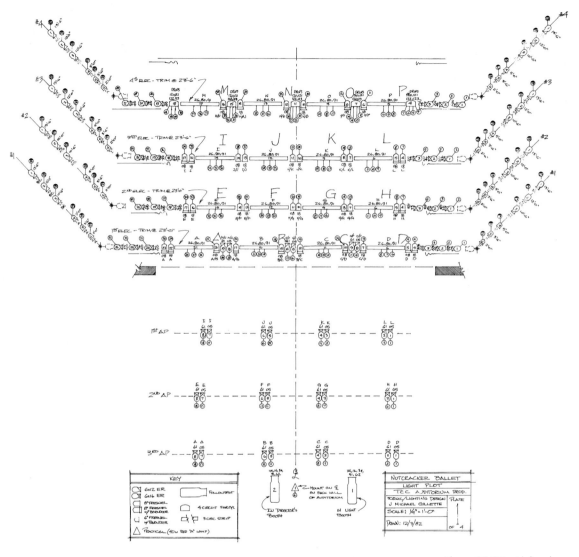

Figure 16.29 Light plot for *The Nutcracker*.

top and in ERSs in the side-front coves to provide the primary color-change mechanisms. The front ERSs (Roscolux 63, Pale Blue) provide a cool visibility light. The side boom ERSs contain Lee 103, Straw; Roscolux 18, Flame; and 62, Booster Blue.

The Lee 103 and Roscolux 18 on the booms, when used in conjunction with the Roscolux 63 from the front, additively mix to yield a white light on the sides of the dancers. The Roscolux 08, Pale Gold, in the top-back ERSs

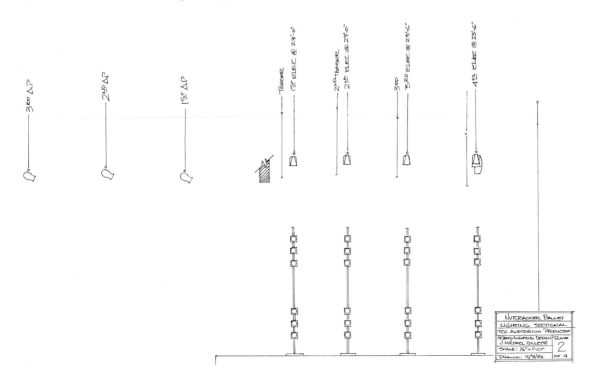

Figure 16.30 Lighting section for *The Nutcracker*.

SAFETY TIP

Dancers are often temporarily blinded by stage lights. As they are exiting the stage, there is a real danger that they may run into a boom. Since the area of the side booms at their eye height rarely holds an instrument, it is a good idea to wrap that part of the boom with white and red tape in a barber-pole pattern so that the dancers can see it.

To avoid becoming dizzy and losing their balance, dancers need a visual reference point when executing pirouettes. If you hang a low-wattage red lamp (light bulb) slightly above eye height on the center line and at the back of the auditorium, you will provide them with that point of focus. If your theatre has a balcony, hang the lamp from the balcony rail. If there isn't a balcony, hang the lamp on the back wall of the auditorium. If possible, put the light on a dimmer so that you will be able to control its intensity and fade it in and out when necessary.

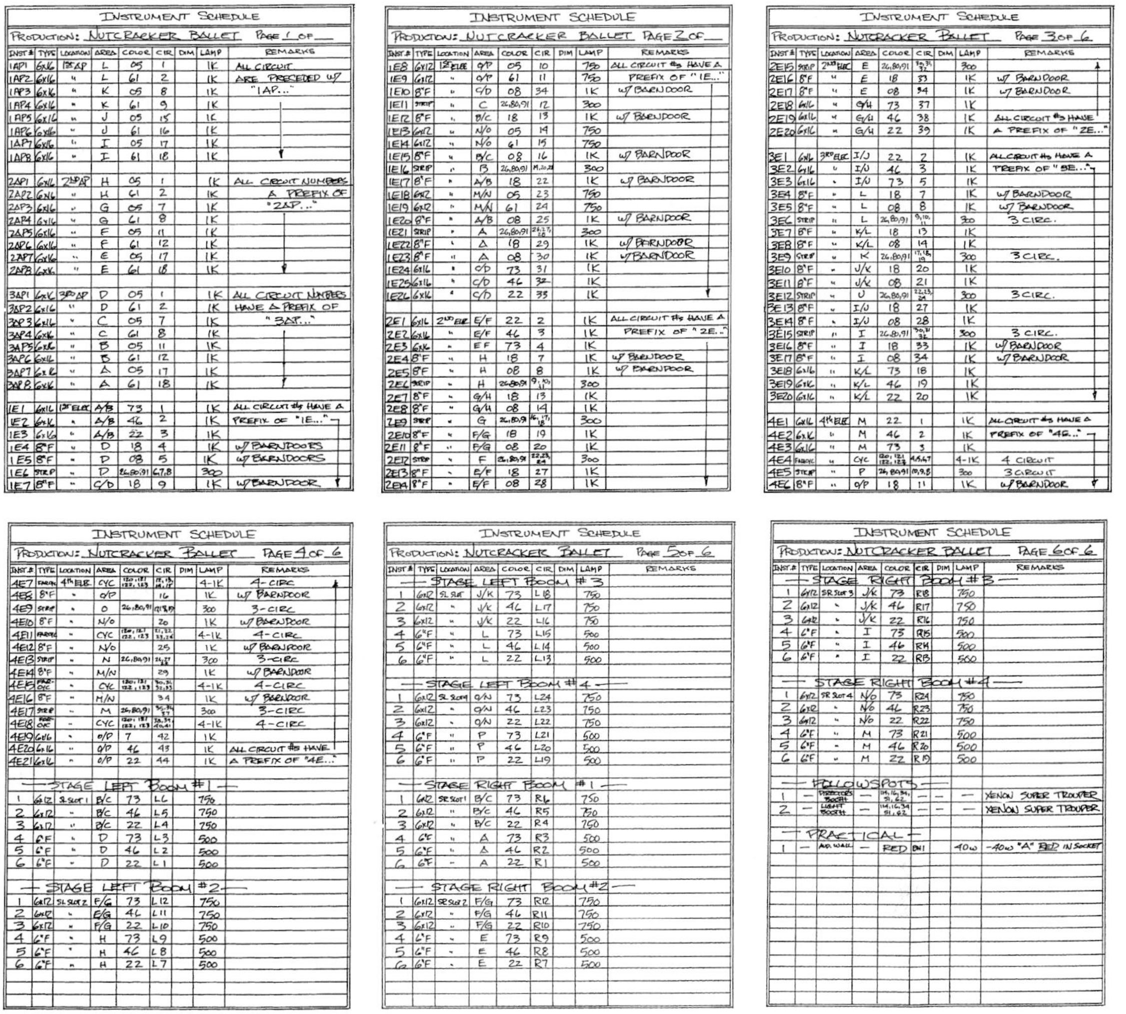

INSTRUMENT SCHEDULE

PRODUCTION: NUTCRACKER BALLET PAGE 1 OF ___

INST #	TYPE	LOCATION	AREA	COLOR	CIR	DIM	LAMP	REMARKS
1AP1	6x16	1ST AP	L	05	1		1K	ALL CIRCUIT
1AP2	6x16	"	L	61	2		1K	ARE PRECEDED W/
1AP3	6x16	"	K	05	8		1K	"1AP..."
1AP4	6x16	"	K	61	9		1K	
1AP5	6x16	"	J	05	15		1K	
1AP6	6x16	"	J	61	16		1K	
1AP7	6x16	"	I	05	17		1K	
1AP8	6x16	"	I	61	18		1K	
2AP1	6x16	2ND AP	H	05	1		1K	ALL CIRCUIT NUMBERS
2AP2	6x16	"	H	61	2		1K	A PREFIX OF
2AP3	6x16	"	G	05	7		1K	"2AP..."
2AP4	6x16	"	G	61	8		1K	
2AP5	6x16	"	F	05	11		1K	
2AP6	6x16	"	F	61	12		1K	
2AP7	6x16	"	E	05	17		1K	
2AP8	6x16	"	E	61	18		1K	
3AP1	6x16	3RD AP	D	05	1		1K	ALL CIRCUIT NUMBERS
3AP2	6x16	"	D	61	2		1K	HAVE A PREFIX OF
3AP3	6x16	"	C	05	7		1K	"3AP..."
3AP4	6x16	"	C	61	8		1K	
3AP5	6x16	"	B	05	11		1K	
3AP6	6x16	"	B	61	12		1K	
3AP7	6x16	"	A	05	17		1K	
3AP8	6x16	"	A	61	18		1K	
1E1	6x16	1ST ELEC	A/B	73	1		1K	ALL CIRCUIT #s HAVE A
1E2	6x16	"	A/B	46	2		1K	PREFIX OF "1E..."
1E3	6x16	"	A/B	22	3		1K	
1E4	8"F	"	D	18	4		1K	W/ BARNDOORS
1E5	8"F	"	D	08	5		1K	W/ BARNDOORS
1E6	STRIP	"	D	26,80,91	6,7,8		300	
1E7	8"F	"	C/D	18	9		1K	W/ BARNDOOR

INSTRUMENT SCHEDULE

PRODUCTION: NUTCRACKER BALLET PAGE 2 OF ___

INST #	TYPE	LOCATION	AREA	COLOR	CIR	DIM	LAMP	REMARKS
1E8	6x12	1ST ELEC	O/P	05	10		750	ALL CIRCUIT #s HAVE A
1E9	6x12	"	O/P	61	11		750	PREFIX OF "1E..."
1E10	8"F	"	C/D	08	34		1K	W/ BARNDOOR
1E11	STRIP	"	C	26,80,91	12		300	
1E12	8"F	"	B/C	18	13		1K	W/ BARNDOOR
1E13	6x12	"	N/O	05	14		750	
1E14	6x12	"	N/O	61	15		750	
1E15	8"F	"	B/C	08	16		1K	W/ BARNDOOR
1E16	STRIP	"	B	26,80,91	19,20,21		300	
1E17	8"F	"	A/B	18	22		1K	W/ BARNDOOR
1E18	6x12	"	M/N	05	23		750	
1E19	6x12	"	M/N	61	24		750	
1E20	8"F	"	A/B	08	25		1K	W/ BARNDOOR
1E21	STRIP	"	A	26,80,91	26,27,28		300	
1E22	8"F	"	A	18	29		1K	W/ BARNDOOR
1E23	8"F	"	A	08	30		1K	W/ BARNDOOR
1E24	6x16	"	C/D	73	31		1K	
1E25	6x16	"	C/D	46	32		1K	
1E26	6x16	"	C/D	22	33		1K	
2E1	6x16	2ND ELEC	E/F	22	2		1K	ALL CIRCUIT #s HAVE A
2E2	6x16	"	E/F	46	3		1K	PREFIX OF "2E..."
2E3	6x16	"	EF	73	4		1K	
2E4	8"F	"	H	18	7		1K	W/ BARNDOOR
2E5	8"F	"	H	08	8		1K	W/ BARNDOOR
2E6	STRIP	"	H	26,80,91	9,10,11		300	
2E7	8"F	"	G/H	18	13		1K	
2E8	8"F	"	G/H	08	14		1K	
2E9	STRIP	"	G	26,80,91	16,17,18		300	
2E10	8"F	"	F/G	18	19		1K	
2E11	8"F	"	F/G	08	20		1K	
2E12	STRIP	"	F	26,80,91	22,23,24		300	
2E13	8"F	"	E/F	18	27		1K	
2E14	8"F	"	E/F	08	28		1K	

INSTRUMENT SCHEDULE

PRODUCTION: NUTCRACKER BALLET PAGE 3 OF 6

INST #	TYPE	LOCATION	AREA	COLOR	CIR	DIM	LAMP	REMARKS
2E15	STRIP	2ND ELEC	E	26,80,91	30,31,32		300	
2E16	8"F	"	E	18	33		1K	W/ BARNDOOR
2E17	8"F	"	E	08	34		1K	W/ BARNDOOR
2E18	6x16	"	G/H	73	37		1K	
2E19	6x16	"	G/H	46	38		1K	ALL CIRCUIT #s HAVE
2E20	6x16	"	G/H	22	39		1K	A PREFIX OF "2E..."
3E1	6x16	3RD ELEC	I/J	22	2		1K	ALL CIRCUIT #s HAVE A
3E2	6x16	"	I/J	46	3		1K	PREFIX OF "3E..."
3E3	6x16	"	I/J	73	5		1K	
3E4	8"F	"	L	18	7		1K	W/ BARNDOOR
3E5	8"F	"	L	08	8		1K	W/ BARNDOOR
3E6	STRIP	"	L	26,80,91	9,10,11		300	3 CIRC.
3E7	8"F	"	K/L	18	13		1K	
3E8	8"F	"	K/L	08	14		1K	
3E9	STRIP	"	K	26,80,91	17,18,19		300	3 CIRC.
3E10	8"F	"	J/K	18	20		1K	
3E11	8"F	"	J/K	08	21		1K	
3E12	STRIP	"	J	26,80,91	22,23,24		300	3 CIRC.
3E13	8"F	"	I/J	18	27		1K	
3E14	8"F	"	I/J	08	28		1K	
3E15	STRIP	"	I	26,80,91	30,31,32		300	3 CIRC.
3E16	8"F	"	I	18	33		1K	W/ BARNDOOR
3E17	8"F	"	I	08	34		1K	W/ BARNDOOR
3E18	6x16	"	K/L	73	18		1K	
3E19	6x16	"	K/L	46	19		1K	
3E20	6x16	"	K/L	22	20		1K	
4E1	6x16	4TH ELEC	M	22	1		1K	ALL CIRCUIT #s HAVE A
4E2	6x16	"	M	46	2		1K	PREFIX OF "4E..."
4E3	6x16	"	M	73	3		1K	
4E4	FAR-CYC	"	CYC	120,121 122,123	4,5,6,7		4-1K	4 CIRCUIT
4E5	STRIP	"	P	26,80,91	10,9,8		300	3 CIRCUIT
4E6	8"F	"	O/P	18	11		1K	W/ BARNDOOR

INSTRUMENT SCHEDULE

PRODUCTION: NUTCRACKER BALLET PAGE 4 OF 6

INST #	TYPE	LOCATION	AREA	COLOR	CIR	DIM	LAMP	REMARKS
4E7	FAR-CYC	4TH ELEC	CYC	120,121 122,123	12,13,14,15		4-1K	4-CIRC
4E8	8"F	"	O/P		16		1K	W/ BARNDOOR
4E9	STRIP	"	O	26,80,91	17,18,19		300	3-CIRC
4E10	8"F	"	N/O		20		1K	W/ BARNDOOR
4E11	FAR-CYC	"	CYC	120,121 122,123	21,22 23,24		4-1K	4-CIRC
4E12	8"F	"	N/O		25		1K	W/ BARNDOOR
4E13	STRIP	"	N	26,80,91	26,27 28		300	3-CIRC
4E14	8"F	"	M/N		29		1K	W/ BARNDOOR
4E15	FAR-CYC	"	CYC	120,121 122,123	30,31 32,33		4-1K	4-CIRC
4E16	8"F	"	M/N		34		1K	W/ BARNDOOR
4E17	STRIP	"	M	26,80,91	35,36 37		300	3-CIRC
4E18	FAR-CYC	"	CYC	120,121 122,123	38,39 40,41		4-1K	4-CIRC
4E19	6x16	"	O/P	7	42		1K	
4E20	6x16	"	O/P	46	43		1K	ALL CIRCUIT #s HAVE
4E21	6x16	"	O/P	22	44		1K	A PREFIX OF "4E..."
— STAGE LEFT BOOM #1 —								
1	6x12	SL SLOT 1	B/C	73	L6		750	
2	6x12	"	B/C	46	L5		750	
3	6x12	"	B/C	22	L4		750	
4	6"F	"	D	73	L3		500	
5	6"F	"	D	46	L2		500	
6	6"F	"	D	22	L1		500	
— STAGE LEFT BOOM #2 —								
1	6x12	SL SLOT 2	F/G	73	L12		750	
2	6x12	"	E/G	46	L11		750	
3	6x12	"	F/G	22	L10		750	
4	6"F	"	H	73	L9		500	
5	6"F	"	H	46	L8		500	
6	6"F	"	H	22	L7		500	

INSTRUMENT SCHEDULE

PRODUCTION: NUTCRACKER BALLET PAGE 5 OF 6

INST #	TYPE	LOCATION	AREA	COLOR	CIR	DIM	LAMP	REMARKS
— STAGE LEFT BOOM #3								
1	6x12	SL SLOT	J/K	73	L18		750	
2	6x12	"	J/K	46	L17		750	
3	6x12	"	J/K	22	L16		750	
4	6"F	"	L	73	L15		500	
5	6"F	"	L	46	L14		500	
6	6"F	"	L	22	L13		500	
— STAGE LEFT BOOM #4 —								
1	6x12	SL SLOT 4	O/N	73	L24		750	
2	6x12	"	O/N	46	L23		750	
3	6x12	"	O/N	22	L22		750	
4	6"F	"	P	73	L21		500	
5	6"F	"	P	46	L20		500	
6	6"F	"	P	22	L19		500	
— STAGE RIGHT BOOM #1 —								
1	6x12	SR SLOT 1	B/C	73	R6		750	
2	6x12	"	B/C	46	R5		750	
3	6x12	"	B/C	22	R4		750	
4	6"F	"	A	73	R3		500	
5	6"F	"	A	46	R2		500	
6	6"F	"	A	22	R1		500	
— STAGE RIGHT BOOM #2 —								
1	6x12	SR SLOT 2	F/G	73	R12		750	
2	6x12	"	F/G	46	R11		750	
3	6x12	"	F/G	22	R10		750	
4	6"F	"	E	73	R9		500	
5	6"F	"	E	46	R8		500	
6	6"F	"	E	22	R7		500	

INSTRUMENT SCHEDULE

PRODUCTION: NUTCRACKER BALLET PAGE 6 OF 6

INST #	TYPE	LOCATION	AREA	COLOR	CIR	DIM	LAMP	REMARKS
— STAGE RIGHT BOOM #3 —								
1	6x12	SR SLOT 3	J/K	73	R18		750	
2	6x12	"	J/K	46	R17		750	
3	6x12	"	J/K	22	R16		750	
4	6"F	"	I	73	R15		500	
5	6"F	"	I	46	R14		500	
6	6"F	"	I	22	R13		500	
— STAGE RIGHT BOOM #4 —								
1	6x12	SR SLOT 4	N/O	73	R24		750	
2	6x12	"	N/O	46	R23		750	
3	6x12	"	N/O	22	R22		750	
4	6"F	"	M	73	R21		500	
5	6"F	"	M	46	R20		500	
6	6"F	"	M	22	R19		500	
— FOLLOWSPOTS —								
1	—	DIRECTOR'S BOOTH	—	114,16,34, 51,62	—	—	—	XENON SUPER TROUPER
2	—	LIGHT BOOTH	—	114,16,34 51,62	—	—	—	XENON SUPER TROUPER
— PRACTICAL —								
1	—	AUD. WALL	—	RED	BH1		40w	-40w "A" RED IN SOCKET

Figure 16.31 Instrument schedule for *The Nutcracker.*

similarly combines with Roscolux 60, No-Color Blue, in the high side ERSs to produce a white result on the head and shoulders of the dancers. Appropriate specials are used to highlight specific set pieces and locations such as the growing Christmas tree and the throne. Two followspots are located in a booth at the rear of the auditorium.

CHAPTER 17

Rehearsal and Performance Procedures

It has been said that any lighting design is only as good as its paperwork. The light plot, lighting section, and instrument schedule or hookup sheet are only about half of that paperwork. The rest of it is associated with the recording of the dimmer intensity levels and other data that are used when running the lights for a production. Much of this additional paperwork is eliminated, or significantly reduced, when using a computer board.

This chapter will present a series of rehearsal and performance procedures, forms, and practices that can be used to assist in the running of the lighting for any production. Every action involving the adjustment of one or more lighting instruments needs to be recorded, either electronically or in writing, to ensure that the intensity settings for those dimmers and the timing of each lighting cue remain the same from rehearsal to rehearsal and performance to performance.

ORGANIZATIONAL TOOLS

The forms and practices suggested in this section are not sacrosanct; many different methods can be used to record the information needed to run the lighting for a production. Any well-organized system that works for the lighting designer and electrician can be used. The important point is the necessity of having a clear, written, systematic method of recording the necessary information.

As indicated above, some of the paperwork that will be described in this section, such as the recording of individual dimmer settings on **preset sheets**, is eliminated with the use of a computer board. But it is still being

Preset sheet: A form used by the electrician to record the intensity levels for each dimmer during major shifts in the lighting.

ELECTRICIAN'S CUE SHEET

Show _Under the Rainbow_ _____ Script Page_____

Cue	Preset	Count	Notations
1	1	—	House preset @ 7:30
2	—	8	House to half
3	—	4	House out
4	2	6	Apartment ↑ (morning)
5	3	1	Kitchen when Hal hits switch
6	4	5	Fade to black

Figure 17.1   An electrician's cue sheet.

included in the text for two reasons: (1) some theatres are still equipped with preset light boards; (2) the process of hand-recording dimmer levels is instructive of the electronic process used by the computer light boards.

Electrician's Cue Sheet

When working with a preset light board, the electrician's cue sheet is the **board operator's** bible. It contains the primary operating instructions (cue number, what specific action the board operator takes, the timing of the cue, and so forth) for every lighting cue, as shown in Figure 17.1. It is also important to note what information the electrician's cue sheet does not contain. It doesn't give the specific channel/dimmer intensity-level settings (commonly referred to as dimmer or channel settings) for major shifts in the lighting. That information is either written on the preset sheet, which will be discussed later, or recorded in the board's memory. But the electrician's cue sheet is often used to record the channel/dimmer levels for minor shifts of intensity that involve only one or two channels or dimmers.

If you carefully study the information written on the electrician's cue sheet shown in Figure 17.1, you will be able to follow the progress of the lighting from the lowering of the house lights through the end of the first scene of the play. It is important to remember that the board operator does not run the lighting on his or her own. The cues to run the lighting are called by the stage manager.

When working with a computer board the information written on the electrician's cue sheet is frequently limited to identifying the cue number and some description of the line or on-stage action as well as the count for that particular cue. (Even though the count for all cues is stored electronically, it is a good idea to have it written on the electrician's cue sheet as a backup. It is also useful information for the board operator.) Sometimes the electrician's

Board operator: An electrician who runs the lighting control console during rehearsals and performances.

cue sheet is replaced with a copy of the script set up like a stage manager's script—the script pages are taped to unlined notebook paper and placed in a three-ring binder—and the cues and associated notes are written adjacent to the appropriate line. The actual type of paperwork used by the board operator doesn't matter that much. What *is* important is that there be some type of written instructions for the board operator that are understandable to not only the operator, but the lighting designer and stage manager as well.

Recording Dimmer Intensity Levels

There are two methods of recording lighting cues: electronically and in writing.

Electronic Cue Storage   Electronic cue storage is a primary advantage of the computer lighting console. Although the capabilities of computer boards vary from manufacturer to manufacturer, they all provide a basic level of computer memory that allows them to electronically store the intensity levels for each channel or dimmer that is used in each cue. Most computer boards also store the time associated with each cue. If the cues are stored in the computer memory, it is *vitally* important that a backup copy of those cues be made *every* time any cue is adjusted or changed. The backup disk should be kept in a safe place in reasonably close proximity to the computer board.

If a production company doesn't have a computer board, the above-described information will have to be recorded manually.

Preset Sheet   In working with a preset board, the preset sheet, Figure 17.2, is used to record the intensity levels for each dimmer during major shifts in lighting. Handwritten preset sheets are not normally used when working with computer boards. Most computer boards can either directly print a list of the intensity levels of each channel for every cue, or they can export that data to a database program like Lightwright for manipulation and printing. Many, though certainly not all, designers consider it essential that some type of paper backup of channel intensity levels be available for every cue in the production.

The layout and content of the preset sheet is dependent on the type of preset control system used for the production. But regardless of the exact form of the sheet, it will have an open space adjacent to each dimmer number to record the intensity level of that particular dimmer for that particular cue.

Each time a major shift in the lighting involves more than two or three dimmers, a preset sheet is completed for that cue. The sheet provides the board operators with the information necessary to accurately adjust the dimmers.

Preset sheets are used in conjunction with electrician's cue sheets. The electrician's cue sheets tell the board operator what action is necessary for

PRESET SHEET

Production:_____

Preset Bank:_____ Cue:_____

1		16	
2		17	
3		18	
4		19	
5		20	
6		21	
7		22	
8		23	
9		24	
10		25	
11		26	
12		27	
13		28	
14		29	
15		30	

Figure 17.2 A preset sheet.

any particular cue, and the preset sheets are inserted between the cue sheets where they are needed. To keep everything tidy, the cue sheets and preset sheets are usually kept in a three-ring binder.

Just as it is extremely important to keep a backup disk of electronically stored cues, it is equally important to keep an accurate and up-to-date copy of the preset sheets and the electrician's cue sheets. Although it may seem to be an unnecessarily boring and time-consuming chore to photocopy the preset and electrician's cue sheets after every rehearsal in which a change is made, the importance of doing so will become crystal clear if you ever misplace or lose the original sheets. Keep the copies in an accessible spot, but *not* in the same place as the originals.

Multipart cues: Cues divided into several parts, each part controlling a portion of the channels in the cue.

Isolation spot: A small, bright spot of light used to isolate that space from other less bright or colored areas onstage

Default programmed: The original "from-the-manufacturer" setting of some aspect of a software program. Generally the user can modify default settings.

Computer Board Cueing Techniques

In designing lights for a production, one of the designer's most important decisions will be to choose a particular approach to cueing a show. Knowledge of the control options available to structure the movement of light plays a significant role in informing that decision. The basic cueing techniques of computer boards were discussed in Chapter 6, "Intensity Control." This section will discuss some advanced control methods that are fairly standard on many computer boards.

Multipart Cues   **Multipart cues** are cues that are divided into several discrete units. They allow the designer to obtain very precise control of the lights. Most boards with this capability allow a cue to be broken into at least four parts with each part controlling some of the channels in the cue. Each portion of the cue is assigned its own fade time. This would be an excellent technique to employ if you wanted to create a "rolling" color wash. Assume that you wanted to bathe the stage in a blue top light that slowly advanced from stage left to stage right. In your plot you'd hang enough blue-colored top lights over the stage to cover the whole stage, and you'd circuit and channel them separately. For this cue you'd assign the channels controlling the stage left top lights to part one of the cue, the left-center top lights to the second part, and so on. You'd assign a fade time to each of the four parts so the blue light would seem to start on stage left and progress across the stage until the entire stage was bathed in blue. The multipart cue allows you to execute this complex maneuver within a single cue.

Cue Follows   Normally, each lighting cue is executed with a press of the "Go" button on command from the stage manager. It is also fairly standard to encounter situations where a number of related cues need to be called in close proximity to each other. Imagine a situation with six **isolation spots** in which each spot begins its 5-second fade-up 1 second before the previous spot has reached full. It would be all but impossible for the stage manager to call these cues, much less for the board operator to consistently execute them as intended. That's where "cue follows" is useful. The cue follows function allows the designer to set up each isolation spot as a separate cue and tie all six cues together so that each successive cue begins automatically in the fourth second of the previous cue's fade-up. That way the operator only has to press the "Go" button one time to start the first isolation spot. The remaining five cues follow, in sequence, automatically.

Insert Cues   As hinted at in some of the previous discussions, most computer light boards are **default programmed** to play cues back in numerical sequence—cue 1 is followed by cue 2, and so forth. Insert cueing involves assigning decimal cue numbers (2.3, 14.7, and so forth) to the new cue that you want to insert into the show cue sequence. When a decimal number is assigned to an insert cue, the computer program automatically inserts that cue after the appropriate whole-numbered cue.

When a lighting designer first begins setting intensity levels for the cues in a show it is fairly common practice to set up several **looks** for various major moments in the play—e.g., the **preshow**, day/night looks for each set, and so forth—and record those looks as cues. Frequently the designer or board operator will separate these looks from the show cue sequence by assigning them cue numbers higher than the anticipated number of cues in the show, e.g., 901, 902, and so forth. With these "look cues" the designer can begin to build the sequence of show cues, modifying the look cues as necessary for the particular moment in the play. Typically, when the designer finishes creating each show cue, it is assigned a whole cue number. If, during rehearsals, the designer decides to insert a new cue between existing cues 12 and 13, she will call up one of the stock look cues, modify it as desired, and insert it between cues 12 and 13 by naming it "12.1." The computer will then activate the show cues in the new sequence—12, 12.1, 13.

Look: The appearance—the way the light looks onstage—of a particular cue.

Preshow: Before the show starts. In this case the preshow cue refers to the settings of the house and stage lights as the audience is entering the auditorium.

Link: An action where a cue is electronically "tied" to another cue. Typically used to create a sequence of cues that automatically follow one after the other.

Linking   During rehearsals designers frequently "hop around" the cue sheet, dropping out-of-sequence cues into the playback sequence. The **link** function allows you to make these inserted cues a permanent part of the show cue sequence. For example, after looking at the show sequence you decide that right after cue 37 you'd like to repeat the look that you had with cue 5. Link cue 5 to 37 and it, rather than cue 38, will fade up as 37 fades out.

Stage and Blind Modes   Most computer boards operate in two modes: stage and blind. A cue is in "stage mode" when it can be seen on stage. Adjustments to intensity and timing are normally done in stage mode because you can see the light on stage. But there may be times when you want to adjust the levels or timing of one cue while another cue is activated on stage. Blind mode allows the intensity and timing levels of a cue to be seen on the computer monitor without activating the onstage lights. Changes can then be made "in the blind." This is normally used when the designer wants to change some element of a cue without disturbing the other onstage activities.

There is one common theme to all of the above-described techniques. They are relatively time-consuming to set up but extremely simple to execute. And that is the preferable technique. A core goal for any lighting design is to achieve the look and feel agreed upon by the production design team *every time the play is performed*. Reaching that goal requires that the execution of the design should be as simple, foolproof, and repeatable as possible. These techniques help you achieve those goals.

✳ Sneaky Trick Number 102

There will be times when you will want to shift the audience's attention from place to place on the set. Sometimes you'll want to make that obvious, as when you're changing from location to location on a unit set. For these types of cues, you'll usually use a timed cross-fade of between 3 and 5 seconds duration. At other times, however, you won't want the audience to be aware of what you're doing, as when you're trying to shift the audience's point of focus from one area of the set to another in a realistic interior. On these occasions, if you boost or drop the intensity of the lights only a little (10 or 15 points on a 100-point scale) and prolong the fade over 60 or 90 seconds, the audience will not consciously *see* the fade but will feel it, and their attention will be drawn to the area of highest intensity.

Designer's Cue Sheet

After the designer has a general idea of the intensity levels for each cue, the levels are recorded on a designer's cue sheet similar to the one illustrated in Figure 17.3. The designer's cue sheet, also known as a cheat sheet, is a form that identifies the function (color, direction) of the light(s) associated with each channel or dimmer and provides a space for recording its intensity level. The cheat sheet allows the designer to record the rough intensity levels and timing of each cue in a systematic manner. Using one page per cue, the designer records the intensity level for each channel or dimmer used in a cue so that he or she will have a clear idea of what changes are being made to each dimmer for every cue. Notations can be made on the sheets to indicate the purpose, function, or effect of that particular cue. Designer's cue sheets should be kept in a loose-leaf binder so that cues can be easily added or deleted by inserting or removing sheets from the binder. As with the other paperwork, copies also should be made of the designer's cue sheets.

It is also possible to program a digitizing tablet to create a designer's cue sheet that interacts with the light board.[1] Part of the tablet's surface is programmed to emulate the various control features of the light board. The remaining space is programmed with needed information such as lighting areas, washes, and so forth. The programmed tablet allows you to remotely make adjustments to instrument intensity and cue timing, as well as control projectors, moving light fixtures, and so forth.

An article, "Cupped in the Hand," in the February 2004 edition of *Stage Directions*, provides information about how to program a Palm Pilot or PDA to wirelessly run a light board controlled by a Windows operating system.[2]

---

[1]This idea supplied by Dr. Richard Gamble, Florida Atlantic University.
[2]Marc Beth, "Cupped in the Hand," *Stage Directions*, February 2004, pp. 22–23.

Figure 17.3 Designer's cue sheet for use with a preset board. Also known as a cheat sheet.

PRODUCTION: MEMORY LANE

CUE #: 38 | MEMORY #: 42A | SCRIPT PAGE: 27

DIM	USE	LVL	DIM	USE	LVL	DIM	USE	LVL	DIM	USE	LVL
1	A↗62	50	11	C↗62	60	21	E↗62	50	31	G↗62	40
2	A↘08	50	12	C↘08	60	22	E↘08	50	32	G↘08	40
3	A→51	70	13	C→51	75	23	E→51	70	33	G→51	45
4	A←51	70	14	C←51	75	24	E←51	70	34	G←51	45
5	A↓CL	60	15	C↓CL	80	25	E↓CL	60	35	G↓CL	30
6	B↗62	60	16	D↗62	60	26	F↗62	60	36	UL DOOR 06	25
7	B↘08	60	17	D↘08	60	27	F↘08	60	37	TABLE 08	10
8	B→51	75	18	D→51	75	28	F→51	70	38	WINDOW 25	—
9	B←51	75	19	D←51	75	29	F←51	70	39	FLASH POT #1	—
10	B↓CL	80	20	D↓CL	80	30	F↓CL	75	40	FLASH POT #2	—

We can only expect more and more of these time- and labor-saving developments in the future.

Magic Sheet

The magic sheet, another organizational tool of the lighting designer, is a method of visually codifying information that will benefit the lighting designer when she or he is adjusting the dimmer settings during the lighting, technical, and dress rehearsals.

The layout of these very important forms is idiosyncratic and personal. While the information a designer puts on a magic sheet—channel, color, direction, focus area, and so forth—is fairly standard, the way that information is laid out on the magic sheet, and what information is emphasized, often changes. Why? Because each production is unique and the designer's approach to each production is similarly individualized. For example, one production may make extensive use of color washes. The design for another show may have no color washes, but may employ a number of isolation specials. Another production may have almost continual motion effects and sky projections, while the next show the designer works on may have almost no lighting changes except for the fade up and fade out at the beginning and ending of each act. Each of these shows requires that different information on the magic sheets be emphasized. How that information is laid out, what

Figure 17.4 Sample areas from a magic sheet (dimmer only).

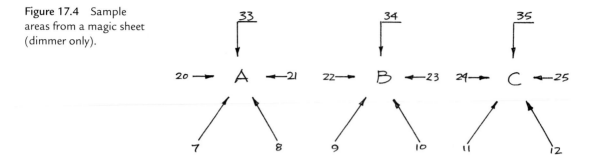

is emphasized, and how it is emphasized is a personal decision made by the designer on a case-by-case basis.

In its most basic form, shown in Figure 17.4, the magic sheet provides a clear picture of which channels or dimmers are controlling the various lights for each area. Typically a magic sheet will be drawn on one sheet of paper with all the lighting areas laid out in their appropriate locations relative to the set. The arrows indicate the direction of the lights while the numbers at the base of the arrows typically represent the channel or dimmer.

Figure 17.5 is a magic sheet for the *Playboy of the Western World* design that was discussed in Chapter 14. The light plot for that design, Figure 14.13, is on page 216. Again, the numbers at the base of the arrows indicate channel or dimmer while the numbers at the head indicate color. Notice the organization of the channel assignments on the magic sheet. Each acting area is assigned its own "decade" of channels. The specials are numerically grouped by function—cyc lighting is in the 150s, windows and doors are in the 160s, the "night light" layer is in the 180s, and so forth. While this is not the only way that these channel assignments could be organized, it is functional and makes it easier for *this* designer to remember what channel controls each individual instrument.

When designs make extensive use of color shifts, it is frequently advantageous to have color indicated on the magic sheet. This can be done in one of several ways. The directional arrows can be overlaid with colors (use wide-tip marking pens) that approximate the hue of each instrument, or the numbers of the color media can be placed in front of the directional arrows as previously mentioned.

Almost all computer boards have monitors that display the intensity levels of the various channels used in each cue. Lighting designers now routinely place additional monitors at their **workstations** in the auditorium during the lighting/tech/dress rehearsal period. The monitor lets the designer see the intensity levels for each channel of every cue. Two monitors can be used, one to show the currently active cue, the other to preview non-active cues. While the monitors show the intensity levels for each channel, they don't provide the other magic sheet information. That information can be laid out on a piece of paper in the same format as the lightboard's monitor. Figure 17.6

Workstation: A table placed in the auditorium for use by the lighting designer and assistants during lighting/tech/dress rehearsals.

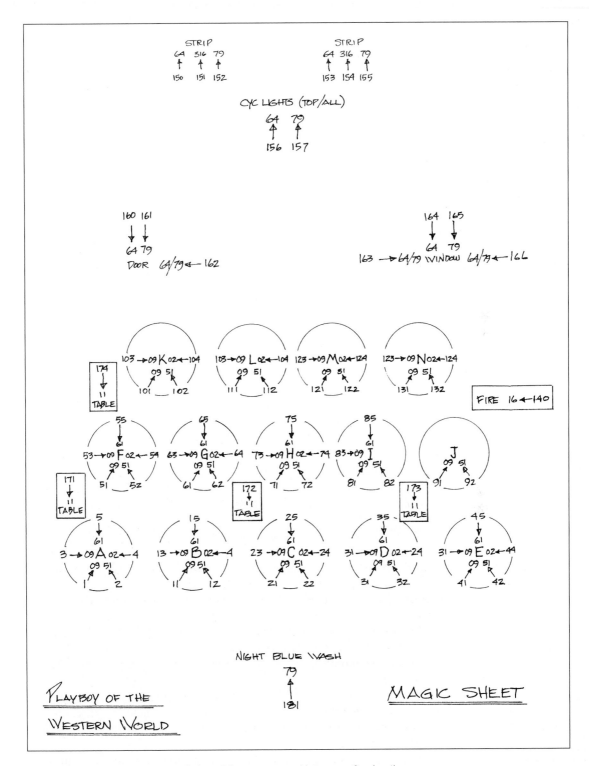

Figure 17.5 A magic sheet for *Playboy of the Western World*. See text for details.

Figure 17.6 A magic sheet can be set up to mirror a light board's channel monitor.

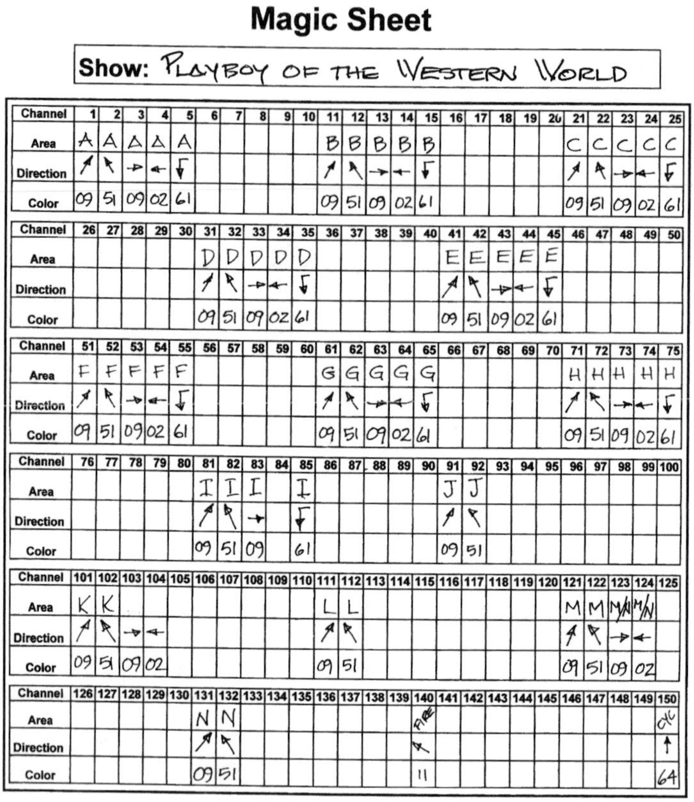

Magic Sheet

Show: PLAYBOY OF THE WESTERN WORLD

Channel	1	2	3	4	5	6	7	8	9	10	11	12	13	14	15	16	17	18	19	20	21	22	23	24	25
Area	A	A	A	A	A						B	B	B	B	B						C	C	C	C	C
Direction	↗	↖	→	←	↓						↗	↖	→	←	↓						↗	↖	→	←	↓
Color	09	51	09	02	61						09	51	09	02	61						09	51	09	02	61

Channel	26	27	28	29	30	31	32	33	34	35	36	37	38	39	40	41	42	43	44	45	46	47	48	49	50
Area						D	D	D	D	D						E	E	E	E	E					
Direction						↗	↖	→	←	↓						↗	↖	→	←	↓					
Color						09	51	09	02	61						09	51	09	02	61					

Channel	51	52	53	54	55	56	57	58	59	60	61	62	63	64	65	66	67	68	69	70	71	72	73	74	75
Area	F	F	F	F	F						G	G	G	G	G						H	H	H	H	H
Direction	↗	↖	→	←	↓						↗	↖	→	←	↓						↗	↖	→	←	↓
Color	09	51	09	02	61						09	51	09	02	61						09	51	09	02	61

Channel	76	77	78	79	80	81	82	83	84	85	86	87	88	89	90	91	92	93	94	95	96	97	98	99	100
Area						I	I	I		I						J	J								
Direction						↗	↖	→		↓						↗	↖								
Color						09	51	09		61						09	51								

Channel	101	102	103	104	105	106	107	108	109	110	111	112	113	114	115	116	117	118	119	120	121	122	123	124	125
Area	K	K									L	L									M	M	M/N	M/N	
Direction	↗	↖	→	←							↗	↖									↗	↖	→	←	
Color	09	51	09	02							09	51									09	51	09	02	

Channel	126	127	128	129	130	131	132	133	134	135	136	137	138	139	140	141	142	143	144	145	146	147	148	149	150
Area						N	N								FIRE										CYC
Direction						↗	↖								↖										↑
Color						09	51								11										64

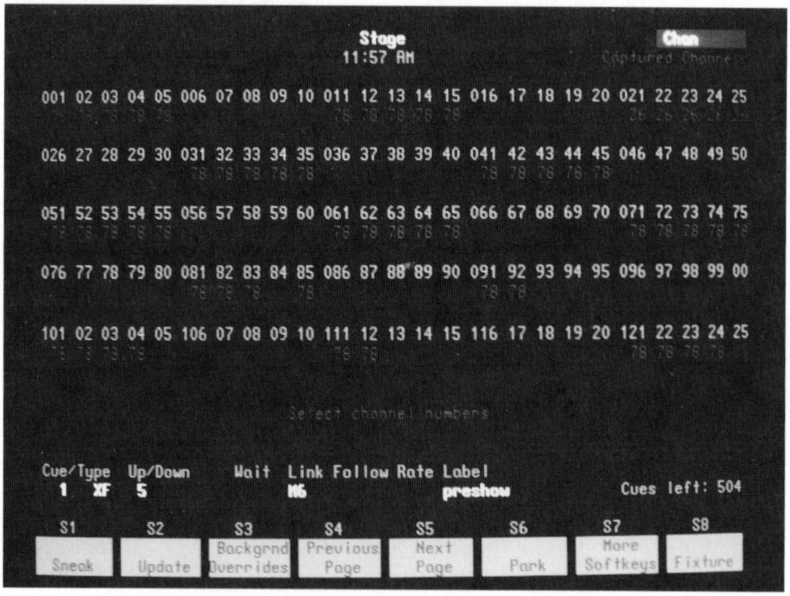

shows this type of magic sheet for the previously discussed *Playboy of the Western World* design. The channel assignments for this magic sheet are the same as those shown in Figure 17.5 to allow you to compare the two types.

The intensity level of every instrument is adjusted, normally many times, during the course of the lighting/tech/dress rehearsal period. To facilitate recognition and recall of what channel or dimmer is controlling which instrument, designers frequently develop an organized system for assigning channels to dimmers. The organization of these systems varies extensively. The only commonality is that they enable the designer to more easily recall the channel numbers for specific instruments or functions. Let's look at several different magic sheet organizational methods that can be used. In the first example, acting area front lights could be assigned channel numbers that end in 1, stage-right side lights 2, stage-left side lights 3, and top lights 4, as illustrated in Figure 17.7A. In the second example channels 1 to 9 are assigned to lighting area A, 10–19 for area B, 20–29 for C and so forth. Within these groups the light from the various directions is repetitively numbered. For example, stage right front lights are assigned channels that end in 1, top-light channels end in 5, and so forth, as shown in 17.7B. Not all the channels within each decade are used because there are only five base lights per acting area. But assigning one decade per acting area makes this type of organization relatively easy to remember.

Specials are frequently grouped together by function and assigned channels that are well removed from the channel numbers used for the acting area lights. For example, if the lighting area lights take up channels 1 to 150, on-set specials such as fireplace effect lights and isolation specials might be assigned to channels in the 200s, cyc lighting the 300s, and so forth.

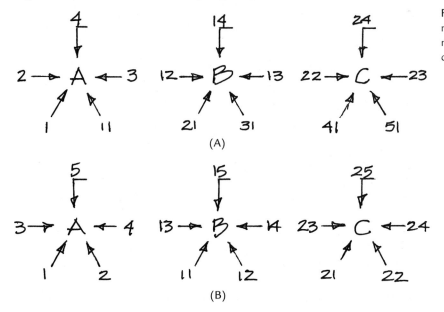

(A)

(B)

Figure 17.7 Two organizational methods for magic sheets. See text for details.

Some designers simply prefer to use the board's default channel assignment function, which, in most cases, assigns channel 1 to dimmer 1, 2 to 2, and so forth, and then work with the resultant random numbering without making any attempt to organize a system of logical sequencing. The point of this discussion is that there isn't a "correct" method of channel assignment. Try different systems. Whatever system best helps you remember what channel/dimmer controls which light is the "correct" solution for that particular design challenge.

It is essential that the lighting designer and master electrician devise some type of organized system that will ensure that the lighting designer's concepts are accurately recorded and reproduced during each rehearsal and performance of the production. It is of utmost importance that the paperwork be clear and current; any changes in the timing, intensity, or location of any cue must be recorded so that they can be duplicated during the next rehearsal or performance.

REHEARSALS

The lighting, technical, and dress rehearsals provide the designer with the opportunity to see and adjust the lighting design.

Lighting Rehearsal

The lighting rehearsal is a period devoted to adjusting the intensity levels and timing for each lighting cue. The lighting designer, electrician (board operator), stage manager, a small crew to shift the scenery (if necessary), and the director are the only members of the production team who need be present for this rehearsal.

Before the lighting rehearsal, the lighting designer will have noted the position of any motivated or unmotivated lighting cues that he or she may want to use in the production. The designer will have discussed these cues with the director during one of the production conferences. The extent of this discussion varies greatly. Some directors want to know the exact location, purpose, and function of every cue, whereas other directors will leave the matter entirely up to the lighting designer. The lighting designer and board operator will have "roughed in" the intensity settings for each cue before the lighting rehearsal.

There are two primary reasons for holding a lighting rehearsal. First, it provides the director and lighting designer with a specific time to discuss the effect, purpose, and content of each cue when they are relatively unencumbered by other elements of the production. Additionally, it gives them an opportunity to discuss any additions, deletions, or other changes that they feel should be made in the location or duration of the cues or anything else

✳ Hanging Cardboards

Hanging cardboards are a great time-saver for the electricians hanging the show. Typically, they are pieces of stiff cardboard with specific portions of the light plot (first electric, first anteproscenium cut, and so forth) taped or glued to them. The master electrician can assign one or two electricians to each position, give them the appropriate hanging cardboard, and send them on their way. With the hanging cardboards (which are mounted on cardboard so that the electricians can put them in their pockets without crumpling them), the crew members will have all the information they need and won't have to constantly refer back to the master plot. If the electricians are assigning circuit numbers to the instruments during the hanging session, they can write the circuit numbers on the hanging cardboards and transfer that information to the master plot when they've finished.

affecting the lighting design. Second, holding a lighting rehearsal provides the designer, director, stage manager, and board operator with an opportunity to make sure that the paperwork affecting the lighting design is correct. Because the stage manager will be **calling** all the cues, he or she can use the lighting rehearsal to make sure that the lighting cues have been noted in their appropriate positions in the prompt script. It also gives the board operator a chance to check the accuracy of the electrician's cue sheets and preset sheets.

Call: To tell specific crew members when to perform their cues.

Technical and Dress Rehearsals

Changes and adjustments to the timing, content, and positioning of lighting cues are normal during the technical and dress rehearsals. Although this can be a very frustrating time, it is essential that the lighting crew understand that the majority of the lighting cues will probably have to be adjusted; intensities and timing will be changed, entire cues will probably need to be added or deleted, instrument focus may need to be shifted, and the color in various instruments may also have to be changed. These adjustments should be considered as normal, rather than extraordinary, because it is part of the lighting designer's responsibility to develop the lighting design to work with the production concept that has evolved during the rehearsal period.

Instrument and Dimmer Check

Several routine equipment checks should be conducted before each technical or dress rehearsal and each performance. All dimmers and instruments need to be checked to determine that they are functioning properly. With the aid

Figure 17.8 A dimmer/
instrument check sheet.

DIMMER/INSTRUMENT CHECK SHEET

Dimmer/ Channel	Number of Instruments	Instrument Location(s)/Color(s)	Area of Focus

of a check sheet (Figure 17.8) two crew members can test all the instruments and dimmers in a short time. As the board operator turns on each channel or dimmer, the other electrician checks to see that all the instruments assigned to it are functioning properly. At the same time, the person checking the instruments can see if any of the color media are bleached out, torn, or otherwise in need of replacement. Each instrument should also be tested to determine if it is focused into its respective area.

The dimmer and instrument check is normally made about an hour and a half before curtain time to allow any necessary repairs, replacements, or adjustments to be made.

CHAPTER 18

An Introduction to Lighting for Film and Video

The basic reason for designing light for theatre—to enhance the mood and spirit of the production—is the same for film and video. The design principles used to design lights for theatre that were discussed earlier in this text apply equally well to film and video. Almost all of the perceived differences between lighting for theatre and lighting for film/video can be explained in terms of how the audiences for the two forms see. The audience for theatre is people. The audience for film and video is cameras.

Humans see with their eyes and their brains. Their brains not only interpret what they see, but remember it as well. The camera is the equivalent of the human eye for film and video. In video, electronic circuitry mimics some of the interpretative functions of the brain, while filters are used to accomplish the same processes in film. The memory sections of the brain store images that people see, while in film those same images are stored on a chemical-based emulsion, and in video they are stored electronically.

Not all film and video requires designed light. Snapshots, family videos, home movies, news footage, and similar situations in which the spontaneity of the action takes precedence over the evocative effects created with designed light would be adversely affected by the time it takes to execute a designed-light setup. But any entertainment, or infotainment, medium such as portrait photography, movies, most broadcast and cable television programming, and studio newscasts all benefit from having designed light. And that's the subject of this chapter—how to create designed light for film and video.

A caveat: This chapter should not be mistaken for an introduction to filmmaking or videography. It isn't. It's an introduction to *lighting* for film and video. It will include, of necessity, a great deal of specialized material about cameras—how they "see" and record images. This information is essential because the choices you make when designing lights for film and video are predicated, to a significant degree, on the technical parameters dictated by the cameras and their recording media. Additionally, it is *strongly* recommended that anyone interested in working in lighting for film or video take, minimally, a beginning production course in film, video, or photography. Hopefully, you'll be able to take all three. Remember that this is a craft and the best way to learn any craft is to practice it.

When discussing designed light for film and video, there are two major elements that need to be considered: the design principles that enable the lighting to visually reinforce the production concept, and technical information that allows the camera to record the scene the way the designer intended.

As mentioned earlier, the design principles discussed in Chapters 11, "The Design Process," 12, "The Image of Light," and 13, "The Lighting Key," apply with equal effect to designing lighting for film, video, and theatre. Those design principles, with examples specific to film/video lighting design, will be discussed toward the end of this chapter. The technical information will be discussed in the following section.

TECHNICAL INFORMATION

Cameras see and record images in a less sophisticated manner than humans. To record images that duplicate what we see, we need to understand how cameras work. This section covers technical information about cameras, film, and tape. Initially, much of it may seem unrelated and disconnected. Hang in there. When, toward the end of the chapter, we begin discussing actual design challenges, you'll see how all of this stuff fits together.

Color Temperature

The basic principles and characteristics of color temperature were discussed in Chapter 4, "Lenses, Lamps, Reflectors, and Lighting Instruments," under "Color Temperature." Here, we deal with additional information you need to know about color temperature when lighting video or film.

When a picture is taken, the color of the light emitted by the sources lighting that object will determine how accurately that object's colors will be reproduced. As described in Chapter 9, "Color," we humans perceive color on the basis of light being reflected to our eyes from whatever we're looking at and our brain interpreting that information. To thoroughly comprehend the discussion that follows, it is essential that you understand that the brain is continuously interpreting and manipulating the information it receives from your eyes.

Whenever you look at something, your brain analyzes the colors it sees. It compares the color information sent from your eyes with memories of similar colors or colors seen in similar circumstances. If you see someone

What Do You Call the Lighting Designer in Film and Video?

In theatre the person who designs the lighting is called a lighting designer. In film the person who designs the light is the cinematographer. He or she is responsible for creating and implementing the lighting design as well as all aspects of camera operation. The decision about the "look"—the overall visual feeling—of the film normally will be decided during discussions involving the director, cinematographer, and others prior to the start of shooting, but it is the cinematographer who is responsible for implementing that "look" once production gets underway. In high-budget feature filmmaking, camera operators and their assistants normally run the cameras, but they do so under the direction of the cinematographer. Electricians—under the direction of the head electrician or gaffer—rig and run the lighting fixtures. The gaffer works under the aesthetic direction of the cinematographer. In low-budget independent filmmaking the cinematographer is frequently the camera operator and may rig and run the fixtures as well.

Network video production frequently lists a "lighting director" in the credits. This person is the video equivalent of the lighting designer. This credit normally appears only on productions that are either studio- or story-based, such as the studio portion of network and local newscasts, and all elements—location and studio—of entertainment programming. In video production, electricians work under the supervision of the lighting director to rig and run all lighting. In those situations where there isn't a credited lighting director the videographer—the camera operator—normally is in charge of the lighting.

strolling around in a white shirt your brain interprets that information. It compares the current viewing of that shirt with memories of white shirts it has seen before. By comparing those memories with what it is currently seeing, your brain determines that the color of the shirt your eyes are looking at is supposed to be white, so it manipulates the information to "see" a shirt that is white. But physical reality is frequently different from perception. The color of light being reflected from the shirt is determined by the color of the light source shining on it. For example, let's look at that white shirt in two different situations. In the first situation it is lit with a sunlight source (color temperature of 5,500 degrees kelvin, or 5,500° K). In the other situation it is lit with studio lights (3,200° K). Because your brain interprets the information it sees, both times you look at that shirt it appears to be white. If your brain wasn't interpreting the information the eye was sending, you would "see" that the shirt lit with the studio lights (3,200° K) looked more reddish than when it was lit with the 5,500° K light. To prove this theory, you need only to look at two identically white shirts, or pieces of white paper, sitting side by side on a neutral gray or black background, one lit with a 3,200° K source, the other with a 5,500° K source. The one lit by the lower color temperature source would definitely look redder than the other.

Almost all video cameras manufactured since the early 1980s have a feature known as "automatic white balancing." This means that the camera has circuitry that mimics the interpretative function of the brain by

Collector plate: The electronic plate of a video or digital camera on which the visual image is focused. The collector plate converts the light image into an electronic signal.

Open sunshine: Refers to the color temperature of sunshine on a cloudless day. In temperate geographic regions this color temperature averages 5,500° K, which is used as the industry standard designation.

White light: Light that contains all wavelengths of the visible spectrum in relatively equal proportion.

electronically adjusting the way the image is perceived by the camera's **collector plate** and subsequently recorded. The theory is that, with automatic white balancing, whites will look white, reds red, and so forth, regardless of the color temperature of the source illuminating the scene. While white balancing works well, it isn't perfect, nor does it "read the scene" as well, or as quickly, as the brain. Almost everyone has seen a home video in which someone in a room moves in front of a sunlit window or open doorway. While the person is in the room, away from the window, the scene is nicely white balanced. As the person moves in front of the window or door he or she is suddenly silhouetted and the color balance swings wildly out of whack—skin tones turn bluish and the interior takes on a reddish tone—until the white-balancing circuitry "catches up" and the color balance goes back to normal again. The same thing happens again if the person moves and the window or door goes out of frame.

Film is not capable of white balancing because the color balance of a particular film stock is fixed by the chemical composition of the film's emulsion. Films to be used outdoors in **open sunshine** are manufactured to accurately render colors when the scene is lit with a 5,500° K source, which is the color of open sunshine. The vast majority of films balanced for incandescent light is manufactured to accurately render colors when the scene is lit with 3,200° K sources.

Although film cannot be white balanced automatically, it can be adjusted manually. The light striking the emulsion can be accurately color balanced to suit the requirements of a particular film stock through the use of filters, which will be discussed a little later.

Light Sources and Their Effects on Film and Video

This section provides a little more detail about the different types of light sources that you will encounter when shooting film or video. You need to know this information because of the color of the light produced by these different sources can adversely affect the color of what you're shooting. Remember that our brains are constantly interpreting and adjusting the colors that we see, but video can't white balance nearly as well, or as quickly, as our brains, and film can't do it at all. Both media record what is actually there, and that reality is often at odds with what we see.

Continuous-Spectrum Sources   Sunlight and incandescent lights are known as continuous-spectrum sources because they emit all colors of the visible spectrum in relatively equal proportion. You'll remember from color mixing theory that when you mix the three primary colors of light—red, blue, and green—together in equal proportion, the resultant mix creates white light. So, by natural extension, when you mix all the colors of the visible spectrum together in relatively equal proportion you'll also create white light. Therefore, a continuous-spectrum source produces, by definition, **white light**.

Images are formed on film when light, reflected from objects in the scene, passes through the camera lens to the film's emulsion. If the light entering the camera is produced by a white-light source, the color of the light reflected from objects in the scene will be an accurate representation of the color of those objects. If the color temperature of the film and the light sources are matched—if they are color balanced or "balanced"—then the recorded image will be an accurate representation of the colors in the scene. An example may help explain this concept. Imagine that you're shooting an outdoor scene during the daytime with a film balanced for 5,500° K. When you look at the processed film the whites will look white, reds red, and so forth. The reason they look "correct" is because the film is color balanced with the source light—the color that the emulsion recognizes as white (5,500° K) is the same color temperature as the sunlight (5,500° K).

The same principles apply when working with incandescent studio lights. The only difference is that film balanced for studio lights recognizes 3,200° K as white. When you shoot a scene lit with 3,200° K studio lights with film balanced for 3,200° K the processed film will be properly color balanced.

Video cameras are capable of white balancing, so the issue of color balancing isn't as critical as it is with film. However, colors will be more accurately recorded when all of the sources lighting the scene have the same color temperature.

Fluorescent Lights   Incandescent lamps and the sun emit all the colors of the visible spectrum in relatively equal proportion. Fluorescent lamps don't. Figure 18.1 graphically depicts the difference between the light produced by incandescent and fluorescent sources. Figure 18.1A shows the relatively smooth emission over the entire visible spectrum of a typical incandescent lamp. Figure 18.1B shows the spiked emission pattern of a hypothetical, but typical, fluorescent lamp. The specific colors of these emission spikes, and their intensity, vary with the color design, (cool-white, warm-white, and so forth) as well as the age of the lamp.

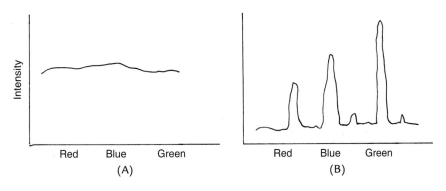

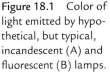

Figure 18.1   Color of light emitted by hypothetical, but typical, incandescent (A) and fluorescent (B) lamps.

Figure 18.2 Typical fluorescent-tubed lighting fixtures. (Courtesy of Lowel-Light and Mole-Richardson.)

Figure 18.2 Typical fluorescent-tubed lighting fixtures. (Courtesy of Lowel-Light and Mole-Richardson.)

Color-correction filters—filters that effectively turn cool-white fluorescent lamps into 3,200° K or 5,500° K white-light sources—are available. These filters snap onto the fluorescent tubes found in typical fluorescent ceiling fixtures. Additionally, several manufacturers offer fluorescent-lamped lighting fixtures for film and video. The lamps in these fixtures, Figure 18.2, are specifically designed for this use and are normally color balanced for either 3,200° or 5,500° K.

Fluorescent lamps require an internally mounted **ballast** to run properly. The fluorescent ceiling fixtures commonly seen in stores and classrooms use ballasts that operate at a relatively low frequency. The "hum" that you sometimes hear coming from a fluorescent fixture is a sonic manifestation of that frequency. Another by-product of that low operating frequency is lamp flicker. Most humans don't notice the flicker, but it can be recorded on film or tape, particularly if the ballast is relatively old. Fluorescent fixtures designed for media lighting use a high-frequency ballast that eliminates both the flicker and the hum.

Ballast: A special type of resistor that maintains an essentially constant current despite fluctuations in line current. Fluorescent tubes require this constant current to opereate.

Aperture: The opening in a lens that allows light to pass through to the film or electronic collector plate. A variable aperture allows the size of the opening to be changed.

F-stop: A numerical indication of a lens aperture setting.

F-Stops

The lens is the device that lets the light into the camera. It has two functions: (1) Control the amount of light entering the camera; (2) focus the image on the film or electronic collector plate. Almost all cameras, except the most basic still photography cameras, have lenses with a variable **aperture**. The size of the aperture is measured in **f-stops**. There is a logarithmic relationship between the f-stop and the size of the opening, but, for those of us who are not mathematically inclined, the important thing to remember is that the f-stop number is an indication of the size of the opening of the aperture, as illustrated in Figure 18.3.

There are additional points to remember about f-stops.

- The lower the f-stop number, the larger the aperture, and/or, the higher the f-stop number, the smaller the aperture.
- The amount of light passing through a lens changes by a factor of 2 as you move from one f-stop to the next. For example, twice as much light passes through a lens when you decrease the aperture from f/16 to f/11 or f/2.8 to f/2. Half as much light passes through a lens when you increase the f-stop from, for example, f/5.6 to f/8 or f/16 to f/22.

Cinematographers and photographers frequently refer to intensity of light in f-stops. For example, a cinematographer may say, "We need to brighten this area two stops." What he or she means is that the intensity of light falling on that part of the set needs to be increased by 2 f-stops. (You'd do this by bringing in supplemental light—either bouncing sunlight into the area if you're outdoors, or rigging additional lights.)

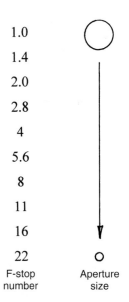

F-stop number
1.0
1.4
2.0
2.8
4
5.6
8
11
16
22

Aperture size

Figure 18.3 The size of a lens' aperture varies with the f-stop.

Shutter Speed

As stated above, one of the functions of the lens is to control the amount of light entering the camera. To accomplish this, most still cameras have variable apertures and variable shutter speeds. To precisely control the amount of light passing through the lens, the operator varies either, or both, the aperture and shutter speed. Most still camera shutters can be varied between at least 1 and ¹⁄₅₀₀ second.

Unlike still cameras, the speed of the shutter on movie and video cameras is relatively fixed. Movie cameras take 24 individual pictures, or frames, per second. Video cameras run at 30 frames per second. The actual shutter speed for most film and video cameras is about ¹⁄₅₀ second, depending on the make and model. When the talent moves, this relatively slow shutter speed causes the image on that frame to be slightly blurred. But remember that the camera is recording either 24 or 30 of these slightly blurred images *per second*. When projected at 24 or 30 frames per second the image will be perceived as moving smoothly.

On some movie and video cameras it is possible to change the shutter speed. As you increase the shutter speed—decrease the time that the shutter is open—of a movie or video camera, you initially sharpen the focus of the recorded image—the image becomes "crisper." If you increase the shutter speed even more, you can actually create a stop-motion effect that mimics movement seen under strobe lights. These effects are just that—effects—and are not used in run-of-the-mill shooting situations. Normally, and for general lighting purposes, the shutter speed of movie and video cameras can be considered fixed.

Gray Scale

A gray scale is simply a way of describing the variations in the reflectivity of gray that range from the total reflectivity of white and to the total absorption of black. A basic gray scale could be represented this way:

> White
> Light gray
> Middle gray
> Dark gray
> Black

In this typical gray scale, middle gray is perceived as halfway between white and black, light gray is halfway between white and middle gray, while dark gray is halfway between middle gray and black.

Middle gray is an important technical term in photography and videography. Specifically, middle gray reflects 18 percent of the light that strikes it. Most humans perceive middle gray as being halfway between white and black, hence its name—middle gray.

Film Latitude

This information is included because knowledge of the latitude of the film stock or video equipment being used on the project is an essential component of the process of lighting design for film or video.

Film latitude is, as the name implies, specifically related to emulsion-based recording media. It refers to the range of acceptable exposure of a particular film stock, which means that any objects whose **reflectance** falls within the latitude of a film will be accurately recorded. This "range of exposure" normally is measured in f-stops or stops. This concept is best explained through example. Let's say that we want to shoot a scene using a hypothetical film stock that has a latitude of four stops. As you recall, middle gray is the midpoint between black and white. It logically follows that middle gray is also the midpoint in the latitude range of any given film. So our hypothetical film with the four-stop latitude will have a range of acceptable exposure two stops **above** middle gray and two stops **below** middle gray. The practical effect of this principle is that anything in the frame that has a reflectance within the film's four-stop latitude will be accurately recorded. When the reflectance of something in the frame moves outside of a film's latitude—becomes brighter or darker than the acceptable range of exposure—then that object becomes progressively more over- or underexposed as it moves further outside the acceptable range of exposure. Generally, when an object is over- or underexposed by about half a stop, you begin to notice a loss of detail—the subtle shadowing created by an actor's cheekbones, noticeable when the shot was correctly exposed, are no longer visible. Additional detail will be lost when a shot is over- or underexposed by one stop—individual hairs on an actor's head, noticeable when the shot was properly exposed, have become a clump.

Film latitude: The range of acceptable exposure of a particular film stock.

Reflectance: The amount of light being reflected from an object. Reflectance is dependent on two elements: the amount of light falling on the object and the color of the object. The color determines how much light is reflected. Light colors reflect more light than dark colors.

Above: In this context, "above" means "brighter than."

Below: In this context, "below" means "darker than."

A two-stop overexposure washes out almost all detail, while a two-stop underexposure results in most of the picture being lost in darkness.

To complicate the situation even further, the latitude of any particular film stock is variable—it can shrink or grow by one or more stops depending on the intensity of the light, its direction relative to the camera, and the **reflectance range** of the objects in the shot. The following generalizations apply to all film stocks, whether used for still photography or movies.

- For any given film stock, film shot with higher levels of illumination will have a wider latitude than scenes shot with a lower level of illumination.

- The narrower the luminance range—the smaller the contrast between the brightest and darkest objects in the scene—the wider the latitude.

- **Negative film** stocks have a wider latitude than **reversal film** stocks.

- The latitude of color films is wider than that of most black and white films. (Historical note: Until the early 1990s the latitude of black and white films was generally wider than color, but recent technological advancements have reversed that situation.)

Determining the specific latitude of a film stock is a complex challenge routinely solved by the cinematographer. It isn't essential that the lighting designer know how to calculate it. Normally, the lighting designer would simply ask the cinematographer the latitude of the film(s) that will be used on the project, which stocks would be used in which setups, and proceed from there. That information may not be readily available on low-budget projects where a professional cinematographer is not part of the production team. If the information isn't available, a call to the technical department of the film's manufacturer will usually provide you with the "beginning point" latitude for any given stock. Using that figure when making your design choices will, in all but the most extreme shot situations, provide you with a very functional number.

The concept of film latitude—the range of acceptable exposure—is applicable to video and digital systems as well as film. All consumer-grade video and digital cameras have coupled exposure meters that provide the cameras with an adequate basic exposure setting in most lighting situations. The latitude of the collector plate systems in most video cameras manufactured since the mid-1990s is generally quite wide—8 to 10 stops. The latitude of many top-of-the-line digital cameras, both video and still, is even better. (Interesting note: In 2001, the image quality of top-of-the-line professional high-definition digital video cameras became sufficiently high that at least three feature films, including the second episode in the *Star Wars* "prequel" trilogy, released in May 2002, were shot with digital, rather than film, cameras.) The wide latitude of the current generation of video cameras allows almost everything within a typical scene to be within the camera's latitude. Only when there are extreme contrasts in the frame—as when shooting inside a room that includes a sunlit window or doorway in the shot—will detail be lost.

Reflectance range: The difference in reflectivity between the brightest and darkest objects in a scene. Normally measured in f-stops.

Negative film: A film that, when processed, provides a negative image in which blacks appear white and so forth. Snapshots are printed from negative film.

Reversal film: When processed reversal film provides a positive image. Slides are an example of reversal film.

☀ Why Not Use Dimmers for Intensity Control?

Dimmers are frequently used for intensity control when working with video because of the automatic white balancing feature of video cameras. But there are two primary reasons why dimmers generally aren't used in film work. First, the rated color temperature of an incandescent lamp is attained only when that lamp is operated at full intensity. If an electronic dimmer is used to lower a lamp's intensity, its color temperature also drops, which results in a "red shift" of the recorded image. The second reason is that many fixtures used for movie lighting have encapsulated arc sources. These lamps cannot be dimmed electronically. Mechanical dimmers, which were discussed in Chapter 10, can be used, but metal neutral density screens are the preferred method of reducing the light output of both incandescent and encapsulated arc sources because they're portable, efficient, effective, and they don't change the color temperature of the light source.

Since the instructions that come with most video equipment do not include information about the equipment's latitude capability, you should determine that with a field test. Working with the videographer, use the camera(s) and recording equipment that will be used on the project. Take several shots that include low-, normal-, and high-contrast settings. While shooting each of these shots, take **reflective light meter** readings of at least ten objects ranging from the brightest to the darkest in the shots.[1] Write down the results of these readings. Identify the objects you metered and note their f-stops. When you look at the tape on a good quality monitor you'll be able to see which objects are properly exposed with good detail. You'll also see those brighter and darker objects where the picture begins to lose detail. The effective latitude of the video equipment will be the number of stops between those two extremes. The latitude of the video equipment is subject to the same variables as film. Those variables were listed as "bullet points" toward the beginning of this discussion.

Reflective light meter: A light meter that measures light being reflected from the subject.

Frame: In this context, frame refers to the scene framed by the camera's viewfinder.

Coupled exposure meter: A reflective exposure meter built into the body of a camera that automatically adjusts the lens aperture to the correct setting for the available light. Also called a coupled exposure system.

Reflex meter: A built-in meter that reads the light after it has passed through the camera's lens.

Light Meters

There are two types of light meters: those that measure light intensity and those that measure the color of light.

Exposure Meters   To design light for video or film you have to be able to determine how much light is entering the camera lens. Exposure meters do

---

[1] See the next section, "Light Meters," for information about reflective light meters. See the section "Shoot the Highlight/Shadow Areas" later in the chapter for information about metering techniques.

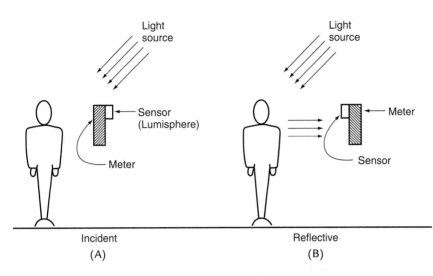

that. They enable us to determine the appropriate f-stop for an individual scene and obtain consistent lighting levels from scene to scene.

An exposure meter is an electronic device that measures the intensity of light. There are two classes of exposure meters—incident and reflective. Incident meters measure light falling on a subject, as shown in Figure 18.4A, while reflective meters measure light being reflected from the subject, as illustrated in 18.4B.

While there are many excellent incident and reflective meters, a combination meter such as the Sekonic L-398M, Figure 18.5A, is accurate in both modes—incident and reflective—and is satisfactory for most media lighting and cinematographic work.

Reflected light meters are manufactured in two types—averaging and spot. The averaging meter is more common and is used in many combination meters, including the Sekonic L-398M. An averaging meter's reading is based on an average of the brightness levels of all elements in its relatively wide angle of view. Averaging meters normally are used to read the reflectance of an entire scene, although they can be used to measure small areas.

A spot meter is an averaging reflective meter with a very narrow angle of view—normally between 1 and 4 degrees. Spot meters, such as the Sekonic L-778 Dual Spot F, Figure 18.5B, normally are used to read the reflectance of small areas, such as bright and dark spots, within the **frame**.

Top-of-the-line digital meters such as the Sekonic L-608 Cine Super Zoom Master, Figure 18.5C, are combination incident/reflective meters with spot meter capabilities along with a number of additional programmable functions.

Coupled exposure meters are averaging reflective meters. They are used on all video and all but the most basic still cameras. Almost all video cameras manufactured since the early 1990s have **reflex meters**—meters

(A)

(B)

(C)

Figure 18.5 Light meters. (A) Sekonic L-398M Studio Deluxe II. (B) Sekonic L-778 Dual Spot F. (C) Sekonic L-608 Cine Super Zoom Master.

☀ Overexposure and Underexposure

An image is recorded on film when light strikes the emulsion. Too much light causes overexposure, too little light causes underexposure. When a film is either over- or underexposed, the image starts to lose detail. For example, if a shot of someone with blond hair is overexposed, the detail of the individual hairs will be lost. If the overexposure is severe, all detail is lost and the overexposed area simply becomes a white outline. Similarly, if you underexpose the face of someone with black hair, you'd begin to lose detail of the individual hairs. If the underexposure becomes se-

vere, all detail will be lost and the underexposed area would become a solid black silhouette.

Video, digital, and most still photography cameras have coupled exposure meters, which are built-in exposure meters that automatically adjust the lens aperture. Because of this feature these cameras rarely over- or underexpose anything. Most movie cameras do not have coupled exposure meters. The reason movie cameras don't have coupled meters is explained in the box, "Determining 'Proper' Exposure."

Center-weighted meter: An averaging reflective meter in which the center of the frame accounts for a greater proportion of the total exposure than the edges of the frame.

Color-correction filters: Filters used to adjust the color of light to match the color of a specific film emulsion.

that read the light after it has passed through the camera lens. All coupled exposure meters are reflective meters. Most consumer-grade video cameras have averaging reflective meters, but many medium- and high-end consumer-grade, and most professional-grade, models employ **center-weighted meters**.

All light meters are calibrated for middle gray. That means when you take a meter reading with an exposure meter, the f-stop recommended by the meter will provide a proper exposure for middle gray. Since middle gray is in the center of the latitude of the film stock that you're using, the recommended f-stop will provide an accurate exposure for those objects whose reflectance is within the latitude of the film. It is important that you fully understand this point. It is a central element in the process of exposure control that will be discussed a little later in the chapter.

Color Meters   Color meters are light meters that measure the color temperature, rather than intensity, of light.

Color meters are available in two types—those that measure two colors (red and blue) and those that measure three colors (red, blue, green). Two-color meters measure only sunlight and incandescent light sources. Three-color meters can measure the color temperature of any light source.

Typical three-color meters not only measure the color temperature of the light, but also recommend specific **color-correction filters** to use on the camera to balance the color temperature of the sources to the color temperature of the specific film stock being used.

Filters

As was discussed in Chapter 9, "Color," filters change the color of light passing through them. They do so by allowing light that is the same color as the filter to pass through the filter, while absorbing light waves of different hues.

Filters are commonly used in two places when shooting film or video—on the source or on the camera.

Source Filters Source filters are mounted on a light source. In the theatre the light source is almost always a lighting instrument. In film and video the light source can also be a lighting fixture, but it may also be sunlight coming through a window when a location interior is shot. In shooting outdoors, the sun is almost always the source.

Plastic source filters are manufactured in 24 × 24-inch sheets (the same as theatrical gels), rolls (approximately 4 × 25 feet), and rigid sheets roughly 4 × 8 feet. Gels for use on fixtures are normally cut from the sheets, while the rolls and rigid sheets are typically used to cover windows.

Plastic source filters should be handled carefully because, if the surface of the filter is abraded, the light passing through it will be diffused.

Camera Filters While a lighting designer doesn't normally work with camera filters, it is important to know about them.

Camera filters are normally mounted either behind the lens (BTL) or in front of the lens (FOL). Camera filters are used to produce specific effects such as increased or decreased contrast, diffusion, color correction, and tinting.

All camera filters need to be handled with great care. BTL filters must be kept scrupulously clean. Any scratch, smudge, or dust will degrade the quality of the image being recorded. FOL filters should be kept equally free of scratches and smudges for the same reasons, but a few stray dust particles on an FOL filter won't adversely affect image quality as they will with BTL filters.

Types of Filters There is a plethora of filters used in film/video production. We are not going to discuss them all. The intent of this section is to focus on those filters most frequently used by a media lighting designer. But it is important for the lighting designer to know about the properties of some other filters as well. These filters, primarily used by the cinematographer, affect various aspects of the lighting designer's work, and so they are included as well.

Neutral Density Filters Grayish in color, neutral density filters reduce the amount of light passing through the filter without altering its color. They are primarily used for exposure control and are available for both sources and cameras.

Neutral density (ND) filters for sources are manufactured as standard plastic filter material and metal screens. The plastic filters are used on lensed fixtures such as fresnels and ERSs. The heat generated by the nonlensed or open-faced fixtures commonly used in film and video location production

✴ Controlling Depth of Field

Neutral density filters are sometimes used to control depth of field. Depth of field is the range of distance that objects within the frame are in focus, as shown in the figure. Depth of field is determined by three criteria:

1. The focal length of the lens: The longer the focal length, the shorter the depth of field—and the converse—the shorter the focal length the greater the depth of field.
2. The aperture of the lens: The bigger the aperture the shorter the depth of field—and the converse—the smaller the aperture, the greater the depth of field.
3. The distance of the subject from the camera: The further the subject is from the lens the greater the depth of field—and the converse—the closer the subject is to the lens the shorter the depth of field.

Controlling the depth of field requires that you have a lens on which the focus and aperture can be manually adjusted. Manually adjustable lenses are not normally found on consumer- and industrial-grade video and digital still cameras. The exception to this generalization involves high-end, and very expensive, digital cameras, both still and high-density (HD) digital video. For these reasons, this technique is usually limited to film cameras, both movie and still, as well as

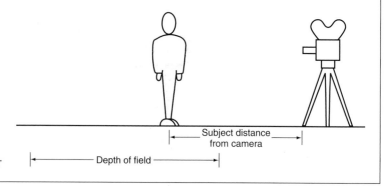

Subject distance from camera

Depth of field

would melt most plastic filters in a matter of seconds. For this reason metal screen ND filters are used on these instruments.

Camera-mounted ND filters are normally manufactured in gradations that correspond to one-third stop reductions up through three stops. A one-stop neutral density filter cuts the light passing through it by half (50 percent). This reduction is equivalent to one f-stop.

Plastic ND source filters are available in one-, two-, and three-stop formulations.

Metal ND filters, called **scrims**, are precisely calibrated metal screens typically available in one-half, one-, and two-stop meshes. They are frequently used in combination to precisely control an instrument's output intensity. These are commonly used in film production for two reasons: (1) if you run an incandescent lamp down on dimmer, you change the output color temperature of that lamp; (2) encapsulated arc lamps, which are common lighting sources for film and video, cannot be electronically dimmed.

In general, neutral density filters are used for exposure control. An example may help explain the concept. Imagine that you're shooting outdoors on a bright day. Your light meter indicates that proper exposure for the scene will be obtained with a lens setting of f/22. Further imagine that the highest

Scrim: In the context of filters, scrim refers to metal screens designed to reduce light in one-half, one-, and two-stop meshes.

✳ (*continued*)

the aforementioned high-end digital cameras. Additionally, the format—size—of the recorded image influences the depth of field. The principle can be stated: The smaller the format, the greater the depth of field. The formats of all but the highest-end video cameras have a smaller image than either 16 mm or 35 mm film. Consequently, the inherent depth of field for these small format video cameras is much greater than movie or still film cameras.

In practical application, after you have selected the particular lens you want to use, you adjust the aperture to control the depth of field. In general, you ignore "distance from the camera" to control the depth of field

because changing the camera-subject distance would require you to change the composition of the shot. Again, an example may help explain the process. You want to take a closeup of a person with the subject's face in focus but everything else out of focus. For this shot you need a very short depth of field. You meter the scene and decide that an aperture setting of f/8 will give you the proper exposure. To shorten the depth of field you'll need to open the aperture. The number of stops that you open the aperture will determine the new depth of field. To keep the proper exposure you need to use an ND filter with a one-stop compensation for each stop that you open the

aperture. For example, if you open the aperture 3 stops, use a 0.9 neutral density filter, which has a 3-stop compensation. To determine the actual depth of field that you want to use, and the number of stops that you'll need to open the lens to achieve that setting, you should consult the depth of field tables in the *American Cinematographer Manual*. The American Society of Cinematographers publishes this book, currently in its ninth edition. It is an invaluable resource for anyone who is serious about filmmaking or still photography. Its companion piece, *American Cinematographer Video Manual*, contains a similar wealth of information about videography.

f-stop on the camera lens is f/11. If shot at f/11 the film will be overexposed. But, if a camera-mounted neutral density filter with a two-stop compensation—the difference between f/11 and f/22—is used and the lens is set at f11, the shot will be properly exposed.

Ultraviolet Filters Ultraviolet (UV) filters remove the ultraviolet portion of the spectrum from the light. UV light technically is not part of the visible spectrum since humans can't see it. Film emulsions, however, are sensitive to it. UV light manifests itself as haze. If a UV filter is used, the haze is significantly reduced. Normally, UV filters are camera mounted rather than source mounted.

Polarizing Filters Polarizing filters, just like polarized sunglasses, reduce glare. They reduce glare because of the physical structure of the filter and the nature of the light that causes glare. A polarizing filter is identical in concept to an extremely narrow set of miniblinds. The only light that can pass through the filter is light whose waveform is moving parallel to the open slits. Since glare is scattered white light, a polarizing filter will allow only a relatively small portion of the reflective glare to pass through it.

Color-conversion filters: Filters used to make large adjustments—generally more than 1,000° K—to the color of the light entering the camera. These are almost always camera filters.

The use of a camera-mounted polarizing filter enhances all colors. This is accomplished by reducing glare. Glare occurs when white light is reflected from the surface of an object. To illustrate this point, let's assume that we're standing in a driveway on a sunny day looking at a red, highly polished, car. There is a significant amount of glare being reflected from the car. The amount of glare is easily equal to, or greater than, the amount of red light being reflected from the red paint of the car. The camera (film or video) records what it sees: a red diluted with the white light of the glare. A polarizing filter reduces the white glare, so more red light strikes the film or collector plate, which results in the red appearing to be more fully saturated than when recorded without a filter.

Color-Correction Filters Color-correction filters are used almost exclusively with film—movie and still—work. Because of their white-balancing capabilities, most video cameras don't use this type of filter.

As was explained earlier in the color temperature section, if the color temperature of a light source and a film emulsion don't match, the color recording will not be accurate. For example, if a film balanced for studio lights (3,200° K) is shot outdoors without the use of an appropriate color correction filter, it will have a bluish tint. The filters used to make these large color-correction shifts are called **color-conversion filters**. A Wratten 85B filter is used to allow indoor-balanced film to be shot outdoors. It changes the color of open sunshine (5,500° K) to 3,200° K. The use of an 85B filter requires a two-third stop compensation—the lens aperture must be opened two-thirds of a stop to compensate for the light removed by the filter.

The conversion of daylight-balanced emulsion for use with studio lights—through the use of an 80A filter—is rarely done because it requires a compensation of two stops.

Film Speed

The concept of "film speed" refers to a film emulsion's sensitivity to light. The more sensitive the emulsion is to light—the quicker an image can be formed on that particular emulsion—the "faster" that film is said to be.

In the United States, the most commonly used film speed rating systems are ASA (American Standards Association) and ISO (International Organization for Standardization). The numerical rating for both of these systems is identical. Generally, a film with an ASA/ISO rating of 25 to 50 is considered "slow." A rating of 50 to 200 is considered "medium," and 200 to 400 is considered "fast." These relatively arbitrary categories were developed more than 25 years ago. Since that time a number of advances in film emulsion technology have suggested that a fourth category—"superfast" for any emulsion rated over 400 ASA/ISO—would be appropriate.

The practical application of the concept of film speed is: Films with faster speeds need less light to record an image. This means that in low-light situations—outdoors at night, dark interiors, and so forth—you would want to use a fast, or superfast film. When shooting outdoors on a bright sunny day, a slow-speed film would be appropriate. You might want to use a medium-speed film when shooting outdoors on a cloudy day.

Typically, cinematographers want to use as few different film emulsions as possible on a project. For this reason, they will frequently choose a fast or superfast tungsten-balanced emulsion and then use color-correction and neutral density filters when shooting outdoors.

The collector plates of modern video cameras are extremely sensitive to light. Since the collector plate is a video camera's equivalent of film emulsion, video cameras essentially can be thought of as having the equivalent of a fast or superfast film speed.

EXPOSURE CONTROL
· ·

Cameras with coupled exposure meters have an effective method of exposure control. As mentioned earlier, some top-of-the-line still cameras and a few movie cameras have extremely sophisticated **center-loaded exposure systems**. However, none of the exposure settings provided by those systems are aesthetically based. These coupled systems generally provide excellent exposure control for individual shots and scenes. However, in shooting a story film, one of the primary goals of the cinematographer/lighting director is to achieve a consistency of skin tone reflectance for the primary actors throughout the film. Generally, that isn't possible with a coupled exposure system because the exposure meter simply reads what it sees and adjusts the aperture accordingly. But an aesthetically based exposure control technique (for lack of a better term) lets the lighting designer make choices. And having the opportunity to make those choices is the basis of lighting design. Light meters provide a great deal of useful and necessary information, but those readings are only part of the information that the media lighting designer uses to make his or her design choices.

As explained at the beginning of this chapter, not all film or video production situations require designed light. But, for those situations that do, the following process is offered as an example of an aesthetically based exposure control system that gives the designer the opportunity to create meaning with light.

Take a Base Reading

After you have all of the lighting in place, and turned on, hold an incident meter in the center of the primary point of focus for the scene. In most cases this will be the face of your talent. Holding the meter just in front of the talent's face, point the lumisphere—the white plastic dome—*toward the camera*. Activate the meter to measure the light intensity, and use that reading

Center-loaded exposure system: A coupled exposure system in which objects in the center of the frame are given precedence over objects outside the center in determining the exposure value. The term center-loaded is synonymous with center-weighted.

to determine the recommended f-stop. This reading is the beginning point for determining the "proper" exposure. For all interior settings, and most outdoor settings except for those shots that have a lot of visible sky in the frame, the f-stop recommended by the incident meter will provide you with a good exposure for middle gray. If you're metering an outdoor shot that includes a lot of sky or bright lights, use a reflective, rather than incident, meter. With the reflective meter, stand beside the camera and point the reflective meter *toward the subject*. The reading this setup provides will give you a good exposure for middle gray when shooting in one of these "bright-light background" situations.

With the f-stop recommended in your base reading, and knowledge of the latitude of the particular film stock or video system with which you're working, you can determine the exposure limits for the shot. An example will help explain this process. Assume that the base reading recommended an aperture setting of f/5.6. The film stock/video system you're using has a latitude of six stops, so your exposure limits will be three stops above and three stops below f/5.6. This means that everything in the scene that has a reflectance or luminance between f/2 (three stops below f/5.6) and f/16 (three stops above f/5.6) will be accurately recorded on the film or tape/disk/chip. Objects with a reflectance or luminance of more than f/16 will begin to be overexposed, with the effects of that overexposure increasing as the amount of overexposure increases. Objects with a reflectance or luminance below f/2 will be similarly underexposed.

Visually Analyze the Scene

Critically look at the variations in brightness—the range of luminance—of the scene that you're shooting. What are the brightest areas within the frame? What are the darkest? Is everything within the frame within the exposure limits of the scene? Frequently, you'll discover that some part of the scene looks really bright or very dark. You need to ask yourself if that object or element contains visual information important to the scene, or, in the case of a really bright object, if it will be a distraction. If the answer is yes, then you need to determine exactly how bright or dark that object or those areas are. You need to meter again, but this time with a reflective meter.

Meter the Highlight/Shadow Areas

Use a reflective light meter to determine the amount of light in the highlight/shadow areas. If using a spot meter, stand beside the camera and "shoot" readings of the highlight and shadow areas. Make notes, either mental or written, of the readings. If using a "non spot" reflective meter—the type that averages the reflectance of everything in its field of view—hold the meter so the sensor is about 1 to 2 feet away from, and pointing at, the object to be metered. Be sure that neither you nor the meter is creating any shadows on, or bouncing any light into, the area you're reading.

If the camera with which you're working has a **coupled reflex meter**, a zoom lens, and some type of readout of the f-stops the meter is sensing, it can be used as a pseudo-spot meter. After framing the scene you can zoom in on the bright and dark spots and meter them to determine if they are within the latitude of the film or video system with which you're working. Even on **max telephoto**, the viewing angle of the zoom lens will never be as narrow as a real spot meter, so it will be difficult to completely isolate any small areas you're trying to read unless you move the camera closer to the subject.

If the brightness levels of the metered highlight/shadow areas in your shot are outside the exposure range of your film or video system, you may want to adjust the lighting to bring the objects back within the film's exposure limits. But remember, if the object's reflectance/luminance is barely outside the film's latitude, most of its detail will still be visible. You need to ask yourself if the detail in the over/underexposed area is critical visual information. If it isn't, leave it alone. If it is, brighten or darken the affected area as necessary.

Completing the above-listed steps will provide you with the information needed to make a decision about what f-stop to use for a shot. The lighting designer doesn't normally make that decision, but you need to know the process to be sure that the design you **rig** will not only reinforce the mood and spirit of the production, but will work for the technical circumstances of the shot as well.

Coupled reflex meter: A meter that senses through the lens of a camera and automatically adjusts the lens to the aperture recommended by the meter.

Max telephoto: A zoom lens that is zoomed all the way to its longest, or maximum, focal length.

Rig: To place lighting equipment on a set. Normally used in reference to film or television sets. Synonymous with the theatrical lighting term "hang."

Location: In the context of lighting fixtures, those instruments designed to be used outside the studio. Typically these fixtures are small, lightweight and are equipped with a telescoping stand.

MEDIA LIGHTING INSTRUMENTS
· ·

Two general classes of instruments are used for media lighting—studio fixtures and those instruments specifically designed for **location** lighting. Just like theatrical instruments, media lighting fixtures are normally designed for lamps with specific characteristics and sizes. Therefore, this discussion of media lighting fixtures will begin with a discussion of the lamps used in these fixtures.

Lamps

Generally, lamps used for media lighting have one of two color temperatures—3,200° or 5,500° K. The 3,200° K lamps are normally incandescent tungsten-halogen lamps, while the 5,500° K lamps are typically encapsulated arc HMI lamps. The operating characteristics of both these types of lamps were discussed in Chapter 4, "Lenses, Lamps, Reflectors, and Lighting Instruments." Additional information about lamps is provided below.

Incandescent Lamps   Whether shooting video or film, the incandescent lamps used in studio and location fixtures normally are rated at 3,200° K. Incandescent lamps for media lighting fixtures are available in a variety of wattages ranging from approximately 100 to 2,500 watts. The envelopes of lamps used in theatrical fixtures almost always are clear. In media lighting, fixture lamps are either clear or frosted depending on their intended use. Clear-envelope lamps typically are used in fixtures where the desired effect is a "punch" of light. Diffused-envelope lamps are almost always used in fixtures designed to create a soft, directionless, fill light.

In addition to lamps designed for use with specific lighting fixtures, lamps that look like ordinary household lamps—A or PS shapes with medium screw bases—with a 3,200° K color temperature are also available. Although originally intended for use in photo reflectors, these lamps can be used in practicals—table or floor lamps, wall sconces, and so forth—to provide a properly color balanced atmospheric lamp.

Fluorescent Lamps   3,200° K and 5,500° K fluorescent lamps are available from many photo supply or film rental companies. On location, the 3,200° K lamps can be used to replace the fluorescent lamps found in typical ceiling lighting fixtures. There are also several soft-light fixtures specifically designed to use fluorescent lamps.

Encapsulated Arc Sources   Encapsulated arc sources for use in media lighting fixtures almost universally have a color temperature rating of 5,500° K to match the color temperature of open sunshine. They are available in wattages ranging from around 200 to 12,000 (or 12 kW).

Studio Fixtures

Studio fixtures are lights designed for use in a studio. The workhorse fixture of studio lighting is the fresnel, which is similar in design and function to the fresnel spotlight used in theatrical lighting. The one significant difference between the two is that the yoke of the studio fresnel is slightly wider and sturdier than its theatrical cousin because studio fresnels, like all studio lights, are designed for use on stands as well as grids. Several types of studio fresnels are shown in Figure 18.6.

Softlights are the second type of workhorse studio fixture. While there are a plethora of softlight fixture designs, as shown in Figure 18.7, they all provide a soft, almost shadowless, fill light. Many of these softlights are used on location setups as well as in the studio.

The lighting instruments used for theatrical lighting—ERSs, fresnels, and so forth—can also be used for lighting film and video, particularly if the location on which you are shooting is a theatre stage. Generally, the light output of theatrical instruments is harsher, and creates sharper shadows, than lights specifically designed for media lighting. However, the judicious use of diffusion gels will soften the light from these instruments. But there are still a few inherent quirks about theatrical lighting instruments that generally make them less than ideal for media lighting.

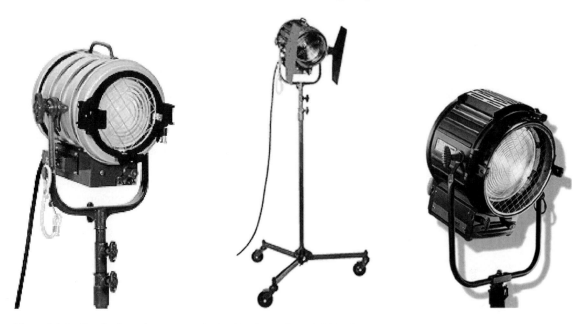

Figure 18.6   Studio fresnels. (Courtesy of Mole-Richardson and Strand Lighting.)

Figure 18.7   Softlights. (Courtesy of Strand Lighting and Mole-Richardson.)

The Pyrex lenses used in some theatrical instruments actually color any light passing through them. Pyrex lenses produce a slight green tint that is visible on film. Many newer instruments are equipped with borosilicate lenses that are fairly colorless. The best way to determine if a lens is going to tint the light passing through it is to look at the lens from the side. Ideally the glass will look clear or gray. If it appears tinted the lens will project that color.

When using theatrical instruments to light for film, the ideal solution would be to equip all the instruments with new 3,200° K lamps. This would be expensive. If the budget doesn't allow for relamping, you can shoot with the extant lamps, as long as they are all of the same color temperature. If all the lamps are *not* the same color temperature, the color of the light will have slight variations. The camera—either film or video—will record those color shifts and they may be noticeable when you look at the film or video. Interestingly, when you look at the lit set you won't notice the color shifts because the brain makes rapid color corrections. But the cameras will see them.

Regardless of the medium—film or video—the use of same-color-temperature lamps in all fixtures provides the most accurate color reproduction. Working with film, a uniform 3,200° K light source would be ideal. Because of its white-balancing capabilities, video can be lit with non–3,200° K sources as long as all the lamps are of the same color temperature.

The color temperature of typical theatrical instrument lamps normally is lower than 3,200° K. Most theatrical lamps are rated between 2,950° and 3,050° K. These lamps can be used when shooting film if an appropriate **light-balancing filter** is used on the camera. The selection of which light-balancing filter to use would be made by the cinematographer.

Because of the color shift that occurs when a lamp is dimmed, if any instruments are to be run on dimmer at less than full intensity, the lighting designer will probably want to use a color meter to take a reading of the overall color temperature, particularly if shooting film. With all of the lights turned on to the desired intensity, the meter would indicate the overall color temperature reading and, if necessary, prescribe an appropriate color-balancing camera filter.

Location Fixtures

There is a plethora of instruments designed for use in location film and video lighting. The following discussion generally will be limited to lighting equipment typically used on student projects or small-scale independent productions. Interestingly, about the only difference between lighting these small-scale productions and lighting large-scale/big-budget made-for-TV movies and feature films involves the size of the areas being lit. The design principles used on both are identical. Small-scale/small-budget productions generally light relatively small areas—the corner of a room, a hallway, part of a porch, a portion of an alley, and so forth, while large-budget productions can afford the equipment, and personnel, necessary to light areas the size of football fields if required.

Light-balancing filter: A filter used to make small adjustments—generally less than 400° K—to the color of the light entering the camera. These are almost always camera filters.

There are two general criteria used for selecting the type of lighting fixture to be used in any particular setup: The type of light to be provided—key or fill; and the size of the area being lit. Small setups typically use fixtures with lamps ranging from 250 to 1,000 watts, with the largest fixtures generally having lamps of approximately 2,000 watts. Typically, the smallest "general use" lamp on a big set will be around 2,000 watts, and the size of the fixtures will range up to the 12,000-watt fresnels that have replaced the open-arc klieg lights used in the past. The primary reason for the discrepancy of wattage is relatively simple: Production units for feature films and made-for-TV movies have the budget required to rent a **generator truck** to power the lights on the production. These trucks generate amazing amounts of the correct type of electricity for every conceivable lighting fixture that might be used on the production. Small-scale productions normally use whatever electricity is available on site. Typically, "location electricity" means a few 120-volt, 15- or 20-amp circuits available in the store, apartment, or home in which the project is being shot. The maximum load that can be placed on a 120-volt, 20-amp circuit is 2,400 watts. For this reason, location fixtures using a maximum lamp size of 1,000 watts are fairly typical in these small-scale production situations.

Most of the location instruments discussed in this chapter are relatively small and lightweight. None of them are designed to be hung from grids, but rather placed on light stands. Some of the lighter units are actually designed to be taped to walls.

The DP Light, Figure 18.8, from Lowel is typical of these small location lights. It is open-faced and has two reflectors, one for "normal" use and one for "long throw" situations. The open face is covered with a wire screen that keeps the operator from accidentally touching the tungsten-halogen lamp. The DP uses 500-, 750-, or 1,000-watt, 120-volt lamps and a similar range of 220/240-volt lamps. A variety of accessories are available, such as a four-way barndoor and scrims. It can be used as a key, back, or **background light**. By adding an **umbrella** or diffusion it can be used as a **soft key** or fill light.

Lowel's Tota-light, Figure 18.9, is a versatile fixture that uses a diffused tungsten-halogen 500- or 750-watt, 120-volt or 800-watt, 220/240-volt lamp.

Generator truck: A large flatbed truck equipped with a well-muffled gasoline- or diesel-powered generator.

Background light: This context means that the fixture can be used for lighting the background of a scene.

Umbrella: A small, silvered umbrella used as a reflector. The umbrella is attached to the stand with a clamp. The light is focused on the umbrella, which acts like a parabolic reflector to create a soft, moderately focused fill light.

Soft key: A diffused key light.

Figure 18.8 DP light. (Courtesy of Lowel-Light.)

Figure 18.9 Tota-light. (Courtesy of Lowel-Light.)

Figure 18.10 Incandescent (tungsten-halogen) fresnels. (Courtesy of Strand Lighting and Mole-Richardson.)

The "winged" reflectors are movable and it can be used with an umbrella or with a **standoff gel frame** and diffusion to provide soft key, fill, back, or background light. As with all of the other fixtures in the Lowel line, there are a wide variety of accessories available for the Tota-light.

Fresnels, in a variety of sizes, are offered by a number of manufacturers such as Mole-Richardson and Strand Lighting. They are available with both incandescent, Figure 18.10, and HMI, Figure 18.11, lamps. The primary difference between the incandescent and HMI fresnels is that the HMI fixtures are equipped with the additional electronic equipment required by the HMI lamp. As with their theatrical cousins, both the incandescent and HMI fresnels produce a focusable, smooth wash of reasonably soft light. Accessories such as two- and four-flipper barn doors, gel frames, and scrims are available.

Light kits, such as those shown in Figure 18.12, are available in a wide variety of configurations. The kits are composed of a carrying case that usually contains two or more lighting fixtures or heads, and the most commonly used accessories such as telescoping stands, cables, barndoors, umbrellas, gel frames, and scrims.

Since the "audience" for a film is the camera, lighting instruments can be placed with much greater freedom than in the theatre. The only "placement criterion" is that the fixture needs to be put where it will do its intended job most efficiently, and it needs to be out of view of the camera frame. It is not at all unusual to see several fixtures on stands in the middle of a set.

Control of "where the light goes" is similarly less restricted than in the theatre. **Flags** are rectangular pieces of black cardboard or frame-mounted

Standoff gel frame: A gel frame that is held some distance, typically 6 to 12 inches, in front of an open-face lighting instrument to keep the lamp from melting the plastic gel.

Flag: Named for its shape. A roughly rectangularly shaped material—transparent, translucent, or opaque depending on function—that is inserted into a beam of light to color, shape, or dim the light.

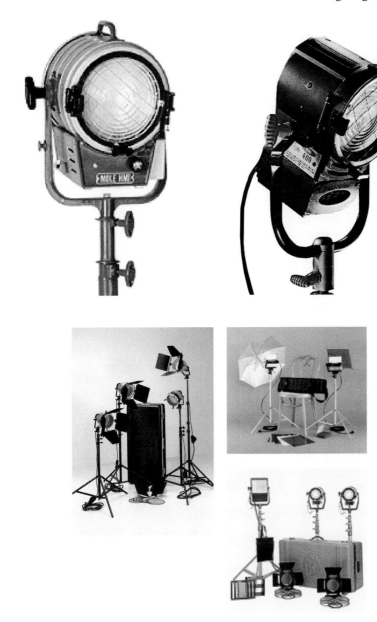

Figure 18.11 HMI fresnels. (Courtesy of Mole-Richardson and Strand Lighting.)

Figure 18.12 Light kits. (Courtesy of Strand Lighting, Lowel-Light, and Mole-Richardson.)

cloth used to block or stop the light. The size of the flag depends entirely on its intended use. They can be as small as an envelope or as large as a blanket. They are normally secured in place by stand-mounted articulated arms that can be moved to almost any position. Flags are used to cast shadows wherever needed. They are used to control the edges of a beam of light in a manner similar to the shutters on an ERS. Additionally, they are frequently used to keep direct light off of the camera lens.

ERSs, equipped with cookies or patterns, are frequently used to project shadow images—leaves, windows, and so forth—on the set. Additionally, patterns can be projected with fresnels and open-faced fixtures by interrupting their beam of light with a shadow pattern cut out of a large piece of cardboard. These large patterns, called cookies after their inventor, one Mr. Cucaloris, are normally stand-mounted and held in position with articulated arms in exactly the same manner as flags.

You are strongly encouraged to scan the information about the wide variety of fixtures, accessories, and light kits on various manufacturers' Web sites, such as www.lowel.com (Lowel Lighting), www.strandlighting .com (Strand Lighting), www.mole.com (Mole-Richardson Co.), and www .altmanltg.com (Altman Stage Lighting Co.).

DESIGN EXAMPLES

When this chapter began it was stated that the design principles discussed earlier in this text apply equally well to film and video. Those principles provide a useful analytical approach to the process of design, whether that design is for theatre, film, or video. As stated at the beginning of this chapter, the only significant difference between designing lighting for theatre and designing lighting for film/video is that the audience for theatre is people and the audience for film/video is a camera. And, as you have seen in this chapter, cameras make a lot more technical demands than people when it comes to seeing. Satisfying the camera's demands makes implementing a lighting design for film/video a different challenge than implementing a theatrical lighting design, but the process of creating those designs is pretty much the same.

The following design examples are intended to demonstrate the process that the cinematographer/director or photography/lighting designer goes through when creating and implementing lighting designs for film or video. Because the technical requirements differ, sometimes substantially, between film and video, separate solutions will be offered for the lighting for each media.

As with the caveat offered in Chapter 16, "Design Examples," the solutions offered for these examples shouldn't be thought of as the only, or correct, solutions to their particular design challenges. Each design team needs to work together to create a lighting design that is the most appropriate solution for the particular design challenge.

Example 1: A Short Film, *Dunston's Discovery*

The Story   This is a story about a young man in search of himself. At the beginning of the story, which is set somewhere in the Midwest in 1993, our hero, Dunston, is consumed with the idea that he's going to be the next Hemingway. During the course of the story, which takes place during the second semester of Dunston's freshman year in college, he discovers that the *idea* of being a writer is much more romantic, and a lot more fun, than the actual work of being a writer. At the end of our story, Dunston meets Sarah, falls desperately in love, forgets all about writing, and moves on to the next chapter of his life.

The Scene   We are in Dunston's room. It is 3:00 A.M. The writing isn't going well. Dunston, a cigarette hanging from the corner of his mouth, stares at the blank sheet of paper in his old Underwood Standard typewriter. (Dunston believes that "real" writers not only dangle cigarettes from the corners of their mouths, but use typewriters as well, not computers. Something about "suffering for their art.")

An old 1930s-style gooseneck lamp casts a dim cone of light as our hero, deep in thought, shifts his eyes from the typewriter to blankly stare into space. Obviously, he's deep in thought. Suddenly, he begins to furiously type. He stops, reads what he's written, rips it out and disgustedly pitches it into the wastebasket beside the table.

The Shot   The **storyboards**, Figure 18.13, depict the shot composition. During the course of the shot the camera moves from A to B.

The Design Concept   The overall tone of the shot is dark. It's 3:00 A.M. and Dunston's writing is suffering from what he likes to think of as writer's block. The only visible source of light is the gooseneck lamp on the table. The rest of the room should be very dim. It doesn't matter if some of the room falls into blackness. There should be hard shadows.

Latitude   The latitude of the film or video equipment—the camera and its associated recording equipment—is a primary element in determining how much light you need on the scene:

> *Video:* The digital video equipment has a latitude of nine stops.
>
> *Film:* Tungsten-balanced (3,200° K) color negative film, with a film speed of ASA 125, and a five-stop latitude.

The Solution   The solution to any design challenge involves compromise—compromise between the design concept and the reality of bringing that concept to life. In lighting for film/video an additional element is added to the

Storyboards:
Thumbnail sketches used in filmmaking to provide a visualization of a shot. Normally storyboards include a ground plan only if it will help explain the shot.

Figure 18.13 Story-
boards for Example 1.

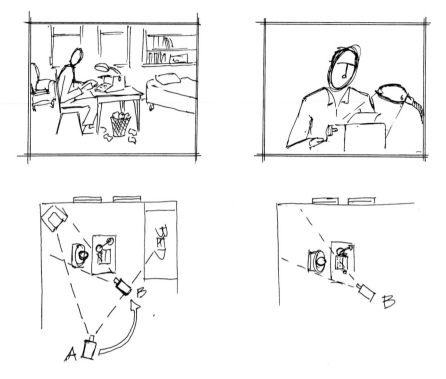

equation. Media lighting is created for the camera. The lighting designer is not in charge of the camera. The cinematographer or videographer makes all the decisions regarding the camera(s)—aperture, focus, filters, and so forth. That's why, in filmmaking, the cinematographer or director of photography has traditionally been responsible for creating and implementing the lighting. In video production there has always been a distinction between the lighting director and the videographer. The lighting director creates the lighting and the videographer runs the camera. At the dawn of broadcast television the lighting director was more an engineering than design position because, at that time, the primary concern in lighting video was simply to get enough light on the scene to allow the cameras, which needed a lot of light and had a very narrow latitude, to properly record the image. But, regardless of the historical reasons, the reality is that a media lighting designer needs to work closely and cooperatively with the cinematographer or videographer.

Video   Given that the nine-stop latitude of the video equipment is extremely wide, we might be able to light the scene just using a 60-watt household lamp in the gooseneck lamp. The light from the gooseneck lamp will bounce off the typewriter onto Dunston's face. The same light will also bounce around the room.

To determine if the reality of the setup matches the design concept, you need to set up the scene and turn on the gooseneck lamp. Have the actor playing Dunston, or a stand-in for Dunston, sit in the chair and look at the typewriter. Ask the videographer to set up the camera and recording equipment and take a shot of the scene. Record the shot. Look at it on a monitor. (Don't just look at a "live" shot. Look at the recorded shot. Normally there is a difference in latitude between the two. You need to see the recorded shot.) When looking at the replay, does the scene look the way you saw it in your mind's eye when you were formulating the design concept? If it does, you're ready to shoot.

If the shot doesn't look the way you envisioned it, analyze *why* it doesn't. Is Dunston's face properly exposed? Can you see the amount of detail in the shadow areas that you wanted to see? Can you see too much detail? Is the room too bright? If the video camera's coupled exposure meter was left in automatic mode during the test shot, the chances are quite good that Dunston's face was a little overexposed and the room was too bright. This is because the automatic exposure meter *averages* the scene. You don't want that. The design concept suggests that the shot should be exposed for Dunston's face and the background should be in shadows.

To achieve that look, you need to go through the exposure control process outlined earlier in the chapter. The following describes the steps you would take to achieve a good exposure, based on the design criteria, for this scene.

With the gooseneck lamp turned on, take an incident reading at Dunston's face. Because the light is coming from a source located very close to the actor's face, be sure to hold the light meter as close to Dunston's face as possible. Since the camera will be tracking during the shot you would want to take the reading with the meter's lumisphere—the white dome—pointing toward the camera's location halfway through its movement arc.[2] Note the meter's recommended f-stop. Then take reflective readings of those parts of the room that will be in the shot. If using a spot meter, simply stand where the camera will be during the shot, point the meter as if it were the camera, depress the "go" button, and walk through the camera's movement pattern.[3] Note the variations in the readings. Average them. If the f-stop of those reflective readings is within 4½ stops—one-half of the video equipment's

---

[2] Another way to take this exposure reading would be: Holding the meter just in front of Dunston's face, with the lumisphere pointing toward the camera's location, move the meter through the arc that the camera will make while holding down the "go" button on the meter. Watch the meter to see if there is any change in the exposure as it is moved. If there is any change, use an average of the highest and lowest readings.

[3] If using a "nonspot" reflective meter, hold the meter so the sensor is about 1 to 2 feet away from, and pointing at, the object to be metered. Be sure that neither you nor the meter is creating any shadows on, or bouncing any light into, the area you're reading.

9-stop latitude—of the incident reading for Dunston's face then the background detail will be visible. The less the difference between the f-stop reading for Dunston's face and the f-stop reading for the background, the brighter that background will appear in the shot.

If the background is brighter than desired, it is because too much light is being reflected from the gooseneck lamp. To reduce the reflected light you could do one, or a combination, of the following. Put a lower-wattage bulb in the lamp. Spray-paint the inside of the lamp reflector flat black.[4] Tape neutral density gel or black metal—not nylon—window screen to the inside of the lamp's reflector. Be sure the gel/screen doesn't touch the bulb and can't be seen by the camera. If Dunston is wearing a white or light-colored shirt, ask if it could be changed to a darker color. Rather than white paper in the typewriter, see if you could use a light gray typing paper or at least another white that is less reflective. Re-meter the background and keep making adjustments until you achieve the f-stop differential that you want between the reading on Dunston's face and the background.

When you get the light balanced the way you want it, ask the videographer to take another test shot. This time ask that the aperture be locked on the f-stop that you determined when you metered Dunston's face. Also suggest that, after getting an initial white-balance reading, that the white-balancing feature also be locked. Ideally, the videographer will be taking test shots throughout the time you're adjusting the lighting. But reality may dictate that she or he can only be there to make the initial and final test shots. Those shots are absolutely critical and need to be taken with the equipment that will actually be used during the shoot, as was suggested earlier in this chapter.

Film   The process of implementing the lighting concept for film is virtually identical to the one outlined under "Video" above. The only significant difference between the two is that, when shooting with film, we need to factor in film speed, balancing the color temperature of the sources and the film stock, and the latitude of the specific film stock with which the project is being shot.

There are several ways to create the lighting look dictated by the image of light—the lighting concept—for this shot. Remember that there are two primary issues that need to be addressed: Replicating the lighting concept and meeting the additional technical demands of shooting on film that were outlined in the preceding paragraph.

Generally, you would want to address the challenge of "replicating the lighting concept" first. The gooseneck lamp is the key light for this shot and

---

[4] Use flat black "engine paint," available at almost any automotive parts store. It is advertised to withstand up to 800-degree heat. "Regular" spray paints will smoke, smolder, or off-gas under the heat generated by the lamp.

we don't want to use any additional lights to reinforce the practical light from the desk lamp because of the multiple shadows this might create. Multiple shadows would make the end of the shot—when the camera moves into a medium closeup on Dunston—look staged or fake, and that is not the look we want.

ASA 125 film is a little slow for low-lit interior scenes such as this one. (Working with a faster film—ASA 400 or faster—would be much easier and would be preferable. But since the producer got a "real good price" on a whole bunch of this ASA 125 film, and the rest of our budget is committed, this stuff is what we have to use.)

Because of the relatively slow speed of the film, the light from the gooseneck lamp probably will not be bright enough to light the rest of the room, so we will need to provide some supplemental light. Probably the most efficient way to create the dim background light would be to bounce light off the ceiling. This can be done by pointing a lighting instrument, such as a Lowel DP with a 1,000-watt lamp, at the ceiling. The resulting bounce light would be relatively dim and directionless. If you wanted the background to have harder, more defined, shadows you could use **wall washers**. Ideally, the wall washers would be hung high on the wall and angled downward to mimic light from the desk lamp bouncing off the ceiling. The intensity differential between the key and background lights—both the ceiling bounce and wall washers—could be adjusted by using scrims on the background lights.

The second issue that must be addressed is color balance. The color temperature of the light needs to be balanced with the 3,200° K film stock. This can be done in several ways. Ideally all the lights will be 3,200° K. If that is the case, then all that needs to be done is meter the scene, adjust the intensity differential between the key and fill lights, and you're ready to shoot.

The wall washer/fill lights probably will be 3,200° K because the location fixtures used for this purpose are normally equipped with 3,200° K lamps. However, the chances are quite good that the gooseneck desk lamp won't come equipped with a 3,200° K lamp. That situation will need to be rectified. This can be done in one of several ways. You could use a household lamp as we did in the video version. The color temperature of household lamps is around 2,500 to 2,800° K, depending on the voltage/wattage ratings and age of the lamp.[5] If a household lamp is used an appropriate color-correcting gel[6] would need to be taped to the inside of the reflector to raise the color temperature of the lamp to 3,200° K. Another possibility would be the use of

Wall washers: Fixtures placed at a shallow angle to a wall to bring out its texture.

---

[5] Household bulbs with low voltage ratings—117 as opposed to some "long-life lamps" rated at 130 volts—have higher color temperatures than their long-life cousins. Higher-wattage household lamps generally have higher color temperatures than lower-wattage lamps. Older lamps of all types (except tungsten-halogen) have lower color temperatures than new lamps.

[6] You would need to meter the color of the household lamp with a color temperature meter. It would also tell you the proper color-correction filter to use.

ECA: The American National Standards Institute (ANSI) identifies lamps with specific characteristics by a code number. ECA is the code for the following lamp: 3,200° K color temperature, PS-shaped, 250 watts, 120 volts, medium screw base.

Edge of visibility: The outside limits of a film's latitude where detail begins to be lost.

an **ECA** lamp. But ECA lamps are too big to fit inside the reflectors of most gooseneck lamps. Even if the lamp does fit inside the reflector, at 250 watts the ECA lamp would probably be too bright for working that close to the talent. You could also rewire the gooseneck lamp to use a small halogen bulb such as those used in small study lamps. This bulb would easily fit inside the reflector. The color temperature of these small tungsten-halogen lamps is normally around 3,000° K. (The exact color temperature may be written on the base of the lamp. If not, it almost always is written on the packing materials for replacement lamps, which can be found in most hardware stores and home centers.) To raise the color temperature to the required 3,200° K, color-correction gel could be taped inside the reflector.[7] Unfortunately, there could be a problem with using a color correction filter. There is a distinct possibility that the heat of the halogen study lamp will melt the plastic filter. Therefore you might consider shooting the shot without using any color correction. The 200-degree difference between the color temperature of the study lamp (3,000° K) and the color balance of the film (3,200° K) isn't very large. If you shot the scene without color correction the resultant picture would have a very slight red shift. But given that the study lamp is the only relatively intense light on Dunston's face,[8] and the background lights are very dim, that color shift may not even be noticeable.

After the "3,200° K conundrum" has been solved, the scene will need to be metered for the shot. In the video solution portion of this design challenge the video equipment had a 9-stop latitude which meant that there was a 4½-stop differential between the incident reading for Dunston's face and the **edge of visibility** of the background material. The color film being used has a 5-stop latitude which means there is only a 2½ stop differential between the two. Using the same techniques explained in the video solution section, an incident reading would be taken at Dunston's face, and a reflective reading would be taken of the background area. The design concept dictates the appropriate contrast ratio, or intensity differentiation, between Dunston's face and the background lighting. The contrast ratio between the key and background/fill lights can be manipulated by using scrims to reduce the output of the fill lights. If the differentiation is less than 2½ stops the background will probably seem too bright. If the differential is 2½ stops, the background will look dark, and all but the darkest background

---

[7] If run at full intensity, tungsten-halogen lamps don't lose color temperature over time. For this method you don't need to use a color temperature meter. If the T-H lamp being used has a verifiable rated color temperature of 3,000° K, then you would simply use a color-correction filter that raised the color temperature of the lamp 200° K.

[8] The color shift would be more noticeable if we were using a second, correctly color balanced, light on Dunston's face. That setup would allow you to visually compare the color temperature of the two sources—3,000° K and 3,200° K—on his skin tone. That side-by-side comparison would make the color shift more apparent.

detail will be visible. If the differential is greater than 2½ stops, the background will be dark and some detail will be lost. It would be up to the cinematographer to make the final decision about the appropriate contrast ratio.

Because shooting film is expensive, some cinematographers like to check the look of the lighting setup by taking Polaroid or digital still shots before they shoot with film. The images on the Polaroid or digital stills don't exactly match the look of the film, but they do provide quick feedback about the contrast range and look of the lighting. It is an excellent way to check the lighting setup before you shoot, and helps train your eye to "see like film."

When the above process has been completed, it's time to shoot the shot.

Example 2: *Julio and Kate*

Exercise 1 demonstrated a process for designing and implementing video/film lighting. While it certainly isn't the only method that can be used, it does work, it requires that you be creative, and it provides you with a process that can be used, and repeated, until you can develop your own lighting design **voice**. The same process will be used for this exercise.

The Story   This story is a tragic romance loosely based on *Romeo and Juliet*. Set in a city in Arizona, the story centers on two young adults, Julio and Kate. Julio comes from a good, working-class family. Kate comes from money. They are both genuinely good people and madly in love. Julio's brother Esteban, the black sheep of his family, is psychotic about Kate. He hates everything about her—her money, her family's social status, her race. During the course of the story Kate discovers that she's pregnant. Both she and Julio are overjoyed. They had planned to marry eventually and the pregnancy just accelerates the wedding. Esteban goes crazy. He hunts them down and confronts them. After a terrible argument Esteban kills Kate. Enraged, Julio attacks Esteban and kills him. During the fight Julio is mortally wounded. He crawls to Kate and cradles her head in his lap as he dies.

The Scene   We are in a dead-end alley. It is night. The pavement glistens from a recent hard rain. Nightlights above several doorways form pools of light on the wet asphalt. Shimmering light from storefront windows and traffic on the cross street spills into the alley.

Esteban has been hunting Julio and Kate. They ducked into the alley in an attempt to avoid him. Esteban saw them enter the alley and has followed them.

The Shot   Julio and Kate have discovered there's no exit to the alley. Julio has protectively moved in front of Kate. He turns to face Esteban. Estaban slowly advances on them. He takes out a switchblade, flicks it open and stops just in front of them.

Voice: In this context, design "voice" refers to the ability to express your own artistic style.

Figure 18.14 Storyboards for Example 2.

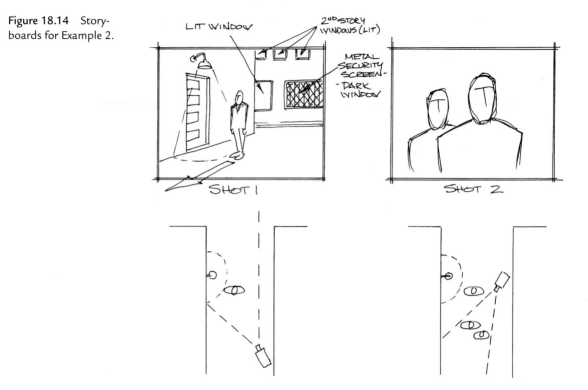

There are two shots we're going to be lighting in this exercise: a medium-long shot of Esteban and a medium closeup of Julio and Kate. The storyboards, Figure 18.14, show the compositions for this two-shot sequence.

The Design Concept The mood is tense and dangerous. The alley is dark and glistening.[9] Esteban is silhouetted against the open end of the alley. One of the overhead doorway lights creates a hard-shadowed key on the side of his face. Julio and Kate are hit with the same hard-shadowed key light, but the shadows are partially filled by light bouncing in from the open end of the alley. The scene is high contrast, both emotionally and visually.

Latitude The latitude of the film or video equipment is a primary element in determining how much light is needed on the scene.

Video: The digital video equipment has a 7-stop latitude.

Film: Tungsten-balanced (3,200° K) color negative film, with a speed of ASA 400, has a 7-stop latitude.

---

[9] Sneaky Trick #739: When shooting outdoors at night and you want to heighten tension, wet the street. The wet surface will both reflect light and make the roadway much darker, thus increasing the visual contrast, which increases the emotional tension in the scene.

The Solution There are many possible solutions to any design challenge. While the primary goal is to create a design that effectively supports the design concept, another goal of almost equal importance is that the solution be practical. In this context practicality relates directly to fiscal and temporal budgets. You have to ask yourself if the proposed solution can be rigged within the confines of the budgets. Is the equipment required for the proposed solution available on site? If not on site, is it available locally? Would we have to have it shipped in? If it has to be shipped in, can it be shipped to arrive when needed? Can we afford the equipment within the existing budget? Can we rig the proposed design in the time we have for the setup? These and similar questions need to be asked for every setup because, if the required equipment isn't on hand, and there isn't enough money in the budget to rent it, or if there isn't enough time to rig it, then the proposed solution simply isn't practical regardless of the brilliance of its concept. And practicality, in most cases, must take precedence.

The solutions offered below should not be thought of as the "only" solutions. After reading them, a good exercise would be to design other practical, effective ways to light the scene.

Video The 7-stop latitude of the digital video equipment should be wide enough to allow the scene to be shot with just a little reinforcement for the practical lamps.

The shot of Esteban has two conceptual keylights: the silhouetting light coming from the open end of the alley and the practical entry light above one of the alley doorways. The keylight for the **two-shot** of Julio and Kate is the practical light above the doorway.

The design of the practical fixture above the doorway will determine whether it could be used as the actual keylight. An ECA lamp would probably provide enough light if it could be used. That will depend on the socket and reflector design. If the extant fixture doesn't have a medium screw base socket, or if the fixture design doesn't have a straight-down light capability, the fixture could be changed if the building owner is agreeable. But, before going to the work of changing the fixture, hang the practical that you would want to use next to the existing fixture, put in an ECA lamp, turn it on (at night), and see if the ECA's output is sufficient for the keylight. If it isn't, then you'll need to rig a light, either fresnel or DP with a 3,200° K, 1,000-watt lamp to provide the downlight that you need. If the 1,000-watt lamp is too bright, you could use either a 750- or 500-watt lamp or "scrim it down." Just be sure that all the lamps you use are rated at 3,200° K because, as stated before, the best picture quality occurs when the color temperature of all fixtures used on a shot match.

The light spilling into the alley will look like it is coming from the windows of the buildings on the far side of the street. The extant fixtures in the stores and apartments across the street from the head of the alley will probably be equipped with a mixture of lamps that aren't rated at 3,200° K. They

Two-shot: A shot with two subjects.

will basically be bright background lights. Their output won't affect the skin tone of the actors. For those reasons, their color temperature probably won't materially affect the shot, so you may not have to do anything with them. If, however, their color temperature is sufficiently different to make them a distraction, or if they are too bright, you might want to cover the windows with appropriate color-correction or neutral density gel after receiving permission from the business/building owners.

Those "across-the-street" lights probably won't be bright enough to fully silhouette Esteban. You could hang a pipe or small truss across, and just inside the mouth of, the alley high enough to be out of camera frame. Fresnels, lamped with 1,000-watt, 3,200° K lamps and equipped with barndoors could be hung from the pipe to provide the backlight needed to "edge" Esteban with light. Again, adjustments to those fixtures' output could be made by equipping them with lower-wattage lamps or by using scrims. If you needed more output you could hang more fixtures or replace them with fresnels that use 2,000-watt lamps. If the alley walls are made of brick, or some other finish that would provide interesting shadow/highlight detail, you might consider hanging wall washers on the pipe in addition to the backlight fresnels for Esteban.

When rigging pipes or trusses such as the setup described above, you must be absolutely certain that the pipe or truss is securely mounted. It could either be hung with cables dropped from the roofs or windows of the buildings, or it could be mounted on booms placed next to the buildings and disguised as drainpipes or something similar. Regardless of the rigging solution chosen, be certain that the equipment is stable and safe before letting any other crew or talent on the set. Remember: safety first.

As mentioned above, the keylight for the two-shot of Julio and Kate will be the same "light-above-the-doorway" key light used for Esteban. In addition, Julio and Kate will need a soft fill light so their faces appear softer than the harsh light on Esteban. Conceptually, this fill light could be thought of as the light coming in the open end of the alley. This light would need to be very soft. Regardless of the type of fixture used—softlight, fresnel, mini-9 light—you would want to use diffusion material to achieve the needed level of softness. To achieve the contrast ratio between the key and fill lights—the key/fill contrast ratio—that was visualized in the design concept scrims would be used to reduce the output of the fill until the desired contrast ratio was reached. As this softlight may interfere with the setup for the silhouette shot of Esteban, the fixture would be rigged, but probably not be set in place until you were ready for the shot of Julio and Kate.

Marks: In this context, "mark" refers to the specific location where the talent needs to stand during a shot. If the mark is out of frame, it is frequently marked with a masking tape "X" to make it easier for the talent to "hit their mark."

After the lighting is rigged, it is time to meter the scene. You would position either the talent, or their stand-ins, on their **marks**. As in Exercise 1, for each of the two shots you would take an incident reading with the lumisphere pointing toward the camera position while holding the meter just in front of the talent's nose. After taking the incident reading you would reflectively meter the background for each shot. The 7-stop latitude of the digital video equipment would give you a $3\frac{1}{2}$-stop differential between the incident reading and the edge of visibility. Compare the reflective readings with the incident readings to see if the differentiation between the subject's faces and the background matches your lighting concept. Then shoot a test shot with the video equipment—both camera and recorder—that will be used on the project. Look at the taped shots on the monitor. When you analyze the shots, you will, in all probability, want to make some adjustments to instrument focus, contrast ratios, and/or the levels of diffusion of both the key and fill lights. After those adjustments have been made, meter the scene again, make another test shot, and keep refining the setup until you have it exactly the way you visualized it or you run out of time.

Film   Because we used location lighting equipment equipped with 3,200° K lamps to light the video setup, and both the video equipment and the film stock have the same latitude, it shouldn't be necessary to make any changes when shooting this project on film. The only possible reason that anything would need to be changed would be because of the speed of the film—ASA 320. If that speed is significantly different than the speed of the video equipment, then you may have to change intensity levels for the key and fill lights. But the basic design and setup of the equipment should not need to be changed.

Again, after making any changes/adjustments to the lights, meter the scene, shoot Polaroid or digital still camera test shots, make any necessary adjustments, and turn the setup over to the cinematographer.

This chapter has provided you with the basic technical information needed to understand the process of designing light for film and video. As has been mentioned numerous times in this text, lighting—whether for theatre, film, or video—is a craft, and the best way to learn any craft is to practice it. Use the processes and technical information provided in this book as a beginning. Practice them. Use that information as a springboard to develop your own processes and methods. That's where the real enjoyment lies. Lighting design is a wonderful challenge and can be a lot of fun. So enjoy!

A Revised Standard Graphic Language for Lighting Design

The material in this appendix is the current draft (Draft Revision 4) of a proposed revision to the USITT Recommended Practice for Theatrical Lighting Design Graphics. Please note that as of this writing (December 2005) this revised standard is a work in progress and has not been adopted by the USITT. It is included in this edition because it contains new information and symbols, as well as modifications to the symbols for some existing instruments, and it shows where the standard is probably headed. Additional changes may be made to this draft before it is adapted as the new official USITT standard. But I felt it was important to provide the most up-to-date information possible, and this draft provides that information.

USITT RP-2, RECOMMENDED PRACTICE FOR THEATRICAL LIGHTING DESIGN GRAPHICS—DRAFT REVISION[1]

PREAMBLE
· ·

The original Graphics Standards Board noted that a standard is an example for comparison and an authority, which serves as a model. It should be noted that this model cannot hope to cover all possible situations encountered during the drafting of a light plot or section and thus should be viewed as a guide that theatrical lighting practitioners use to create their drawings. This document, therefore, represents a "recommended practice." The terms

---

[1]Reprinted with permission. © 2006, United States Institute for Theatre Technology Inc.

instrument and *luminaire* are used interchangeably throughout the document to designate lighting luminaries while other equivalent designations may also include fixture and unit. This document also does not seek to represent a specific manufacturer of lighting equipment but suggests common instruments in general use. The result is a group of generic instrument types that can be adapted to specific uses as necessary rather than an attempt to present a symbol for each luminaire available.

The purpose of this document is to establish a standardized language among lighting designers and anyone else who needs to understand or execute such a design. In practical terms, this document is intended to provide guidelines so that anyone, ranging from technicians who hang the luminaires to other members of the production team, can clearly understand the intent of the lighting designer.

1.0 INTRODUCTION

Legibility and consistency should determine the graphic choices made in the drafting of both CAD and hand-drafted drawings. USITT, or modified ANSI three-line thickness standard drafting practices, may be employed as set forth in the USITT Scenic Design and Technical Production Graphic Standard of 1992 (reissued April 15, 1999). Complex drawings may require the use of three- or four-line thicknesses. Luminaire outlines should take visual precedence over other information on the lighting design drawings.

The graphical representation of a lighting design normally consists of two categories of documents: the Light Plot and the Lighting Section. Preferably, the documents are produced in 1/2″ = 1′-0″ scale. Other scales, such as 1/4″ = 1′-0″, 3/8″ = 1′-0″, 1:25 or 1:50 (if working in SI or metric) maybe used after considering the size of the architectural space, the overall size of the document and reproductions, the number of individual luminaries, and the desired legibility of their text and numeric attributes. A complete lighting design requires additional paperwork such as channel hookups and shop orders not addressed in this document. Generally, the light plot should include all information necessary to assure clear understanding of the designer's intentions.

1.1 SPECIAL CONSIDERATIONS FOR CAD DRAWINGS

Computer assisted drawings should follow the same recommended practice as those drawn by hand. However, three additional considerations should be made. Layer, class designation, line weight, and color assignment must be coordinated with other members of the production team who are using the same document to create other drawings. This avoids confusion between the draftspersons or the end users. When a lighting graphic symbol is created with "labels," attention must be paid to the relative orientation of both the symbol and its associated text. When a symbol is inserted into a drawing, the associated text should be properly oriented with the rest of the text in the drawing. The luminaire symbols that are included in some computer applications may be specific to various manufacturers' equipment rather than the generic symbols provided in this document. Nevertheless, the size and designation of the luminaires used should follow these generic symbols as closely as possible.

2.0 THE LIGHT PLOT

The Light Plot is a composite plan drawing that provides the most descriptive possible view of the luminaries so that the production staff can most efficiently execute the design intent. It may consist of more than a single plate; however, all plates should be the same size to facilitate reproduction. Distances between front of house hanging positions and the playing area can be compressed in a light plot.

2.1 INFORMATION CONTAINED IN THE LIGHT PLOT

Normally, the light plot should include all information necessary to assure clear understanding of the designer's intentions. The location and identification data of every luminaire, accessory, and specialty unit should be represented on the light plot, along with the following information:

- The centerline
- A lineset schedule when appropriate
- A ruler or some other indicator of distance left and right of ceterline in scale
- A ruler indicating on-stage distances up and downstage (or the 90° axis to centerline) in scale
- A drawn representation of the edge of the stage where applicable
- A drawn representation of the edge of the playing area where applicable
- Basic scenic elements
- All scenic masking

- All architectural and scenic obstructions
- The proscenium arch, plaster line, smoke pockets, or other architectural details necessary to orient the lighting design in flexible spaces
- Trim measurements for movable mounting positions should read from the stage level surface (or other common point of reference) to the pipe (or mounting position)
- Trim heights to boom positions measure from bottom of the boom base to the side arm
- Identification (label) of hanging/mounting positions
- The legend or instrument key designating symbol type and notation in the light plot
- The title block (see Section 4)
- Sightlines
  Additional information may include:
- Lighting areas
- Template key
- Color key
- Liability disclaimer
- Union stamp

2.2 LUMINAIRE SYMBOL INFORMATION

The luminaire symbols used on the light plot should represent the approximate size and shape of the luminaires in scale (except where computer applications supply more specific symbols). The symbol should be placed so that its location reflects its exact hanging point. Unless otherwise noted, the default spacing between typical fixed focus luminaries is 18″ (or 45 cm) to allow for adequate focus range of each luminaire. When the symbols are placed in relative locations other than the default, dimension lines or other measuring notations should be added between the symbols to indicate the distance and to facilitate mounting the luminaires. It is acceptable to visually orient the angle of each drawn luminaire to either focus points or 90° axes.

Normally, each symbol should be accompanied by the following information:

- Luminaire number
- Indication of focal length or beam spread as part of the symbol (where appropriate)
- Indication of any accessories such as templates, irises, scrollers, top hats, barn doors, etc.

- Channel (or control designation)
- Axis notation for PAR lamps

  Additional information may include:

- Focus
- Wattage
- Circuit and/or dimmer number or space for the electrician to add this information
- Indication of "two-fers"
- Color notation
- Color notation for scrollers
- Template notation

2.3.1 DESIGNATION AND NUMBERING OF CONVENTIONAL MOUNTING POSITIONS

- Front of House (FOH) positions begin numbering from the position closest to plaster line.
- Onstage electrics number from downstage to upstage.
- Onstage booms number from downstage to upstage.
- All hanging locations not intersecting centerline are subnamed by their location relative to centerline. Ladders, box booms, booms, and such are divided between stage left and stage right; stage left listed first.

2.3.2 NUMBERING LUMINAIRES WITHIN CONVENTIONAL MOUNTING POSITIONS

Each luminaire receives a unique whole number. If a luminaire has an attachment that alters the beam of an instrument, the attachment will often not receive its own whole number but rather the host instrument's number. Luminaires that are inserted between previously numbered fixtures are assigned the lower luminaire's unit number plus an additional letter (e.g., 3A or 3B). At the designer's discretion, decimal or letter suffixes may also be added to a luminaire's number. In common practice, multi-circuited luminaries such as striplights will be assigned a letter with a corresponding number for each circuit (e.g., A1, A2 and A3 while luminaries with multiple control channels or attributes will often be represented through a whole number designation of the unit number followed by a decimal point and number representing specific attributes for the luminaire (e.g., 23.1, 23.2 and 23.3).

- Luminaires on hanging positions perpendicular to centerline (e.g., battens) are numbered from stage left to stage right.
- Luminaires on onstage booms or other vertical hanging positions are numbered from top to bottom, downstage to upstage.
- Luminaires mounted on FOH positions parallel to centerline should number starting with the units nearest to plaster line.
- Luminaires mounted on FOH positions non-parallel to centerline (box booms) should number starting with the units closest to centerline.

2.3.3 DESIGNATION AND NUMBERING OF MOUNTING POSITIONS IN NON-PROSCENIUM VENUES

- Pipe grid positions should be designated by numbers on one axis of the grid and by letters on the other axis.
- Other atypical mounting positions may be designated by compass points or numbering in a clockwise manner.
- Mounting positions that repeat should be numbered from a consistent starting point.
- Other atypical hanging positions should be designated in a fashion that is sensible to the electricians. Luminaires hung in these positions should be numbered in an intelligible fashion compatible with other luminaire designations on the plot.

3.0 THE LIGHTING SECTION

The Lighting Section is a sectional view in which the cutting plane intersects the theatre, typically along the centerline but may intersect any plane that best illustrates the mounting positions. This drawing provides the most descriptive view of the hanging positions relative to the architectural and scenic elements of the production. While it may be appropriate to compress distance (horizontal or vertical) in a presentational section, doing so in the working version reduces its effectiveness.

3.1 INFORMATION CONTAINED IN THE LIGHTING SECTION

The purpose of the lighting section is to communicate spatial information and relationships of all other elements relative to the lighting design. The following information should be represented on the lighting section:

- Definition of where the section is "cut"
- Stage floor, deck, or "vertical zero" location (indication of which one is being used as reference zero)
- Proscenium, plaster line, smoke pocket, or the "horizontal zero" location
- Back wall or upstage limitation of the performing space
- Vertical audience sight points and/or sightlines
- Downstage edge of stage floor and/or edge of playing area
- Architectural details necessary to orient the lighting design in non-proscenium spaces
- All hanging positions including side elevation of booms, ladders, etc.
- Trim height for all hanging positions that can change height
- Identification of all lighting positions
- Architectural and scenic obstructions
- Sectional view of scenery
- All masking
- Title block (See Section 4)
- Scaled representation of the luminaire that determines batten height mounted in each position.
- Human figure (or "head height") in scale

  Additional information may include:

- Vertical ruler in scale
- Horizontal ruler in scale
- Defined distance to other elements not shown on the drawing (to follow spot booth, other sightlines, etc.)
- Liability disclaimer
- Union stamp

4.0 TITLE BLOCK

Acceptable locations for the title block are:

- Lower right-hand corner of the drawing
- Vertical banner on the right side of the drawing

4.1 INFORMATION CONTAINED IN THE TITLE BLOCK

To be placed in the order deemed most important by the lighting designer:

- Name of the producing organization
- Name of the production
- Name of the venue
- Drawing title
- Drawing number (i.e., "1 of 4")
- Predominant scale of the drawing
- Date the plate was drafted
- Designer of the production
- Draftsperson of the drawing
  Additional information may include:
- Location of the venue
- Director of the production
- Other members of the production team
- Lighting assistant and/or Master Electrician
- Date and revision number
- Approval of the drawing
- Contact information (telephone and fax numbers, e-mail addresses)

5.0 LEGEND OR INSTRUMENT KEY

Placement is acceptable in any location that does not conflict with other information.

5.1 INFORMATION CONTAINED IN THE LEGEND OR INSTRUMENT KEY:

- Pictorial representations (symbols) of all luminaires and devices shown on the plot with identifying descriptions of each.
- Beam spread (in degrees or focal length) for each luminaire type if the numeric value is not part of the luminaire's name
- Designation of all notations associated with each luminaire.
- Color manufacturer designation (e.g., R = Rosco, L = Lee, G = Gam, etc.)
- Template manufacturer designation (when applicable)
- Wattage (total luminaire load) and/or ANSI lamp code
- Symbols for any accessories—templates, irises, color scrollers, top hats, barn doors, etc.

  Additional information may include:
- Luminaire manufacturer
- Representation of "two-fers"
- Indication of voltage

6.0 SYMBOL GUIDELINES

These guidelines represent a selection of standard generic symbols that approximate the size and shape of stage luminaires. Further differentiation or notation may be necessary to distinguish between luminaires of approximately the same size. This may include shading the symbol, making the "front" of the symbol a heavier line, and other individual techniques. Detailed luminaire symbols specific to each manufacturers' products and supplied by computer drafting programs may be substituted, provided they allow the specialized markings needed to exactly specify the luminaire and provided they are properly explained by the instrument key (see Section 5).

These symbols are presented as a guideline. Specific choices should be considered to differentiate between different manufacturers of the same type of luminaire. It is USITT policy not to specify any manufacturers in the Symbol Guidelines.

Because of the number and complexity of attributes in automated fixtures, each designer must determine a logical notation system for the luminaire used.

USITT RP-2, Recommended Practice for Theatrical
Lighting Design Graphics—Draft Revision 4   **DRAFT**   6.0 Symbol Guidelines

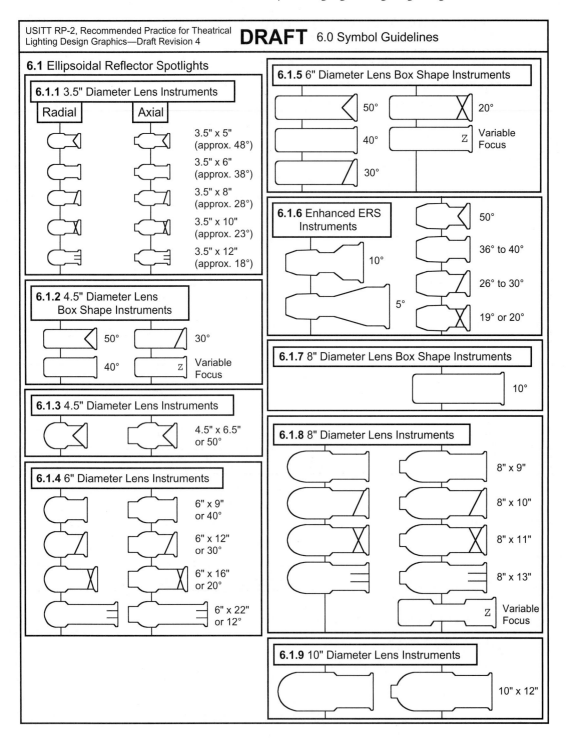

6.1 Ellipsoidal Reflector Spotlights

6.1.1 3.5" Diameter Lens Instruments

Radial   Axial

3.5" x 5"
(approx. 48°)

3.5" x 6"
(approx. 38°)

3.5" x 8"
(approx. 28°)

3.5" x 10"
(approx. 23°)

3.5" x 12"
(approx. 18°)

6.1.2 4.5" Diameter Lens
Box Shape Instruments

50°   30°

40°   Variable
z   Focus

6.1.3 4.5" Diameter Lens Instruments

4.5" x 6.5"
or 50°

6.1.4 6" Diameter Lens Instruments

6" x 9"
or 40°

6" x 12"
or 30°

6" x 16"
or 20°

6" x 22"
or 12°

6.1.5 6" Diameter Lens Box Shape Instruments

50°   20°

40°   Variable
z   Focus

30°

6.1.6 Enhanced ERS
Instruments

50°

36° to 40°

10°

26° to 30°

5°

19° or 20°

6.1.7 8" Diameter Lens Box Shape Instruments

10°

6.1.8 8" Diameter Lens Instruments

8" x 9"

8" x 10"

8" x 11"

8" x 13"

Variable
z   Focus

6.1.9 10" Diameter Lens Instruments

10" x 12"

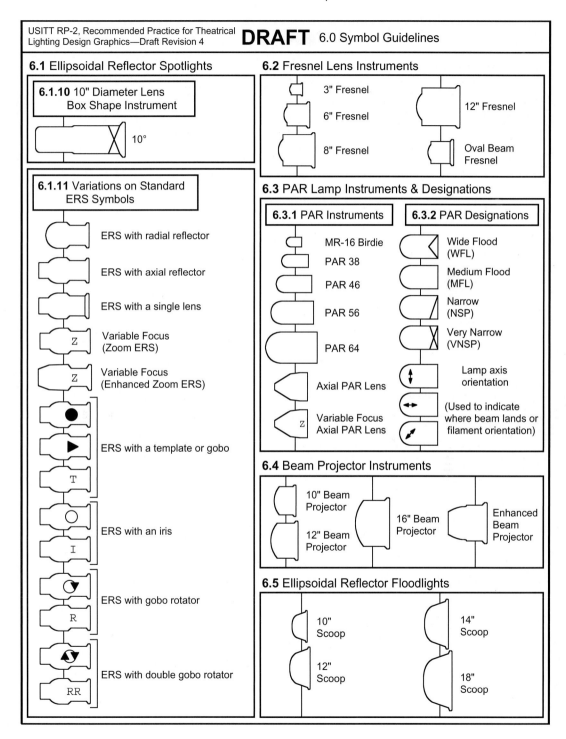

6.1 Ellipsoidal Reflector Spotlights

6.1.10 10" Diameter Lens Box Shape Instrument

10°

6.1.11 Variations on Standard ERS Symbols

ERS with radial reflector

ERS with axial reflector

ERS with a single lens

Variable Focus (Zoom ERS)

Variable Focus (Enhanced Zoom ERS)

ERS with a template or gobo

ERS with an iris

ERS with gobo rotator

ERS with double gobo rotator

6.2 Fresnel Lens Instruments

3" Fresnel

6" Fresnel

8" Fresnel

12" Fresnel

Oval Beam Fresnel

6.3 PAR Lamp Instruments & Designations

6.3.1 PAR Instruments

MR-16 Birdie

PAR 38

PAR 46

PAR 56

PAR 64

Axial PAR Lens

Variable Focus Axial PAR Lens

6.3.2 PAR Designations

Wide Flood (WFL)

Medium Flood (MFL)

Narrow (NSP)

Very Narrow (VNSP)

Lamp axis orientation

(Used to indicate where beam lands or filament orientation)

6.4 Beam Projector Instruments

10" Beam Projector

12" Beam Projector

16" Beam Projector

Enhanced Beam Projector

6.5 Ellipsoidal Reflector Floodlights

10" Scoop

12" Scoop

14" Scoop

18" Scoop

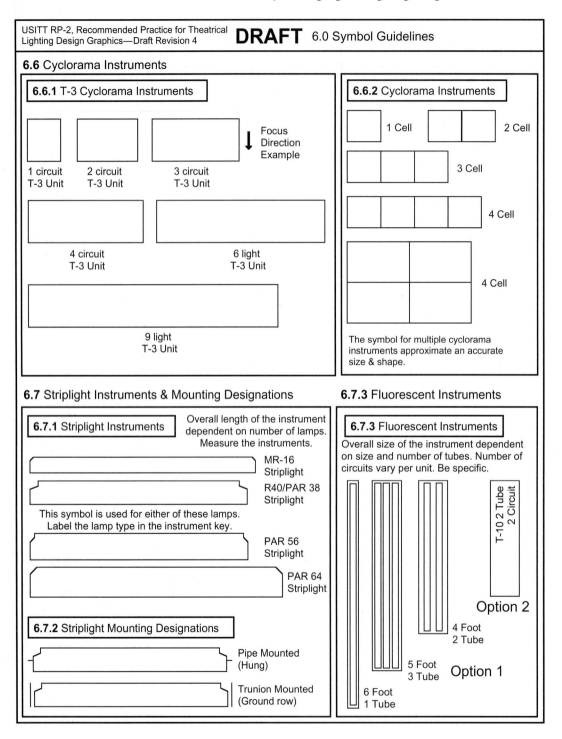

USITT RP-2, Recommended Practice for Theatrical Lighting Design Graphics—Draft Revision 4   **DRAFT**   6.0 Symbol Guidelines

6.6 Cyclorama Instruments

6.6.1 T-3 Cyclorama Instruments

↓ Focus Direction Example

1 circuit T-3 Unit   2 circuit T-3 Unit   3 circuit T-3 Unit

4 circuit T-3 Unit   6 light T-3 Unit

9 light T-3 Unit

6.6.2 Cyclorama Instruments

1 Cell   2 Cell

3 Cell

4 Cell

4 Cell

The symbol for multiple cyclorama instruments approximate an accurate size & shape.

6.7 Striplight Instruments & Mounting Designations

6.7.1 Striplight Instruments

Overall length of the instrument dependent on number of lamps. Measure the instruments.

MR-16 Striplight

R40/PAR 38 Striplight

This symbol is used for either of these lamps. Label the lamp type in the instrument key.

PAR 56 Striplight

PAR 64 Striplight

6.7.2 Striplight Mounting Designations

Pipe Mounted (Hung)

Trunion Mounted (Ground row)

6.7.3 Fluorescent Instruments

6.7.3 Fluorescent Instruments

Overall size of the instrument dependent on size and number of tubes. Number of circuits vary per unit. Be specific.

T-10 2 Tube 2 Circuit

Option 2

4 Foot 2 Tube

5 Foot 3 Tube   Option 1

6 Foot 1 Tube

USITT RP-2, Recommended Practice for Theatrical
Lighting Design Graphics—Draft Revision 4 **DRAFT** 6.0 Symbol Guidelines

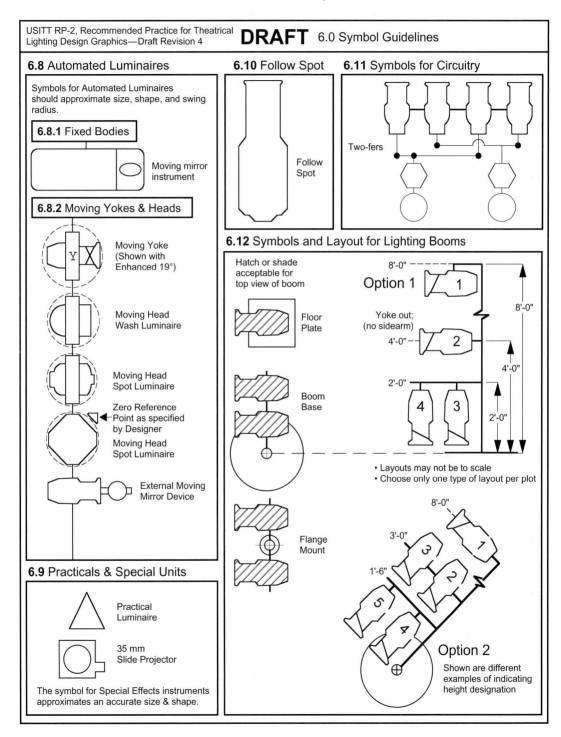

6.8 Automated Luminaires

Symbols for Automated Luminaires
should approximate size, shape, and swing
radius.

6.8.1 Fixed Bodies

Moving mirror
instrument

6.8.2 Moving Yokes & Heads

Moving Yoke
(Shown with
Enhanced 19°)

Moving Head
Wash Luminaire

Moving Head
Spot Luminaire

Zero Reference
Point as specified
by Designer

Moving Head
Spot Luminaire

External Moving
Mirror Device

6.9 Practicals & Special Units

Practical
Luminaire

35 mm
Slide Projector

The symbol for Special Effects instruments
approximates an accurate size & shape.

6.10 Follow Spot

Follow
Spot

6.11 Symbols for Circuitry

Two-fers

6.12 Symbols and Layout for Lighting Booms

Hatch or shade
acceptable for
top view of boom

Floor
Plate

Boom
Base

Flange
Mount

Option 1

8'-0"

Yoke out;
(no sidearm)

4'-0"

2'-0"

1

2

4   3

8'-0"

4'-0"

2'-0"

• Layouts may not be to scale
• Choose only one type of layout per plot

8'-0"

3'-0"

1'-6"

1

3

2

5

4

Option 2

Shown are different
examples of indicating
height designation

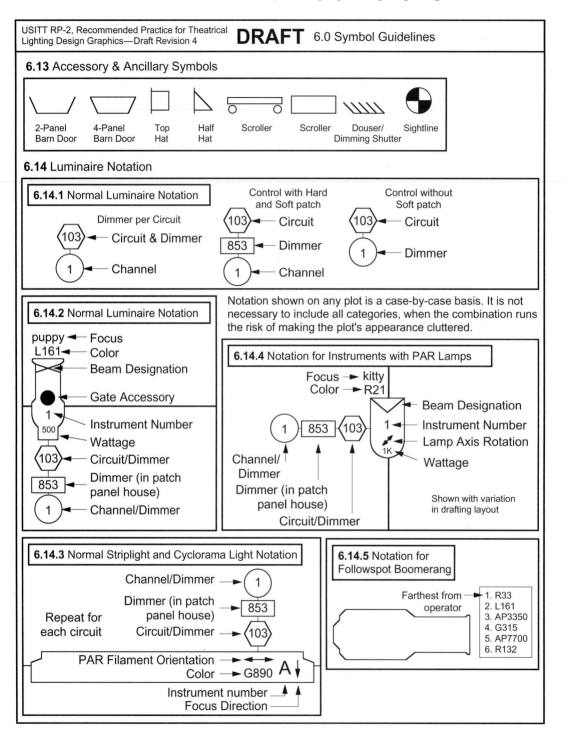

USITT RP-2, Recommended Practice for Theatrical Lighting Design Graphics—Draft Revision 4   **DRAFT** 6.0 Symbol Guidelines

6.13 Accessory & Ancillary Symbols

2-Panel Barn Door | 4-Panel Barn Door | Top Hat | Half Hat | Scroller | Scroller | Douser/ Dimming Shutter | Sightline

6.14 Luminaire Notation

6.14.1 Normal Luminaire Notation

Dimmer per Circuit

〈103〉◄— Circuit & Dimmer

（1）◄— Channel

Control with Hard and Soft patch

〈103〉◄— Circuit

[853]◄— Dimmer

（1）◄— Channel

Control without Soft patch

〈103〉◄— Circuit

（1）◄— Dimmer

6.14.2 Normal Luminaire Notation

puppy ◄— Focus
L161 ◄— Color
◄— Beam Designation
● ◄— Gate Accessory
1 ◄— Instrument Number
500 ◄— Wattage
〈103〉◄— Circuit/Dimmer
[853] ◄— Dimmer (in patch panel house)
（1）◄— Channel/Dimmer

Notation shown on any plot is a case-by-case basis. It is not necessary to include all categories, when the combination runs the risk of making the plot's appearance cluttered.

6.14.4 Notation for Instruments with PAR Lamps

Focus ►— kitty
Color ►— R21

（1） [853] 〈103〉

1 ◄— Beam Designation
◄— Instrument Number
◄— Lamp Axis Rotation
1K ◄— Wattage

Channel/ Dimmer
Dimmer (in patch panel house)
Circuit/Dimmer

Shown with variation in drafting layout

6.14.3 Normal Striplight and Cyclorama Light Notation

Channel/Dimmer ►— （1）
Dimmer (in patch panel house) ►— [853]
Circuit/Dimmer ►— 〈103〉

Repeat for each circuit

PAR Filament Orientation ►—◄
Color ►— G890 **A** ↓

Instrument number
Focus Direction

6.14.5 Notation for Followspot Boomerang

Farthest from operator ►—

1. R33
2. L161
3. AP3350
4. G315
5. AP7700
6. R132

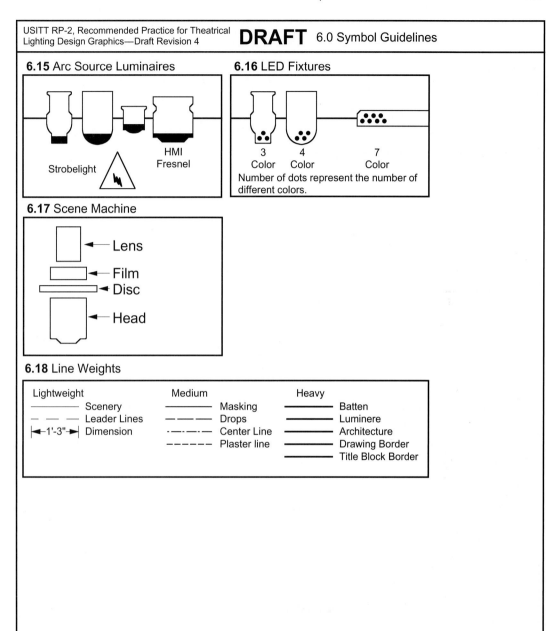

6.15 Arc Source Luminaires

Strobelight

HMI Fresnel

6.16 LED Fixtures

3 Color 4 Color 7 Color

Number of dots represent the number of different colors.

6.17 Scene Machine

Lens

Film

Disc

Head

6.18 Line Weights

Lightweight		Medium		Heavy	
———	Scenery	———	Masking	———	Batten
– – –	Leader Lines	– – –	Drops	———	Luminere
◄–1'-3"–►	Dimension	·–··–··	Center Line	———	Architecture
		– – – – –	Plaster line	———	Drawing Border
				———	Title Block Border

A Selected Bibliography

Books

Bennette, Adam, *Recommended Practice for DMX512: A Guide for Users and Installers*. PLASA, 1994.

Cardena, Richard, *Automated Lighting: The Art and Science of Moving Light*, Focal Press, 2006.

Carter, Paul, *Backstage Handbook: An Illustrated Almanac of Technical Information*, 3rd edition, Theatre Crafts International, 1994.

Donovan, Harry, *Entertainment Rigging: A Practical Guide for Riggers, Designers & Managers*.

Moody, James, *Concert Lighting*, 2nd edition, Focal Press, 1998.

Schiller, Brad, *The Automated Programmer's Handbook*, Focal Press, 2003.

Simpson, Robert, *Lighting Control*, Focal Press, 2003.

Vasey, John, *Concert Sound and Lighting Systems*, 3rd edition, Focal Press, 1999.

IESNA Lighting Handbook: Reference and Application, 9th edition, IESNA, ed. Mark S. Rea, 2000.

Magazines

Entertainment Design, Primedia, Inc., 745 Fifth Ave., New York. Web address: www.entertainmentdesignmag.com.

Lighting Dimensions, Primedia, Inc., 745 Fifth Ave., New York. Web address: www.lightingdimensions.com.

Projection, Lights & Staging News Magazine, Timeless Communications Inc. 18425 Burbank Blvd, Suite 613, Tarzana, CA. Web address: www.plsn.com.

Stage Directions, Lifestyle Media, Inc., 110 William St., 23rd Floor, New York. Web address: www.stage-directions.com.

Note: When trying to find information about a specific product or process, do an online search. All manufacturers now have excellent Web sites and you can discover an amazing amount of information on the Web. Enjoy exploring!

Glossary

above   In the context of film latitude, "above" means "brighter than."

acting areas   Those areas of the stage on which specific scenes, or parts of scenes, are played.

additive color mixing   The transmission of light of varying hues to the eye and the brain's interpretation of the ratio of the light mixture as a specific hue.

aerial perspective   An optical phenomenon in which objects that are farther away appear less sharply in focus and less fully saturated in color.

aircraft cable   Extremely strong, flexible, multistrand, twisted metal cable; $\frac{1}{8}$-inch aircraft cable has a breaking strength of one ton.

amperage   A term denoting current flow within an electrical circuit.

ampere   The unit of measurement of electrical current.

aperture   The opening in a lens that allows light to pass through to the film or electronic collector plate. A variable aperture allows the size of the opening to be changed.

arc   An electric current that leaps the gap between two closely placed electrodes.

arena stage   A stage completely surrounded by the audience.

atom   The smallest particle of a chemical element that retains the structural properties of that element.

atomic theory   A generally accepted theory concerning the structure and composition of substances.

autotransformer   A type of dimmer that increases or decreases lamp intensity by varying the voltage within the circuit.

background light   This context means that the fixture can be used for lighting the background of a scene.

ballast   A special type of resistor that maintains an essentially constant current despite fluctuations in line current. Fluorescent tubes require this constant current to operate.

barn door   An accessory for a fresnel spotlight whose movable flippers are swung into the beam to control it.

beam angle   That point where the light emitted by an instrument is diminished by 50 percent when compared with the output of the center of the beam.

beam projector   A lensless instrument with a parabolic primary reflector and a spherical secondary reflector that creates an intense shaft of light with little diffusion.

below   In the context of film latitude, "below" means "darker than."

board operator   An electrician who runs the lighting control console during rehearsals and performances.

boom   A vertical pipe with a heavy base, frequently equipped with horizontal crossbars. Used as a hanging position for lighting instruments.

bring up   Synonymous with fade-in.

bulb   The Pyrex glass or synthetic quartz container for a lamp filament and gaseous environment.

bump   An instantaneous cue. In this case, refers to bumping from one color to another as opposed to fading from one color to another.

cable   An electrical extension cord used to connect instruments to dimmers or instruments to permanent stage circuits.

call   To tell specific crew members when to perform their cues.

candela   An international unit of luminous intensity. Also called a candle. The luminosity of a light source is often expressed in candles per square foot (footcandles) or candelas per square meter.

cassette tape   Audio recorder tape, used in computer storage.

center line   A leader line that runs perpendicular to the set line from the midpoint or center of the opening of the proscenium arch.

center-loaded exposure system   A coupled exposure system in which objects in the center of the frame are given precedence over objects outside the center in determining the exposure value. The term center-loaded is synonymous with center-weighted.

center-weighted meter   An averaging reflective meter in which the center of the frame accounts for a greater proportion of the total exposure than the edges of the frame.

changeover   Changing from one play to another in a repertory theatre situation. Involves exchanging sets, costumes, and properties and making adjustments to lighting and sound.

channel control   An electronic patching system in which one or more dimmers can be assigned to a control channel, which in turn controls the intensity level of those dimmers.

circuit   A conductive path through which electricity flows.

circuit breaker   A device to protect a circuit from an overload; has a bi-metal device that trips open when heated by excess current, breaking circuit continuity.

circuiting   The process of connecting a lighting instrument to its specific stage circuit.

club   In the context of lighting, refers to night clubs in which high-energy music (live or recorded) is the prime attraction.

collector plate   The electronic plate of a video or digital camera on which the visual image is focused. The collector plate converts the light image into an electronic signal.

color   One of the four controllable qualities of light; a perception created in the brain by the stimulation of the retina by light waves of certain lengths; a generic term applied to all light waves contained in the visible spectrum.

color-conversion filters   Filters used to make large adjustments-generally more than 1,000° K-to the color of the light entering the camera. These are almost always camera filters.

color-correction filters   Filters used to adjust the color of light to match the color of a specific film emulsion.

color frame   A lightweight metal holder for color media that fits in a holder at the front of a lighting instrument.

color fringes   A rainbow effect seen at the edges of some beams of light. Caused by refraction of the projected light.

color media   The plastic or glass materials used to color the light emitted by lighting instruments.

combination circuit   Typically, a circuit where the elements are in a parallel configuration and the controls are placed in series with the load.

company switch   A disconnect box to which portable dimmers may be connected. Normally, has 240-VAC power, sometimes higher. Usually located in the wings adjacent to stage.

complementary colors   Two hues that, when combined, yield white in light or black in pigment; colors that are opposite each other on a color wheel.

computer board   A lighting control console that uses a computer to store and recall dimmer intensity levels and fade times for each cue; it also stores and recalls various other functions.

concert   In the context of lighting, primarily refers to touring rock and country shows.

condensing lens   A device that condenses the direct and reflected light from a source and concentrates it on the slide plane aperture of a projector.

conductor   Any material with many free electrons, such as copper, silver, gold, and aluminum.

cones   Nerve cells in the retina that are sensitive to bright light; they respond to red, to blue, or to green light.

connecting strip   An electrical gutter or wireway that carries a number of stage circuits; the circuits terminate on the connecting strip in female receptacles.

control board   A console containing controls for a number of dimmers. Also called a control console.

coupled exposure meter   A reflective exposure meter built into the body of a camera that automatically adjusts the lens aperture to the correct setting for the available light. Also called a coupled exposure system.

coupled reflex meter   A meter that senses through the lens of a camera and automatically adjusts the lens to the aperture recommended by the meter.

crashes   In the context of computers, refers to the hard disk becoming inoperable and the data stored on it nonretrievable.

cue   A directive for action: for example, a change in the lighting.

cueing   Designing the light cues. Manipulating, and recording, the distribution, intensity, movement, and color of the lights for each cue to create an appropriate look for that moment in the play.

cut list   A list that details the number of gels of specific size and color that will be used on a production; for example, 12 pieces of Roscolux 09 for 6-inch ERSs, 6 pieces of Lee 154 for 8-inch fresnels, and so forth.

cyc   Cyclorama. A large drop used to surround the stage.

cyc light   A lensless instrument with an eccentric reflector used to create a smooth wash of light on a cyclorama or sky tab from a relatively close distance.

cyclorama   A large expanse of cloth or drop used to surround the stage. Also called a cyc.

daisy chain   to connect, one to another, in a continuous line, like a chain of daisies.

default programmed   The original "from-the-manufacturer" setting of some aspect of a software program. Generally the user can modify default settings.

delay   Refers to the time interval that the second part of a split time fade follows the first.

depth of field   The range of distance that objects within the frame are in focus.

designer's cue sheet   A form used by the lighting designer to record pertinent information (dimmer levels, timing, and so forth) about every cue in the production.

dichroic filter   A filter that reflects, rather than absorbs, unwanted wavelengths of light while allowing the desired wavelengths to pass through the filter.

diffuse   To soften the appearance of light by using a translucent filtering element to scatter the rays.

dimmer An electrical device that controls the intensity of a light source connected to it.

dimmer circuit An electrical circuit terminating on one end at a dimmer. The other end terminates at either a patch panel or on stage. Synonymous with stage circuit when it terminates on stage.

disconnect box Contains a main disconnect, but no circuit breakers for individual circuits. Used as a power source for, normally, 220-VAC equipment.

discrete Separate and complete; in this case, pertaining to information represented by binary code.

distribution One of the four controllable qualities of light; the direction, shape and size, quality (clarity or diffusion), and character (texture) of light.

double hang To place two instruments adjacent to each other to light an area that normally would be lit by one instrument. Normally done to allow a color shift during a scene or to provide an additive color mix.

double plano-convex lens train Two plano-convex lenses placed with their curved surfaces facing each other; creates a system that has a shorter focal length than either of its component lenses.

douser A mechanical dimming device used in followspots.

Dremel tool A hand-held router similar to a dentist's drill, which can be equipped with a number of bits for grinding, cutting, or carving of wood, plastic, and metal.

dress rehearsal A run-through with all technical elements, including costumes and makeup.

drop-and-wing set A setting primarily composed of two-dimensional scenery, normally one or more drops upstage and a series of portals placed between the drops and the proscenium.

drop box A small connecting strip, containing four to eight circuits, that can be clamped to a pipe or boom.

ECA The American National Standards Institute (ANSI) identifies lamps with specific characteristics by a code number. ECA is the code for the following lamp: 3,200° K color temperature, PS-shaped, 250 watts, 120 volts, medium screw base.

edge of visibility The outside limits of a film's latitude where detail begins to be lost.

effect A specialty device designed to give the appearance of being a light source such as a fire effect, candle, torch, or lightning.

effects head A motor-driven unit capable of producing relatively crude moving images with a scenic projector.

efficient In this case, refers to a comparison of the intensity of light emitted by the lamp with the intensity of light emitted by the instrument.

electric Any pipe that is used to hold lighting instruments.

electrical current The flow or movement of electrons through a conductor.

electricians Those who work on the stage lighting for a production.

electrician's cue sheet A form used by the board operator that contains the primary operating instructions for every lighting cue in the production.

electricity A directed flow of electrons used to create kinetic energy.

electron A negatively charged fundamental particle that orbits around the nucleus of an atom.

electronics The field of science and engineering concerned with the behavior and control of electrons within devices and systems and the utilization of those systems.

ellipsoidal reflector floodlight A lensless instrument with a conical ellipse reflector; used for lighting cycloramas and drops; also known as a scoop.

ellipsoidal reflector spotlight (ERS) A lighting instrument characterized by hard-edged light with little diffusion; designed for relatively long throws, it is manufactured with fixed- and variable-focal-length lenses; the light beam is shaped with internally mounted shutters.

fade To increase (fade-in) or decrease (fade-out) the intensity of the lights.

fade-in A gradual increase. In lighting, usually from darkness to a predetermined level of brightness. Synonymous with fade-up.

fade-out A gradual decrease. In lighting, usually from a set level of brightness to darkness.

fader A device, usually electronic, that effects a gradual changeover from one circuit to another; in lighting it gradually changes the intensity of one or more dimmer circuits.

fiber-optic material Material made of thin transparent fibers of plastic that conduct light throughout their length by internal reflections.

field angle That point where the light output diminishes to 10 percent of the output of the center of the beam.

filament The light-producing element of a lamp; usually made of tungsten wire.

fill light Light used to fill the shadows created by the key light.

film latitude The range of acceptable exposure of a particular film stock.

first ante-proscenium (AP) cut A hanging position for lighting instruments; also known as beamport; the slot or opening in the auditorium ceiling closest to the proscenium arch. The second AP is second closest to the proscenium arch, and so on.

first electric The onstage pipe for lighting instruments that is closest, from the onstage side, to the proscenium arch.

fixed In the context of fixed trim height, fixed means unmovable.

flag Named for its shape. A roughly rectangularly shaped material—transparent, translucent, or opaque depending on function—that is inserted into a beam of light to color, shape, or dim the light.

flash pot   A device used to detonate flash powder.

flat   Refers to a beam of light, the output of which is essentially smooth from edge to edge when measured perpendicular to the axis of the beam.

floor pocket   A connecting box, usually containing three to six circuits, the top of which is mounted flush with the stage floor.

floppy disk   A thin piece of plastic coated with metal oxide, used to record the information stored in a computer's memory.

flush mounted   Attached so that the box is recessed into the wall and the face of the box is flush with the wall surface.

focal length   The distance from the lens at which the light rays converge into a point; for lenses used in stage lighting instruments, the focal length is most frequently measured in even inches.

focus   In stage lighting, the location onstage where the light from an instrument is directed.

fog   A low-lying smoke effect.

followspot   A lighting instrument with a high-intensity, narrow beam of light; mounted on a stand that allows it to tilt and swivel so that the beam can "follow" the actor.

footcandle   An international unit of illumination. One footcandle equals one lumen of light falling on a surface area of one square foot.[1]

foot-lambert   An international unit of brightness. The average brightness of a perfectly diffusing surface emitting or reflecting light of one lumen per square foot.

form   In the context of theatre, elements that have similar physical characteristics. For example, arena, thrust, and proscenium theatres have different *forms* of stage configuration.

frame   In the context of light meters, frame refers to the scene framed by the camera's viewfinder.

free electron   An electron that has broken away from its "home" atom to float free.

fresnel lens   A type of step lens with the glass cut away from the convex face of the lens.

fresnel spotlight   A spotlight that produces a soft, diffused light; the fresnel lens is treated on the plano side to diffuse the light.

front-of-house   Describing lights that are hung on the audience side of the proscenium arch.

front projection screen   An opaque, highly reflective, usually white material used to reflect a projected image; the projector is placed on the audience side of the screen.

f-stop   A numerical indication of a lens aperture setting.

---

[1]Boylan, Bernard R., *The Lighting Primer*, Iowa State University Press, Ames, Iowa, 1987, p. 7.

funnel   An accessory for a fresnel or ERS spotlight that masks the beam to create a circular pattern; also called a snoot or top hat.

fuse   A device to protect a circuit from an overload; has a soft metal strip that melts, breaking circuit continuity.

gating principle   A rapid switching on and off of electrical power.

gel   (verb) To insert color media in a color frame and place on a lighting instrument. (noun) Color media made from gelatin.

generator truck   A large flatbed truck equipped with a well-muffled gasoline- or diesel-powered generator.

ghost-load   To connect an offstage, unseen load to the dimmer. An instrument, usually a 500- or 1,000-watt fresnel, is two-fered with the small onstage load to provide sufficient wattage for the dimmer to operate properly.

gobo   A thin metal template inserted into an ellipsoidal reflector spotlight to project a shadow pattern of light.

grid   A network of steel I beams supporting elements of the counterweight system.

grounding plug   A plug that connects to ground in addition to electrical service. The grounding pin is longer than the energized pins to complete the ground before the electrical service is connected.

ground plan   A scale mechanical drawing in the form of a horizontal offset section with the cutting plane passing at whatever level, normally a height of 4 feet above the stage floor, is required to produce the most descriptive view of the set.

ground row   Generally low, horizontal flats used to mask the base of cycs or drops; frequently painted to resemble rows of buildings, hedges, or similar visual elements.

group   The grouping of two or more dimmers/channels under one controller.

hanging   The process of placing lighting instruments in their specified locations.

hanging crew   Those responsible for the hanging, circuiting, patching, focusing, and coloring of the lighting instruments; they are under the supervision of the master electrician.

hanging positions   The various locations around the stage and auditorium where lighting instruments are placed.

hard disk   A device for storing/retrieving digital information. Usually mounted inside a computer.

hard drive   A device for storing/retrieving digital information.

haze   A smoke effect that fills the entire stage space.

head   A housing that holds scenic projector lenses in fixed positions to project images of a specific size.

heat filter   A dichroic glass medium that removes much of the infrared spectrum from light.

heat sink   A metal device used to draw heat away from heat-sensitive electronics and vent heat to the air without the use of fans.

heat welding   The use of a heat gun (a high-temperature air gun, visually similar to a hand-held hair dryer) to fuse two pieces of plastic.

hookup sheet   Another name for instrument schedule.

hot spot   An intense circle of light created when a projector lens is seen through a rear screen.

house plot   A scale plan view of a theatre's stage and auditorium showing all hanging positions and related circuiting information.

hue   The qualities that differentiate one color from another.

image of light   A picture or concept of what the light should look like for a production.

instruments   Lighting fixtures designed for use in the theatre.

instrument schedule   A form used to record all the technical data about each instrument used in the production; also known as a hookup sheet.

insulator   Any material with few free electrons, such as rubber, paper, glass, and certain types of plastics.

intensity   One of the four controllable qualities of light; the relative brightness of light.

iris   A device with movable overlapping metal plates, used with an ellipsoidal reflector spotlight to change the size of the circular pattern of light.

isolation spot   A small, bright spot of light used to isolate that space from other less bright or colored areas onstage.

key light   The brightest light in a scene.

keystoning   The linear distortion created when a projector is placed on some angle other than perpendicular to the projection surface.

kinetic   Having to do with movement. In the case of lighting design, having to do with moving light.

ladder   A vertical pipe with horizontal crossbars hung from the end of an onstage electric pipe. Used as a hanging position for lighting equipment.

lamp   The stage term for "light bulbs" used in stage lighting instruments.

law of charges   The law: Like charges repel and unlike charges attract.

legitimate theatre   Refers to plays that rely on the spoken word to convey their message. Does not include musicals, reviews, dance, opera, or concerts.

lensless projector   A projector that works by projecting a shadow image without a lens, such as the Linnebach and curved-image projectors.

lens train   The path taken by light as it passes through the lens into the camera and onto the film or electronic receptor.

light-balancing filter   A filter used to make small adjustments—generally less than 400° K—to the color of the light entering the camera. These are almost always camera filters.

light board   A generic term used to describe all types of lighting control consoles.

light cue   Generally, some type of action involving lighting; usually the raising or lowering of the intensity of one or more lighting instruments.

light plot   A scale ground plan drawing that details the placement of the lighting instruments relative to the physical structure of the theatre and the location of the set.

lighting area   Cylindrical space approximately 8 to 12 feet in diameter and about 7 feet tall; the actual size is roughly determined by the diameter of the beam of light of the instruments that are being used to light the area.

lighting designer   Person responsible for the appearance of the lighting during the production.

lighting key   A drawing that indicates the plan angle and color of the various sources that illuminate the image of light.

lighting production team   The personnel who work on lighting for a production.

lighting rehearsal   A run-through, without action, attended by the director, stage manager, lighting designer, and appropriate running crews to look at the intensity, timing, and placement of the various lighting cues.

lighting sectional   A composite side view, drawn to scale, of the set, showing the hanging position of the instruments in relation to the physical structure of the theatre, set, and stage equipment.

line   The wires in low-voltage control systems are frequently called "lines" rather than "wires."

link   An action where a cue is electronically "tied" to another cue. Typically used to create a sequence of cues that automatically follow one after the other.

load   A device that converts electrical energy into another form of energy; a lamp converts electrical energy to light and heat; an electrical motor converts electricity to mechanical energy.

location   In the context of lighting fixtures, those instruments designed to be used outside the studio. Typically these fixtures are small, lightweight and are equipped with a telescoping stand.

look   The appearance—the way the light looks onstage—of a particular cue.

lumen   An international unit of measurement of light output. The light emitted by a source of power of one candela that falls on one square unit of surface at one unit of distance from the source. Example: The light output of a 100-watt household lamp is 1,750 lumens.[2]

lux   An international unit of luminous intensity. One lux equals an illumination of a surface, all points of which are one meter from a point source of one candela.

---

[2]Boylan, Bernard R., *The Lighting Primer*, Iowa State University Press, Ames, Iowa, 1987, p. 7.

marks In the context of making a video or film, "mark" refers to the specific location where the talent needs to stand during a shot. If the mark is out of frame, it is frequently marked with a masking tape "X" to make it easier for the talent to "hit their mark."

mask To block the audience's view—generally of backstage equipment and space.

master electrician Person responsible for ensuring that the lighting equipment is hung, focused, and run according to written and verbal instructions from the lighting designer.

maximum throw distance The point at which the output of a stage lighting instrument drops to 50 footcandles.

max telephoto A zoom lens that is zoomed all the way to its longest, or maximum, focal length.

microcassette tape A tape cassette approximately $1\frac{1}{4}$ by 2 inches, used in computer storage; identical to microcassette audio tape.

microwatt One millionth of a watt.

modeling One of the four functions of stage lighting: the ability of light to reveal form.

momentary-on switch A push-button switch without a locking feature. The circuit remains on only as long as the button switch is depressed.

mood One of the four functions of stage lighting: the ability of light to create a mood.

moon box A device, basically a wooden box with lights inside, for re-creating the moon.

motivated light cue Indicated or caused by some specific action within the script, like the beginnings and endings of scenes and acts or a character's turning a light switch on or off.

movement (in light) One of the four controllable qualities of light; refers to the timing of lighting cues as well as to the movement of onstage and offstage sources.

multipart cues Cues divided into several parts, each part controlling a portion of the channels in the cue.

multiplex (1) To transmit two or more messages simultaneously on a single channel. (2) To carry out several functions simultaneously in an independent but related manner.

negative film A film that, when processed, provides a negative image in which blacks appear white and so forth. Snapshots are printed from negative film.

neutralization The result of mixing complementary hues. In light, the creation of white. In pigment, the creation of dark gray.

neutron A fundamental particle in the structure of the nucleus of an atom; possesses a neutral charge.

objective lens A device to focus a projected image on a screen or other surface.

Ohm's law   The law that states: As voltage increases, current increases; as resistance increases, current decreases.

open arc   Light source in which two electrodes operate in the open air.

open sunshine   Refers to the color temperature of sunshine on a cloudless day. In temperate geographic regions this color temperature averages 5,500° K, which is used as the industry standard designation.

orthographic projection   A series of elevations, drawn to scale, that show each side or face of an object.

paint chip   A small rectangle of paper or thin cardboard painted in a specific hue.

pan   To rotate horizontally.

parabolic aluminized reflector   A sealed-beam lamp similar to the headlight of an automobile.

parallel circuit   A circuit in which only a portion of the electricity flows through each of the branches of the circuit.

PAR   Acronym for parabolic aluminized reflector. A sealed-beam lamp with a parabolic-shaped reflector covered by a thin, reflective aluminum coating.

PAR can   A holder for a parabolic aluminized reflector (PAR) lamp; creates a powerful punch of light with a relatively soft edge; the PAR 64 is commonly used for concert lighting.

patch   To connect a stage circuit to a dimmer circuit.

patch panel   An interconnecting device that allows you to connect any stage circuit into any dimmer.

PDA   Personal Digital Assistant. A small, hand-held computer.

peak   Refers to a beam of light, the output of which has a noticeable hot spot in its center when measured perpendicular to the axis of the beam. Peak field reading taken at the center of the hotspot.

pigment   Material that imparts color to a substance such as paint or dye.

pigtail   The electrical cable containing hot, neutral, and ground wires used to connect a lighting instrument to a power source such as a dimming system.

pipe   A counterweighted batten or fixed metal pipe that holds lighting instruments or equipment.

plan angle   The ground-plan view of an object.

plano-convex lens   A lens with one flat and one outward-curving face.

plano-convex spotlight   An archaic instrument with a relatively hard-edged light quality. So called because it used a plano-convex lens.

plotter   A computer-controlled machine that draws graphic representations on large-sized paper.

plug   The male portion of a connecting device.

point source   A theoretical concept: All light emanates from a single point that has no dimensions. In the real world all light sources, such as filaments, have height, width, and depth.

pop riveter   A tool used to secure rivets in thin metal.

potential   The difference in electrical charge between two bodies; measured in volts.

practical   An onstage working light source such as a table lamp, wall sconce, or oil lamp.

preset light board   A lighting control console that uses electromechanical variable-resistance switches to control the output of the dimmer.

preset sheet   A form used by the electrician to record the intensity levels for each dimmer during major shifts in the lighting.

preshow   Before the show starts. In this case the preshow cue refers to the settings of the house and stage lights as the audience is entering the auditorium.

primary colors   Hues that cannot be derived or blended from any other hues. In light, the primaries are red, blue, and green; in pigment, the primary colors are red, blue, and yellow.

prismatic lens   The surface or interior of the glass is scored or beveled to create the desired effect.

production concept   The creative interpretation of the script that will unify the artistic vision of the production design team.

production design team   The producer; director; and scenic, costume, lighting, and sound designers who develop the visual and aural concept for the production.

production meeting   A conference of appropriate production personnel to share information.

profile   A fade profile is a linear, graphic representation of a fade. See the box "Fade Profiles" on page 162 for further explanation.

proscenium stage   A stage configuration in which the spectators watch the action through a rectangular opening (the proscenium arch) that resembles a picture frame.

proton   A fundamental particle in the structure of the nucleus of an atom; possesses a positive charge.

rear projection screen   Translucent projection material designed to transmit the image through the projection surface; the projector is placed in back of the screen.

receptacle   The female portion of a connecting device.

reflectance   The amount of light being reflected from an object. Reflectance is dependent on two elements: the amount of light falling on the object and the color of the object. The color determines how much light is reflected. Light colors reflect more light than dark colors.

reflectance range   The difference in reflectivity between the brightest and darkest objects in a scene. Normally measured in f-stops.

reflex meter   A built-in meter that reads the light after it has passed through the camera's lens.

relay   An electromechanical device in which a low-voltage circuit is used to control the opening and/or closing of contacts in a high-voltage on/off system.

repatch   To remove one circuit from a dimmer and replace it with another during a performance.

repertory theatre   A company that presents several different plays alternately in one theatre in the course of a season. In the context of lighting design, adjustments are normally made to the focus and color of lighting instruments for each play each time it is performed.

resistance   The opposition to electron flow within a conductor, measured in ohms; the amount of the resistance is dependent on the chemical makeup of the material through which the electricity is flowing.

resistance dimmer   An archaic dimmer that functioned as a variable resistor.

reversal film   When processed reversal film provides a positive image. Slides are an example of reversal film.

rig   To place lighting equipment on a set. Normally used in reference to film or television sets. Synonymous with the theatrical lighting term "hang."

rise time   The time that it takes the filament of a lamp to heat to full incandescence.

rods   Nerve cells in the retina that are sensitive to faint light.

Roto-lock   Specialized clamps used to fasten pipes together for temporary structures such as scaffolding and temporary hanging positions for lighting instruments.

roundel   A glass color medium for use with striplights; frequently has diffusing properties.

running   Controlling or operating some aspect of a production.

running crew   Those electricians responsible for operating lighting equipment during rehearsals and performances.

saturation   The relative purity of a particular hue.

scenic projector   A high-wattage instrument used for projecting large-format slides or moving images.

scenographic designer   A designer responsible for the entire artistic look—scenery, costumes, lighting, properties—of a production.

SCR (silicon controlled rectifier)   A heavy-duty power transistor.

SCR dimmer   A dimmer that uses two SCRs in a back-to-back configuration to control the load circuit. A low-voltage control circuit uses the gating principle to switch the SCRs to a conducting state.

scrim   In the context of filters, scrim refers to the metal screens designed to reduce light in one-half, one-, and two-stop meshes.

secondary colors   The result of mixing two primary colors.

second electric   The onstage pipe for lighting instruments that is second closest, from the onstage side, to the proscenium arch.

sectional   A drawing, usually in scale, of an object that shows what it would look like if cut straight through at a given plane.

sectional angle The angle of intersection between the axis of the cone of light emitted by an instrument and the working height—usually the height of an actor's face (about 5 feet 6 inches)—of the lighting area.

selective focus One of the four functions of stage lighting: the ability of light to direct the audience's attention to a specific location.

series circuit A circuit in which all the electricity flows through every element of the circuit.

service panel Also called fuse box or panel box. Normally contains a primary power switch (called the main disconnect) for the area being served by the panel as well as circuit breakers or fuses for the individual circuits in that area.

shade A color of low value; usually created by mixing one or more hues with black.

short circuit A short circuit, or short, is created when a very large surge of current causes a portion of a conductor to explosively melt.

shutter A lever-actuated device used to control the height of the top and bottom edges of a followspot beam; also called a chopper.

shutter cut The straight-line edge created when an ERS's shutter is inserted into its beam of light.

side In the context of lighting, "side" refers to one of a paired set of faders; e.g., one "side" of the fader dims a cue out while the other side fades in the next cue.

sidelight Any light striking the side of an object relative to the view of the observer.

sky tab Also sky drop. A large drop made to be hung flat, without fullness; used to simulate the sky.

slide plane aperture The point in a projection system where a slide or other effect is placed.

slide projector A reasonably high-output instrument capable of projecting standard 35-mm slides.

snoot Another term for funnel.

soft key A diffused key light.

source The origin of electrical potential, such as a battery or 120-volt wall outlet.

source light The apparent source of light that is illuminating a scene or an object.

spec sheets Specification sheets. Data sheets providing information about equipment such as lighting instruments, dimmers, and so forth.

spectrometer A device for measuring specific wavelengths of light.

spidering Running a cable directly from the dimmer to the instrument; also known as direct cabling.

split time fade A fade in which the fade-up and fade-out are accomplished at different rates or speeds.

stage circuits An electrical circuit terminating on one end in a female receptacle in the vicinity of the stage. The other end is connected to a dimmer or patch panel. Synonymous with dimmer circuit when it terminates at a dimmer.

stage picture The visual appearance of the stage during a specific moment in a play.

standoff gel frame A gel frame that is held some distance, typically 6 to 12 inches, in front of an open-face lighting instrument to keep the lamp from melting the plastic gel.

step-down transformer A transformer whose output voltage is lower than its input voltage.

step lens A plano-convex lens with the glass on the plano side cut away in steps that are parallel with the plano face.

stepper motor An electric motor whose movement consists of discrete angular steps rather than continuous rotation. Precision movement is achieved by programming the motor to run, in either direction, for a specific number of steps.

step-up transformer A transformer whose output is higher than its input voltage.

storyboards Thumbnail sketches used in filmmaking to provide a visualization of a shot. Normally storyboards include a ground plan only if it will help explain the shot.

stream-of-consciousness questioning Asking whatever relevant questions pop into your mind in the course of a discussion.

striplight A long narrow troughlike instrument with three or four circuits controlling the individual lamps; each circuit is normally equipped with a separate color; used for blending and creating color washes; also known as an X-ray.

style In this context, refers to the specific compositional characteristics that distinguish the appearance of one type of design from another. Using this definition, the various design styles—realism, expressionism, surrealism, and so forth—are delineated by the differences in their compositional principles.

subtractive color mixing The selective absorption of light by a filter or pigment.

surface mounted Attached to the wall so that the entire unit protrudes from the wall.

system ground The grounding point—usually a metal rod driven into the earth outside the building or an underground metal water pipe—for an electrical system.

take out Synonymous with fade-out.

technical rehearsals Run-throughs in which the sets, lights, props, and sound are integrated into the action of the play.

texture The relative roughness or smoothness of the finish of an object.

third pipe When lighting instruments are hung on a batten over the stage, the terminology changes and the batten becomes a pipe. The third pipe is the third batten upstage of the proscenium arch that holds lighting instruments.

3½-inch floppy disk A floppy disk 3½ inches in diameter.

throw distance How far light from an instrument travels from its hanging position to the center of its area of focus.

thrust stage A stage projecting into, and surrounded on three sides by, the audience.

tilt To rotate vertically.

tint A color of high value; usually created by mixing one or more hues with white.

tone A color of middle value achieved by mixing one or more hues with black and white.

top hat Another term for funnel.

top light A directional term meaning light that approaches the stage from above, or on top of, the stage floor.

transformer A device that changes the voltage in an electrical system; the output voltage of a step-down transformer is less than its source; a step-up transformer increases it.

trim height Height above the stage floor at which an instrument will be hung.

truss An engineered structure, usually made out of metal tubing, suspended above the stage or auditorium. Used as a hanging position for lighting equipment.

two-fer An electrical Y that has female receptacles at the top of the Y and a male plug at the bottom leg of the Y; used to connect two instruments to the same circuit.

two-shot A shot with two subjects.

umbrella A small, silvered umbrella used as a reflector. The umbrella is attached to the stand with a clamp. The light is focused on the umbrella, which acts like a parabolic reflector to create a soft, moderately focused fill light.

unit set A single set in which all of the play's locations are always visible and the audience's attention is usually shifted by alternately lighting various parts of the set.

unmotivated light cues Changes in the lights that are not specifically called for in the script.

valence shell The outermost plane of orbiting electrons in the structure of an atom.

value The relative lightness or darkness of an object.

variegated gel   A multicolored gel made in the shop from strips of color media of differing hues.

visibility   One of the four functions of stage lighting: to make the stage selectively visible.

voice   Design "voice" refers to the ability to express your own artistic style.

volatility   Nonpermanence; in computers, a volatile memory will be lost if the computer loses its power supply.

volt   The unit of measurement of electrical potential.

wall pocket   A connecting box similar to a floor pocket but mounted in the wall.

wall washers   Fixtures placed at a shallow angle to a wall to bring out texture.

watt   The unit measurement of power required to do work.

white light   Light that contains all wavelengths of the visible spectrum in relatively equal proportion.

working sectional   A drawing showing the sectional angle for a lighting instrument; used to determine its trim height or hanging position; not to be confused with the lighting section.

work light   A lighting fixture, frequently a scoop, PAR, or other wide-field-angle instrument, hung over the stage to facilitate work; generally not used to light a production.

workstation   A table placed in the auditorium for use by the lighting designer and assistants during lighting/tech/dress rehearsals.

X-ray   Another term for striplight.

zoom   Widening or narrowing of the cone of light emitted by the instrument.

zoom ellipse   An ellipsoidal reflector spotlight with movable lenses that allow the focal length to be changed.

zoom lens   A lens that has a continuously variable focal length from wide angle to telephoto.

Index

Italic page numbers refer to illustrations